ARCHITECTURAL
RESEARCH METHODS

ARCHITECTURAL RESEARCH METHODS

LINDA GROAT AND DAVID WANG

JOHN WILEY & SONS, INC.

Library of Congress Cataloging-in-Publication Data

Wang, David C., 1954–
    Architectural research methods / David Wang and Linda Groat.
        p.   cm.
    Includes index.
    ISBN 0-471-33365-4 (cloth : alk. paper)
    1. Architecture—Research. 2. Architecture—Study and teaching. I. Groat, Linda N.
II. Title

    NA2000.W36 2001
    720′.1—dc21

Printed in the United States of America

10 9 8 7 6 5 4 3 2 1

Contents

Preface

LINDA GROAT

As a designer just starting out and working for a Bay Area architecture firm, I had never given much thought to how research might contribute to the design quality of the projects I was working on. But I remember well the growing sense of unease I had as the schematic design for a major computer and software corporation proceeded. The lead architects had developed a scheme that included a set of exterior courtyards situated between a series of office pavilions; and the concept was to coat the courtyard facades with a series of bold primary colors. Among my responsibilities was to develop the color palette.

I was torn. On the one hand, I was enthusiastic about the concept—the project was sure to be an award winner (which it eventually was). But on the other hand, what was it going to feel like for someone working there to have reflected primary colors bouncing into their office and onto their desk? Or even just to look out and see a wall of shimmering bright red or orange? I didn't have any answers, but my response was to start reading. First about the psychology of colors; and then gradually anything I could find about the impact of different formal choices on people.

A few years later, armed with many more questions about the impact of design decisions on people, I found myself in a M.Sc. program champing at the bit to study people's reactions to different architectural styles. There was one big problem though. First I had to take several required courses, including one on research methods. Certainly I recognized that I needed to learn how to conduct research properly; that's why I was there. But why did I have to spend so much time learning about all those other methods besides the ones I might want to use for the study I had planned?

Now, quite a few years later, I continue to see the same restlessness in many of my students. Like me (and like David Wang, whose preface follows), most students I work with have come to the research enterprise because of questions and issues raised by their professional work or experiences in school. Questions such as: To what extent can a more informed choice of building products and mechanical systems by architects contribute to the goal of sustainability? How is it that a choice of plan configuration for a building might either support or impede an organization's strategic goals and cultural values? In what way might new computer software enhance collaboration among dispersed teams of architects and other professionals? How might an understanding of why Modernism was widely accepted in one country help us identify the conditions under which other "elite" architectural styles might be accepted elsewhere?

Many of my students become impatient when they have to learn about research methods beyond the one they initially deem most relevant to their research interests. When pressed for reasons why they should, I have two complementary answers. The first is this: Although I believe that there will always be a place for very focused research using the methods traditionally associated with particular subject area (e.g., experimental research in technical areas), I also strongly believe that some of the most innovative research in architecture will be interdisciplinary, requiring atypical or unexpected combinations of methods. My second answer is directed more at the student's individual experience. I suggest they think about the methods course as an experience in "clothes shopping." Of course they aren't going to be forced to "buy" a method that doesn't "fit" their research question, but I do insist that they at least "try each one on." To this end, they are asked to study and evaluate the strengths and weaknesses of the full range of research methods presented in this book. And for their final project, each student must develop a research design for his/her topic area that makes use of at least two of the methods studied. This ensures that each student will at least "think out of the box" enough to identify a less conventional method for studying his/her topic.

This book has been developed very much in the spirit of that invitation to think outside the box. While we recognize that each reader is likely to gravitate to the chapters that describe methods most typical of his or her research interests, we invite everyone to "try on" some of the other modes of research they are less familiar with. In his classic book, *The Conduct of Inquiry*, Abraham Kaplan wrote of the tendency for researchers to frame their research questions in terms of the methods they know best:

I call it the law of the instrument, and it may be formulated as follows:

Give a small boy a hammer, and he will find that everything he encounters needs pounding. . . . What is objectionable is not that some techniques are pushed to their utmost, but that others, in consequence, are denied. . . . The price of training is always a certain "trained incapacity." . . . I believe it is important that training in [one's field of research] encourage appreciation of the greatest possible range of techniques.*

---

*A. Kaplan, *The Conduct of Inquiry* (San Francisco, Calif.: Chandler Publishing Co., 1964), 28–29.

Ultimately, any researcher who is able to wield an array of tools, not just the hammer she is most familiar with, gains an enormous power to begin to answer all those troubling questions that led her to the research enterprise in the first place. I have seen this happen many times with the students I advise. After struggling for quite a while with how to investigate a particular problem or question, their facility with the methods of inquiry eventually kicks in, and they are able to launch much more incisive and robust projects. It is our hope that this book may contribute to such a process for our readers. More important still, if architecture as a field can be strengthened and enriched through research, then the power of architecture to enhance people's lives will be strengthened as well. This is a goal to which we can all aspire.

Finally, a word about how David and I have chosen to collaborate on this book. The overall organization of the book and its constituent chapters is the product of long and frequent discussion, as well as a slow evolution to its current form. Within this common framework we have chosen to speak with our individual voices; this is in part because we have complementary expertise in different areas of architectural research. But this does not mean that we have developed our chapters in isolation; rather, we each inhabit each others' chapters in many ways. Sometimes it is a matter of reviewing and critiquing each others' efforts: other times we have suggested key sources and research examples; and in some instances, we have reworked or added significant segments. In this regard, I want to acknowledge David's special contributions to two of the chapters I have written, Chapter 1 and Chapter 7.

DAVID WANG

I practiced architecture for fifteen years before embarking on teaching architecture full time. This transition was marked by a decision to pursue a Ph.D. in the field. To make a long story short, I sold my five-bedroom, three-and-a-half-bath house in the Philadelphia suburbs and moved our family of five into graduate student housing at the University of Michigan. Our unit in "Northwood Five" was some 1,000 square feet in size—still spacious by housing standards in many parts of the world, mind you, but let us say it was a step down from what my family was used to. We had to make do, for instance, with only one bathroom. This was not a convenient thing in the mornings, or after a serious Asian meal.

Some years after earning my Ph.D., after we had moved from Ann Arbor and settled again into a more spacious home (3 bathrooms) in Spokane, Washington, I asked one of my sons whether he liked our new house, or whether he still preferred the cramped quarters at Northwood Five. Without hesitation, the answer was Northwood Five. "Why?" I asked. "Well," he said, "there is no dumpster here."

You see, our unit at Northwood Five was located right next to the communal dumpster. Often in the predawn hours we would be awakened by the beep-beeps of the garbage truck backing up to unload the darn thing. But that dumpster was the community information center. For my sons Jeremy and Andrew, the dumpster offered them opportunities for making some spending money. They would tape flyers on it to hawk their services, next to all the other flyers announcing everything from piano lessons to furniture sales. Jeremy, for instance, made a few bucks fixing bicycles. My sons weeded gardens, babysat, ironed shirts for pay, all thanks to their flyers taped to the dumpster. Over the few years we lived in that housing complex, the dumpster made the difference in terms of "a sense of place" for my kids.

That someone would prefer one locale over another because of a dumpster is one reason why I think a book like this is needed. Let me elaborate. My years of practice led me to conclude that the relationship between the human being and the built environment was not a simple one, but rather composed of multiple connections, and richly and profoundly so. On the other hand, early in my education as an architect, I had somehow picked up an implicit message that goes something like this: If you can only come up with a nifty physical form, one that excites the eyes, one that is deemed worthy of "the magazines," then, to adapt a phrase from John Ruskin, *that* is architecture! In short, if the physical form is really nifty (and "nifty" kept changing in meaning, like a flavor-of-the-week sort of thing. What chance do you think Frank Gehry's museum in Bilbao would have had to even see the light of day in the 1960s? But now it is considered by many to be great architecture.)—if the form is really nifty, all of the positive subjective feelings of identity, communal well being, and so on, would ensue. It took me some years to realize that this idea may not be fully true. The answer to what comprises the relationship between the human being and built environments, in terms of what makes such relationships rich and successful, is much more complex. At least the answer must somehow accommodate that dumpster.

This book addresses research methodologies that, in essence, grapple with the multiple connections between human experience and built form. The seven strategies we survey in Part II offer a variety of perspectives from which to understand this relationship. These range from experimental ways of knowing, to appreciating our place in the world from a historical perspective, to social-cultural interpretative approaches, to simulation studies. Architectural research allows us to understand, at least a little better, that successful built environments are successful not just because of their physical attributes, but also because of many *human* considerations. These include subjective preferences, memory, physical comfort (variously defined), a sense of one's social roles, and so on. By understanding human relationships with built forms at these levels, we enhance our ability to create meaningful architecture and deepen our appreciation of relating to our present environments.

Two further points can be made about the perspectives we examine in Part II. First, each of these have traditionally been used to make linkages between human experience and built form. In other words, Linda and I did not set out in this book to propose new theory or to offer any new approaches to tackling this large theme. Our aim in this book was to cull different perspectives from diverse literatures, to bring them together into one volume, *and to make the contents of each perspective applicable more specifically to architecture and architects.* Each of these perspectives may or may not have the explicit goal of focusing upon connections between human beings and built form. In their home domains, they address many other foci. Our aim was to take some of the research material other domains offer and to train it explicitly upon the human–to–built environment relationship.

The second point flows from the first: Research into architectural realities is necessarily an interdisciplinary matter. Perhaps the word should be "trans-disciplinary," but here I do not want to fret over fine semantic distinctions. That is because there is a fair amount of fluidity in how the academic community is coming to terms with what these words can mean. And far from being a frustrating fact, this diversity of opinion on the exact nature of knowledge that transcends disciplinary bounds, I think, represents a new frontier for architecture and architectural education. It is one reason why research-oriented degrees in architecture have proliferated in recent years. The simple truth in all of this is not hard to see; namely, that architecture encompasses so many different disciplines that architectural *research* must engage with what all of them have to offer. For our purposes, then, architectural research is interdisciplinary in the sense that it harnesses strategies and tactics from other disciplines to achieve its own ends in gaining knowledge about how built environments could enhance human life. In my teaching, I have tried to describe this reality with the following diagram:

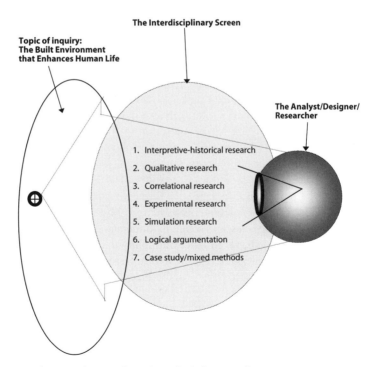

Figure P.1 Architectural research: an interdisciplinary reality.

The diagram is pretty self-explanatory. The designer/researcher/analyst seeks to understand a topic of inquiry, almost always related to built environments, via research. The contents of the research are located within a domain in between the analyst and the topic. I call the domain an interdisciplinary screen, for two reasons. First is simply because of the variety of research strategies that the analyst can use to "see through" in architectural inquiry. The diagram lists the seven strategies we address in Part II, although I hasten to add that these seven do not represent an exhaustive listing of the possibilities. Second, as will become clear at multiple places in this book, the term "interdisciplinary" is appropriate because often the analyst will need to depend upon more than one type of strategy to perform his or her work. In these instances, often one strategy becomes subservient to another strategy, taking on the more supportive aspects of a research tactic. This will be explained in the chapters to come.

I wish to say a few words about Part I. In addition to containing chapters of an introductory nature (Chapter 1 defines our audience, Chapter 2 considers some general "ways of seeing," and Chapter 3 deals with literature review), Linda and I felt that dealing with research methodologies for architects required addressing two related themes. One is the relationship between systems of methodology, on the one hand, and how they relate to what we call "theory in general," on the other; we address this in Chapter 4. The other is the relationship between research activity and design activity; we address this in Chapter 5. While none of the chapters of Part I cover research strategies in the sense that the seven chapters of Part II cover them, we urge the reader to be familiar with our positions in these beginning chapters, for their content is related to the material in Part II of this book.

Now, a few words about authorship. Linda and I believe we have put together a useful single-source reference on architectural research for the variety of readers addressed in Chapter 1. We also feel it would be informative for each of us to identify the chapters we wrote. This not only clarifies our contributions, it also helps the reader to be aware of who is speaking through the words of any particular chapter. Although we did comment upon each other's chapters, and in some cases actually worded certain sections, for the most part the authorship of each chapter is very much the work of one or the other of us. For my part, I wrote:

Chapter 3. Literature Review

Chapter 4. Theory in Relation to Method

Chapter 5. Design in Relation to Research

Chapter 6. Interpretive-Historical Research

Chapter 10. Simulation and Modeling Research

Chapter 11. Logical Argumentation

I am particularly grateful to Linda for her comments, as well as recommendations for literature, related to the writing of Chapters 4 and 5.

Finally, as far as Linda and I are aware, this is the first book-length work explicitly dedicated to architectural research. We are satisfied to have been a part of it. But as any architecture student who presents first on jury day knows, "going first" can get you an inordinate amount of comments and criticism. As this book is now added to the literature, I am sure I speak for Linda when I say that we look forward to the suggestions and constructive criticism of our colleagues and students. And we invite others to contribute to the literature on architectural research as well.

Acknowledgments

LINDA GROAT

First and foremost, I want to thank David Wang, who is not only my co-author, but the person who got this book project going. Without his initiative, enthusiasm, and sustained commitment, this book would not have been conceived or written. Throughout the process, I have valued his polite prods to action, his thoughtful critiques, his substantive suggestions for various references and examples, and especially his sense of purpose.

My gratitude also goes to all the folks at John Wiley and Sons. I have greatly appreciated the steadfast guidance and encouragement we received from Amanda Miller, our editor. Her assistant, Nyshie Perkinson, has been extremely helpful to us in sorting out various loose ends and complications.

I have been very fortunate in my academic career to have encountered so many people whose insights at critical moments have contributed mightily to the ideas presented in this book. First among these is David Canter, now of the University of Liverpool, my doctoral adviser, as well as a friend and colleague of over twenty years. It was David who first exposed me to the distinction between strategy and tactics as applied to research methods. That distinction has been fundamental to my thinking ever since and is a foundation of the material in this book.

Likewise Robert Johnson, formerly a colleague at University of Michigan and now at Texas A & M, developed an invaluable conceptual framework that served as the springboard for the research methods course I've been teaching at Michigan. Over the years during which I modified and reconfigured much of it, my students and I continued to refer to it as "Bob Johnson's matrix." Without that original seed, the contents of the course, and now this book, might have evolved quite differently.

Early on in the evolution of the course, many of my other colleagues at Michigan were generous in either sharing their relevant publications with me or pointing me to other illustrative examples of particular research methods. Some of those now figure as important references and examples in this book. I am very grateful to Harold Borkin, Kurt Brandle, Colin Clipson (now deceased), J. J. Kim, Bob Marans, Rod Parker (who is now pursuing a medical career), Lee Pastalan, Anatole Senkevitch, Jim Snyder, Sharon Sutton (now at University of Washington), and Manos Vakalo (now deceased). Colleagues J. J. Kim and Jean Wineman were especially helpful in reviewing drafts of several of the research design chapters.

In addition, I wish to thank my many former colleagues at University of Wisconsin-Milwaukee who helped to create an environment that was so supportive of research. And I especially want to thank Sherry Ahrentzen, my friend and coauthor on other projects, who early on shared her own research methods syllabus with me. Some of her suggested readings have become central to discussions in this book.

There are many others at Michigan who have been instrumental in supporting this work. Jean Ellis, the doctoral program secretary, has cheerfully carried out all manner of miscellaneous typing, formatting, and phoning for me. The university provost office and the office of the vice president for research kindly agreed to support the work of my doctoral assistants, Fernando Lara and Leonard Temko; their untiring commitment to seeing the project through was invaluable to us. I am grateful to Dean Douglas Kelbaugh and Doctoral Program chair Jean Wineman, both of whom have provided support for this project. Colleagues in my research study group at Michigan's Institute for Research on Women and Gender (Jane Dutton, Martha Feldman, Jane Hassinger, Lora Lempert, Beth Reed, Carolyn Riehl, and Raven Wallace) have also given me insights on the methodological terrain across many disciplines.

Above all, I wish to thank and celebrate my students. They have been insightful critics and "doubting Thomases" who have prodded me to refine the ideas and to explain things more clearly. And they have been collaborators in figuring out better and more robust methods for tackling research questions. This book is dedicated to them.

Finally, I want to thank my husband, Lawrence Stern, and daughter, Laura, for their patience, support, and love.

DAVID WANG

There are many people to thank for helping make my efforts bear fruit in this book. First is my coauthor Linda Groat. Linda was my doctoral adviser at the University of Michigan. And as my teacher in research methods during that time, she gave me my first awareness of these things. I have learned more from her in the process of writing this book.

My thanks and gratitude go to Amanda Miller at John Wiley Publishers, whose confidence in this project was unwavering. Her advice was always just what was needed, and her gentle firmness kept both Linda and me on task. Thanks also go to Amanda's assistant, Nyshie Perkinson.

I wish to thank many colleagues and student assistants. Two colleagues in particular are Brian Schermer, now of the University of Wisconsin-Milwaukee, and Keith Diaz Moore, of Washington State University Spokane. At different times, they occupied the office next to mine, and both were very helpful in their encouragement, suggestions for literature, and constructive criticism. Thanks also go to other colleagues at Washington State University for their contributions and encouragement: Suzanne Snowdon, Kerry Brooks, Catherine Bicknell, Darlene Septelka, Tracy Grover, Nancy Clark Brown, Henry Matthews, Ken Carper, John Abell, Ayad Rahmani, Douglas Menzies, Joanne Asher Thompson, Phillip Tabb, and Forster Ndubisi. Michael Neville, chair of WSU's department of philosophy, offered me detailed advice on Chapter 11, for which I am grateful. I am also grateful to Kathy Schwanz and her staff at the CALS library at WSU Spokane, who supplied me punctually with the endless stream of books and journal articles I requested. Ann Warrington at WSU's main architecture library in Pullman was also helpful. And then there are the graduate student assistants who helped me: Eliot Price, Nicole Alexander, Angela Feser, and Daniel Pontius—thanks guys; I simply could not have done this without you. Linda's assistants Fernando Lara and Leonard Temko at the University of Michigan also made my task a lot easier—thank you.

Much thanks go to my friend Catherine Goodman, whose prayers, counsel, and expertise in the field of textbook writing remained a steady source of encouragement.

And of course, my thanks and love go to my wife Valerie and our sons, Jeremy, Andrew, and Joshua.

I dedicate my efforts in this book to my graduate students, who always keep me learning.

ARCHITECTURAL
RESEARCH METHODS

Part I

The Domain of Architectural Research

Chapter 1

The Scope of This Book

1.1 INTRODUCTION: THE AUDIENCE FOR THIS BOOK

The aim of this book is to provide an introductory guide for anyone wishing to conduct research on an aspect of the built environment—from a building component to a room, a building, a neighborhood, or an urban center.

By this we mean to suggest that this book is intended to be both *comprehensive* and an *entry point*. Our intent is to be comprehensive by providing a single text that addresses the full range of research methods available and applicable to the diverse array of topics germane to architectural research. We also want to offer an entry point by introducing readers to the major characteristics and applications of each research method, and to provide references to more specific books and articles on the methods of interest. Indeed, a plethora of materials already exists on how to conduct research either in specific design-related areas (e.g., socio-cultural issues or architectural history) or in related disciplines (e.g., the sciences or humanities). Yet to date, architectural researchers have not had the benefit of a single source that assembles this material within a clearly articulated framework. This book aims to provide such a framework.

With this goal in mind, we envision an audience for this book that includes at least four types of readers:

Architectural Students in Ph.D. and M.Sc. programs. There are now over 20 Ph.D. programs and at least an equal number of M.Sc. programs offered in architecture throughout North America. Numerous other research programs in architecture exist worldwide, although the exact numbers are difficult to come by. Many degree programs in architectural research offer multiple areas of specialization or emphasis, so there is an obvious need for a comprehensive book that introduces a range of methods across multiple topic areas. What is more, "research methods" is typically a required course in the curricula of these programs; yet, many of these courses use compilations (or "coursepacks") of readings from neighboring disciplines such as history, engineering, and the social sciences. Although this practice recognizes that many disciplines are concerned about issues related to human interactions with the built environment, we are motivated to provide a text that is explicitly aimed at the graduate research student in architecture. To this end, this book takes material from those neighboring disciplines and applies the information in ways more directly useful for classes in *architectural* research methods.

Faculty Scholars and Researchers in Architecture and Architecture-related fields. For at least 25 years now, a number of architectural faculty have chosen to concentrate their creative work on scholarship and funded research rather than on practice. For those who have themselves graduated from doctoral or research masters programs, this book may provide a kind of "refresher" text in methods. Others may have had to develop and pursue their research projects with guidance from colleagues or the few easily available published sources. This book is intended to aid such independent work for interested faculty.

Upper Level M.Arch and B.Arch Students. Many architectural students are asked to undertake some form of research project in the final years of their professional program. For some, it may be the programming segment of a final thesis project (see our first example in Chapter 5). For others, it may be an expanded project or research paper on a specialized topic of interest. This book provides some basic guidelines for any professional program students who expect to carry out such assignments.

To this segment of our audience we wish to say explicitly that this book is our earnest attempt to bridge the gap between design and research. This gap, as some of the following pages will argue (for instance, see Chapter 5 on the relationship between design and research), is both perceived and real. While we do not use forced arguments to erase the real differences between the two domains, we do make the case that a knowledge of research methods can inform the design process.

Architectural Practitioners. Although relatively few firms have established research divisions, many practitioners will at some point feel the need to conduct research in the course of a design project. Such research may consist in the development of a survey questionnaire for a client/user group, or an extended investigation of a historic style for a preservation project. While such studies are certainly more limited than a typical research project in academia, the practitioner will still need to spend some time structuring and organizing the inquiry. This book aims to provide the practitioner with a variety of strategies and tactics to use in his or her endeavor.

All Together Now. In conceptualizing the diverse readership outlined above, we have found the diagram in Figure 1.1 particularly useful. Overall, the diagram suggests the complementary nature of research and design. (Again, for a more extended discussion of this issue, please see Chapter 5.) It also suggests the relative proportion of these two activities in different contexts. The left-hand third of the diagram suggests that professional program students and practitioners are likely to emphasize design-related activities, while employing research less frequently and more episodically. The middle third of the diagram suggests that students in research masters pro-

DESIGN		
		RESEARCH
B.Arch / M.Arch	M.Sc.	Ph.D.
Practitioners	Consultants	Research faculty
	Specialist firms	Research scientist

Figure 1.1 The complementary nature of research and design.

grams, practitioners in consulting roles and firms specializing in more focused areas are likely to experience a more equal balance of activities. Finally, the right hand segment of the diagram represents the context in which doctoral students, research-oriented faculty, and research lab practitioners are more likely to find themselves. For them, the research activity is likely to dominate, even while the research questions may well flow directly from architectural design questions.

In sum, our goal is for each reader to find this book a valuable resource for whatever type and quantity of research activity she or he pursues. Our firm belief is that whatever our individual contributions to architectural research may be, ultimately these efforts will not only complement each other but also substantially further the long-term vitality of the architectural field.

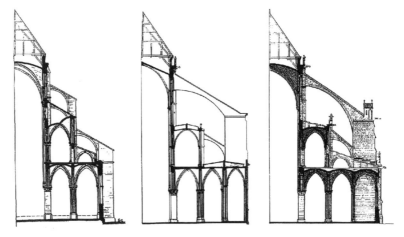

Figure 1.2 Flying buttress. (Left to right) After Sanders and Clark; Clark, after Leconte; Clark, after Chaine. Courtesy of William Clark.

1.2   WHAT IS RESEARCH IN ARCHITECTURE?

In one sense, architectural research has been conducted throughout the history of architecture. The development of particular structural forms and building materials over the centuries is the outcome of trial and error experimentation, systematic observation, and application of such building principles to other building projects. Take for example the development of the flying buttress, the first visible external examples of which are attributed to the nave of Notre Dame de Paris.[1] A combination of archaeological reconstruction and structural analysis conducted by authors William Clark and Robert Mark demonstrates the technical validity of the original buttress design. However, the authors argue that structural stress points resulting from that design, in conjunction with associated maintenance requirements, seem to have led to major alterations to the buttress system early in the 13th century. Continued modifications and systematic observations in subsequent cathedral projects led to further innovations, and so on. Parallel developments in all manner of materials and structural innovation can be cited throughout the history of the field.

On the other hand, the conduct of architectural research outside the confines of specific building projects is a much more recent phenomenon. Although climate and structural studies seem to have been a focal point of research in the 1950s, architectural research emerged more broadly across a range of topic areas—including socio-behavioral issues, design methods, and energy conservation—in the 1960s and early 1970s.[2] It was during this period that funding from an array of federal agencies from the National Science Foundation to the National Endowment for the Arts became more widely available; university programs provided internal support for architecture faculty to pursue research topics; doctoral programs in architecture began to emerge in greater numbers; architecture-affiliated organizations such as the American Institute of Architects and the Association of Collegiate Schools of Architecture sponsored joint ventures to promote research; a few major architectural firms developed research-oriented divisions; and the professional journals began to publish evaluation studies and offer research award programs.

Over the last two decades, this great variety of research activity has continued, but often in a more variegated way. Many areas of research have experienced an ebb and flow of funding and interest. Energy conservation, for example, was a dominant feature of much technical research in the 1970s because of the energy crisis, but received much less attention in the 1980s. Over the last decade, however, research interest in sustainability has reintroduced many of the earlier issues, but framed within a new conceptual model.

Similarly, research in architectural history has over the years moved from an almost exclusively art historical model into a more conceptually expansive terrain that includes design 'theory' and criticism. Interest in historic preservation seemed to be overtaken in the late 1980s by a concern for the architectural implications of deconstruction and critical theory.

And in the realm of practice, the early emphasis on a relatively systematic cycle of programming, design, and evaluation led a number of larger firms to establish programming research units. This emphasis coincided with a trend in the professional journals, which started publishing evaluation articles on notable design projects on a relatively regular basis. In the last decade, however, predesign services have been transformed and reconceptualized; they may no longer consist simply of programming, but include facilities planning integrated with real estate services, organizational development, and business strategy. According to a 1997 AIA firm survey, expanded nondesign services accounted for a large portion of architectural firms' growth nationally.[3]

Given this staggering breadth, then, what is architectural research? In a 1984 edited book titled *Architectural Research*, at least two chapters address this question. James Snyder, who edited the book, suggests that research is "systematic inquiry directed toward the creation of knowledge."[4] Two elements of this definition are significant.

First, the inquiry is systematic in some way. Although one might unconsciously acquire important information simply by strolling down the street observing the array of buildings in view, the notion of systematic inquiry suggests that there is a conscious demarcation of how particular information is culled from the rest of our experience, how it is categorized, analyzed, and presented. The term *systematic* need not be equated with *experimental* or *positivist*, terms that many critics associate with work they consider "reductionist." While it is true that structuring a study around precisely defined variables is reductionist, it is just as true that culling or coding key themes from an in-depth interview is also reductionist. The truth is that all research is a reduction of some kind or other. Research necessarily involves reducing lived experience or observed phenomena to chunks of information that are noted and categorized in some way. Choosing between an experiment and a qualitative study is a matter of choosing one reduction strategy over another.

Second, knowledge creation is frequently cited as characteristic of the research endeavor. To many readers this may seem to imply something on the scale of the grand theories of the sciences, such as Einstein's theory of relativity or geological theories of plate tectonics. Although such theories certainly encapsulate new knowledge, they are not the only model of knowledge creation. Rather, we would argue that new knowledge can also emerge in relatively small increments and be attained through a variety of means, including: assessing the outcome of fusing two previously distinct functional building types; testing materials through a series of built projects; and evaluating the success of particular building forms in communicating intended meanings to different stakeholders.

Moreover, though much architectural research focuses on the physical outcomes of design—from the scale of building components to neighborhood and urban design—research on the process of design and the practices of architectural firms is just as vital. This is partly a consequence of the use of computer technology in multiple phases of the design process. As well, global economic trends are causing changes in so many professions that research on the structure and scope of architectural practice has taken on a special urgency.

1.3   THE IMPERATIVE FOR ARCHITECTURAL RESEARCH

We believe that architectural research is mightily important to the success and ultimate viability of the profession, and should be pursued both for reasons of self-interest and more broadly for the common good. Although some researchers have argued that embracing a research model will lift the status of architecture to the level of other professions, such as engineering or medicine, we believe this is not the most persuasive argument to advance.[5] This is because each profession operates within a context that has its own dynamics and constraints. The context of medicine or engineering is substantially different in many particulars from the context of architecture.

Others have argued that the increasing pace of "post-industrial technological change has exploded the knowledge base" required for the architectural profession.[6] Although in a general sense this is true, it is still also true that many building and design projects can be based on existing, well-articulated and known typologies (e.g., big-box stores or single-family homes). In addition, many projects involving greater uncertainty can be developed with relative ease because they involve a limited array of stakeholders from social circumstances familiar to the architectural team.

Our argument for the essential importance of research is that an ever-increasing proportion of architectural practice involves unfamiliar circumstances beyond the expertise of individual practitioners, and beyond the conventional wisdom of the profession as a whole. This is the case, for example, if the requirements of a project—perhaps a multi-use complex or an innovative manufacturing plant—are extraordinarily complicated. Great uncertainty is also likely if unconventional aesthetic principles (e.g., derived from poststructuralist or deconstructivist philosophy; see Figure 1.3) are being used in a setting involving conflicting stakeholder values. Or if the project is for a specialized user group, such as people with spinal cord injuries, whose particular requirements for the physical environment are not well documented.

1.4   DEFINING THE TERMS OF METHODOLOGY:
STRATEGY AND TACTICS

In his classic book *The Conduct of Inquiry*, Abraham Kaplan defines methods as the study of the process, rather than the product, of inquiry.[7] More specifically, he argues for using the term *methodology* for "mid-range" aspects of the research process that are common to a broad range of disciplines. Thus he is seeking to articulate the

Figure 1.3 A deconstructivist interior in a well-known public building. Research can inform us on the many issues that innovative ideas, like this one, bring up. Courtesy of Katherine Keane.

processes of inquiry that are simultaneously more *general* than the specific techniques of interviewing, archival searches, or data collection and analysis, and more *specific* than broad epistemological perspectives such as positivism, structuralism, or post-structuralism.

Following Kaplan's lead, we use the terms *method* and *methodology* to focus on research processes that are common across the entire range of architectural research, including content areas from the technical fields to the humanities, and from the pragmatic to the most theoretical. Although critical theory and poststructuralist thought have been very influential in architectural research in recent years, these philosophical stances are more usefully understood as *systems of inquiry* within which more specific choices about methodology are made. Within any particular system of inquiry (i.e., postpositivism) there are multiple methodologies, or choices for structuring the research (see Figure 1.4).

To clarify the relationship between the 'mid-range' of methodology and the more specific level of techniques, we distinguish between *strategies* (methods) and *tactics* (techniques). This distinction has been adopted by many other authors writing about research methods.[8] The term *strategy* is defined as "the skillful management and planning of anything."[9] This contrasts with the more detailed level of *tactics*, defined as "any skillful move." In the military usage of these words, *strategy* refers to a nation's overall war plans, whereas *tactics* refers to the disposition of armed forces in combat.[10]

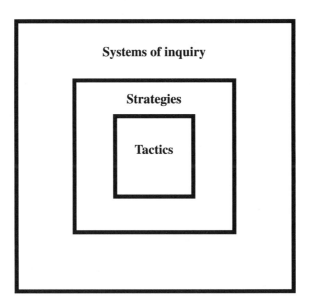

Figure 1.4 A system of inquiry frames both strategies and tactics.

In the context of our discussion, the *strategy* is the overall research plan or structure of the research study. In contrast, the *tactics* are the specific techniques used, such as data collection devices, response formats, archival treatment, and analytical procedures.

Thus we have defined a conceptual model of concentric frames (see Figure 1.4). The broadest frame is that of the system of inquiry. Assuming, for example, that we have adopted a structuralist perspective, this would then frame—but not predetermine—our choice among a range of strategies. Similarly, the choice of strategy then frames—but does not predetermine—the choice among a range of tactics. However, there should be a coherence and continuity among the system of inquiry, strategy, and tactics.

Another term we will frequently use as a synonym for strategy is *research design*. A research design is "an action plan for getting from here to there,"[11] where *here* describes the investigator's research question(s), and *there* describes the knowledge derived from the research. In between the *here* and the *there* are a set of steps and procedures that may be highly prescribed or emerge as the research proceeds.

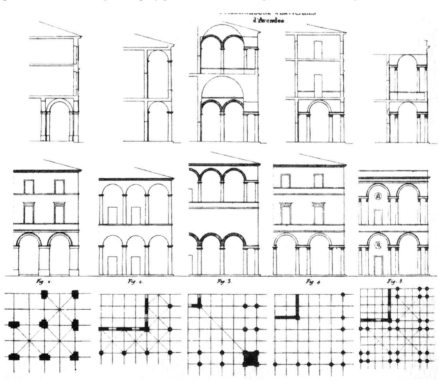

Figure 1.5 The notion of research design as a "type" is analogous to Jean-Nicolas-Louis Durand's development of formal types in architecture.

The term *research design* is one that is particularly appropriate for a readership trained in architecture and/or other design disciplines. In architecture, we often speak of a "parti" when describing the formal organizing concept of a design scheme. Similarly, we often refer to a variety of formal "types"—such as a courtyard form or nine-square plan—that specify generic spatial relationships. The important point is this: Just as a courtyard plan can be used for such varied purposes as college dorms, houses, museums, or office buildings, so too a given research design can be employed for a variety of topic areas of architectural research, from thermal comfort studies to analyses of aesthetic theories.

1.5 THE ORGANIZATION OF THIS BOOK: AN INTEGRATIVE FRAMEWORK

Our focus on the formal structure of research designs across a variety of topic areas is consistent with our goal of providing an integrative framework for architectural research. A common tendency in architecture has been to divide knowledge into domains associated with particular subdisciplines. As a consequence insights derived from research in energy-efficient technologies cannot easily be integrated with insights drawn from aesthetic analyses of exemplar buildings.[12] And yet, we believe that much innovative and needed research in architecture will result from integrating such apparently discrete topic areas. By organizing this book in terms of common research designs, we hope to make the commonalities shared by different kinds of architectural research more apparent.

In the subsequent chapters of the book, we will address seven major research strategies. We have purposefully chosen substantively neutral terms for each of these research strategies because our intention is to describe of the *structure* of the strategy, and to eschew any assumptions about the subject matter of the research. Readers who scan the table of contents will not see chapter titles containing such familiar terms as *theory/criticism research* or *human behavior research*. Indeed, we hope that this will encourage all of us to think *out of the box*.

As we have already mentioned, architectural research can be undertaken for different purposes and in different contexts. Sometimes research is initiated primarily for scholarly purposes, with its outcome being a published report, journal article, or dissertation. In this case, the researcher will need to be very clear about the overall structure of the study, being careful to choose a research strategy that is consistent with the nature of the research question. Readers who are most likely to follow the scholarly research model will likely find the discussion of individual research strategies in the seven central chapters of this book of particular value.

In other instances, architectural research may form an integral component of the design process, perhaps during the programming phase, or as a part of materials specification, or in the evaluation of schematic designs. In such situations, the nature of the inquiry is likely to be much more pragmatic, and the necessity of answering research questions as they arise in the design process often means that the inquiry is more episodic. Research of this more limited scope and duration is likely to concentrate on specific tactics by which the required information can be derived, whether from archives and documents, buildings and artifacts, or observations and conversations with people. Thus, within each of the chapters on research strategies, we provide a number of concrete examples of techniques through which the design researcher can discover the information s/he seeks.

1.6   AN OUTLINE OF THE CHAPTERS

Chapter 2 begins an exploration of common attributes among research strategies by addressing two foundational issues. First we discuss the range of paradigms—or systems of inquiry—that can serve as the epistemological basis for any research study. Within this discussion we consider several frameworks for clarifying the relations between these systems of inquiry. Second, we then examine the similarities and differences among the criteria for assessing research quality within these different systems of inquiry. Discussion of these criteria is framed by examples of specific research studies.

In Chapter 3, we move on to discuss the first step in almost all research endeavors—the literature review. After a general introduction, we discuss the variety of purposes that the literature review serves. Next we present a number of tactics for accomplishing this essential first step in research.

In Chapter 4, we introduce the role of theory in research. This chapter is paired with Chapter 5, which focuses on the nature and role of design. Our purpose for pairing these chapters is to emphasize that theoretical generalizations and practical interventions in design are both possible and desirable outcomes of research. Taken together, Chapters 4 and 5 form an introduction to the seven chapters on specific research strategies. In the theory chapter, we first discuss the role of theory in research generally. We next consider different ways to categorize different kinds of theory. And finally, we use exemplary research studies to demonstrate the role of theory within each research strategy.

With Chapter 5 we discuss design as both outcome and generator of research. The chapter begins with a discussion of the general qualities and challenges of the relationship between design and research. Next we present several alternative models for the episodic incorporation of research in the design process. Finally, we argue that design or action research outcomes can play a role in any of the seven research strategies we have presented in earlier chapters; and exemplar studies are presented and discussed for each.

Each of the next seven chapters (6–12) has a common organizational structure. After a short introduction, we present several well-known exemplars of architectural research that represent the particular strategy being examined. In the main body of the chapter we discuss the basic characteristics of the strategy, citing further examples of architectural research. With the contours of the strategy clearly in mind, we discuss some of the common tactics for information gathering and analysis. Along the way, we describe examples of recent and current research conducted by students, faculty, and practitioners. A general discussion of the strengths and weaknesses of the strategy and a list of recommended readings concludes each chapter.

Beginning with Chapter 6, we address, in turn, each of seven major research strategies. As a means of previewing the nature of each research design, we use the example of research on windows to describe below the next seven chapters.

Chapter 6, then, explores the nature of the interpretive research strategy, which typically draws upon evidence derived from archival or artifactual sources. This is so usually because the research question focuses on a setting or circumstance from the past. For example, Kim Dovey wondered about the complex cultural associations that have been attached to window openings over time.[13] To this end, he analyzed the evolution of window shutters, and the meanings that have come to be attached to them. While operable shutters were once a necessity, they are largely decorative today, so much so that, in many instances, the size of the shutters obviously bear no relationship to the size of the windows they adorn. And yet we feel that something is missing without them. The fact that they are the wrong size does not even occur to us, much less bother us. And so Dovey raises real questions regarding "authenticity," and the shades of meaning that this word takes on in describing built environments that are so often constructed of "fake" things, but things that we nevertheless want to be there. Research helps us to understand why this is so.

Chapter 7 introduces the qualitative research design. Like interpretive research, qualitative research seeks to understand settings and phenomena in a holistic and full-bodied way. But whereas interpretive research seeks discovery through archival and artifactual material from the past, qualitative research typically focuses on contemporary social and cultural circumstances. A good of example of a qualitative analysis is presented in Clare Cooper Marcus's book *A House as a Mirror of Self*.[14] Cooper Marcus sought to understand the way in which people "express aspects of their *unconscious* in the home environment."[15] One of the hallmarks of qualitative research is its emphasis on understanding how people make sense of their own experience. Among the many examples in Cooper Marcus's book is this commentary by a woman about her bedroom and its window:

> I loved my room because of the large window and the view out the backyards. I rearranged it so that my bed was by the window and I lay in my bed gazing at the stars. I felt philosophical and wondered about the universe, UFOs and the existence of other forms of life. I felt very much at peace with myself and my surroundings. I tried to pick out constellations. I would write "Good morning world" backward on the window through the dew.[16]

Figure 1.6 Window shutters analyzed by Kim Dovey, 1985. With permission from David Seamon and Robert Mugerauer, *Dwelling, Place & Environment* (Malabar, Fla.: Krieger Pub., 2000).

Figure 1.7 The bedroom window as a place of reverie and withdrawal. From Clare Cooper Marcus, *House as a Mirror of Self*, copyright © 1995 by Clare Cooper Marcus, by permission of Conari Press.

Next, with Chapter 8, we move on to the correlational strategy. The signature characteristic of this research design is the discovery of patterns or relationships among specified variables of interest in a particular setting or circumstance. In a study of people's perceptions of window quality, Stephen Kaplan and his colleagues were interested in finding out whether there was a consistent pattern of similarity or differences in the way designers and laypeople experienced windows.[17] Their findings showed, among other things, that nondesigners tended to prefer window places with a sense of enclosure, while designers did not register any such preference. This raises very interesting questions regarding how design training on the part of the experiencing subject—never mind any questions about what culture he or she comes from—can significantly affect how a "window place" can be perceived and experienced.

With Chapter 9 we explore the nature of the experimental strategy, the research design that is the most completely codified in the research methods literature. For many researchers it stands as the preeminent standard for empirical research. In others' eyes, however, it is viewed as being inappropriately "reductionist" because of its emphasis on the careful manipulation of variables (often in a lab setting), with the goal of attributing causality. In architecture, the experimental strategy is the bedrock of much materials and building component testing, including, of course, windows. Among the many tests of window performance there are tests for wind resistance,

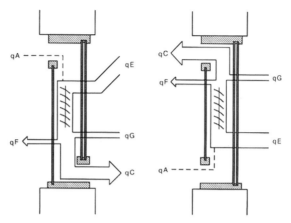

Figure 1.8 Ventilation and thermal gain/loss diagrams for windows. From R. Boehm and Kurt Brandle, "Testing of Air-Flow Windows for Evaluation and Application." Drawing courtesy of Kurt Brandle.

thermal transmission, tightness of seal against both air infiltration and water leakage, and so on. The images in Figure 1.8 are from a study conducted by R. F. Boehm and K. Brandle for the U.S. Department of Energy;[18] they used experimental methods to compare the performance of triple-glazed "airflow" windows, which have a higher initial installation cost, with a more standard double-glazed design. The window units were mounted side by side in a mock room that could simulate a variety of sun angles and heating/cooling conditions. Boehm and Brandle found that the triple-glazed airflow windows indeed performed better in terms of thermal transmission and retention during the extreme summer and winter seasons, but their superiority during the transition seasons of spring and autumn was not noticeably better than the double-glazed unit. Their conclusion was that the cost effectiveness of the airflow unit over a prolonged period, at least at their level of investigation, was not demonstrable.

Chapter 10 introduces the simulation strategy. The essential characteristic of this research design is that some aspect of the physical environment is recreated in one of a variety of modes, from a highly abstract computer simulation to a full-scale, real life mock-up. Some simulations—such as models, mock-ups and now computer-generated imaging and walk-throughs—are of course also used in architectural design practice. In practice, the very pragmatic goal is to determine by means of the simulated environment the likely success of the design according to any number of criteria from client satisfaction to earthquake resistance. In scholarly research, simulation is increasingly used as an alternative to lengthy and perhaps costly physical experiments. In a research study on heat transfer in double-pane window designs, Medved and Novak sought to evaluate window panel designs using numerical simulation software.[19] To accomplish this, they first developed the simulation software, then validated it through a series of physical experiments. Once they had validated the simulation model, they then used it to evaluate the designs.

In Chapter 11, we present the logical argumentation strategy. The hallmark of this strategy is the sequence of logical steps within a closed system. The most typical examples of this derive from the disciplines of philosophy and math. Although philosophy uses words or sentences and math uses numbers, both employ relatively pure forms of logical argumentation. In architecture, this strategy can be used, for example, in a philosophical treatise on architectural aesthetics. Or, working from the mathematical model, much of the research in computer-aided design involves the development of computer software generating long sequences of coding. An example of this is Caldas and Norford's recent paper,[20] which reports on their development of a genetic algorithm for the design of fenestration patterns in buildings. Their goal was to create a "generative and goal-oriented" computer tool that could help designers generate and evaluate window designs according to environmental performance criteria. (See Figure 1.9)

In Chapter 12, the last of the research strategy sequence, we discuss mixed-method strategies and case studies. Increasingly, it appears that researchers across many disciplines are seeking ways to marshal the benefits of two or more research designs. In a similar vein, many other scholars are gravitating toward case study research, a strategy in which a particular setting or circumstance is investigated holistically using a variety of data collection and analysis tactics. Lara's investigation

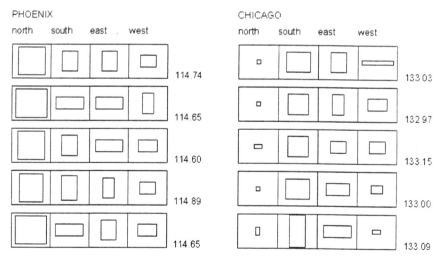

Figure 1.9 Window patterns generated from algorithms. From Luisa G. Caldas and Leslie K. Norford, "A Genetic Algorithm Tool for Design Optimization," in *Proceedings of ACADIA'99.* Drawing courtesy of Luisa G. Caldas and Leslie K. Norford.

of the popularization of modernist architecture in Brazil during the 1950s is a good example of such a case study.[21] In addition to archival data and in-depth interviews with residents of 1950s houses, he also conducted a physical inventory of housing within two multiblock areas of Belo Horizonte. In his formal analysis of the facades, the findings indicate that while the houses tend to have asymmetrical window compositions like their modernist models, they also tend to be of medium size and vertical orientation like the vernacular Brazilian examples.

An epilogue brings this book to a close. In it we review and summarize the major themes discussed in the course of the earlier chapters. We also offer a diagrammatic model of the domain of architectural research methods. At a minimum it may serve as a heuristic device, guiding scholars and practitioners as they consider their choices for research methods in their future research endeavors. Finally, we close with an optimistic perspective on the potential of architectural research for sustaining the vitality of architecture.

1.7   RECOMMENDED READINGS

Readers interested in understanding the status of architectural research as of 1984 may want to consult James Snyder, ed., *Architectural Research* (New York: Van Nostrand Reinhold, 1984). Two chapters were cited in the preceding discussion: Michael Joroff and Stanley Morse," A Proposed Framework for the Emerging Field of Architectural Research," and Roger Schluntz, "Design + Energy: Results of a National Student Design Competition."

For a classic discussion of research inquiry and methodology in general, readers may want to consult: Abraham Kaplan, *The Conduct of Inquiry* (San Francisco: Chandler, 1964).

NOTES

1. William Clark and Robert Mark, "The First Flying Buttresses: A New Reconstruction of the Nave of Notre Dame de Paris" *Art Bulletin* 66, no. 1 (1984): 47–65.

2. Roger Schluntz, "Design + Energy: Results of a National Student Design Competition" (Washington, D.C.: ACSA, 1984).

3. Clifford Pearson, "How to Succeed with Expanded Services," *Architectural Record*, January 1998, 50–55.

4. James Snyder, *Architectural Research* (New York: Van Nostrand, 1984).

5. Michael Joroff and Stanley Morse, "A Proposed Framework for the Emerging Field of Architectural Research," in *Architectural Research*, ed. J. Snyder (New York: Van Nostrand, 1984), 15–28.

6. Snyder, *Architectural Research*.

7. Abraham Kaplan, *The Conduct of Inquiry* (San Francisco: Chandler, 1964).

8. Groat was first introduced to this vocabulary early in her research career by David Canter, then of the University of Surrey. Although the strategy/tactics distinction is not universally used by research methodologists, a number of authors do make use of it as well, e.g., Denzin and Lincoln, 1998; Mertens, 1998.

9. C. L. Barnhart, *The World Book Dictionary* (Chicago: World Book, 1995).

10. Ibid.

11. Robert K. Yin, *Case Study Research* (Newbury Park, Calif.: Sage Publications, 1984): 19.

12. Julia Robinson, "Architectural Research: Incorporating Myth and Science," *Journal of Architectural Education* 44, no. 1 (1990): 20–32. See also Joroff and Morse, "A Proposed Framework for the Emerging Field of Architectural Research."

13. Kim Dovey, "The Quest for Authenticity and the Replication of Environmental Meaning," in *Dwelling, Place and Environment: Towards a Phenomenology of Person and World*, ed. D. Seamon and R. Mugerauer (Dordrecht, Netherlands: Nijhoff, 1985).

14. Clare Cooper Marcus, *The House as a Mirror of Self* (Berkeley, Calif.: Conari Press, 1995).

15. Ibid., 10.

16. Ibid., 26–27.

17. Stephen Kaplan, D. Foster, and R. Kaplan, "Pattern Hypothesis: An Empirical Test," *Proceedings of the Environmental Design Research Association* (1986): 188–193.

18. R. Boehm and Kurt Brandle, "Testing of Air-Flow Windows for Evaluation and Application" (prepared for the U.S. Department of Energy, contract #W-7405-ENG-48).

19. Saso Medved and P. Novak, "Heat Transfer Through a Double Pane Window with an Insulation Screen Open at the Top," *Energy and Buildings* 28 (1998): 257–268

20. Luisa G. Caldas and L. K. Norford, "A Genetic Algorithm Tool for Design Optimization," in *Proceedings of ACADIA '99* (The Association for Computer-Aided Design in Architecture, 1999), 260–271.

21. Fernando Lara, "Popular Modernism: An Analysis of the Acceptance of Modern Architecture in 1950s Brazil" (Ph.D. diss., University of Michigan, 2001).

Chapter 2

Systems of Inquiry and Standards of Research Quality

2.1   INTRODUCTION

In Chapter 1, we argued that any researcher's choice of a particular research design is necessarily framed by the researcher's own assumptions about both the nature of reality and how one can come to apprehend it. We have used the term *system of inquiry* to describe these sets of assumptions;[1] another term that is frequently used to describe such assumptions is *paradigm*.[2] Both terms convey the notion of a worldview, the ultimate truthfulness of which cannot be established.

For example, in one study, Medved and Novak present an analysis of heat transfer through a double-pane window.[3] They aim to evaluate the performance of specific double-pane window designs through a combination of computer simulation and experimental testing. They introduce the research question this way:

> An element [double-pane window] with a semi-open cavity and a siphon of different shapes as an integral part of the window was developed [on the basis of previous research]. The cavity is formed by lowering blinds or closing screens over the outer side of the window. The siphon at the top of the cavity is formed by the housing and always has the same shape, while the bottom of the cavity can be opened or closed. . . . In this way a cavity with different siphons is established. . . . Different cavities are presented in Fig. [2.1]. Heat transfer through a closed cavity with a 'y' shaped siphon was analyzed in this study [positions a and c in Fig. 2.1].[4]

21

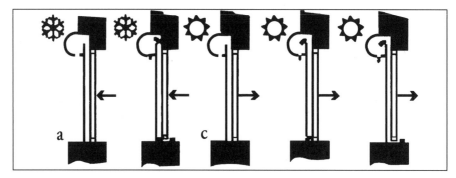

Figure 2.1   Window diagrams. From Saso Medved and Peter Novak, "Heat Transfer through a Double-Pane window with an Insulation Screen Open at the Top," *Energy and Buildings* 28 (1998): 257–268. With permission from Elsevier Press.

From this short excerpt, it is clear that the authors have conducted their research within a system of inquiry that assumes the physical reality of objects, whose properties can be accurately specified, their performance measured by calibrated instruments, and the outcomes compared in quantifiable terms. In other words, there is a reality "out there" that we can know and define systematically.

Next is the example of Benyamin Schwarz's study of the design process in the development of nursing homes, examined through three case study projects.[5] (See Figure 2.2) The ontological assumptions that frame his research are stated this way:

> [T]his inquiry . . . [allowed] access to the inherent complexity of social reality. . . . A design process cannot be regarded as a world made up of totally objectified elements and observable, measurable facts. Therefore, an effort was made to avoid simplification of the social phenomena of the design process.[6]

Schwarz's commentary reflects his assumption that reality is nuanced by the complexity of social relations, rather than being limited to the objectively measured reality posited by Medved and Novak.

Third, and last, is the example of Diane Favro's study of the well-known early-twentieth-century California architect Julia Morgan (1872–1957).[7] By way of introduction, Favro cites a quotation from a 1931 interview with Julia Morgan in which she is asked about women's contribution to the field of architecture. Morgan demurs and comments that women professionals have so far contributed little or nothing, though they might in the future. Favro then compares these comments with the response of Linda Nochlin, who in 1972 was asked why there had been no great women artists; to which Nochlin replied that "as a disenfranchised group, women artists had limited opportunities for greatness."[8] Favro then goes on:

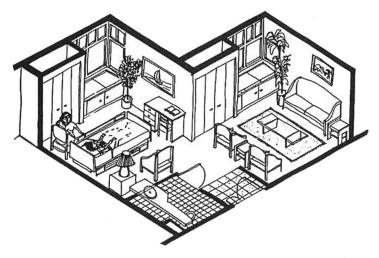

Figure 2.2 Axonometric drawing of the nursing home, the design process for which was analyzed by Benyamin Schwarz. Drawing courtesy of Benyamin Schwarz.

Thus, Nochlin correctly deduced, the question itself is inappropriate. Women architects similarly have been evaluated according to masculinist criteria. To be accurate, every evaluation of female practitioners must consider how gender affected their careers, designs, and recognition.[9]

With this introduction, Favro is clearly signaling that her study of Morgan will challenge existing orthodoxies regarding how the careers of architectural practitioners in general, and women in particular, are assessed.

These three examples clearly demonstrate the great variety of paradigms—or systems of inquiry—within which architectural research is typically conducted. Although both Schwarz and Favro, for whatever reasons, chose to be quite explicit about the systems of inquiry underlying their particular studies, it is far more often the case that researchers are relatively inexplicit about their study's ontological assumptions (e.g. Medved and Novak). While the experienced researcher is likely to be able to infer the paradigmatic frame of a given study, less experienced readers may be left wondering or confused about why the study was structured and presented in a particular way.

Thus the goals of this chapter are twofold: 1) to provide a conceptual framework for understanding the range of paradigms commonly employed in architectural research; and 2) to clarify the way in which standards for evaluating research quality are substantially dependent on the system of inquiry employed by the researcher.

Figure 2.3   One of Julia Morgan's well-known buildings at Asilomar, California. Photo courtesy of Melissa Harris.

2.2   FRAMEWORKS FOR UNDERSTANDING MULTIPLE SYSTEMS OF INQUIRY

Because the practice of architecture requires knowledge of a vast array of phenomena—from the physical properties of materials to principles of visual perception—it is hardly surprising that the research subdisciplines within architecture bring with them a broad range of paradigms. Indeed, this is also the case within entire disciplinary families—e.g. within the natural sciences, the social sciences, or the humanities. From the perspective of someone in the humanities, "science" may seem to represent a rather monolithic system of inquiry within which a highly standardized set of procedures is adopted; but from a scientist's point of view, there are vast differences between scientific disciplines with respect to the typical methods employed and their standards for the credibility of evidence.[10] As a consequence, many scholars of research methodology from a variety of disciplines have developed models or frameworks for clarifying the similarities and differences among systems of inquiry.

In the following chapter segments, we will briefly review several of these frameworks, and then introduce a three-part framework that we will utilize throughout the remainder of this book.

2.2.1 A Dichotomous Framework

In a 1990 *Journal of Architectural Education* article, Julia Robinson characterized the then current state of architecture research as one in which a dichotomous set of paradigms predominated. (Even now, the circumstances she describes are not so very different.) While the stated goal of her article was to offer a means of resolving this dichotomy into a more integrated framework for architectural research, she nevertheless offered a rather stark differentiation of the two contending research paradigms. Two fairly distinct communities of architectural researchers "find different explanations acceptable," according to Robinson. Their ideas "of acceptable explanation do not necessarily coincide."[11]

The terms by which she chooses to describe these two systems of inquiry are *science* and *myth*. Although both science and myth "are used to explain," the way they do so is quite different. A scientific explanation is typically portrayed as a mathematical description made up of linked fragments; it is thereby atomistic, reductionist, and convergent. Architectural research on technology, engineering, or behavioral issues are seen as representing the scientific paradigm. On the other hand, mythic or poetic description is seen as continuous, holistic, divergent, and generative; this paradigm is usually associated with architectural research drawn from an arts and humanities base. This would include much of the scholarly work in architectural history and design theory.

Although Robinson's use of the "science vs. myth" terminology is relatively idiosyncratic, the notion of a dichotomous set of research paradigms is commonplace in architecture and other research disciplines. Perhaps the most common device for framing such a dichotomous model employs the terms *quantitative* vs. *qualitative*. At its most basic level, this terminology assumes that quantitative research depends on the manipulation of phenomena that can be measured by numbers; whereas qualitative research depends on nonnumerical evidence, whether verbal (oral or written), experiential (film or notes about people in action), or artifactual (objects, buildings, or urban areas).

Unfortunately, the quantitative/qualitative terminology, though beguilingly simple, places the emphasis on distinctions at the level of tactics, i.e. the techniques for gathering or interpreting evidence or data. But, distinctions between research methods at this level are often not nearly so clear cut. Many research studies employ

Figure 2.4 In her studio teaching, Julia Robinson had her students evaluate institutional living environments, the results of which were subjected to statistical, "scientific" analysis. © ACSA Press, Washington, D.C., 1993.

a combination of quantitative and qualitative tactics. Even research areas normally associated with a qualitative paradigm, such as architectural history, may necessarily require significant quantitative techniques. For example, in Fernando Lara's study of the acceptance of modern architecture by the Brazilian middle class, a quantitative analysis was conducted based on documentation of the facade elements of 460 houses in Belo Horizonte.[12] In this case, the quantitative analysis complemented interviews and archival material that focused on how and why the houses were built as they were. (For more details on this study, see Chapter 12.)

At another level however, the quantitative/qualitative framework entails certain ontological and epistemological assumptions, as well as implications for methodological choices, that mirror those described by Robinson. Figure 2.6 represents an abbreviated version of John Creswell's matrix for differentiating quantitative and qualitative research paradigms in the social sciences.[13] Within this model, quantitative research assumes an *objective* reality and a view of the researcher as *independent of the subject of inquiry*. Qualitative research, on the other hand, assumes a *subjective* reality and a view of the researcher as *interactive with the subject of inquiry*. On a methodological level, the quantitative paradigm is seen as involving a *deductive* process of inquiry that seeks *cause-and-effect explanations*; whereas the qualitative paradigm

Figure 2.5 Robinson also had her students sketch a sociable home environment based on the "mythic" qualities that were evoked. Drawing by Michela Mahady. © ACSA Press, Washington, D.C., 1993.

Assumption	Question	Quantitative	Qualitative
Ontological Assumption	What is the nature of reality?	Reality is objective and singular, apart from the researcher.	Reality is subjective and multiple as seen by participants in a study.
Epistemological Assumption	What is the relationship of the researcher to that researched?	Researcher is independent from that being researched.	Researcher interacts with that being researched.
Methodological Assumption	What is the process of research?	Deductive process Cause and effect	Inductive process Mutual simultaneous shaping of factors.

Figure 2.6 Quantitative and Qualitative Paradigm Assumptions. Adapted from John Creswell, *Research Design: Quantitative and Qualitative Approaches* (Thousand Oaks, Calif.: Sage Publications, 1994, p. 5). By permission of Sage Publications.

necessitates an *inductive* process of inquiry that seeks clarification of *multiple critical factors* affecting the phenomenon.

Even within the family of physical sciences, this dichotomous framework for differentiating systems of inquiry is frequently employed. When the terms *quantitative* and *qualitative* are employed in the sciences, they are often associated with the corresponding terms *hard* vs. *soft*.[14] The implication is that the sciences that depend on numerical measurement (e.g., physics) are hard, while those that rely on description and classification (e.g., biology or geology) are soft.

In our view, however, this dichotomous framework is often misleading. First, as indicated earlier, the quantitative/qualitative terminology places undue emphasis on the level of tactics, instead of that of ontological and epistemological assumptions. As numerous examples of architectural research throughout this book will demonstrate, both numerical and nonnumerical evidence can be deployed in the service of more than one system of inquiry.

Secondly, at least as characterized by Creswell's framework and others like it, there is an assumption that each of the two paradigms necessitates a particular research methodology. For example, the quantitative system of inquiry is assumed to be manifested in deductive methodology that seeks to discover cause-and-effect explanations. While we do not deny that there may frequently be such an association of quantitative data and deductive methods, this is not an invariate and necessary relationship. A system of inquiry will indeed frame the articulation of a research question, but there is not a one-to-one relationship between that system of inquiry and a particular research design. Indeed, in the chapters that follow, we will intentionally include examples of architectural research that employ research designs atypical of that particular topic area and system of inquiry.

2.2.2 A Continuum Framework for Multiple Systems of Inquiry

In their 1980 review of the state of architectural research, Joroff and Morse map out the range of architectural research methods along a nine-point continuum from informal observation on the one hand to laboratory research on the other.[15] (See Figure 2.7) While this framework identifies what appears to be a full range of architectural research areas representing different systems of inquiry, the organizing concept for the continuum is essentially consistent with the dichotomous model described above. This is because the underlying concept that organizes the scalar order is the degree of "systematization" that characterizes the different methods. In clarifying this concept, the authors suggest that systematization entails two basic ideas: 1) the idea that there is a reality "out there"; and 2) the assumption that to know this reality requires "objective" methods.

In effect, then, Joroff and Morse's proposed scalar framework mirrors the objective vs. subjective concept of the dichotomous model. The left side of the model represents the more "subjective" paradigm, and the right side the more "objective" paradigm. Although they introduce the framework as "an overall integrating context for divergent research efforts,"[16] they also propose that such a framework is needed "to distinguish research from other activities in which architects may engage."[17] Indeed, in discussing the examples on the left side of the scale, Joroff and Morse invoke a variety of qualifiers and cautions, none of which are applied to the more objective and systematic examples on the right. For example, they write that when architects review precedents during the design process, "it is an assessment of knowledge gained by others rather than research in the strict definition of the term."[18] Moreover, by equating research with the term *systematic*, and systematic with the belief that there

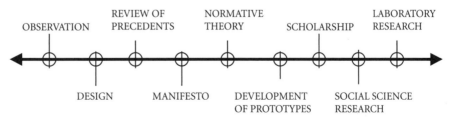

Figure 2.7 Michael Joroff and Stanley Morse's conceptual framework for architectural research. By permission of Michael L. Joroff.

is a reality "out there," they are essentially arguing that "real" research exists only at the objective end of the scale.

Like Joroff and Morse, many scholars in other disciplines have also sought to provide a more fine-grained conceptual framework than the dichotomous model based on the quantitative vs. qualitative distinction. One especially instructive example is provided by Morgan and Smircich writing for a diverse audience of social scientists, who, like architectural researchers, are likely to represent the a full range of ontological stances.[19] Morgan and Smircich explicitly argue that "the dichotomization between quantitative and qualitative methods is a rough and oversimplified one."[20] Their concern is that particular "quantitative" or "qualitative" tactics for gathering or interpreting evidence might be employed for their own sake, without reference to the paradigmatic frame of reference within which they are used. They go on to emphasize the "need to approach discussions of methodology in a way that highlights the vital link between theory and method."[21]

The framework that Morgan and Smircich propose is, like Joroff and Morse's, a continuum, with the terms *subjective* and *objective* framing the end points. (See Figure 2.8) Within this framework, they identify and label six paradigmatic positions, indicating for each their core ontological assumptions and assumptions about human nature. Notably, however, they refrain from specifying particular strategies or tactics that might be associated with these positions. Indeed, they argue that such a one-to-one correspondence between a given system of inquiry and a particular strategy or tactic would be counterproductive.

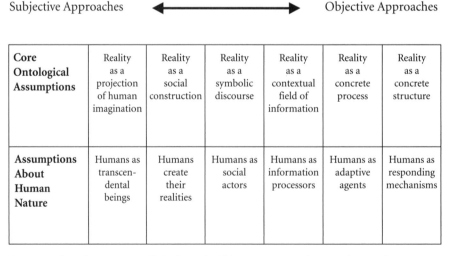

Subjective Approaches   ⟵⟶   Objective Approaches

Core Ontological Assumptions	Reality as a projection of human imagination	Reality as a social construction	Reality as a symbolic discourse	Reality as a contextual field of information	Reality as a concrete process	Reality as a concrete structure
Assumptions About Human Nature	Humans as transcendental beings	Humans create their realities	Humans as social actors	Humans as information processors	Humans as adaptive agents	Humans as responding mechanisms

Figure 2.8 Gareth Morgan and Linda Smircich's continuum of research paradigms, 1980. Reproduced by permission of Copyrights Clearance Center.

[A]ny given technique [tactic] often lends itself to a variety of uses according to the orientation of the researcher. For example, participant observation in the hands of a positivist may be used to document the number and length of interactions within a setting, but in the hands of an action theorist the technique may be used to explore the realms of subjective meaning of those interactions.[22]

Our own position regarding the relation of systems of inquiry to strategies and tactics is consistent with that articulated by Morgan and Smircich. On the one hand, there should be a coherence and consistency among these characteristics within any given research study. But on the other hand, when a researcher adopts a particular system of inquiry, that decision does not automatically determine either the strategy or the tactics for the study. Rather, a variety of both strategies and tactics can be orchestrated in ways consistent with the chosen paradigm.

To illustrate this point, we invoke a rather humorous analogy to a child's toy where a variety of heads, bodies, and legs can be interchanged to create a host of assembled characters. To be sure, some result in improbable combinations of mixed genders and incongruous body forms, just as not all combinations of strategies and tactics make sense within a particular system of inquiry. On the other hand, given the selection of a particular "head" (system of inquiry), many different bodies and legs (strategies and tactics) can be linked to form a credible and coherent character (research study).

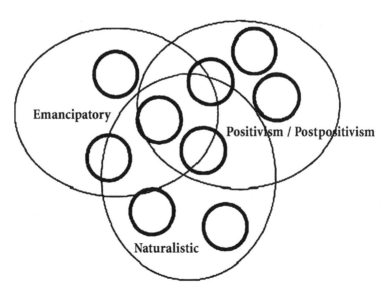

Figure 2.9   Clusters of systems of inquiry. Drawn by Fernando L. Lara.

2.2.3 An Alternative Framework: Tripartite Clusters

As an alternative to the two most frequently used models—the dichotomy and the continuum, we propose here the notion of three paradigmatic clusters: postpositivist, naturalistic, and emancipatory. (See Figure 2.10) This tripartite model has been proposed by several methodologists (e.g., Le Compte and Preissle; Mertens), albeit with slightly different nomenclature.[23] By cluster we mean to suggest that there are any number of very particularized systems of inquiry (e.g., critical theory and feminist theory) that share some common ontological and epistemological assumptions. One advantage of this framework is that it does not postulate a particular ordering along a unitary dimension. The matrix in Figure 2.10 summarizes the nature of these three paradigmatic clusters.

Postpositivism. Many research theorists use this term to describe a system of inquiry that emerged from the earlier traditions of positivism.[24] Whereas positivism was characterized by what many would describe as a "naive" belief in a reality "out there" that can be fully known, postpositivism is characterized by a more nuanced belief in an "out there" reality that can only be known within some level of "probability." And whereas positivism assumes that objectivity can be achieved in the research process, postpositivism presumes that objectivity is a legitimate goal that may be imperfectly

Basic Beliefs	Positivism / Postpositivism	Interpretive / Constructivist	Emancipatory
Ontology (nature of reality)	One reality; knowable within probability	Multiple, socially constructed realities	Multiple realities shaped by social, political, cultural, economic, ethnic, gender, and disability values
Epistemology (nature of knowledge; relation between knower and would-be-known)	Objectivity is important; researcher manipulates and observes in dispassionate, objective manner	Interactive link between researcher and participants; values are made explicit; created findings	Interactive link between researcher and participants; knowledge is socially and historically situated

Figure 2.10 Tripartite framework of research paradigms. Adapted from Donna Mertens, *Research Methods in Education and Psychology* (Thousand Oaks, Calif.: Sage Publications, 1998, p. 8.) By permission of Sage Publications.

realized. Postpositivists also acknowledge that the experimental model often used in the natural sciences is often inappropriate for research involving people. As a result, modifications and accommodations may have to be made in research practices, particularly in the use of quasi-experimental procedures. (See Chapter 9 for details.)

Naturalism. The naturalistic paradigm has gradually emerged to greater prominence over the last two or three decades. Although we have adopted the term *naturalism*, other authors have proposed a variety of other names for this paradigmatic cluster, including qualitative, phenomenological, hermeneutic, and interpretive/constructivist (Guba and Lincoln; Mertens).[25]

The basic ontological premise of naturalistic research is that there are multiple, socially constructed realities. The corresponding epistemological position is that it is neither possible nor necessarily desirable for research to establish a value-free objectivity. Rather, naturalistic researchers recognize the value and reality of the interactive dynamics between the inquirer and the people or setting being studied. In a similar vein, they also make sure they are explicit in stating the theoretical position and values inherent in their work, and acknowledge the role of interpretation and creation in reporting their findings.

Emancipatory. The emancipatory paradigm emerged over the last two or more decades in response to growing discomfort with the dominant research paradigms and procedures, particularly the postpositivist system of inquiry. In particular, a variety of researchers in a number of disciplines began to point out the unconscious dominance of racial, ethnic, gender, and Western-focused biases in the vast majority of research. Although we have chosen to use the term emancipatory, this paradigmatic cluster includes research from several research streams across many disciplines, including: critical theory–based, feminist, race-specific, participatory, and transformative.[26]

Emancipatory research shares with the naturalistic cluster a recognition of multiple realities, but it also stresses the role that social, political, cultural, ethnic, and gender issues play in the social construction of reality. There is as well a tendency to focus on the dynamics of power and marginalization as they affect less dominant groups. At an epistemological level, emancipatory researchers also share with the naturalists a recognition of the interactive dynamics between researchers and participants. But in addition, they highlight the historically and socially situated context in which the study respondents find themselves.

2.2.4 The Complementary Nature of Research Framed by Diverse Systems of Inquiry

Finally, and most importantly, the larger intent of Figures 2.9 and 2.10. is to convey the stance to which we are committed in writing this book, specifically that each system of inquiry can provide an appropriate and useful frame of reference for architectural research. Good research that yields important theory or significant practical applications can be achieved within any one of these paradigmatic clusters. Likewise, adherence to a particular system of inquiry—however esteemed within a particular subdiscipline of architectural research—is no guarantee for achieving high-quality research. In that, the analogy to architectural style is directly pertinent; though we may individually prefer to design in a particular style, we have to acknowledge that there are both good and bad exemplars of that style. Adherence to either classicism or art deco, postmodernism or neomodernism, does not in and of itself assure quality.

2.3   MEASURES OF RESEARCH QUALITY

In an inherently interdisciplinary field, such as architecture, a common tendency is for researchers, who might work primarily or only within one system of inquiry, to evaluate research from a different system of inquiry according to the standards of quality they know best. For example, researchers whose work falls clearly within an objective paradigm may tend to judge research done in either a naturalistic or emancipatory paradigm by the standards they employ for "objective" research. Not surprisingly, this can lead to a lot of heated arguments about whose work is really "research" and whose is not. In such instances, the potential benefits of tackling research topics in architecture from a variety of perspectives is virtually negated.

Instead, we believe it is far more productive to evaluate quality in architectural research according the standards that have been developed by methodologists working within the various paradigmatic traditions. Figure 2.11 presents a comparative analysis of quality standards that are representative of two of the three paradigmatic clusters: the postpositivist and the naturalistic. The emancipatory is not represented in this figure because advocates of this position generally question the relevance of the standards set by the postpositivist tradition in the first place; instead they advocate quite a different set of standards, to which we will turn later.

A second important feature of the matrix in Figure 2.11 is that the relevant quality criteria (in the left column of the matrix) have been identified using "generic" terms that are not associated with any particular system of inquiry.[27] The obvious purpose in doing so is to avoid privileging the terms and concepts associated with any one of the three paradigm clusters. Nevertheless, it might be objected that this matrix still privileges the postpositivist paradigm standards because the terms proposed for the naturalistic paradigm have been devised as comparable and equivalent to those postpositivist standards. Indeed, even the originator of Figure 2.11, Egon Guba, has since critiqued its formulation for precisely these reasons.[28] While we acknowledge this point, we believe that Figure 2.11 is still a useful framework for understanding important similarities and differences between these two systems of inquiry. In addition, our discussion of research executed within the other paradigmatic traditions (both in this and subsequent chapters) should allow other indicators of quality to be

Standard	Positivism / Postpositivism	Naturalistic
Truth value	*Internal validity* Equivalence of data of inquiry and phenomena they represent	*Credibility* Check data with interviewees; triangulation — multiple data sources of data collection
Applicability	*External validity* Generalizability	*Transferability* Thick description of context to assess similarity
Consistency	*Reliability* Instruments must produce stable results	*Dependability* Trackability of expected instability of data
Neutrality	*Objectivity* Methods explicated; replicable; investigator one-step removed from object of study	*Confirmability* Triangulation of data; practice of reflexivity by investigator

Figure 2.11   Comparative Analysis of quality standards, 1981. By permission of Egon Guba.

represented. To this end, a discussion of quality standards for each of the research strategies we examine will be presented in Chapters 6 through 12.

2.3.1 Quality Standards within a Postpositivist System of Inquiry

For better or worse, many readers are likely to be at least somewhat familiar with the standards of quality identified with the postpositivist paradigm. This is because they have been codified, discussed, and presented in methodology texts for many years. And as suggested earlier, because the standards within the other two paradigmatic clusters have been less explicitly codified, or codified more recently, there is often a tendency among researchers to apply the "postpositivist" standards to research executed within the other systems of inquiry. Although we believe this tendency is a mistake, we have nevertheless chosen to begin with the postpositivist paradigm, simply because it already is a starting point for many researchers.

Internal Validity. Although there are many subcategories of internal validity, the fundamental issue is whether the key concepts and operations of the study are truthful representations of the object of study. For example, we might ask whether a housing satisfaction questionnaire really measures residents' satisfaction with their housing. This requires a clearly stated definition of what would constitute housing satisfaction, and a rationale for the correspondence between the question items and that definition. Or perhaps we have reason to develop a new housing questionnaire. We might want to make sure that the results using that questionnaire correspond to a previously developed questionnaire on housing.

In the case of Medved and Novak's study of double-paned windows, the authors carry out their testing of the windows' performance primarily through a computerized, numerical simulation model.[29] But how can we trust the validity of the simulation model? The authors describe in considerable detail a validation process using physical experimentation based on actual window pane assemblies. Among their several goals in doing so is "to prove the agreement of numerical values and experimentally established heat flux and temperatures in selected areas in which sensors are located."[30] Having subsequently established the validity of the numerical model, the authors then proceed to use the numerical model to test the performance of a set of window pane designs.

External Validity. The question behind this criterion is whether the results of the study are applicable to the larger world, or at least whether there are defining contextual constraints within which the results are valid. In the case of the window pane study, the authors are quite specific and clear in stating that the window designs were tested using meteorological data for the central European climate. Within these climatic conditions, the authors conclude that window pane designs using a cavity with a "y" siphon are highly efficient, and comparable in efficiency to closed cavity designs.[31]

What if we want to use this window pane design in New York or California? We have two choices. At a more informal level, we might compare the climate data for New York or California with that of central Europe; and we would then make a calculated judgment about the degrees of similarity in climate. We might well conclude that the climates of New York and central Europe are similar enough to expect the same results; and similarly, we might conclude that the California climate is too dissimilar to assume comparable results. In that case, we might seek to expand the original study and to run the numerical simulation using the California climate data.

Reliability. The concept of reliability is concerned with the consistency of the measurements or findings. Within the postpositivist paradigm, the assumption is that the research methods would yield the same results if the study were conducted under the same conditions in another location or at another time. What might we say then about the reliability of the window pane study? In this case, since the research concerns relatively stable physical objects and properties, the window performance data would be expected to be quite reliable, so long as the physical conditions of the experiments and simulation remain the same. Nevertheless, the authors conclude their article by acknowledging that additional experiments should be carried out over a sustained time period to test for the effects of material degradation. Still, they suggest that since today's building materials are of high quality, the window performance data would likely remain stable.

On the other hand, other architectural studies using an "postpositivist" system of inquiry may involve conditions or social phenomena that require a more detailed examination of reliability. If, for instance, we consider again the example of housing satisfaction research, we might expect similar results in a study in which a sample of residents are surveyed initially, and then again a week or two later. In this instance, such similar results would suggest reliability; inconsistent results would suggest that the questionnaire was unreliable. However, if the survey were administered to the same group a year or two later, after major changes in the housing management occurred, then we would expect that changes in the survey results might well occur. We would then attribute the lack of consistent or stable results to a fundamental change in the conditions of the study rather than to a lack of reliability.

Objectivity. Within the "postpositivist" paradigm, the goal for the research procedures is to keep the potential bias or interference of the researcher out of the process. This is achieved by strict specification and administration of the relevant procedures. Typically, the researcher utilizes standardized measurement instruments—whether questionnaires or calibrated equipment; and the sequence and process of experimental manipulation are highly regulated. In the case of the Medved and Novak study, the researchers carefully specify the experimental procedures; detailed diagrams of the window pane designs and the "hot boxes" in which they were tested are provided. Information such as the dimensions, materials, and devices for regulating air temperature are also provided. Armed with these specifications, another researcher could choose to replicate the study, providing yet another test of the results.

2.3.2 Quality Standards within a Naturalistic System of Inquiry

In 1981, Egon Guba proposed a new set of quality standards for what he termed naturalistic inquiry.[32] In introducing what he calls "criteria for assessing trustworthiness," Guba has identified a number of key characteristics of naturalistic (or "constructivist," in his current terminology) inquiry, among them: the recognition of multiple realities, as opposed to a single reality; the assumption that generalizations are not necessarily possible in all instances; the understanding that a research design may emerge as the research proceeds; and the belief that the researcher and the respondent influence and are influenced by each other. Although Guba has subsequently proposed an alternative set of quality standards for naturalistic research, he and Lincoln concede that these quality standards are not well resolved.[33] Because of the heuristic value of the originally developed criteria, we will present them here for discussion and comparison to the postpositivist standards.

The standards of quality that Guba has proposed represent substantially different criteria—though presented in parallel structure—from those associated with the postpositivist system of inquiry. Moreover, Guba provides examples of several procedures for meeting each of these criteria; but given the summary nature of this discussion, we will simply highlight the most essential points.

Credibility. The idea behind credibility is to establish truth value by taking into account the natural complexities inherent in the situation or circumstance being studied. In other words, credibility entails a holistic approach to the research problem. Two particularly important ways of demonstrating truth value are triangulation and member checks. The former involves the use of a variety of data sources, multiple investigators, and/or a combination of data collection techniques in order to cross-check data and interpretations. The latter involves checking the data and interpretations with the respondents and groups from whom the data was solicited, a process that Guba claims "goes to the heart of the credibility criterion."[34]

If we return now to Schwarz's study of nursing home design, we find that he reports triangulation, but not the use of members checks. Schwarz achieves triangulation in two distinct ways. First, although he provides details of three separate case studies, he reports that these are three of a total of eight case study facilities. In other words, his conclusion that the architectural model used for nursing homes is misguided and unduly compromised by code regulations and reimbursement systems is strengthened by his ability to demonstrate this dynamic in multiple instances. Secondly, within each case study, Schwarz indicates that his data derive from:

> [M]ultiple means such as open-ended interviews, document collection, participatory observation, and visits to built facilities. . . . Key informants included care-providers, owners, architects, gerontological consultants, staff members, committee and board members, state regulators, residents of nursing homes and their families.[35]

Transferability. Like generalizability—its corresponding term in the postpositivist paradigm, transferability has to do with the extent to which the conclusions of one study can be applied to another setting or circumstance. To achieve transferability, Guba argues, one must provide a sufficiently "thick" description that the relative similarity of the two contexts can be adequately assessed. In the nursing home study, Schwarz is careful to emphasize the particularities of the settings he studied, while at the same time suggesting that similar themes would likely emerge in research on other nursing home settings:

> In [this] tradition . . . researchers are cautious not to generalize because of the personal nature of their observations and specificity of the measurements made in the fieldwork. In most cases, fieldwork can produce results that would not necessarily be replicated by other researchers. Because of the nature of in-depth studies, the themes, results, and conclusions are real and accurate, primarily within their original context. Although no comprehensive generalization was intended in this study, it is safe to assume that the themes described in the three cases are not unique in other design processes of nursing homes.[36]

Dependability. The notion of dependability suggests that there is a fundamental consistency within the data, but it also takes into account "apparent instabilities arising either because different realities are being tapped or because of instrumental shifts stemming from developing insights on the part of the investigator-as-instrument [of research]".[37] The primary device for ensuring dependability is, according to Guba, the establishment of an "audit trail." The audit trail documents all the processes by which data were collected, analyzed and interpreted; this might include interview and observation notes, drawings and diagrams that track people's activity patterns in a building, the investigator's daily journal notes, etc.

Schwarz's study does not specify the extent to which he established a comprehensive audit trail. However, one can infer from his discussion of the data analysis that his audit trail may well have been substantial:

> The analysis process followed the grounded theory approach [See Chapter 7 for details] in the steps described by Chesler.[38] The data were transcribed, coded, and categorized in a search for themes. Due to the limited scope of this article, the themes from the three cases presented here depict only issues related to regulations and the reimbursement system of long-term care settings. These themes are major anchoring points of the world's [sic] views of the actors in the design process. Quotes are given in their natural form to capture the character of the fieldwork.[39]

Confirmability. Rather than demanding objectivity, Guba argues that the investigator's data and interpretations should be confirmable. This, he maintains, can be achieved through a combination of triangulation and reflexivity on the part of the researcher. We have already discussed the use of multiple methods, sources, and investigators to establish triangulation. Reflexivity requires the investigator to reveal his or her epistemological assumptions, their influence on the framing of the research question, and any changes in perspective that might emerge during the course of the study.

In the example of Schwarz's study, his efforts to establish triangulation have already been noted. And although he does not provide the full measure of reflexivity suggested by Guba, he nevertheless makes his stance clear by articulating the system of inquiry within which his research is situated.

2.3.3 Quality Standards within the Emancipatory System of Inquiry

Compared to the quality standards in postpositivist and naturalistic research, the quality standards pertinent to emancipatory research are conceived in more holistic terms, less tied to specific issues of the actual research procedures. Guba and Lincoln describe three general quality concerns of emancipatory (or in their terminology, "critical theory") research: 1) the historical situatedness of the inquiry; 2) the extent to which the inquiry acts to erode ignorance and misunderstanding; and 3) the transformative potential of the inquiry.[40]

Historical Situatedness. This concern has to do with the extent to which the inquiry takes into account and highlights the political, gender, ethnic, and racial aspects of the situation or setting under investigation. In Favro's study of Julia Morgan, she very explicitly weaves throughout the article the gender issues that affected women during Morgan's lifetime.[41] For example, she notes that Morgan was one of the few Americans among an almost entirely male group of students to earn a diploma from the Beaux Arts Academy in Paris. Morgan, Favro argues, was determined to do so "to overcome the disadvantages incumbent with her gender."[42] Favro then goes on to suggest that other characteristics of her professional life—such as her decision to downplay her gender, maintain a low profile, and develop a repeat business with influential women clients—were strategies adopted because of the social construction of gender at that time.

Eroding Ignorance. Guba and Lincoln (1998) argue that emancipatory research attempts to uncover and make explicit social, cultural, and physical dynamics that have previously gone unnoticed. To this end, Favro makes the point that previous research had often criticized Morgan for the attitudes and practices described above, including, for instance, her lack of "a signature style or theory."[43] Favro argues instead that "her accommodation was a logical response to the professional situation faced as a trailblazer."[44]

Transformational Impulse. In this quality standard, there is an imperative to action, a desire to somehow transform existing situations or practices.[45] In this regard, Favro makes it clear that she is not only challenging the historically situated value system evident during Morgan's lifetime, but also arguing that the values Morgan embraced and promoted deserve to be at the heart of architecture today. Favro concludes her article this way:

Morgan deserves recognition for all her skill at crafting a profitable, large-scale, and enduring career despite the obstacles presented by her gender. . . . Reacting to preconceptions about women's roles . . . [she] emphasized livability, cost effectiveness, durability, client-satisfaction, and user needs. Difficult to document, non-visual in content, transient, and associated with women, these concerns historically have earned little praise. . . . If these aspects of architecture are thought unimportant, then perhaps the priorities of the architecture profession, not the gender of the architect, should be evaluated.[46]

There is no doubt that Favro seeks to provoke changes in the values, attitudes, and practices of architecture as it is currently conceived and practiced.

2.4   CONCLUSIONS: LOOKING AHEAD

Over the course of this chapter, we have sought to demonstrate how the researcher's affinity for a particular system of inquiry is likely to frame the way in which the research question is posed, the selection of the research design, the tactics of information gathering and analysis, and even the practices of the researcher as s/he conducts the inquiry. Although we will not always attempt to identify the operative research paradigms in the seven chapters on research strategies (Chapters 6 through 12), we suggest that readers keep the paradigms in mind as they consider the strengths and weaknesses of the various strategies.

2.5   RECOMMENDED READINGS

Readers interested in reviewing the variety of research paradigms in architecture may wish to consult: Michael Joroff and Stanley Morse, "A Proposed Framework for the Emerging Field of Architectural Research," in *Architectural Research*, ed. James Snyder (New York: Van Nostrand Reinhold, 1984); Julia Robinson, "Architectural Research: Incorporating Myth and Science," *Journal of Architectural Education* 44 no. 1 (1990).

Those interested in the range of research paradigms across multiple disciplines may find the following texts valuable: John Creswell, *Research Design: Qualitative and Quantitative Approaches* (Thousand Oaks, Calif.: Sage Publications, 1994); Egon Guba and Yvonna Lincoln, "Competing Paradigms in Qualitative Research," in *The Landscape of Qualitative Research*, ed. Norman Denzin and Yvonna Lincoln (Thousand Oaks, Calif.: Sage Publications, 1998); Donna Mertens, "An Introduction to Research," *Research Methods in Education and Practice* (Thousand Oaks, Calif.: Sage Publications, 1998); Gareth Morgan and Linda Smircich, "The Case for Qualitative Research," *Academy of Management Review* 5 no. 4 (1980).

Readers interested in reviewing the exemplar studies discussed in this chapter should consult: Diane Favro, "Sincere and Good: The Architecture Practice of Julia Morgan," *Journal of Architectural Education* 9 no. 2 (1992): 112–128; Saso Medved and Peter Novak, "Heat Transfer through a Double Pane Window with an Insulation Screen Open at the Top," *Energy and Buildings* 28 (1998): 257–268; Benyamin Schwarz, "Nursing Home Design: A Misguided Architectural Model," *Journal of Architectural and Planning Research* 14 no. 4 (1997): 343–359.

NOTES

1. Donald Polkinghorne, *Methodology for Human Sciences* (Albany, N.Y.: SUNY Press, 1983).

2. Norman Denzin and Yvonna Lincoln, *Handbook of Qualitative Research* (Thousand Oaks, Calif.: Sage Publications, 1998).

3. Saso Medved and Peter Novak, "Heat Transfer through a Double Pane Window with an Insulation Screen Open at the Top," *Energy and Buildings* 28 (1998): 257–268.

4. Ibid., 257.

5. Benyamin Schwarz, "Nursing Home Design: A Misguided Architectural Model," *Journal of Architectural and Planning Research* 14, no. 4 (1997): 343–359.

6Ibid., 347.

7. Diane Favro, "Sincere and Good: The Architectural Practice of Julia Morgan," *Journal of Architectural Education* 9, no. 2 (1992): 112–128.

8. Ibid., 113.

9. Ibid., 113.

10. Henry H. Bauer, "Scientific Literacy and the Myth of Scientific Methods," in *The So-called Scientific Method* (Urbana: University of Illinois Press, 1992), pp. 19–41.

11. Julia Robinson, "Architectural Research: Incorporating Myth and Science," *Journal of Architectural Education* 44, no. 1 (1990): 20.

12. Fernando Lara, "Popular Modernism: An Analysis of the Acceptance of Modern Architecture in 1950s Brazil" (Ph.D. diss., University of Michigan, 2001).

13. John Creswell, *Research Design: Qualitative and Quantitative Approaches* (Thousand Oaks, Calif.: Sage Publications, 1994).

14. Bauer, "Scientific Literacy," p. 29.

15. Michael Joroff and Stanley Morse, "A Proposed Framework for the Emerging Field of Architectural Research," in *Architectural Research*, ed. J. Snyder (New York: Van Nostrand, 1984), 15–28.

16. Ibid., 21.

17. Ibid., 21.

18. Ibid., 22.

19. Gareth Morgan and Linda Smircich, "The Case for Qualitative Research," *Academy of Management Review* 5, no. 4 (1980).

20. Ibid., 499.

21. Ibid., 499.

22. Ibid., 498.

23. M. Le Compte and J. Preissle with R. Tesch, *Ethnography and Qualitative Design in Educational Research*, (2d ed.) (New York: Academic Press, 1993); Donna Mertens, *Research Methods in Education and Psychology* (Thousand Oaks, Calif.: Sage Publications, 1998).

24. Mertens, *Research Methods*.

25. Egon Guba, "Criteria for Assessing the Truthworthiness of Naturalistic Inquiries," *Education Communication and Technology Journal* 29, no. 2 (1981): 76–91; Egon Guba and Yvonna Lincoln, "Competing Paradigms in Qualitative Research," in *The Landscape of Qualitative Research*, ed. Norman Denzin and Yvonna Lincoln (Thousand Oaks, Calif.: Sage Publications, 1998); Mertens, *Research Methods in Education and Psychology*.

26. Mertens, *Research Methods*.

27. Guba, "Criteria for Assessing."

28. Guba and Lincoln, "Competing Paradigms," 213.

29. Medved and Novak, "Heat Transfer," 258.

30. Ibid., 258.

31. Ibid., 267.

32. Guba, "Criteria for Assessing," 80.

33. Guba and Lincoln, "Competing Paradigms, 213, 214.

34. Guba, "Criteria for Assessing," 85.

35. Schwartz, "Nursing Home Design," 347.

36. Ibid., 355, 356.

37. Guba, "Criteria for Assessing," 86.

38. Mark Chesler, *'Professionals' Views of the 'Dangers' of Self-Help Groups*, Working Paper 345 (Ann Arbor: Center for Research on Social Organizations, University of Michigan, 1987).

39. Schwarz, "Nursing Home Designs," 347.

40. Guba and Lincoln, "Competing Paradigms," 213.

41. Favro, "Sincere and Good," 112–128.

42. Ibid., 114.

43. Ibid., 112.

44. Ibid. 112.

45. Guba and Lincoln, "Competing Paradigms," 213.

46. Favro, "Sincere and Good," 125.

Chapter 3

Literature Review

3.1   INTRODUCTION

There are occasions when we cannot depend upon knowledge we already possess. Something comes up, and we must seek out new information in order to know what to do. Say, for instance, we decide to go to Paris. Most likely we would need information on times to go, airfares and connections, where to stay, exchange rates, places to see in Paris, and so on. Where would we go to find this information? Nowadays, we would probably turn to the Internet or visit the travel section at the bookstore. We can talk to a travel agent. We might watch a film on Paris, maybe something associated with the city: its art, its parks, its cuisine. This is all research of a kind. What is more, it is a "literature review," a survey of various sources. But a trip to Paris comes and goes. The information we found to make our trip possible tends not to have applicability beyond the single event of *our* trip, although we can give anecdotal advice to others when they decide to go in the future.

The information gathering this book addresses is of a kind aimed to produce knowledge that is more lasting and has more widespread usefulness. Because of this quest for widely useful knowledge, the literature review is a very important part of the research process. It is essential not only at the beginning of the process, but throughout it.

The information coming out of research should have the following attributes:

1. The information should address a specific topic of inquiry; by specific, we mean that the topic can usually be summarized in several sentences, or at most a concise paragraph or two. (The abstract of a research paper usually fulfills this role,

although the core focus of a research project can often be even more condensed than the wording of a formal abstract.)

2. The research result on this topic of inquiry ought to find its place in a larger domain of relevant literature, or at least be deemed qualified to do so by a representative community of informed people. In other words, the research results should constitute a contribution to (an addition to, an expansion of, a deepening of) a larger body of information related to the topic of inquiry.

3. When completed, the research result should be able to stand on its own for the use of others, independent of the researcher who initially formulated it.

The literature review plays an important role in achieving these goals, where there is always a certain cyclical process at play: A researcher must be informed about the existing literature his or her research needs to draw from, because the outcome of the research will expand that body of literature. The *next* researcher in this topical area will take from the (now expanded) literature and make further contributions to it, and so on.

3.1.1 Literature Review as an Exploratory System

We define "the literature" as *a body of information, existing in a wide variety of stored formats, that has conceptual relevance for a particular topic of inquiry.* A literature review, then, is the totality of activities the researcher undertakes to use that body of information in such a way that a topic of inquiry can be competently defined and addressed. Thus, a literature review is not synonymous with a "general" sense of what exists in the literature of a field. A literature review exists only after the general material has been arranged into a coherent system, one that has been customized to fit the research question. Such a system can be in the researcher's mind; it will be more useful if put in some kind of written or diagrammatic form (which expands or changes as the research progresses). Chris Hart lists various issues that a systematic exploration of the literature should address, among them:

1. What are the key sources?
2. What are the key theories?
3. What are the major issues and debates about this topic?
4. What are the epistemological and ontological grounds for the discipline?
5. What are the main questions and problems that have been addressed to date?[1]

Embedded in these questions is the search for a response to the literature, the generation of a topic of inquiry that will be recognizable by all informed persons as a legitimate and original approach to the subject at hand. "The literature" therefore has fluid boundaries; its scope depends upon the topic of inquiry. Formulating the topic in such a way as to determine the initial scope of the literature is one of the first creative steps a researcher takes.

3.1.2 Annotated Bibliography versus Literature Review

A literature review is often confused with an annotated bibliography. An annotated bibliography is an intermediate point toward the literature review. By means of a listing of references obtained from searching a field's literature (or more commonly the literature of several fields), a researcher begins to amass a body of information that shapes the investigation. The aim of an annotated bibliography is to respond to each reference cited with a descriptive paragraph of the work's goals, its theoretical stance, and most importantly, its relevance for the investigation. This process helps focus the emerging research question.

From the annotated bibliography, the literature review proper can then be produced. This is more than an itemized list of existing references; it is rather a narrative document, making use of the references in the annotated bibliography, but going beyond it to include the following information:

1. An introductory statement of the general intent of the literature exploration. This includes suggestions for the ultimate direction of the proposed research to come.
2. A summary of the lines of existing research that provide background for the proposed research; this usually involves grouping the annotated items into larger common themes (see Section 3.2).
3. Observations on the state of the literature in terms of how it can be expanded by the proposed research. In other words, the reviewer needs to identify specific areas that have not been covered by the extant literature, arguments that he or she wishes to challenge, or subjects of study that can be reconfigured by a new conceptual framework.

3.1.3 Diagrammatic Structure for a Research Study

To situate literature review in relation to the overall research process, we offer the diagram in Figure 3.1. The researcher looks in two directions. On one hand there is the question being pursued; on the other there is the audience that must ultimately receive the research results. The research question is accessed by means of research strategies and tactics. The strategy/tactic distinction is elaborated in the previous chapters, and is the format for the seven chapters in Part II. We depict two bodies of literature because usually at least two are consulted in the course of a research project; often there are many more. One of the bodies of literature is often emphasized more than the other, and the results will most probably contribute to that realm. The arrows drawn from the literature to the various junctures of the research process indicate literature review; it is evident that literature review contributes to every aspect of the process. Additionally, the research result relates to the literature by expanding it. Indeed, the success of the research depends upon whether the audience deems it worthy as an expansion of the literature. Finally, the process is a dynamic one. The relationship between the topic of inquiry, the actions taken to access it, and the

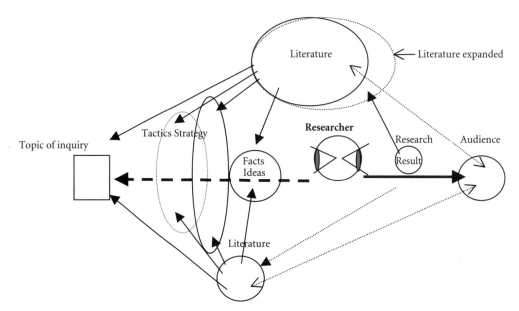

Figure 3.1   An overall diagrammatic of a research project.

researcher's own thinking is an ever-changing reality; the literature review is thus an ongoing activity. It is wrong to limit "lit review" to the beginning of the research process only and to assume that after 20 or 30 titles have been listed, that part of the process is complete. This is simply insufficient.

In keeping with the framework of the chapters in Part II, this chapter considers literature review with a strategy-tactic approach as well. We do not suggest by this that literature review is one kind of research strategy on par with the seven we cover in Part II. Literature review is necessary for any research strategy. Here, we merely follow the strategy-tactic format as a means of organizing our material. Section 3.2 addresses the uses of literature review. Section 3.3 addresses some general tactical considerations for the use of literature review, and Section 3.4 addresses available resources. But before proceeding with the uses of literature review, we first consider some differences between fact-finding for design and fact-finding for research.

3.1.4 Literature Review for Designers and for Researchers

The audience of this book includes designers as well as researchers, two groups that often have different needs. Yet if literature review is understood as fact-finding as such, then it is certainly practiced by both. The chart in Figure 3.2 offers some comparisons between design and research that have a strong bearing on the ways designers and researchers make use of literature review.

	Design Inquiry	**Research Inquiry**
Aim	Usually culminates in an empirical object located in a particular place and time	Usually culminates in an explanatory conceptual system with use beyond the confines of one place and time
Use of literature review	To develop case-specific programmatic information To gain familiarity with typological precedents To garner facts for normative action	To identify and connect topic of inquiry to disciplinary sources To ground the project in the proper theoretical / philo-sophical / epistemological starting points To respond to, or in some other way contribute to, the state of knowledge on the subject To focus methodological approaches
Outcome in relation to "the literature"	Loose connection, in the sense that the designed object can be evaluated on its own with or without reference to a larger literature	Stricter connection, in the sense that the new explanatory system is almost always evaluated on the logic of how it relates to the body of literature it aims to contribute to

Figure 3.2 Similarities and differences in literature review between design inquiry and research inquiry.

While the wording in Figure 3.2 probably does not accommodate all *possible* cases of design or research, it offers some serviceable oppositions. The design task culminates in a built form, while the research task usually results in a written text. Unlike the former, the latter is not yoked to a particular place or time; rather, it is usually applicable regardless of locale. Also, the design task seeks information that applies to a specific case, sometimes with reference to precedents, and always for the purpose of taking normative design actions. The design task is thus more loosely tied to the literature initially consulted. The very physical presence of designed objects calls for evaluative criteria rooted in the objects themselves (e.g., functional criteria, client satisfaction, approval of the community, and so on). Whether or not the literature referenced plays a key role in that evaluation is usually a contingent matter. This is not so with research outcomes. Not only must they be affirmed or denied by subsequent tests at times, they must also meet the logical and qualitative demands of the literature they aim to expand. Here, for instance, are some comments on a well-known example of research, Kevin Lynch's *The Image of the City*; these comments can be found on the back cover of the 27th edition of Lynch's book (MIT Press, 2000):[2]

> City planners and urban designers everywhere will be taking account of his work for years to come. . . . The importance of this book in the literature of urbanism is obvious. (Leonard K. Eaton, *Progressive Architecture*)

> This small and readable book makes one of the most important modern contributions to large-scale design theory. (David A. Crane, *Journal of the American Institute of Planners*)

It is clear from these comments that Lynch's work is considered valuable insofar as it is deemed a *contribution* to a literature. Because it is research, rather than design, that demands a more systematic engagement with "the literature," our observations below are largely given with that domain in view.

3.2   USES OF LITERATURE REVIEW

A large part of the education of researchers involves gaining familiarity with the literature of their fields. This is the reason why masters and doctoral programs in almost all disciplines require a period of coursework before the thesis research is undertaken. The coursework aims not only to expose the student to the extant literature, it also aims to cultivate the ability to interact with it. Research questions emerge out of such interaction. This section addresses ways a working familiarity with the literature can be used.

3.2.1 Using Literature Review to Identify the Research Question

The literature can be "mined" in active ways to identify topics of inquiry; here we list some of those ways. Our list is not comprehensive, but hopefully it is of sufficient variety to stir the mind toward additional possibilities.

First, topics of inquiry can emerge from analyzing, critiquing, and suggesting improvements to an extant work. Consider again Lynch's *The Image of the City*. Lynch limits his study to American cities, but his analytical categories of city image (paths, edges, districts, nodes, landmarks), with their implicitly universal scope, raise the question of whether or not they apply to non-Western cities as well.[3] Would they apply, for instance, to a Bombay or a Shanghai? Lynch's lack of analysis of non-Western cities opens room for further work. As to methodology, Lynch himself critiques his method of interview.[4] The groups he interviewed were so small that their city "images" may not have been truly representative. Certainly a theory with such widespread acclaim ought to be re-examined with a larger sample; this is one example where a critique of existing literature can lead to new ideas for research.

Second, research questions can emerge from a comparison of representative works in the literature. Why does Laugier's *Essay on Architecture* (1751) posit one origin for the built form—the hut—but Quatremere de Quincy's theory of origins (1800) posits three separate origins: hut, cave, tent?[5] What happened in those 50 years to alter the theoretical emphasis from one to three? In a slightly different twist, Michael O'Neill, in a paper on computer simulation of human way-finding, compares an extant theory in the literature (the computational process model) with a new one he proposes (the biological model).[6] Comparison, the exploration of the implications of two related but different realities, offers fertile ground for new topics of inquiry.

Third, a topic of inquiry can emerge when an existing theory is used to assess a related theme. Take Stewart Brand's *How Buildings Learn*, a work that theorizes why the physical attributes of buildings never stay the same, but change due to a variety of factors, among these economics, technology, and fashion.[7] In a current master's thesis under one of the authors' direction, a student is taking Brand's theory of building change and applying it to the scale of a large city block over 100 years of its history. Do Brand's six indicators of change (site, structure, skin, services, space plan, stuff—see Figure 11.8) have the same explanatory relevance at the level of a city block?[8] Can they be attributed to the same factors, or do other factors come into play on a larger scale?

Fourth, extant theories in the literature can always be *tested*. An instance of this can be found in the work of Stephen Kaplan, *et al.*, who tested Christopher Alexander's claims that certain patterned arrangements in physical environments conduce positive subjective responses in people.[9] For his part, Alexander says of a given pattern: "we have a general sense that something is 'right' there; something is working; something feels good."[10] Kaplan took one of Alexander's patterns, the window, and tested this claim, producing qualified results. One can see how the addition of Kaplan's work to a literature that already contains Alexander's *Timeless Way of Building* deepens the body of knowledge in this area.

Fifth, a topic of inquiry can attempt expansions of an existing concept or theory. Take for instance Christian Norberg-Schulz's work in applying Heidegger's phenomenology to the experience of built environments, specifically, to an explanation of "spirit of place" (*genius loci*).[11] Norberg-Schulz's work made two substantial contributions to the literature in architectural theory. First, his "phenomenology" became an explicit way of critiquing the modernist movement in architecture. More importantly,

Norberg-Schulz's ideas on "spirit of place" and "dwelling" have become a kind of primary source for both architects and architectural theorists in their explorations of subjective identities with physical locales.

There are many more possible ways for "mining" the literature to develop a research question. They all involve imagination and creativity, which can be characterized as an ability to seek new thematic connections. Research creativity is the ability to derive new implications from existing positions, critique past stances from an awareness of present positions, or even project future conditions based upon learned premises. This creativity is of course not equal in all people. But it certainly can be cultivated, and that cultivation starts with gaining familiarity with the existing literature, and then gaining dexterity in reacting to it.

One example of the creative imagination working in conjunction with a knowledge of the literature may be seen in Clare Cooper Marcus's own account of how she came upon the methodology for researching subjective experiences of identity with home. She recounts how early in her career she had been frustrated by extant approaches to this topic. It was not until a friend of hers "talked to the desert" that she discovered a way by which precognitive realities of the "house-self dynamic" could be unearthed.[12] She then embarked on a method that involved asking a subject to talk to her house, and then to have the house "talk" back to her, supplemented by attempts to capture the feelings in graphic form. The point for us is that while Cooper Marcus found the literature in her field lacking, it formed the basis by which her imagination was able to identify something new when the opportunity presented itself. The result is her book *House as Mirror of Self*.

3.2.2 *Using Literature Review to Focus the Topic of Inquiry*

A topic of inquiry should not be too general. Here is an overly general topical question: *How do built forms affect people?* This is akin to asking what it is like to be an American. There are so many possible answers that a study based on it is likely to be amorphous. At the other extreme, a topic cannot be so restrictive that the answer will prove to have limited use. Consider this question: *How does Mary like this modernist building?* We may well find out how Mary responds, but this information is not useful in any widely applicable way; it pertains only to the affections of one person.

An indicator that a topic of inquiry may be either too broad or too restrictive is *the inability to clearly and simply identify a body of literature to which the topical question can be referred.* In the general case above, almost anything related to built form may be relevant. What is *driving* the question? Thermal considerations? Quality of life issues? Historical and/or cultural considerations? Aesthetics? Psychology? The question is too broad to furnish a direction. Box 3.1 illustrates the fact that, at the initial stages of identifying a topic of inquiry, the questions tend not only to be too broad, but as a consequence, to cover many different literatures. At the other extreme, how a limited sample (Mary) responds to a built form may not be addressed by

BOX 3.1

What Is the Right Question? A Case from a B.Arch. Design Project

Julie Keen's B.Arch. thesis project is motivated by a concept she wishes to capture in material form. That concept is "the in-between." The project is a cultural center to be located on the grounds of a private Catholic university. In a review early in the design process, she presented her concept to the reviewers. However, she presented several possible definitions of "the in-between," and because she did not precisely define the term, other versions of what "in-between" can mean began to proliferate during the discussion:

1. In between the past and the present (we are forever in the NOW).
2. In between two cultures of the region.
3. In between the cultures of her own background (Julie's background is Asian and Western).
4. In between two physical objects (the actual siting of the building).
5. In between earth and sky.

It is clear that many different literatures can be examined in her project, depending upon the precision of her question. Here is a sampling of the literatures possible for each item above:

1. Phenomenology: Heidegger, Gadamer, perhaps Eliade and Bergson.
2. In this case: Northwest American Indian culture vs. general American culture.
3. Korean vs. American culture; family historical documents.
4. Architectural exemplars of "in-between" solutions.
5. Mystical literature/eastern writings and exemplars; Heidegger.

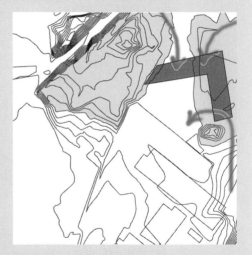

Figure 3.3 A student preliminary study of a structure somehow expressive of "in-between." Here an "elbow-shaped" form is placed on the site "in between" some strategically formed topological conditions. Drawing courtesy of Julie Keen, Washington State University at Spokane. John Abell, instructor.

"a literature" at all. The single case is simply too localized to need any written material (which, again, is motivated by a need to share observations and/or results that are relevant in a broad sense). Now, consider a question that is somewhat intermediate between the two extremes: what is the length of stay of nursing home occupants in "homey" interior environments versus the length of stay in facilities with more "institutionalized" interior décor? *This* is a good beginning for a research question because it easily conjures up available literature. And one additional indicator of a good question is that it quickly conjures up certain methodological possibilities as well. For instance, in this case, we can immediately devise paths of action: defining "homey" and identifying sample environments; identifying "nonhomey" exemplars; surveying records, designing questionnaires, planning for statistical sampling and analysis, and so on.

Consider this question: How does the everyday person on the street in Boston respond to Boston City Hall? This question immediately leads to the following considerations:

1. History of Boston City Hall
2. Modernist architecture
3. Boston, Boston downtown, architecture of Boston
4. Opinion surveys in architecture

Figure 3.4 Boston City Hall. Though the building was hailed by the critics, Ellen Berkeley's research found that everyday passersby had much less positive impressions of the building. Photograph courtesy of Brian Schermer.

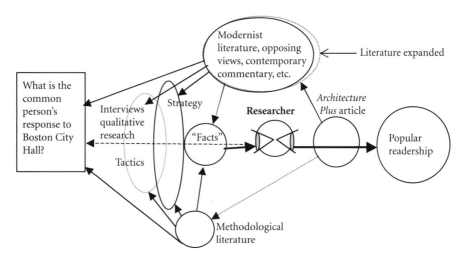

Figure 3.5   A diagrammatic of Ellen Berkeley's research on Boston City Hall.

This question, which is neither too general nor too restrictive, was asked by Ellen Berkeley. The results were communicated to a popular audience, appearing in the February 1973 edition of *Architecture Plus*.[13] Berkeley makes note of the literature on modernism (e.g., she cites Le Corbusier), contemporary commentary (e.g., she cites Ada Louise Huxtable and other critics), details of recent planning policies for the site produced by I. M. Pei and Partners (and commentary on it), and data about the building itself (publicity brochures, etc.). In addition, she was aware of the kind of survey she was conducting with passersby ("it was undoubtedly not a 'scientific' investigation—I did not stop every tenth person for instance—and these brief interviews went off in whatever directions seemed a good idea").[14] Figure 3.5 customizes the general conditions of research for Berkeley's case. The point, again, is this: A focused topic of inquiry can be formulated as a question that makes evident connections to relevant bodies of literature, including literature that can aid in framing the methodology of the study.

3.2.3 Using Literature Review to Understand the Makeup of the Research Question

This subsection and the next two (3.2.4, 3.2.5) address the makeup of the topic of inquiry in terms of the literature or literatures it draws from. Consider again Lynch's *The Image of the City*. What is the topic of inquiry? Lynch aims to understand what attributes of physical city form can produce clear images of the city in the experiencer. Hence his technical term *imageability*: "that quality in a physical object which gives it a high probability of evoking a strong image in any given observer."[15] What might those qualities be? Is this the question? Well, yes, but there is more. Lynch does not want to limit his research to individual experiences of imageability. Rather, he wants to address *public* imageability, that is, experiences of a city's imageability that hold true for a community of people.[16] But what is the literature that informs this investigation? From his association with the field, Lynch's knowledge of the literature on city form is no doubt substantial. His preface graciously mentions several people and their work in this area. But what is striking is that Lynch draws much from a variety of works having to do with *perception* and *orientation* (under the headings of "legibility," "structure and identity," "building the image," etc.) and not necessarily from the literature on city form. In other words, the literature referenced reveals the fact that Lynch's topic of inquiry involves something quite distinct from the material furnishings of city form. Rather, it intimately involves the subjective perception of those furnishings. Thus:

> Structuring and identifying the environment is a vital ability among all mobile animals. . . . Psychologists have also studied this ability in man . . . [Lynch gives nine references after this statement.][17]

> Brown remarks that a maze through which subjects were asked to move blindfolded seemed to them at first to be one unbroken problem. . . . DeSilva describes the case of a boy who seemed to have 'automatic' directional orientation. . . . Shipton's account of the reconnaissance for the ascent of Everest offers a dramatic case of such learning. . . . Kilpatrick describes the process of perceptual learning. . . . Stern . . . Langer . . . [etc.][18]

Appendix A of his book cites many other sources from literature addressing perception and orientation.[19] Lynch is also extensive in describing his research methodology, itself rooted in a body of literature (see Figure 3.6).

From a literature point of view, then, we see that Lynch built his theory by drawing from three bodies of literature: perception/orientation, city planning, methodology. He is most explicit with his connections to the perception and orientation literature; knowledge from the other two is embedded in the work. Lynch had to grapple with his topic of inquiry, recognizing that it was not the physical object of the city only, but rather the subjective images that a city can produce in a community of people. This subtle and pivotal distinction in the makeup of the question led to an association with certain bodies of literature and not others.

How is this accomplished? There is no easy answer to this question; we have already noted the creative back-and-forth between the literature and the formation of a topic in the researcher's mind. Experience indicates that the back-and-forth process is itself key. It is rare that an initial attempt at stating a topic ends up being the final one. Usually the topic gets restated several times, often after discussion with others, as

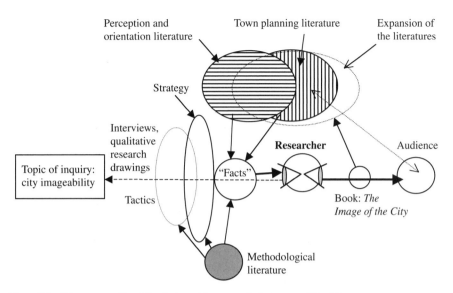

Figure 3.6 Diagrammatic of Kevin Lynch's research in *Image of the City*.

recommendations for perspectives and approaches, not to mention literature, help to sharpen the research focus.

3.2.4 Using Literature Review to Understand an Idea's Genetic Roots

A topic of inquiry tends to have a historical lineage, and the literature will contain its family tree, as it were. In other words, "the literature" is not only a conceptual domain of contemporary material, it is also a reservoir of historical information that contains the genetic links of an idea's background. The topic at hand, then, should be networked not only to its contemporary connections but also to its genetic ones. Indeed, without the history, it is often difficult to make sense of the contemporary state of affairs. With this in view, it is always helpful to diagram the family tree of an idea during the literature review. As familiarity with existing sources increases, additions can be made to the tree. Figure 3.7 shows a family tree that situates Norberg-Schulz's attempts to develop a theory of "dwelling" from the phenomenological literature.

This tree is by no means complete; further investigation will uncover other sources. But the diagram is the beginning of a map that helpfully traces the genetic roots of the theme. During literature review, one task is to "grow the tree" by mapping additional connections as they are uncovered. Uncovering these connections not only gives confidence that the problem is situated in the correct conceptual network, it also

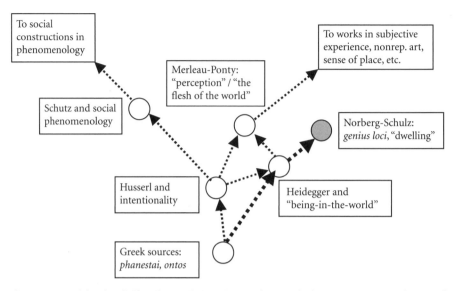

Figure 3.7 An (abridged) "family tree" situating Norberg-Schulz's attempts at a theory of "dwelling" or "architectural phenomenology."

generates material for critique. For instance, knowing on what foundation Norberg-Schulz built his theoretical arguments, how well he actually grasped Heidegger's phenomenology becomes a point of critique, if the goal is an analysis of his theory. Can Norberg-Schulz's argument be better framed by referencing material from a neighboring thinker that he does not cite (perhaps because he was not as familiar with it): Merleau-Ponty? The tree diagram is often able to draw out such questions.

3.2.5 Using Literature Review to Understand the Current Conceptual Landscape

If awareness of a literature's historical roots is important, so is knowledge of the literature in its contemporary context. This is true in two ways. First, within a discipline, one must be aware of current points of view relating to the topic. For instance, on the subject of town growth, it is clear that some literature affirms growth management policies, while other literature opposes them. Any contemporary cross-section of a literature can reveal *competing* views for getting to one result, *opposing* agendas, *nuanced* vantage points, and so on. Of course, nuances can be mapped in diagrams as well to gain an overall "lay of the land" in graphic terms.

Second and equally important is this: During any period, there are overarching intellectual agendas that tend to inform (or color) diverse investigations independent of disciplinary domain. Poststructuralism, for instance, is not really the domain of any one discipline (at least no longer), but rather describes an important *general* way of perceiving reality at the end of the twentieth century. Now, one indicator that a researcher is up against a transdisciplinary theme is that a "buzz-word" is usually used to stand in for a reality that many have bought into, but far fewer people can actually define. In the design fields, *deconstruction* is surely such a word. *Sustainability* is another one. The researcher should identify these buzz-words, and be familiar with a cross-section of bodies of literature that traffic in them. Each body of literature will apply the term in its own way, and a rich understanding of the overall theme can be gained by grasping the nuances. Deconstruction, for example, should lead the researcher into the literature in linguistics, semiology, structuralism and poststructuralism, philosophies of meaning, political science, and so on. All of this cross-disciplinary sampling of common themes goes towards situating the topic of inquiry in a contemporary arena; it also assures that a research result will be well rounded in its ability to confront challenges from neighboring disciplines.

3.3   GENERAL TACTICS

In this section we distinguish between facts and ideas, define primary and secondary sources, and discuss using literature review to understand research methodology. The aim is to elucidate different ways that the literature can be organized to help clarify the goals of the research.

3.3.1 Facts and Ideas

Literature can be organized in terms of facts and ideas. Jacques Barzun and Henry Graff, in their well-known text *The Modern Researcher*, make this useful distinction. In brief, a fact is "a clear and distinct relation held to be so by tacit agreement" (e.g., President Garfield was shot by Charles Guiteau), while an idea is a statement of inference or hypothesis (e.g., Guiteau was a disappointed office-seeker).[20] Put another way, facts are quantifiable and certifiable pieces of information, while ideas, even though they may well be procured in the same ways by delving into the literature, tend to have more of an illustrative or interpretive role. In generating the research report, the integration of facts and ideas is important. This is particularly true in qualitative and interpretive-historical studies, where the researcher needs to get "into" a social-cultural situation not his or her own. Figure 3.8 lists a variety of extant sources that can serve to bring the researcher "into" another place or period. Newspaper articles, letters, material objects, etc., are not facts in themselves; these merely serve to represent more intimately the ideas of the day, from which the researcher can frame a more robust narration. The headings in Figure 3.8 come from

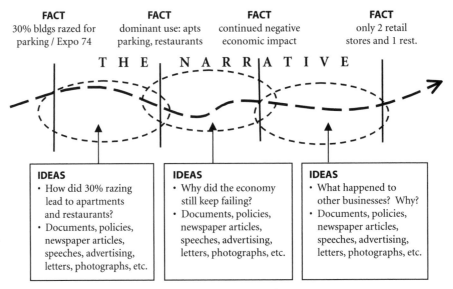

Figure 3.8 Facts and ideas: Literature review in relation to searching for the ideas that integrate a narrative.

the example in Box 3.2, which is an early M.Sc.Arch. thesis draft that was fact-intensive but idea-light.

3.3.2 Primary and Secondary Sources

Another way to divide the literature is into primary versus secondary sources. [Primary sources are *original* sources that, relative to the topic, are not essentially commentary *about* the topic. Primary sources usually *are* the topic that other sources comment *upon*. Those other sources, then, are the secondary sources.] The identification of primary sources is important for the definition of a topic of inquiry. Consider again the family tree in Figure 3.7. The primary source for Norberg-Schulz is Heidegger. For Heidegger, on the other hand, the primary sources are the works of the early Greeks. Depending upon the research strategy chosen, there are nuances in what "primary" can mean. In what we call interpretive-historical research (Chapter 6), that is, investigation into past conditions, primary sources would be those that "give the words of the witness or the first recorders of an event."[21] In qualitative research (Chapter 7), a primary source is any information that is contemporary with the period under study.[22]

An identification of primary and secondary literature can be strategically used to frame the contents of the research. Consider the example of one of the present authors' doctoral dissertations, which used the research strategy of logical argumentation

BOX 3.2

Facts versus Ideas in an M.Sc.Arch. Thesis Draft

This paragraph comes from a draft of a student thesis chapter. The research is an application of Brand's theory: the formal evolution of a major street in Spokane, Washington, over a period of 100 years. Here, the student is referring to a particular segment of the street toward the edge of the downtown area:

"To prepare for Expo 74, more than 30% of the buildings in this block were razed to make room for parking. Since this period, the city texture in this vicinity became discontinuous. The dominant uses were apartments, parking, restaurants. The economic environment continued to negatively affect this segment of Riverside Avenue. Between 1970 and 1990, only one restaurant and two retail establishments continued in operation."*

Figure 3.9A A portion of Riverside Avenue, Spokane, Washington. Image taken in the mid 60s when the structure was a hotel.

This statement is abundant in facts. (But note that the student provides no references to document the claims—for instance, where did the 30% figure come from? We assume that documentation is available. At this point in the research, the student had shown an ability to dig into the literature containing facts: Sanborn maps, census data, etc.) Our aim here is to address how the literature can be used to access ideas as well, and this is what the statement lacks. Ideas connect the facts into a believable narrative. How did the construction of more parking lots lead to apartments and restaurants? We do not know. How did apartments and restaurants lead to an economic downturn? We do not know. Somehow, we have to get from fact to fact by accessing what was going on in that temporal context.

Figure 3.9B The same building as it appears in 2000, now as an apartment building. Other changes to the street elevation are evident. Courtesy of the Northwest Room, Spokane Public Library. Courtesy of Zhenyu Wang.

---

*Courtesy, Zhenyu Wang, M.Sc.Arch. student, Washington State University, fall 2000.

(Chapter 11). The topic of inquiry: How can Kant's aesthetic philosophy yield an explanation for why people feel a "sense of place," and how can this explanation be more robust than the theory put forth by the "phenomenology" of Christian Norberg-Schulz? This is of course no place to answer the question, but a map of the literature review summarizes how primary and secondary sources played key roles in generating the answer. The operative portion of the map is shown in Figure 3.10.

The diagram maps the flow of the original philosophical material in Kant's works, how this material was digested by a network of commentators and analysts (the secondary sources), and finally how a new theory was framed from material taken from both the primary and secondary sources. Also shown is the necessary engagement with the line of thinking proposed by Norberg-Schulz, to which the new theory was a response. Note the designation of Heidegger as a secondary source. Although a primary source for Norberg-Schulz, Heidegger was a secondary source for the research on Kant. This does not mean that original Heidegger material did not play a part in the dissertation; certainly it did, because the critique of the Norberg-Schulz material demanded it. But relative to the topic of inquiry centered on Kant's philosophy, Heidegger's works were secondary sources. This dynamic raises the point that "primary" and "secondary" can easily blur in meaning, depending upon the exact

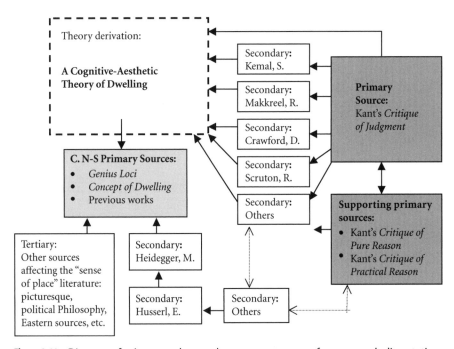

Figure 3.10 Diagram of primary and secondary source structure for a research dissertation.

intent of the research.[23] Ultimately, however, an arrangement of the literature into primary and secondary (and even tertiary) sources is integral to framing the logic of a research project. During the literature review as well as into the first drafts of the project, this diagramming should be going on, until clarity on a hierarchy of the source material emerges.

3.3.3 *Methodology by Theory and by Application*

A topic of inquiry is accessed by way of a research methodology. In the literature, there exist works that describe methodologies as well as works that simply apply them. A fine example where both of these realities are found in one volume is a work we refer to in our chapter on simulation research (Chapter 10), *Environmental Simulation*, edited by Robert Marans and Daniel Stokols. In this work, the first two chapters, by Stokols and Colin Clipson, are obviously *about* the methodology, while the subsequent chapters provide specific instances of how the strategy has been applied. Or again, in our chapter on interpretive-historical research (Chapter 6), the reader will see how the works by Arthur Danto, W. B Gallie, R. G. Collingwood, and others are clearly theories *about* method, while the example given of Jean-Pierre Protzen's work is one of an application. The researcher would do well to identify both categories in the literature review. One purpose of the present text is to provide both the theory and examples of applications for a variety of research strategies in one source.

3.4   SPECIFIC TACTICS: WHERE TO GO, WHAT TO DO

The practical "how-to" of a literature review consists of three parts: 1) knowing where the resources are; 2) having an organizing and retrieving system; 3) bringing motivation and imagination to the task. Whether these three ingredients are always equally represented in any effort at literature review is not the point. A great deal of effort spent in locating resources and amassing titles may end up in very limited original results. Conversely, swift and fortuitous location of the needed materials coupled with a clearly defined aim and an acute imagination can produce much fruit. Suffice it to say that while percentages probably vary from case to case, it is difficult to imagine a good literature review—and a good research result—without a competent knowledge of the resources, a clear organization of accrued information, and a good imagination.

3.4.1 *Where to Go: Resources*

In this subsection we address the *Internet* as a powerful information identifier, the *library* as still the primary source of literature, *archives* as distinct from libraries, *organizations* and *agencies*, and the *popular media*. We use web site addresses here as the initial means to identify sources for literature in all of these categories. This is because the Internet makes available at the fingertips of today's researcher an array of sources that would have astounded a researcher merely 20 years ago. We address it first because more and more it is used to find out where the resources are. The following tools are usually used:

Internet Search Engines. Even without knowledge of any specific web addresses, typing a key word into an Internet search engine can lead to innumerable web sites containing that word. Common Internet search engines include Altavista http://www.altavista.com/, InfoSeek http://www.go.com/, and MetaCrawler http://www.metacrawler.com/index.html. A generally recognized "meta–search engine," or a search engine that searches search engines, is DogPile http://www .dogpile.com/. We typed "city image" into Altavista and found addresses for more than two million web pages. At this point, a search engine can usually narrow the search by domain. Under the "education" domain in Altavista, we located a site from Florida State University addressing the following themes related to city image: cognitive maps, sense of place, characterless places, and a questionnaire on cities void of sense of place.[24] Another link led us to an entire book in electronic form on a case study of the changing city image of Heusden in the Netherlands, with due mention of Lynch's work.[25]

Specialized Search Engines. Academic institutions usually subscribe to a variety of services offering specialized search engines in various disciplinary domains. The Avery Architectural Index, attached to the Avery Architectural & Fine Arts Library, Columbia University, and operated by Research Libraries Group, is an example; the general web address is http://eureka.rlg.org/, although an additional password is needed per institution. Other useful specialized search engines are Arts and Humanities Search, First Search More (under Art Abstracts), and PsychINFO, which leads to many works relevant to environment-behavior research.[26] For instance, we searched "environmental aesthetics" in this engine, and the first article to come up was one on community meanings of town character, which makes use of material from Lynch.[27]

Full Text Services. Complete texts of journal articles or even books can be accessed via the specialized search engines. For instance, the article above from Psych-INFO is available in full text format via the Internet. The terms *eJournal* and *eBook* refer to this service. ProQuest Direct, Science Direct, Ideal, and NetLibrary are just a few of these full text services. Again, university (research) libraries subscribe to these services, so users of their systems can generally download a complete text without charge. In the case of entire books, the site is generally open to the user for a limited period of time, after which a charge may be required.

Library Databases. Most library catalogues are now accessible via the Internet. One example is the catalogue of the Library of Congress at www.loc.gov/catalog/

with the largest collection in the world. A keyword search for "city image" at this site produces the following response: "Your search retrieved more records than can be displayed. Only the first 10,000 will be shown." Item 15 in this search happened to be "Lynch, Kevin, 1918–, Image of the city, 1960." While of course the works themselves cannot be accessed through the Internet, these listings are useful research tools in that they allow many topical connections to emerge.

Specific Web Sites. There are of course specific web sites that researchers become acquainted with in various ways. A handy listing of architecture sites can be found at http://www.bc.edu/bc_org/avp/cas/fnart/archweb_noframes.html.

The *library* is still the place to conduct most research. *Research libraries* are usually attached to universities, and these reflect the research interests and strengths of the particular institution. The holdings of *public libraries* reflect the town or city in which they are located. For the researcher in architecture, this may be of particular importance if the research question has to do with a community's history. *Special libraries* are attached to institutions such as hospitals or corporations, and have holdings that pertain to that particular organization.

A tendency among research libraries is to cross-list their holdings in one centralized system, so that all materials are available via interlibrary loan. For instance, the Big 12 Plus Libraries Consortium is a network of university research libraries in the Midwest and West whose member number continues to increase. The catalogues of libraries in this consortium can be accessed as one source on the Internet. The homepage for the Big 12 Consortium can be found at http://www.big12plus.org/.

Literature review can involve *archival* materials. An archive is a limited-access repository of materials, usually connected to a particular entity (government body, organization, institution, even individual), organized and maintained for long-term safekeeping and for selective review and use. These "traces of past human activities" can include "letters, diaries, confidential memos, lecture notes, transcripts, rough drafts, unpublished manuscripts, and other . . . records."[28] Generally, the topic of inquiry will lead a researcher to identify organizations that may have the relevant archives. Then, contact must be made with the archive to learn what the requirements for accessing the material are. Not surprisingly, this task is again made easier by the Internet, as more and more archivists are putting their information on the web. Furthermore, universities are beginning to link catalogues of their archival holdings with their library information retrieval systems. A National Archive of the United States can be accessed at http://www.nara.gov/.

Documents from *organizations and agencies* are another source for literature review. *Government agencies* such as the Department of Housing and Urban Development http://www.hud.gov/ are a source for literature related to housing. The HUD web site connects to http://www.huduser.org/, which leads to publications, periodicals, ongoing research, bibliographic databases, and so on. *Professional organizations* offer literature pertaining to their disciplines, a significant amount of it research-oriented. One example is the American Institute of Architects' website at http://www.e-architect.com/. This site connects to other sites with relevant research interests; for example, a search led to sites published for a summit on "Communities of Tomorrow," the AIA Center for Advanced Technology Design, an international conference on architecture and health, AIA market research, and many more. Similarly, many disciplines related to the building trades publish extensive information on research; one example is the American Society of Heating and Refrigerating and Air Conditioning Engineers (ASHRAE) at http://www.ashrae.org/. This site offers connections to an abstract center, position papers, publication updates, comment on publications, and continuing education. *Testing agencies* also generate literature. For example, the National Fire Protection Association (NFPA) web site http://www.nfpa.org/ links to codes and standards, conferences, research and reports, a special journal on fire research, fire data analysis, the Charles S. Morgan Technical Library, and the NFPA archives. Literature is also developed by many *private companies* serving the architectural profession. For example, the web site for the furniture systems company Herman Miller http://www.hermanmiller.com/ links to a page that contains case studies, research papers, and issues papers: http://www.hermanmiller.com/us/index.bbk/US/en/WR.

The *popular media* is also a rich source for literature review. The researcher usually needs to situate popular materials within a larger theoretical venue of analysis or criticism; but given this, particularly in the realm of interpretive research, materials from popular media often lend depth to a research report. We leave the kinds of popular sources to the researcher's imagination because they are abundant: newspapers, popular magazines, reviews of theater and other entertainment productions, advertisements and other marketing literature, novels and other forms of fiction, editorials, political commentary, documentary films, and so on. Again, many of these sources can be accessed through the Internet. For instance, a search of www.Amazon.com is as valid as any other literature source. Many newspapers and periodicals update their web sites daily.

3.4.2 *What to Do: Organization and Retrieval*

Locating the resources is one thing, but organizing them and making some sort of conceptual sense out of the information is quite another. We recommend Barzun and Graff's *The Modern Researcher*, already cited above, as perhaps the definitive work on this topic. Our comments here are distillations of their recommendations with some personal experience added. In brief, the researcher must digest the gathered information in order to frame the research report. This takes an organizing schema that includes note taking and cataloguing for retrieval, all admixed with a creative imagination.

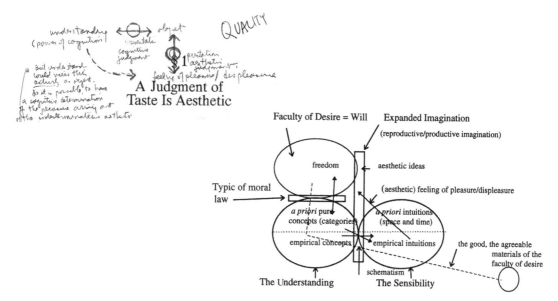

Figure 3.11 On the left, annotations from the author's copy of Kant's *Critique of Judgment*, showing the initial ideas that emerged regarding how Kant's theory of aesthetic judgment can be diagrammed on graphic terms. On the right, an explanatory diagram of the cognitive powers according to Kant; the diagram is from the final research product (the author's doctoral dissertation). The importance of the initial thought, with the sketch on the margin of the text, is evident when placed next to the final product.

As to note taking, pieces of information found in the literature deemed relevant for an emerging topic of inquiry need to be noted in a systematic way. The mode by which this is done is less important: by index cards, by a notebook, or by the laptop computer. Notes need to record all of the bibliographic information of the source. In addition, as Barzun and Graff point out, the writing of a note is the first step toward framing an idea.[29] Initial notes can also be taken by annotating the source material itself. Of course this requires ownership of the material. The proliferation of full text services on the Internet, along with the availability of inexpensive editions of many texts, makes this a small price to pay for research results that may be lasting. Such notes also serve as a permanent record of sorts—referring to a passage in an annotated text will always link to the research idea connected with it. Figure 3.11 is from the present author's annotated copy of Kant's *Critique of Judgment*, the primary source of his dissertation work. The penciled diagram in the top margin was the beginning of an idea that eventually led to one of the explanatory diagrams in the final work (reproduced at right).

Barzun and Graff stress that the researcher must have a "love of order."[30] Operationally, this means having a system that allows for any piece of information to be *retrieved*. During the initial "hunt" through the literature, whether on the Internet, in a library, or in some other venue, the present author simply keeps a notebook with jottings recorded chronologically. Figure 3.12 is one page from the notebook containing

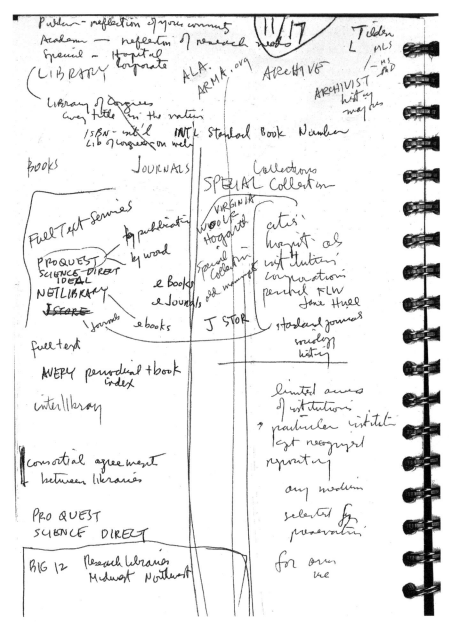

Figure 3.12 Page from the author's notebook generated during the research involved in developing this chapter.

information for this chapter—in fact this very section. (The messiness of this page, taken during an interview with a librarian, illustrates the tension between the ideal of taking neat systematic notes and the "real" of the situation; so we include it as illustrative. The facts should subsequently have been organized in a more coherent way.) As the research process advances, the initial notes can be further distilled or expanded into brief sentences or paragraphs which are in turn organized either by literature area, by subtopic, or by chapter concentration of the research report, once that structure begins to emerge.

Operational considerations aside, note taking and note organization mean nothing without the ability to engage in concept formation. This is also part of "what to do," but it necessarily mixes with issues of creativity and imaginative thinking. We have discussed this earlier in the chapter, suggesting that, even though imagination is hard to quantify, disciplined interactions with the literature can be good training. Barzun and Graff's initial chapters ("The ABC of Technique," "The Searcher's Mind," etc.) are difficult to add to, so we refer the reader to that work.

3.5   RECOMMENDED READINGS

As noted, Jacques Barzun and Henry Graff's *The Modern Researcher* ought to be in the personal library of all researchers, particularly those involved in more qualitative and interpretive research. We have cited this work often in this chapter.

Although not written for the design fields, we recommend referring to the mapping diagrams provided by Chris Hart in *Doing a Literature Review*.[31] We have cited this book earlier in this chapter. Hart goes into more depth than we do on different kinds of mapping. For instance, *feature maps* result from organizing articles by their bibliographic information, along with key theoretical standpoints; a collection of these reveals useful patterns that can be captured in a diagrammatic map. *Tree constructions* diagram major ideas and sub-ideas (different from our "family tree" of Figure 3.7 in that they do not require the temporal element). *Subject relevance maps*, *taxonomic maps*, and *concept maps*, are some others Hart covers, and these can no doubt be helpful to those doing architectural research.

Two works by Paul Leedy that we did not cite in this chapter are: a) *A Key to Better Reading* (New York: McGraw-Hill, 1968); although an older book, this has general pointers for reading that are timeless; and b) *How to Read Research and Understand It* (New York: Macmillan, 1981); this is useful for those doing quantitative research.

Chapter 5 ("Reading Other People's Research") of W. Lawrence Neuman's *Social Research Methods* (Boston: Allyn and Bacon, 1997) is also worthwhile.

NOTES

1. Chris Hart, *Doing a Literature Review* (Thousand Oaks, Calif.: Sage Publications, 1998), 14.

2. Kevin Lynch, *The Image of the City* (Cambridge, Mass.: MIT Press, 2000). Comments are from the back cover of this 27th edition.

3. Lynch, *Image of the City*, 46–90.

4. Ibid., 140, 152–154.

5. Marc-Antoinne Laugier, *Essay on Architecture* (1752), trans. Wolfgang and Anni Hermann (Los Angeles: Hennessey and Ingalls, 1977). See also Silvia Lavin, *Quatremère de Quincy and the Invention of a Modern Language of Architecture* (Cambridge, Mass.: MIT Press, 1992).

6. Another example is Michael O'Neil, "A Biologically Based Model of Spatial Cognition and Wayfinding," *Journal of Environmental Psychology* 11 (1991): 299–320.

7. Steward Brand, *How Buildings Learn* (New York: Penguin, 1994), 5.

8. Ibid., 12–23.

9. S. Kaplan, Dale Foster, and R. Kaplan, "Pattern Hypothesis: An Empirical Test," in *Proceedings of EDRA 18*, 1986.

10. Christopher Alexander, *A Timeless Way of Building* (New York: Oxford University Press, 1979), 249.

11. Christian Norberg-Schulz, *Genius Loci: Towards a Phenomenology of Architecture* (New York: Rizzoli International, 1991).

12. Clare Cooper Marcus, *House as a Mirror of Self* (Berkeley, Calif.: Conari Press, 1995), 3–11.

13. Ellen Berkeley, "Boston City Hall," *Architecture Plus*, February 1973, 72–77, 98.

14. Ibid., 72.

15. Lynch, *Image of the City*, 9.

16. Ibid., 7.

17. Ibid., 3.

18. Ibid., 11, 13.

19. Ibid., 123–139.

20. Jacques Barzun and Henry Graff, *The Modern Researcher* (Fort Worth, Tex.: Harcourt Brace Janovich, 1985), 135.

21. Ibid., 114.

22. W. Lawrence Neuman, *Social Research Methods* (Boston: Allyn and Bacon, 1997), 96.

23. John Tosh, "The Raw Materials," in *The Pursuit of History* (London and New York: Longman Group Limited, 1984), 29–30.

24. Lisa Waxman, "Cities and Towns" (Florida State University, 1999). Available at http://ind4601-01.sp00.fsu.edu/citytownabb/sld013.htm

25. Patricia Alkhoven, "The Changing Image of the City" (Heusden: Canaletto, The Netherlands 1993/1996). Available at http://pablo.library.uu.nl/~proefsch/01754573/hfdheus.htm

26. http://newfirstsearch.oclc.org/WebZ/FSPrefs?entityjsdetect=:javascript=true:screensize=medium:sessionid=sp02sw11-34306-cfsyfx6c-kdhx2w:entitypagenum=1:0

27. Ray Green, "Meaning and Form in Community Perception of Town Character," *Journal of Environmental Psychology* 19 (1999): 311–329.

28. Michael Hill, *Archival Strategies and Techniques* (Newbury Park, Calif.: Sage Publications, 1993), 3. The reference to archives as "traces of past human activities" is cited by Hill from E. J. Webb, D. T. Campbell, R. D. Schwartz, R. D. & L. Sechrest, *Unobtrusive Measures: Non-reactive Research in the Social Sciences* (Chicago: Rand McNally, 1966).

29. Barzun and Graff, *Modern Researcher*, 25–29.

30. Ibid., 44–45.

31. Hart, *Doing Literature Review*, 142–171. See "Mapping and Analyzing Ideas."

Chapter 4

Theory in Relation to Method

4.1 INTRODUCTION

Consider the woodcut below by Albrecht Dürer. This image is useful for considering both theory and theory's relationship to method. It is a good representation of the meaning of the Greek word *theoria*, from which our word theory comes. The Greek word suggests the active contemplation of an object, rather than the passive reception of external effects. This tendency for active contemplation is a significant development in the West because it marks the point when explanations of natural behavior began to be rooted in rational constructions rather than in mythical ones. For instance, when it rained, the new way of thinking was not that the gods were crying; rather, an explanation was sought in the way natural elements interact in accordance

Figure 4.1 A woodcut by Albrecht Dürer (1471–1528). We use it here as a graphic illustration of the separation between a subject's thought and the object contemplated in theory making.

73

with natural processes. A theory emerges when this explanation is set forth systematically, usually in the form of language, or by means of other signs and annotations.

Starting from its origins in *theoria* (active contemplation), theory has become much more developed in meaning. It has never lost its basic characteristic as a removed and systematic accounting of an object. But nowadays every discipline tends to have definitions of theory that are a particular fit for that discipline. For instance, in the natural sciences, the demand for exact prediction is very high. Einstein's $E=mc^2$ is a scientific theory not only because it describes and explains a certain relationship between energy, mass, and the speed of light. Its real status as a theory is rooted in our ability, in the next experiment, to demonstrate that the relationship between these factors is what the theory says it is. If the relationship cannot be demonstrated, in Karl Popper's words, it has been falsified, and its status as a theory becomes obsolete.[1] In the human sciences, the demand for a theory to have this kind of predictive power is not as strong. The emphasis is rather on statistical probabilities that can generalize upon human behavior; we see this, for instance, in correlational research (see Chapter 8). Or the emphasis can be upon very detailed and in-depth descriptions of a particular social-cultural context, as in Geertz's idea of "thick description" (see Chapter 7).[2] Finally, in the fine arts, theories of art and art production tend to depend upon systematic philosophical constructions, as in Dewey's biologically based theory of art or Langer's theory of art as "symbolic form" (see Chapter 11).[3]

This chapter aims to avoid an explicit focus upon theories of just one discipline. Rather, it seeks to outline what it means to theorize *as such*, independent of what is being theorized *about*. We will therefore use the term "theory in general" to denote our concern for theorizing as such. Theory in general is directly related to research methodology in two ways. First, theory in general seeks to describe, explain, and predict. Research methodologies, on the other hand, may be viewed as prescribed ways to test those descriptions, explanations, or predictions. Second, theory in general seeks to develop descriptions, explanations, and predictions that hold true in all cases of a behavior under study, and not just in this or that specific case. Research methodologies offer means by which this claim to applicability beyond the particular case can be affirmed, modified, or rejected.

Refer again to Dürer's woodcut. The artist-observer is not only contemplating the object in the abstract. He is also drawing that object according to a prescribed method: He uses a grid through which to view the object, confident that this measuring instrument can provide for him data that is dependable for a reproduction of the image on paper. What is the basis of his confidence in this grid? It is that he accepts certain presuppositions about the empirical universe, to wit, that the objects that make it up can be understood by certain geometric relationships that hold constant. What he assumes is theoretical. What he does based upon those assumptions is methodological.

A theory does not necessarily have to prescribe the means by which its claims can be verified or tested. (This is a separate issue from the fact that a good theory is usually framed in a way that facilitates the testing of its claims, as we shall address shortly.) On the other hand, it is a role of research methods to verify or test theories. Theories tend to offer generalized descriptions about a condition that claim to fit all instances of the behavior of that condition. Research methodologies, however, tend to be much more specific. At the level of research strategy, a specific "way of knowing" the world is usually selected to test the claims of a theory. Depending upon the theory in question, there are usually "good fits" between that theory and the research strategy chosen to test it. For instance, it is fairly easy to conceive of an experimental research strategy to test the claims of $E=mc^2$; however, it would be much more of a stretch to access Einstein's theory of special relativity by means of, say, qualitative research. Furthermore, at the level of research tactics, specific means are defined to operationalize the investigation. For example, as John Boslaugh has noted in reference to Einstein's theory, "that special relativity works, that mass and energy are indeed interchangeable, has been demonstrated thousands of times in particle accelerators." In this example, clearly, special relativity is the theory, while particle accelerators are part of the methodological apparatus that demonstrate the veracity of the theory. The particle accelerator is of the same category of thing as Dürer's artist's grid; it is a measuring instrument for the purposes of research. Boslaugh goes on to address how Einstein's general relativity theory, which posited the bending of light by gravitation, was also demonstrated in research:

> About three years after the publication of general relativity . . . an expedition was launched by the Royal Society to Principe, an island off the West Coast of Africa. And during the eclipse, British physicist Arthur Eddington found deflection in starlight that nearly matched Einstein's calculations.[4]

Again, the theory itself did not necessitate a trip to faraway Principe; the *testing* of the theory, however, required such an expedition, which involved all sorts of measuring instruments to be taken along.

4.2   THE FRAMEWORK OF THEORY IN GENERAL

Gary Moore defines theory as "a set of interrelated concepts held as an explanation for observable phenomena by recourse to unobserved, more abstract principles." His focus is upon theories in environment-behavior research, but he parses this definition into six components that we suggest can be a descriptive framework for theory in general. Moore's six components are:[5]

1. A set of propositions or observational terms about some aspect of the universe.
2. Logical connections between the propositions.
3. A set of conclusions drawn from components 1 and 2.
4. Linkages to empirical reality.
5. A set of assumptions or presuppositions underlying the theory.
6. The connections of all of the above should be phrased in such a way that the theory is testable in principle.

In a later article Moore expands this list to eight components, adding a requirement for a disciplinary domain and unquestioned philosophical axioms.[6] For our purposes, it is sufficient to focus on the six listed above. It is to be noted that the sixth component is the most obvious gateway to implementing a research design that can generate or test a given theory.

In the case of the artist in Dürer's woodcut, a theoretical framework along the lines of Moore's six points can be understood as follows:

1. *Propositions/observations about some aspect of the universe:* that the human eye can see objects in the empirical realm dependably, and that what is seen can be reported dependably by means of graphic projections.
2. *Logical connections:* that the empirical realm is a system that can be mapped in terms of an objective matrix consisting of geometric location, extension (dimension), magnitude, and so forth.
3. *A set of conclusions drawn from components 1 and 2:* that looking through a matrix that includes the factors described in component 2 can accurately reproduce what is seen in component 1.
4. *Linkages to empirical reality:* an assumption that the abstract factors described in component 2 accurately represent empirical realities, and that the tools used can aid in accurate depiction of those realities.
5. *A set of assumptions or presuppositions underlying the theory:* that the empirical realm, as accessed by the human eye, is a coherent system of parts having predictable relationships to each other, and that any specific vantage point in this system will yield the same view of the system.
6. *Testability of the theory:* The testability of a theory is related both to its internal logical coherence (so that another party can understand its claims and its utility independent of the theorist) and its applicability to other cases (so that its explanatory utility is applicable in all cases of the behavior it purports to explain). Dürer's artist-observer, after he has produced his results (the drawing), can claim that another person sitting at the same spot with the same grid and viewing the same object should be able to reproduce the same view.

Consider a fairly well-known theory from the literature in environmental design research, David Canter's theory of place. Canter posits that physical environments

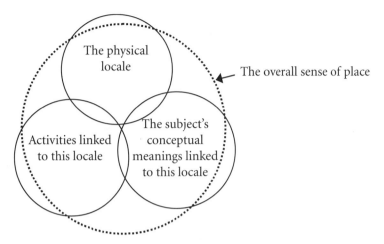

Figure 4.2   A diagram of the factors in David Canter's three-fold "sense of place."

take on significance as a result of the interaction of three domains: the physical locale, the activity performed in that locale, and the meanings assigned to that union of place with activity. Together these are termed the "constituents of places."[7] This could be diagrammed as in Figure 4.2. Canter's proposal certainly meets the requirements of Moore's six-component model for what constitutes a theory. It makes a set of explicit propositions with logical connections that work together (e.g., that locality, activity, and assigned meaning must work together for a sense of place). It also has obvious connections to empirical reality. And underlying the theory are fairly straightforward philosophical assumptions (for instance, the reality of the empirical world, the unity of perception with determinations of moral and aesthetic judgment, and so on).[8] As to testability, Canter in his more recent writings has been particularly careful to note that his ideas are "open to empirical test."[9] Certainly documented research based upon Canter's theory can be readily found in the existing literature. One example is a study of the city as a "multi-place" system, by Mirilia Bonnes, et al.; the authors of this study specifically credit Canter's work as the "theoretical footing" for their study.[10]

4.3   DIFFERENT WAYS TO CONCEPTUALLY DIVIDE THEORY IN GENERAL

Even though theory in general may have certain common attributes, it is difficult, perhaps impossible, to conceive of it as one conceptually homogeneous domain. The difficulty reflects the complex unity that is the human mind, with its ability to receive and explain empirical experience in multiple ways—and simultaneously. In this section we summarize some ways that the *non*-homogeneity of theory has been divided. We will address positive versus normative theory, different scales of theory, theory in relation to design, and the cultural dimensions of theory, which take in factors such as audience and rhetorical persuasion.

4.3.1 Positive versus Normative Theory

One way to map theory in general is to separate it into positive theories and normative ones. Positive theories are descriptive and explanatory systems that, because they can identify causal links, can predict future behaviors of the objects in question. Scientific theories are of this kind. Normative theories, on the other hand, include a wide range of ways-of-doing that belong to the realm of convention, or "rules of thumb." Action is taken based upon such tacit factors as "this is how we've always done it," or "this way is tried-and-true." Normative theories also describe, explain, and even predict (in the sense that a "tried-and-true" approach will most likely yield a competent product). However, they cannot be said to have the logical rigor of positive theories, and they can lead to a great variety of empirical outcomes.

Normative theory is largely what motivates actions taken in design practice. Gary Moore has proposed that positive theories are testable according to the laws of empirical reality, while normative theories (for instance, those related to design practice) are testable only by measures of professional acceptance, or longevity.[11] In short, normative theory is often not as conducive to rigorous testing as positive theory is. Another way to look at it is this: Because normative theory is demonstrated by conventional practices that have withstood the test of time, it is arguable that any normative theory has *already* been tested—repeatedly, and every day, in the field. For instance, that the standard wood frame house in the United States uses wood studs at 16 inches on center is not something that needs testing; it is just the way it is, or else the idea would have been rejected long ago.

In the architectural literature, perhaps the best-known work to make the distinction between positive and normative theory is Jon Lang's *Creating Architectural Theory*.[12] By "architectural theory" Lang largely means behavioral concerns related to the process of designing environments. Lang's argument is that normative theories abound in the design fields, and that they can be pushed more toward positive theory for the betterment of environmental design practice. Although a well-established contribution to the literature, Lang's work is cumbersome in some respects. For instance, he works from the assumption that the normative theoretical domain is often less reliable as a guide to practice. But more important, Lang is not clear in his text on what a practice based upon a "positive" theoretical framework would actually look like. But we do not wish to critique Lang's position here in depth; we only note it as one means of conceptually dividing "theory in general" into the positive and normative domains.

A more fruitful way to relate normative design practice to research can be seen in Peter Rowe's study of three design teams as they produced their designs (see Figure 4.3).[13] Rowe's methodology is largely ethnographic (see Chapter 7): He "lived with" the design teams as they developed their designs. He documented their sketches, talked with them, took notes, and finally interpreted what they said and did in a "thick description" of each process. In short, Rowe accepted the fact that much of design practice is driven by normative theories (for instance, reference to precedent,

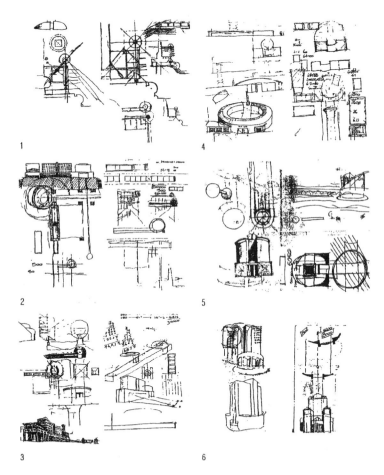

Figure 4.3   Progress sketches from the third of the design teams Peter G. Rowe studied. Here, the drawings sought to resolve the tension between a desire to conform to Burnham's Chicago master plan, on the one hand, and a programmatic wish to extend the project into the lake. Rowe numbers the sketches to catch temporal sequence. Courtesy of MIT Press.

reference to typology, working out conflicting themes, etc.). His research sought not to change this reality, but rather to understand it, as it were, *in vitro*.

4.3.2 Big, Medium and Small Theories

Another way to conceptualize theory in general is to consider the scope of applicability. At one extreme are very ambitious theories that are large in scope. The theory of gravity, which explains both the drop of a coin and the movement of planets, is such a theory. Relativity theory is also such a theory. A truly large scope of coverage is envisioned by Stephen Hawking's search for a "grand unified theory" (GUT). Hawking aims to link the fundamental forces in the cosmos (the strong nuclear force, the weak nuclear force, and the electromagnetic force) to a single explanatory framework.[14]

At the other extreme are small, localized explanations for things. "I get depressed when the sky is overcast" may be a kind of small theory. It explains a very localized reality that by definition has no larger application. It meets all of the requirements of a theory; but its explanatory utility is of very limited scope. At this scale, as Moore points out, there may be little functional difference between theory and fact-gathering. In other words, if I get depressed when the sky is overcast, the localized domain of applicability (in other words, me) does not require systematic theorizing or, for that matter, research. If the phenomenon is consistent, the relationship between overcast sky and how I feel is sufficient as a set of related facts, and can be simply relied on as a working hypothesis.[15]

Following R. K. Merton, Moore then suggests theories of the "middle range," that is, ones with a scope not grand but also not small. These will not have wide applicability across disciplines; but they will have sufficient applicability to make their claims useful within a discipline. Because of this larger scope, they cannot simply remain working hypotheses; the demand is greater that they be tested and either affirmed or rejected. Moore's concern is chiefly with environment-behavior issues, and he argues that much of the theories generated in this literature (for instance, of privacy, personal space, territoriality, aging and the environment, environment and crime, and so on) can be regarded as "explanatory theories of the middle range."

Now, because of the disciplinary scope of middle-range theories, they by definition have a coverage that is not merely local or case-specific. Consider Dana Cuff's theoretical claim about excellent buildings: "I maintain that there are three principal evaluators of any building's quality and these are the consumers or the public at large, the participants in the design process, and the architectural profession."[16] This statement, even though it is not a fully elaborated theory such as Canter's, nevertheless exhibits Moore's elements of theory-making. At least, it is the kind of premise from which a systematic theory can be attempted. What is more, Cuff's premise targets a particular aspect of the architectural discipline; it is making a claim that, if correct, can have applicability beyond any specific building, taking it clearly out of the range of specialized (small) instances. Tests of the claim can easily be envisioned. Cuff goes

BOX 4.1

Dana Cuff's Three Categories of Excellent Practice

Here again is Cuff's formulation: "I maintain that there are three principal evaluators of any building's quality and these are the consumers or the public at large, the participants in the design process, and the architectural profession." Here is a suggestion as to how her method for evaluating "excellent practice" can be considered a theory, according to Moore's six categories.

1. *A set of propositions or observational terms about some aspect of the universe:* Certainly the formulation meets this criterion: Cuff is dealing explicitly with architectural practice.
2. *Logical connections between the propositions:* The three categories form a commonsensical triad as interrelated components of any instance of architectural practice.
3. *A set of conclusions drawn from components one and two:* She posits simply that success in each area directly affects whether or not a practice can be assessed as "excellent."
4. *Linkages to empirical reality:* Cuff's thesis links to the built forms themselves. (In fact, one weakness of her theory is this: There is so much emphasis upon the empirical buildings that sometimes it is unclear whether or not she is theorizing on excellent practice or excellent buildings; there is, of course, a difference at the theoretical level.)
5. *A set of assumptions or presuppositions underlying the theory:* These assumptions range from the fact of architectural practice as a distinct endeavor to the possibility of measuring, at some level, a communally acceptable understanding of "excellence."
6. *The connections of all of the above should be phrased in such a way that the theory is testable in principle:* Cuff tests her own claim with three case studies, and it is easy to envision more studies based upon her theory.

Figure 4.4   The Monterrey Bay Aquarium, Monterrey, California. One of Dana Cuff's three case studies. Photograph from authors' collections.

on to do just that: She assesses three projects in California through the lenses of these three constituencies. In fact, one potential flaw in her theory is how limited her sample tests are: only three projects in California.

4.3.3 Polemical Theories of Design

By design in this case we mean the production of figural schemes drawn on paper or computer that, through many different iterations, ultimately become built environments. There are of course many theories associated with design in this sense, and we will take a closer look at this topic in Chapter 5. Here we address theories that are related to design activity, and that tend to take a polemical stance that sets normative guidelines for what to do. Among these are systematic works that usually promote or defend a particular set of visual attributes often by refuting other opinions (for instance, A. W. Pugin's treatise on "pointed [Gothic] architecture"), or a particular interpretation of how a cultural time should be expressed in architectural form (for instance, Mosei Ginzburg's *Style and Epoch*, or Robert Venturi's *Complexity and Contradiction in Architecture*), or a particular view of how natural processes ought to be expressed in material form (e.g., Louis Sullivan's "form ever follows function," see Box 4.2). Consider Marc Antoine Laugier's very well-known *Essay on Architecture* of 1753. It is one of a series of treatises based upon the premise that architecture began with the primordial hut, when primitive men huddled under trees during rain and thunder (bad idea!) and eventually evolved a structure framed out of tree trunks and branches (Figure 4.5). These "theories of the hut" have had a remarkable run, from Vitruvius through Laugier and Quatremère de Quincy, to R. E. Dripps today, with commentary by Rykwert thrown in (who added something like a wine cellar to the original hut).[17]

Can these polemically based design theories be considered theories, on the basis of Moore's six components of a theory? A theory like Laugier's can arguably meet the first five of Moore's standards; but is Laugier's theory testable? Is Venturi's theoretical statement "less is a bore" testable? Is Sullivan's theoretical position "form ever follows function" testable (see Box 4.2)? This question seems to be a point of contention in the present literature on the subject. Paul-Alan Johnson starts *The Theory of Architecture* by suggesting that architectural theory (by which he largely means polemically based design theories) "may not be theory at all."[18] He cites those who suggest that architectural theory can be reinterpreted just as "talk" about theory, or theory-talk, and no more.[19] Martin Symes, who considers the possibility that the definitions of theory are diverse, suggests that "designers tend to discuss 'theories' of what should be done, while scientists refer to 'theories' of what might be the case."[20] Linda Groat and Carole Despres seek a linkage between scientific theories and theories of design. They first show that design theories from the Renaissance through the postmodern period have emerged from the same cultural roots as scientific ways of knowing the cosmos. They then go on to say, for instance, "while it is not feasible to test a belief in

Figure 4.5   Laugier's hut. This well known illustration has become emblematic of a series of theories, from Vitruvius to the present day, that draw from the idea that architecture begins with a primordial hut.

beauty (as prescribed by Alberti's treatise of 1450), it is possible to test whether the use of Renaissance-baroque principles of hierarchical ordering actually produce buildings that are interpreted as beautiful by a given set of people."[21] This sentence is representative of their larger argument, which is that "architectural theories," by which they mean polemically oriented theories that prescribe the visual attributes of designed forms, offer conceptual material that can be framed into researchable questions. They offer five foci where this can take place: style, composition, type, morphology, and place. This section of their article is particularly useful for its citations of extant research in these areas, and we recommend it for further study.[22]

4.3.4 *Prediction versus Persuasion*

We now cite Paul-Alan Johnson's comment more fully:

> My own long-standing concerns that what I hear, read, and see taught as archi-
> tectural theory may not be theory at all in the sense of broad and all-encompassing
> generalizations about architecture have led me to suspect that . . . *what is called
> theory has more to do with certain arguments and ideas aimed at persuading others
> to particular beliefs and values* [our italics].[23]

Johnson touches upon an important distinction, or demarcation, within the domain of theory in general. Because positive theory identifies causal links that lead to
predictions of future behavior, and because the emphasis upon this in natural sciences has been widespread since the Enlightenment, it has influenced how "theory"
tends to be conceived. This is one reason for the debate on whether design-oriented
theories are even theories at all, because they have fewer powers of prediction. The
claims of design theories tend to depend upon rhetoric and polemics and not upon
empirically demonstrable proofs.

Johnson's suggestion that architectural theories are theories *because of their persuasive function* is significant in light of this state of affairs. We suggest that this idea
itself constitutes a worthy focus for more research, for it may provide the key to what
constitutes a design theory. This is so for two reasons. First, persuasion may be the key
to a reinterpretation of what "testability" can mean for polemically based design theories. Positively oriented theories are anchored in causality, so agreement from the
community they are directed toward is more of a logical imperative. For instance, if
$E=mc^2$ can repeatedly predict certain astronomical behaviors, it demands assent from
its audience. Polemically oriented theories lack the ability to demonstrate causality, so
there is no imperative that an audience agree. In this instance, persuasion becomes
much more important.[24] When a wide audience is persuaded by a design theory, it
gains its own kind of legitimacy. This act of persuasion is, in a sense, a kind of test.
The test of audience acceptance is not scientifically describable or predictable; on the
other hand, the *fact* of wide audience acceptance demonstrates at least two things.
One is that the proposed theory is somehow striking a deep and appropriate chord in
the culture at the time. For instance, Mies's theoretical claim "less is more"—a
polemical formulation—influenced design practice for almost two generations
worldwide. It somehow captured the reverence for the machine aesthetic of the culture of that time. We will return to cultural considerations shortly. The other is that
the proposed theory may even be striking chords of human identity that transcend
the temporal cultural context. For instance, we may still retain certain preferences for
the meanings that the classical orders can communicate. When Groat and Despres
suggest that the beauty of Renaissance order and hierarchy can be tested for "a given
set of people" today, such a test can lead to hypotheses as to whether there are universal tendencies within the human being that can respond to those orders.

This leads to the second reason why Johnson's reference to persuasion is important, and this is particularly relevant for research considerations. Persuasion may be the key to reinterpreting what "generalizability" can mean for polemically based design theories. In a positively oriented theory, generalizability is dependent upon whether research can demonstrate the claims of the theory independent of subjective

BOX 4.2

Louis Sullivan's "Form Ever Follows Function"

Sullivan's dictum deserves a separate focus for several reasons. First, it illustrates a typical feature of polemically based design theories, the ability to capture a theoretical position in a short, concise saying or epigram. Mies's "less is more" and Venturi's "less is a bore" are other examples. Sullivan's saying, usually abridged to "form follows function," is perhaps one of the most enduring epigrams in architectural theory.

This brings up another reason for taking a closer look at Sullivan's saying: It has received wide assent from generations of designers. In other words, it captures in words what a community of informed people would agree is an essential reality about design. This is a trait of polemically oriented design theories: their ability to represent a wide base of feeling.

The third reason for singling out Sullivan's epigram is this: It has inadvertently served as the theoretical banner for very different architectural camps. Sullivan's original point is that the forms of nature always express the organic "inner life" of their essences. It is this reality that we call "natural." Therefore, architecture must also bring out the inner essence of materials. But "form follows function" has also been used to argue for efficiency and mechanical functionalism: Given a function, come up with the most utilitarian form to suit that need.

A Sullivan-designed panel is shown in Figure 4.6. The intricacies of the panel design illustrate the original meaning of the epigram, to wit, that form ought to bring out the essential qualities of a material.

Figure 4.6 Sullivan panel. "Form ever follows function," in Sullivan's original meaning of the phrase, underlines his conviction that beautiful physical form emerges if the design is able to express the inner natural essence of the material. Photograph courtesy of Anna Mutin.

or contingent considerations. This is because causal links, once established, ought to hold true regardless of audience or locale. In a polemically based design theory, on the other hand, generalizability is heavily dependent upon how subjectively universal it can claim to be, that is, how much the experience the theory purports to explain can be understood by a wide community of human beings. This distinction is important not only for theories in the design realm (such as Laugier's hut theory); it is also important for several of the interpretively oriented research strategies to be addressed in this book. For instance, in qualitative research, the narrative that the researcher weaves must stand the test of acceptance by a wide audience of people. This is not incidental to its credential as a robust example of research; it is at the core of its claims to validity. Ian Hodder makes an additional observation in his article "The Interpretation of Documents and Material Culture." Hodder is concerned here about the bases upon which an audience should accept a researcher's narrative:

> The success of interpretations depends upon peer review . . . and on the number of people who believe, cite, and build on them. But much depends too on the trustworthiness, professional credentials, and status of the author and supporters of an interpretation. Issues here include how long the interpreter spent in the field and how well she or he knows the data. . . . Has the author obtained appropriate degrees and been admitted into professional societies? Is the individual an established and consistent writer, or has he or she yet to prove her- or himself? Does the author keep changing her or his mind?[25]

Hodder makes his point with a bluntness that is not often seen in scholarly literature. But his argument is very apropos: Considerations of how audience acceptance is gained are relevant to the design realm in general, and to the legitimacy of design-related theories in particular. They address the question of the relationship between culture and theory.

It is our view that both positive theories and polemically oriented design theories emerge out of cultural contexts. The above argument maintains that cultural receptivity is essential for the success of design theories, in terms of their "testability" as well as their "generalizability." Much more subtle, and hence also more controversial, is the notion that positive theories are also complicit with cultural roots. In other words, "scientific method" may not be as culturally transcendent as it has been assumed to be. The work of Thomas Kuhn and Imre Lakatos are well-established examples of literature in the philosophy of science that show how scientific inquiry is also governed by cultural inertias, by "research programmes," "positive heuristics," "anomalies" (Lakatos),[26] and "normal science" (Kuhn).[27] In both instances, the authors argue that the progress of science is not a smooth reality in which improvements to existing theories are instantly recognized and incorporated. The real case is a lot messier. Once a "dominant paradigm" is in place, it influences how a community receives and perceives new data; it is difficult to motivate the development of new theories, as well as to recognize good ones when they emerge. Space (and the mission of this book) does not allow us to delve into these issues here; we only make note of this as one final indication of the complexity of the domain that we call theory in general.

4.4   "SNAPSHOTS" OF THE CHAPTERS TO FOLLOW

In sum, we offer the following diagram to situate theory in general in the larger context of philosophical foundations, research strategy, and research tactics. Figure 4.7 shows the interrelatedness of the various components we are concerned with in this chapter and in this book. Theory in general is in a kind of Janus position; that is to say, it looks in two directions. On the one hand, it draws from philosophical underpinnings for its own sense of legitimacy and coherence. On the other hand, it posits specific explanations about something in nature or the social/cultural world and makes its claims amenable to testing and analysis by means of research. A strategy for research, or system of inquiry (see Figure 2.1), is then identified to best conduct these tests, which in turn call for specific tactical and instrumental means for their realization.

We conclude this chapter with a survey of some of the research designs to be addressed in this book, with a view toward highlighting the theoretical underpinnings of each. The seven "snapshots" offered here are given in the sequence of the seven chapter headings in Part II of this book: interpretive-historical, qualitative, co-relational, experimental, simulation, logical argumentation, and case study research. It is of course not our aim to exhaust these topics here. Our aim here is to outline ways in which theory is enacted in research in each case.

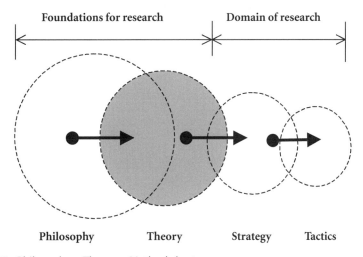

Figure 4.7   Philosophy = Theory = Method chart.

4.4.1 Interpretive-Historical Research

In Chapter 6, we address history research as part of the larger system of inquiry we call *interpretation*. The philosophical possibilities behind the interpretation of either past or present social situations are rooted in assumptions of a coherent world that can be known. Theoretically, much depends upon the construction of the narrative that makes that world known.

At the tactical level, interpretive-historical research makes use of empirical evidence from the past. This evidence can be found in a wide variety of sources, including archival material as well as many other public and private documents, the material evidence available at the site, and interviews of eye witnesses. It can also be drawn from comparisons to similar situations or re-enactments of key actions or events.

Witold Rybczynski's *Home: A Short History of an Idea* is a useful example of interpretive-historical research. Rybczynski draws from a variety of written material both public and archival, along with visual objects such as prints and paintings (each one of his chapters begins with a frontispiece dating from the period to be examined) to weave a narrative that interprets the evolution of "home" from the medieval period to the late twentieth century. From these sources, the author posits reasons why certain Western ideas first emerged, such as privacy, intimacy, comfort, hygiene, even the idea of a family home itself. For instance, during the medieval period, "it was unusual for someone . . . to have his own room. It was more than a hundred years later that rooms to which the individual could retreat from public view came into being— they were called "privacies."[28] As we will see in the Chapter 6, Rybcyznski's account of the evolution of home is what Hayden White calls an "emplotment," and what Arthur Danto calls a composition of "narrative sentences."

4.4.2 Qualitative Research

Qualitative research deals in the interpretation of contemporary situations. It places particular emphasis upon the role of the researcher as a vital part of the research outcome. In this sense it is very different from experimental and correlational research, both of which assume an "objective eye" on the part of the researcher. In qualitative research, the researcher's background, gender, point of view, and so forth, all come into play. This does not mean that personal elements can randomly affect the findings, but it does promote the view—and it is essentially a philosophical stance—that "pure objectivity" is impossible. This is particularly true of complex social-cultural settings.

Herbert Gans's study of life in Levittown, New Jersey, is a good example of qualitative research.[29] The years after World War II saw a boom in housing in the United States, which led to planned communities in Pennsylvania, New Jersey, and New York. Gans was among the first wave of buyers for homes in Levittown, New Jersey, when it was first built. At the theoretical level, Gans wanted to find answers to some questions he had about these new community developments. These included such concerns as how much of the town plan was affected by the builders and how much by the residents; and whether or not suburban life was as bad as some of the commentators of the day were positing.[30] Gans's introduction to his book is very clear as to his tactics: He simply moved to Levittown, New Jersey for two years (October 1958–September 1960) as a member of the community. He was a "participate-observer":

> I planned to observe the development of neighbor relations and social life and to be on hand when organizations and institutions were being set up. In addition to observing at public meetings, I would also be able to interview founders and members, and once having gotten to know them, follow their groups as they went through their birth pains.[31]

Gans also got to know "doctors, lawyers, local reporters, and the Levitt executives." He observed the life of his own street, "making the rounds . . . to find out what was happening." He also [sent out open-ended questionnaires] at the inception of the community, and interviewed the same people again two years later. Finally, he wrote copious notes, often from memory of the events that transpired that day, and organized them into the narrative that is the published book. Research such as Gans's also demonstrates how new theory can come out of research findings. For instance, Gans found that advocates of "rapid growth" generally had their way in private organizations such as churches and volunteer groups. However, in public agencies such as school boards and government programs, advocates of slow growth tended to control the situation.[32]

4.4.3 Correlational Research

Correlational research asks two fundamental questions revolving around the philosophical notion of "necessity." (We will address the definition of necessity in Chapter 11; for now, we ask that the reader take the word in its everyday meaning.) Both of these questions underline the fact that much of life experience cannot be explained purely by causal connections. The two questions are as follows:

1. Is cause the *necessary* explanation for all possible behavior?
2. Even if it is, is it *necessary* to identify a specific cause before an explanation of behavior can have utility?

Behind both of these questions is the one championed by the British empiricist philosopher David Hume: Is causality itself a *necessary* conception?[33] In situations involving human beings, reducing experience down to specific causal variables is often particularly hard to do, and it is sometimes downright unethical. Correlational research is useful because it recognizes that there are many instances in the "real world" where explanatory value can be obtained by showing that certain variables have strong relationships with other variables, without the need to demonstrate that one variable causes another. Consider this: Can we study the effects of daily exercise upon IQ scores by depriving one group of children of all physical exercise while giving a comparison group every opportunity? This is ethically impossible to do. On the other hand, if we identify certain children who tend not to exercise and compare their IQs over time to other groups of children who are more prone to regular exercise, we may be able to find some correlation between the two variables.

At the strategic level, correlational research attempts to identify venues in which a research focus can be framed in such a way that well-defined variables can be specified for study, but that the final outcomes, while useful, do not have to ascribe cause to any one of them. Oscar Newman's study of high-rise versus low-rise public housing in New York City, summarized in his book *Defensible Space*, is an example of this kind of strategy.[34] Newman found that the height of buildings has a clear relationship to the crime rate in public housing venues (crime in interior spaces in buildings of 13 stories or higher is 38% higher than incidents of crime in three-story buildings).[35] In his now well-known comparison between two public housing developments adjacent to one another, one with high-rise buildings and the other with low-rise buildings (Van Dyke and Brownsville, see Figure 8.11), Newman's research found significantly less crime in the low-rise development. This is an example of a correlation between a formal variable (height of building) and a sociological variable (rate of crime).

Tactically, Newman uses a variety of means to give his study traction. These include analyses of data from the New York City Housing Authority (at the time of his research, New York's housing units comprised 19% of all public housing in the country).[36] Interviews were also used; from these it was found that even the quality of interactions between residents and the housing authority police force (1,600 in number at the time of the research) were affected by physical form. Interactions were much more confrontational in the high-rise living units than in the low-rise units.[37]

In sum, Newman's work is important in bringing focus to issues related to crime frequency and built form. It underlines the importance of built forms that maximize such factors as visibility in public circulation, group areas that conduce feelings of ownership, low-rise forms that minimize anonymous vertical travel routes, and so on. These are all factors that have clearly demonstrated correlational ties to crime rate.

4.4.4 *Experimental Research*

Experimental research seeks causal connections between two or more variables. By the manipulation of a variable within a controlled setting, the effect of that variable's behavior upon other variables is observed, and certain conclusions are drawn from these observations. Experimental research is more prone to be summarized by numerical data than by narrative. While experimental research is most suited to testing the behavior of inanimate objects (we give such an example in Chapter 1; refer to Brandle and Boehm's research on the triple-glazed window), it can also be used in studying behavior in people. In his well known work *Inquiry by Design*, John Zeisel cites an example in which a researcher interviewed 352 persons who had applied to live in a senior citizens' residence before they knew the outcomes of their application. 204 eventually were accepted and became residents, while 148 applications were rejected. Treating this latter group as her "control," the researcher interviewed both groups one year after the move-in and found, for instance, that the residents showed a decrease in desire for medical care while the nonresidents doubled their stated need.[38] In Chapter 9, we examine further instances of this kind of research.

4.4.5 Simulation Research

Simulation has a long lineage as well as a wide scope of coverage in the history of philosophy. It is related to the question of how "reality" is actually constituted and how we can come to know it. Plato's view that any empirical thing is merely a copy of its immaterial and ideal form is in essence a question of *simulacra* (the traces or shadows of things) and substance. In *Republic X* for instance, he argues that there are three levels of "bed": the ideal and immaterial form of the bed, the actual empirical bed, and the (by definition) poor copy of a bed that an artist would draw.[39] Descartes, who contributed much to the definition of scientific method, was also very concerned with how the "I think" portion of his famous dictum can actually guarantee the "therefore I am" conclusion.[40]

For our purposes, the theoretical presupposition for simulation research is that knowledge of "a reality" can be obtained by reproducing that reality in some substitute medium. This is usually understood in the context of an anticipated (that is, future) reality. Simulations of past events we call *reenactments*, and we address these in the chapter on interpretive-historical research (Chapter 6). Colin Clipson identifies four general types of simulation: iconic models (physical representations of proposed products), analogue models (which simulate an environmental condition—e.g., a flight simulator), operational models (human interactions with a setting—e.g., war games), and mathematical models.[41]

Tom Porter, in a book essentially devoted to issues of architectural reproduction, *The Architect's Eye*, provides various examples of an increasingly important form of simulation, one that seems to transcend Clipson's typologies: computer simulation.[42] The image in Figure 4.8 shows a computer simulation of airflow in an interior space; this information can help the architect place diffusers in an optimal location. Of course one pressing question today is whether computer modeling will one day replace models built three-dimensionally. More research is needed into the pros and cons of the two approaches. For example, it can be hypothesized that the tactile engagement with building, or even with viewing, three-dimensional models can result in more of an "embodied" sense of the ultimate form. On the other hand, Porter describes an informative research project that depicts on a television screen an actual space from Mackintosh's Glasgow Art School, along with the image of the same space taken from a model. Subjects were asked to identify which image came from the actual space, and they "universally accepted the model simulation." Porter's point is

Figure 4.8   Tom Porter's computer image. Simulated airflow shown on the computer screen can help designers and HVAC engineers understand the consequences of such decisions as diffuser location. Courtesy of Tom Porter and Routledge SPON.

that a television screen seems to mediate our experience of seeing a model, rendering a simulated space much more believable.[43] We address these matters further, along with what a wide array of simulation venues can mean for strategy and tactics, in Chapter 10.

4.4.6 *Logical Argumentation Research*

The main characteristic of logical argumentation is that of *system*: its definition, its component parts and how they relate, what delimits the system, and how the system is connected to other systems that, in total, make up the cosmos in a logical manner. In Chapter 11, we address some of the key components of logical argumentation, including necessity and contingency, induction versus deduction, *a priori* and *a posteriori* formulations, and so on. Suffice it here to say that, while other research typologies implicitly assume system on their way to demonstrating other things, research in logical argumentation aims to frame the system itself.

Logical argumentation attempts to situate a well-defined thing or issue in a systemic framework that can have explanatory or utilitarian power over all instances of that thing or issue. In other words, one important strategic consideration is to know exactly *what* the systemic theory to be developed is going to be *about*. For instance, shape grammar research, such as the work of L. March and G. Stiny, is *about* a certain systemic way that formal composition can be understood by the dictates of formal logic.[44] Once the "about" is determined, tactics both internal and external can then be deployed. Internal tactics are just the logical components of argumentation trained specifically on the "about." For example, March and Stiny's work depends almost totally upon the mathematical connections that describe geometric shapes. External tactics look outside the logical system being framed for supporting material. March and Stiny look to precedents and arguments in eighteenth-century studies in biological morphology (Goethe) and nineteenth-century theories of crystal growth (Froebel) to lend historical continuity to their work. Shown in Figure 4.9 is a window lattice; March and Stiny argue that patterns such as this can be generated by a system of logical rules.

Figure 4.9 Shape grammar rules have been shown to be able to reproduce lattice patterns similar to what is shown here. Photograph from authors' collections.

4.4.7 Case Study Research

Our view of case study research is that it is often a kind of conceptual container. It can be used to contain one or more other research approaches (in which instance it is a strategy). Gans's *Levittowners*, for instance, is case study at a strategic level. Or case study can be used as one of several devices under the umbrella of a single research design (in which instance it can be called a tactic). Several case studies can be compared to reach a general set of observations. This is the approach taken by Rudolph Moos and Sonne Lemke in their study of group housing for the aged.[45] Case studies can also be used as illustrative examples highlighting larger abstract principles. In a recent Master of Science in Architecture thesis, Eliot Price used the design approaches to the Audubon House in New York City (Figure 4.10) and William McDonough's Gap Headquarters in San Francisco as case studies to illustrate general principles of sustainable design.[46] We address case study research in Chapter 12.

Figure 4.10 Audubon House, New York. A case study in sustainable architectural design. Photograph courtesy of Eliot Price.

4.5   CONCLUSION

This chapter considered theory in general and its relationship to research. We have situated theory between its philosophical foundations, on the one hand, and research strategies and tactics, on the other (see again Figure 4.7). Theory and method, as we have shown, are intimately related. Before moving on to the chapters of Part II of this book, which will address more explicitly the seven research strategies surveyed above, we turn now to the relationship between design and research.

4.6   RECOMMENDED READINGS

As we suggested at the outset of this chapter, "theory" can mean different things in different disciplines. We have addressed (what we call) theory in general, that is, the content of theory as such as opposed to theory *about* this or that. A text that does a credible (albeit somewhat involved) job of organizing different kinds of architectural theories is Paul-Alan Johnson's *The Theory of Architecture: Concepts, Themes and Practices* (New York: Van Nostrand Reinhold, 1994). Our use of this text was mainly limited to Johnson's discussion of the relationship between architectural theory and persuasion; however, the book overall is a worthy reference on different types of architectural theory.

Another text of significant help to us in this chapter is one edited by Gary T. Moore and Robert Marans: *Advances in Environment, Behavior, and Design.* This volume is the fourth in a series published by Plenum Press (1977). It is particularly useful for its observations on theories of "the middle range"—theories having explanatory scope at the disciplinary level.

In 4.3.3, we referred to several works under the heading "Polemical Theories of Design" (Laugier, Ginzburg, Venturi, etc.); these will be addressed again in Chapter 11, and the citations for these works are included in that chapter.

"The Significance of Architectural Theory for Environmental Design Research," by Linda Groat and Carole Despres, surveys some major design theories, or design perspectives, from a historical point of view, and then proposes ways they can be tested through the lens of five categories: style, composition, type, morphology, and place. See *Advances in Environment, Behavior, and Design*, eds. Ervin H. Zube and Gary Moore, Vol. 3 (New York: Plenum Press, 1987).

NOTES

1. Karl Popper, "Falsificationism versus Conventionalism," in David Miller, ed., *Popper Selections* (Princeton, N.J.: Princeton University Press, 1985), 143–151.

2. Clifford Geertz, "Thick Description: Toward an Interpretive Theory of Culture," in *The Interpretation of Cultures* (New York: Basic Books / HarperCollins, 1973), 3–30.

3. John Dewey, *Art as Experience* (New York: Berkley Publishing Group, 1959). Susanne Langer, *Philosophy in a New Key* (New York: Mentor Books, 1964).

4. John Boslaugh, *Stephen Hawking's Universe* (New York: Avon Books, 1989) 23–34.

5. Gary T. Moore, "Linking Environment-Behavior and Design Theories: Framing the Debate," in *EDRA 22* (Oaxtepec, Mexico, March 1991), 1–2.

6. Gary T. Moore, "Toward Environment-Behavior Theories of the Middle Range," in *Advances in Environment, Behavior, and Design*, vol. 4, ed. Gary Moore and Robert Marans (New York: Plenum Press, 1997), 6–7.

7. David Canter, *The Psychology of Place* (London: The Architectural Press, 1977), 157–158.

8. For a paper by this book's authors that sought to strengthen Canter's theory of place with Kant's philosophy of cognition, see D. Wang and L. Groat, "Towards an Interdisciplinary Theory of Place," in *1998 ACSA International Conference Proceedings, Rio de Janeiro*, pp. 225–229. The paper makes note of Canter's reference to "cognition" and "perception" and suggests that, while Canter may have identified cognition as an important component of his theory, he does not go into depth on it in any philosophical sense. The authors proposed that Kant's critical system, in which "cognition" includes the theoretical, moral, and aesthetic workings of the human mind, can provide the needed philosophical underpinnings for his theory.

9. David Canter, "The Facets of Place" in *Advances in Environment, Behavior, and Design*, vol. 4, ed. Gary Moore and Robert Marans (New York: Plenum Press, 1997), 114.

10. Mirilia Bonnes, Lucia Mannetti, Gianfranco Secchiaroli, and Giancarlo Tanucci, "The City as a Multi-Place System: An Analysis of People–Urban Environment Transactions," in *Readings in Environmental Psychology: Giving Places Meaning*, ed. Linda Groat (London and New York: Academic Press, 1995), pp. 58–85.

11. Gary T. Moore, "Linking Environment-Behavior and Design Theories: Framing the Debate," in *EDRA 22* (Oaxtepec, Mexico, March 1991), 4.

12. Jon Lang, *Creating Architectural Theory* (New York: Van Nostrand Reinhold), 1987.

13. Peter G. Rowe, *Design Thinking* (Cambridge, Mass.: MIT Press, 1987), 1–37.

14. Stephen Hawking, *A Brief History of Time* (New York: Bantam Books, 1988), 74.

15. Gary T. Moore, "Toward Environment-Behavior Theories of the Middle Range," 19–20

16. Dana Cuff, *Architecture: The Story of Practice* (Cambridge, Mass.: MIT Press, 1993), 196.

17. Joseph Rykwert, *On Adam's House in Paradise* (Cambridge, Mass: MIT Press, 1993), 13. Other references in this paragraph can be found in the notes for Chapter 11.

18. Paul-Alan Johnson, *The Theory of Architecture: Concepts, Themes & Practices* (New York: Van Nostrand Reinhold, 1994), 13.

19. Ibid., 10–11.

20. Martin Symes, "Relationship between Research and Design: A Commentary on Theories" in *Advances in Environment, Behavior, and Design*, vol. 3, ed. Ervin H. Zube and Gary Moore (New York: Plenum Press, 1987), 106.

21. Linda Groat and Carole Despres, "The Significance of Architectural Theory for Environmental Design Research" in *Advances in Environment, Behavior, and Design*, vol. 3, ed. Ervin H. Zube and Gary Moore (New York: Plenum Press, 1987), 29.

22. Ibid., 30–48.

23. Paul-Alan Johnson, *Theory of Architecture*, 13.

24. The space of this book, and its mission, does not allow for an in-depth consideration of the specific components of rhetoric (although these will be referenced in Chapter 11). We do recommend a seminal text, which needs to be connected to the architectural literature much more than it has been. See Chiam Perelman and L. Olbrechts-Tyteca, *The New Rhetoric: A Treatise on Argumentation* (South Bend, Ind.: University of Notre Dame Press, 1969).

25. Ian Hodder, "The Interpretation of Documents and Material Culture," in *Collecting and Interpreting Qualitative Materials*, ed. Norman K. Denzin and Yvonna S. Lincoln (Thousand Oaks, Calif.: Sage Publications, 1998), 126.

26. Imre Lakatos, *The Methodology of Scientific Research Programmes* (Cambridge, UK: Cambridge University Press, 1986).

27. Thomas Kuhn, *The Structure of Scientific Revolutions* (Chicago: University of Chicago Press, 1986).

28. Witold Rybczynski, *Home: A Short History of an Idea* (New York: Penguin Books, 1986), 18.

29. Herbert Gans, *The Levittowners: Ways of Life and Politics in a New Suburban Community* (New York: Random House, 1967).

30. Gans identifies four major questions. In addition to the two recited here, the third is: If living in Levittown did change people's perspectives, did that change occur because of the move to Levittown from the city, or was it due to other causes (and how much of it was unintended change)? And fourth, Gans wanted to research the political workings of planners and their policies, to see how they affected the "birth pains" of a new community. Ibid., xviii–xxi.

31. Ibid., xxi.

32. Ibid., 125.

33. Hume's famous example involves a billiard ball being struck by another billiard ball. That the first moves upon being struck by the second is empirically obvious; what is not visible (empirically obvious) is the assignment of an abstract notion of cause to the event. We do not see cause, says Hume, we merely see billiard balls moving. And that they do move upon every such incident only proves that it is a habitual occurrence, and so we develop customary ways of explaining the phenomenon. See David Hume, *An Enquiry Concerning Human Understanding* (Indianapolis: Hackett Publishing Company, [1748] 1977), 16–18.

34. Oscar Newman, *Defensible Space: Crime Prevention Through Urban Design* (New York: Collier Books, 1973).

35. Ibid., 27–33.

36. Ibid., 10.

37. Ibid., 12–13.

38. John Zeisel, *Inquiry by Design* (Cambridge, Mass.: Cambridge University Press, 1981), 70–71.

39. Plato, *Republic X*, 596–598.

40. Descartes' solution was to claim that God would assure that accuracy: ". . . the things we grasp very clearly and very distinctly are all true, is assured only because God is or exists, and

because he is a perfect Being." René Descartes, "Discourse 4" in *Discourse on Method and the Meditations*, trans. F. E. Sutcliffe (New York: Penguin, 1968), 58.

41. Colin Clipson, "Simulation for Planning and Design," in *Environmental Simulation*, ed. R. W. Marans and D. Stokols (New York: Plenum Press, 1993), 30–34.

42. Tom Porter, *The Architect's Eye* (London: E & FN Spon, 1997).

43. Ibid., 111–112. Porter notes that the problem of believability in seeing a small-scale model is called the Gulliver Gap (i.e., the sense of our own size as compared to the smallness of the mock-up). Viewing the spaces of the model through a screen can reduce or eliminate the Gulliver Gap.

44. L. March and G. Stiny, "Spatial Systems in Architecture and Design: Some History and Logic," *Environment and Planning B: Planning and Design*, vol. 12 (1985), 31–53.

45. Rudolph Moos and Sonne Lemke, *Group Residences for Older Adults* (New York: Oxford University Press, 1994).

46. Eliot Price, "Heidegger's 'Question Concerning Technology': A Philosophical Basis for Evaluating Sustainable Architectural Design" (master's thesis, Washington State University, 2000), 37–44.

Chapter 5

Design in Relation to Research

5.1   INTRODUCTION

For his bachelor of architecture thesis, Austin Dickey decided to design a wedding facility. The impetus for the project was as follows: Austin himself was to be married the summer after his graduation from architecture school and he had been looking for a non-church-based location for the wedding. Austin drove all over looking for a site. He wanted it to be by the river because, for Austin, water represented "the essence of timelessness." For him, this resonated well with the meanings associated with marriage. One day he happened upon an old concrete railroad abutment jutting 40 feet into the air; the tracks themselves had been removed. Austin sensed that this was the right site. The abutment could act as a base for the wedding facility, providing a panoramic view of the valley immediately to the west of the city.

Austin "sketched for a month" before he drew the image shown in Figure 5.1. "Once I sketched that, I had a little light bulb go on," recalled Dickey several weeks after he had graduated (one week, by the way, before his wedding). When asked why this sketch was significant, he said he had seen a project by Zaha Hadid (a garden pavilion in Weil am Rhein, Germany—see Fig. 5.2A) in a magazine and was inspired by her use of plastic concrete forms.[1] Also, an instructor had suggested that a swale on the site be used as the basis for a promenade connecting the parking area to the wedding hall (see Figure 5.2B). These factors motivated a design process that culminated in what is shown in Figures 5.3 and 5.4.

During our postgraduation interview with him, without being asked, Dickey had this to say about the relationship between design and research: "I never thought of design as research. Design is 'off the page' from facts, and research is a fact-based activity. Design is 'subjective research,' in the sense that I must preface my opinion

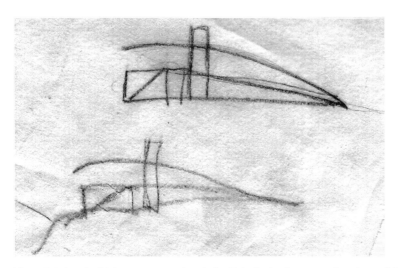

Figure 5.1 Austin Dickey concept sketch for B.Arch thesis: a nonchurch wedding facility. "Once I sketched *that*, I had a little light bulb go on." Courtesy of Austin Dickey.

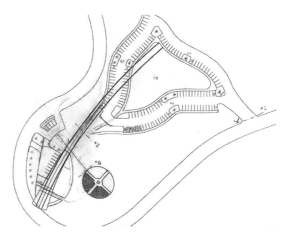

Figure 5.2A This is an image from the article Dickey saw in an issue of *Architecture*. The image is of Zaha Hadid's garden pavilion in Wein am Rhein, Germany. Courtesy of Helene Binet.

Figure 5.2B Dickey sketch plan two weeks after the "light bulb" section. This one shows the linear form of the promenade idea inspired by the swale. Courtesy of Austin Dickey.

Figure 5.3   Dickey's final presentation drawing. Courtesy of Austin Dickey.

of a design by saying, '*I* think this is what should be done, or '*I* think this is what looks good.' "

In this chapter, we examine the relationship between design and research. By design we mean the generative production of figural schemas that lead to built forms. That is, by design we mean what architects do every day: conceiving of built forms by responding to clients, programs, budgets, and other "real-world" factors. These are intermingled with the designers' conceptions and visions, and ultimately translated into graphic representations that increase in detail until they become the guiding images used to construct the actual project.

The connection between design thus defined and research is fraught with difficulties. Dickey's distinction between research as "a fact-based activity" and design as a series of subjective commitments illustrates a philosophical principle that we aim to summarize shortly to make positions like Austin's clearer. Dickey's view seems to be a common one. In the minds of many designers and architects, there seems to be an inherent divide between design and research.[2]

Figure 5.4   Dickey's final presentation section of the wedding facility. Courtesy of Austin Dickey.

It is our position that design, *as such*, is not research, *as such*. But we would add two quick caveats to this view. First, research can aid the design process in many ways. Second, the two domains are equal in intellectual significance. It is our hope that this chapter will serve to refute any position holding, pejoratively, that what designers do is "not research."

5.2   DIFFICULTIES IN RELATING DESIGN TO RESEARCH

The factors that contributed to Dickey's decision to design a wedding facility, as well as the influences upon him during the design process, are clearly contingent realities lacking *necessity* (see the treatment of this word in Chapter 11). These factors include personal history (he was getting married), what he saw in books and magazines (he happened upon a project by Hadid), what instructors told him ("this swale can be interpreted as a promenade"), and numerous sketches until the "light bulb." Someone else in his position would easily have done other things, influenced by other chance factors, to design something totally different. Dickey's experience looks like a very typical design process (see Box. 5.1).

BOX 5.1

Ronchamp Chapel and the Crab Shell

The roof of Le Corbusier's Notre Dame du Haut, according to the architect himself, was inspired by a crab shell he had "picked up in 1946 on Long Island, near New York."* The crab shell was lying next to his drawing board when the initial "birth sketches" for the project were evolving. As we can see from this example, it is very difficult to isolate a theory of design that can explain how chance occurrences can result in architectural designs.

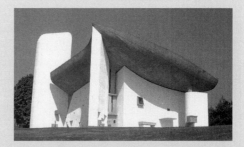

Figure 5.5 Notre Dame du Haut. Years before this project, Le Corbusier spotted a crab shell on a beach, and hung on to it. Later, when he was working on the design of the roof, the crab shell happened to be lying next to his drawing. Photograph from authors' collections.

*Le Corbusier, *Texts and Sketches for Ronchamp*. First published by Jean Petit, 1965. Association oeuvre de N.D. du Haut, Ronchamp. No pagination. This quote is on p. 20 if pagination starts at first page.

But some have posited necessary connections in the design process; theories have been framed about such connections, and research has been conducted to test those theories. For instance, A. Newell and Herbert Simon have posited that design activity can be likened to the workings of an information processor: Input goes into the human mind, and design is the processing of many discrete decisions that produces a figural outcome.[3] Omer Akin has conducted research seeking to demonstrate this kind of theory; for example, in one study, he sought to develop rule-based protocols that chart every decision an architect made during the design of a carriage house.[4] The implication is that, once the rules are known, computers can be programmed to reproduce such processes. The work of Margaret Boden also has this possibility in view.[5] The human images in Figure 5.6 are drawn by a computer named Acrobat-AARON, which is programmed in a rule-based fashion that allows it to generate human forms in an unlimited variety of poses.[6]

These efforts notwithstanding, there is much in the literature refuting the idea that generative design processes can be *completely* explained by means of rule-based protocols. Bill Hillier, et. al., simply states: "A *complete* account of the designer's operations during design would still not tell us where the solution came from."[7] Alan Chimacoff argues that design involves figural as well as systemic considerations. While a system may be programmable and predictable, the capacity for figural generation is not. Chimacoff is "skeptical" of theories holding that the design process *as a whole* can be empirically defined; he therefore opts for the inclusion of "inspiration, so to speak" in explications of how figural designs emerge.[8]

Figure 5.6 A "painting" by a computer program. This image is generated by the computer program that Boden writes about; it is a more recent example of what the program is able to do in the way of creative designs. Courtesy of Harold Cohen, University of California San Diego.

In this section, we consider three aspects of the difficult connection between the generative design process and research. We first offer a philosophical explanation for why the domains of design and research do not have to be considered coterminous. We then distinguish between the notion of design *as* research and that of research *about* the design process. Finally, we suggest ways the gap between design activity and research activity can be bridged.

5.2.1 Generative versus Analytical: A Philosophical Distinction

It is our view that the generative design process is indeed a "subjective" process—in the sense that it cannot be fully captured by rule-based propositions. As such, the process of designing is different from the process of researching, which we hold to be rooted in rule-based (or, to use Dickey's term, "fact-based") frameworks. We propose the following philosophical explanation of this position.

The dominance of scientific method in the West has placed a premium on propositional understanding and has historically tended to devalue subjective experience. In the early eighteenth century, for instance, subjective feelings such as judgments of beauty were held to be "obscure or confused representations" while the faculty of understanding (that is, the mental power that frames specific propositions) was considered capable of "distinct" knowledge.[9] One can see the effects of this attitude in theories related to the art of that day. Edmund Burke, for instance, held that beauty can be broken down into a list of empirical attributes. His list included curves, smooth things, small shapes, and so on; hence, little birds and "fine women" qualified as beautiful.[10] The problem with theories such as this one (aside from any distaste for them) is simply that one person can consider an object or form beautiful while another person does not.

By the end of the eighteenth century, a shift in ideas took place. Simply put, our experience of beauty was no longer attributed to empirical attributes of physical forms. What emerged was much more of an emphasis upon each person's subjective experience as determinative of how that person will hold something to be beautiful—and, ultimately, of what kind of art production (read: design) that person can produce. The "critical philosophy" of Kant, emerging in the late eighteenth century, played a pivotal role in this shift in thinking.[11] For instance, in his *Critique of Judgment*, Kant held that our enjoyment of art is inherently "indeterminate," that is, not definable in propositional terms. According to Kant, the faculties of reason are aligned in fundamentally different relationships when engaged with aesthetic judgments than when engaged with determinate (sometimes called "scientific") ones.[12] And yet art enjoyment and, as we shall see, art production, is a *reasonable* reality without having to be affirmed as such by determinate (scientific) judgments. In other words, with Kant, aesthetic experiences are part of the domain of reason—even though they cannot be fully captured by formulas, words, or other determinate modes of communication.

Now, within his system, Kant proposes that art productions (which include figural schemas) emerge out of the experience of aesthetic pleasure. Kant holds that during aesthetic pleasure, the mental faculties sense a heightened "membership with nature," and this leads to all the mental faculties being engaged "in play." [13] This play produces a "purposive momentum" that in turn generates "aesthetic ideas."[14] It is these aesthetic ideas that strive for expression in empirical forms. This, in short, is how figural schemas emerge to produce what Kant calls "a completeness for which no example can be found in nature."[15] In other words, they are products of art. Kant calls this process a "poetic drive," but Rudolf Makkreel simply puts it this way: "what Kant calls the . . . poetic drive may be applied to the painter, *the architect*, and composer, as well as to the metaphysician."[16] Thus, art and architecture, in the generative sense, emerge out of this process.

The point is this: The entire process of art production (under which figural design production can be subsumed) is indeterminate; that is, it cannot be fully captured by determinate descriptions, *and yet it is within the domain of reason*. For our purposes, Kant's aesthetic theory provides grounds for the idea that generative productions of art and architecture are rooted in different regions of the human faculties of reason. These generative productions do not play "second fiddle" to the analytic processes of the faculty of understanding, which itself is only another manifestation of the workings of reason.

This brief explanation sheds more light on Austin Dickey's account of his design experience. His encounters with the site in nature, his sense of water expressing the essence of timelessness (which is really a determination that involves the moral faculty),[17] the empirical input he received from images, the suggestions from teachers,[17] all contributed to the play of his mental faculties to produce the figural scheme that represented "a light bulb going on." These complex factors all represent the workings of reason, although a reason that is not limited to (and cannot be limited by) pure propositional definitions.

5.2.2 Design as Research versus Research about the Design Process

Research activity tends to be defined by propositional components: strategy, tactic, hypotheses, "the literature," measuring instruments, data, and so forth. As argued above, the generative design process, on the other hand, emerges from other workings within human reason, workings that cannot be fully explained in a propositional way. (Chimacoff's appeal to "inspiration," for instance, finds much support in Kant's formulation of "the supersensible realm." This realm, as something that is beyond the capacity of reason to comprehend, nevertheless underlies "both nature and our ability to think.")[18]

In this light, we can make a distinction between design as research, which we hold to be at best a difficult conceptual union of all the mental faculties, and research *about* the design process. The former seeks to subsume a reality that is inherently nonpropositional (generative design as a mode of art production) under the domain of a propositional activity (analytical research), which raises logical difficulties. The latter seeks, by well-defined propositional frameworks, to understand more deeply the processes involved in the nonpropositional process of design. There is no logical problem with this notion.

Consider two examples for comparison. In the May 1979 edition of the *Journal of Architectural Education*, Chris Arnold makes the claim that a 1927 Aalto sketch of the reading room at the Viipuri Library is "a beautiful example of a designer's research" (Figure 5.7).[19] This is a difficult claim. At minimum, it raises the question of

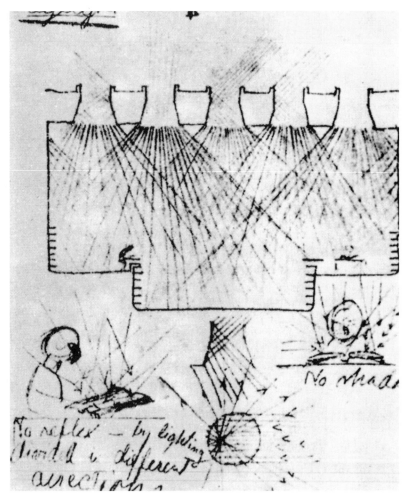

Figure 5.7   Aalto sketch (1927) of the reading room in the Viipuri library. Permission for use granted by the Alvar Aalto Saatio Stiftelsen Foundation.

when a sketch is "research" and when a sketch is, well, just a sketch. Now, there is no doubt that sketching may constitute a tactic in a larger research strategy. For instance, as we note elsewhere in this book, Clare Cooper Marcus's tactic of having her informants sketch their feelings about their homes yielded valuable data for interpretation.[20] But this kind of sketching is different from the generative process of design. The Aalto sketch is a small part of a much larger and (as we saw in Dickey's case) much more complex mix of contingent factors that go into the generation of a design. Is this overall process a process of inquiry? No doubt it is, and at least some architects have recognized that "inquiry" is a much more comfortable word than "research" to describe what they do.[21]

On the other hand, Peter Rowe's study of three design projects, already cited in Chapter 4, is an example of research *about* the design process (see Figure 4.3). Through a variety of tactics (ethnographic involvement, interviews, formal analyses of the drawings, etc.), Rowe documents the way designs emerge. He still cannot get inside the "black box" of the design process itself to witness design ideas emerging; but based upon his research Rowe is able to clarify and explain certain sources (for instance, the use of archetypal forms) that seem to stimulate design ideas.[22] Rowe's study is research *about* the design process.

It is our position that research *about* the design process can help inform the design process itself; this is one argument for reading this book. But research *about* the design process is different from holding that design itself is research. Again, we see the two as equally worthwhile but different functions.

5.2.3 Design Activity versus Academic Credentials

This chapter is not the place for a prolonged consideration of the *political* implications of the distinction between design activity and research activity. But to pass it by without mention at this juncture would be remiss. We are of course referring to the tendency in academic venues to consider research a more legitimate form of scholarly inquiry than design. This is documented by Boyer and Mitgang and is certainly a phenomenon familiar to many architects in the academy.[23] We offer no easy solutions to this problem, except for the following consideration.

Efforts should be made to encourage the view that design activity and research activity are of equal value. The suggestions Boyer and Mitgang make for increasing the scope of what "scholarly work" can mean for architectural faculty are generally good in this regard. Particularly worthwhile is the recommendation that work across a lifetime, broken down into definable segments, can be used as a means to evaluate "creativity."[24] (However, the terms they use—"scholarship," "creativity," etc.—really stop short of declaring design and research of equal worth; the additional words, which in themselves evidence an awareness of the *non*similarity between generative design and analytical research, in fact cloud the issue.)

Howard Gardner, while he does not call what creative individuals do *research*, does propose a means for evaluating the robustness of their output. His model is a basis for evaluating the lifetime productions (or portions thereof) that Boyer and Mitgang call for. Gardner makes the distinction between *idiographic* research and *nomothetic* research:

> In idiographic work, the focus falls sharply on the individual case study, with its peculiar emphases and wrinkles. In nomothetic work, the focus falls instead on a search for general laws; such work . . . overlooks individual idiosyncrasies, searching instead for those patterns that appear to apply to all, or to the vast majority of cases.[25]

Gardner uses this distinction as a means to measure the creative individual and his or her work under the general heading of idiographic research. From the biographies of seven creative people, he posits a life history of a composite Exemplary Creator (E.C.). This paradigm includes certain environmental, relational, and developmental traits that he observed in all seven biographies. (See the recommended readings at the end of this chapter for elaboration.) Gardner's paradigm not only can offer a template for understanding a pattern of creative production over a long period of an individual's life, it can also provide some research underpinnings to Boyer and Mitgang's call for an academician's creative work to be evaluated.

5.3   DIFFERENT MODELS FOR "EPISODIC" RESEARCH WITHIN GENERATIVE DESIGN ACTIVITY

Having delineated the difference between generative design and analytical research, we now summarize some different ways for conceptualizing their coexistence. We will examine programming and postoccupancy evaluation, action research and "design-decision" research, design as a learned skill, and collaborative models for design process. None of these represents any kind of master strategy that can subsume "design" under a "research" umbrella that negates the philosophical differences between the two. On the other hand, all of these are gateways for bringing research into the design process. It is our view that they provide opportunities for *episodic* research within the larger domain of generative design. We also suggest that these approaches can be combined in various ways depending upon the design situation.

5.3.1 Design as Analysis and Evaluation

John Chris Jones's term *the black box* takes the position that the design process is shielded from the eye of research. One way to reduce the mystery of the black box is to know as much as we can going into the project, and then evaluate the outcomes of the project after completion so that we can be more informed about the next design effort. This is what is meant by programming, in the best sense of the word. Much more than leafing through magazines, studying existing types, or working from a client's wish list, programming can be understood as an effort to maximize the amount of information about a project so that the figural concepts generated can optimally respond to those criteria. These can include an almost boundless list of factors, but Gerald Weisman, writing in the 1980s, points out that most of the literature on programming as a research focus has concentrated on "user needs" as well as energy conservation.[26]

The idea of programming as an effort to maximize knowledge about design conditions may be seen in Donna Duerk's *Architectural Programming: Information Management for Design*.[27] It is instructive that she spends some time defining what "the scientific method" can be for architectural programming: "the purpose of the scientific method is to create exact, reproducible results so that we might 'prove' that a report, a theory, or a fact is true or false."[28] Her scientific method breaks down to such components as: ask a relevant question, build a hypothesis, operationalize definitions . . . gather all data, organize and interpret the data. Two of her diagrams are particularly relevant. The first is a series of hierarchical cycles that envision *mission*, *goal*, and *performance requirement* each as an iterative process (Figure 5.8). Within these cycles, the procedures of scientific method give traction to the process of identifying

Figure 5.8 Duerk's cyclical model of inquiry in architectural programming. "How" and "why" questions in each cycle enable the programmer/researcher to clarify the task in a hierarchical fashion, from mission to goal to performance. All of this leads to the (figural) concept. Courtesy of John Wiley & Sons.

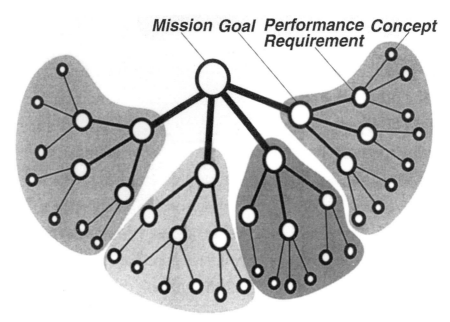

Figure 5.9 The same idea expressed by Duerk in a network-flow format. The relative sizes of the nodes are interesting, implying that if the programming preliminaries (mission, goal, etc.) can be well defined, the concepts will follow as more manageable decisions. Courtesy of John Wiley & Sons.

questions, collecting data, etc. The second diagram (Figure 5.9) illustrates the same relationships, but is instructive because of the relative scales of the nodes. That is to say, by the time the (figural) concept is developed, the nodes representing those realities are smaller, suggesting that the big questions of mission, goal and performance have been propositionally defined.

At the other end of the design process is post-occupancy evaluation, or POE. After-the-fact data collection is another way of reducing the unknowns of the "black box" of the design process, at least for future projects. Craig Zimring and Polly Welch point out that three kinds of clients tend to commission POEs. They are those accustomed to developing a series of buildings, those venturing into an new situation with uncertainty, and organizations characterized by an openness to new information.[29] POEs can lead to a greater understanding of the existing design, with cost-savings ramifications. The authors give the example of a $2.4 million savings to the California Department of Corrections after a POE revealed that equipment rather than walls can be changed to meet occupant needs. Another POE found that columns in a Phase I office building prevented optimal allocation of secretarial work stations, a problem alleviated in the Phase II design stage. POEs can even be coupled with simulation research. The authors cite an example of a major engineering firm that directed the architect to design their new facility with open office planning. The architect persuaded the client to first study this idea in a 30-person mock-up of such a space; the resulting noise levels changed the owner's mind back to enclosed office planning.[30]

Wolfgang Preiser, et al., have written on the methods and procedures of POE studies.[31] They divide POEs into three levels of complexity. An *indicative* POE is one that analyzes as-built drawings, indexing them to such factors as safety and security records. It conducts interviews of building occupants with a view toward understanding the performance of the building. An *investigative* POE goes one step further by comparing an existing situation with comparable facilities, as well as with a summary of what the current literature prescribes. Both lead to more focused recommendations for consideration and change. A *diagnostic* POE involves multimethod tactics (surveys, observations, physical measurements, etc.) all conducted in comparison to other "state of the art" facilities. Readers are referred to the original text for more details on each POE type.

The problem with pre- and post-data collection is obviously that the episodes of research are limited to the introduction and the epilogue. The "middle zone," that is, the design process itself, is left unaddressed. The next model seeks to venture into this middle zone.

5.3.2 Design as Action Research

"Action research" is a term given to studies that examine a concrete situation, particularly the logic of how factors within that situation relate to each other as the process moves toward a specific empirical goal. The emphasis is upon knowledge emerging from localized settings, as opposed to abstract knowledge applicable for many settings. Action research arises out of the social sciences; it has roots in the work of the sociologist Kurt Lewin's notion of *field theory*, which basically holds that theoretical knowledge and practical knowledge must inform each other in a concrete context for the establishment of a true domain (field) of endeavor.[32] The applicability of this notion to the generative design process is quite evident.

Donald Schon's term *reflection-in-action* comes under this heading. The term denotes the *actual* need in the professions to solve problems arising out of practical life-contexts.[33] Schon proposes that design activity is a particular instance of reflection-in-action.[34] Schon looks for patterns within context-specific design venues (e.g., a project in a design office, or the history of interactions between instructor and student in the studio and its effect on the design). The emphasis is upon the specific design venue as a kind of microculture, complete with ways of doing, implicit understandings, technical terms, and so on, that all arise in the midst of creating a design. What results is a product that is the sum of the reflective actions taken in response to the factors unique to the concrete context.

Gerald Susman puts it this way: "I am presented with a problem occurring in an existing concrete setting, rather than a problem raised by theory [which] then leads me . . . to create a setting within which to understand the problem better."[35] In this statement, Susman is basically differentiating between theoretical knowledge that can be tested later by research, and in-context actions that are concretely relevant for that context. In addressing the in-context case, Susman promotes a cyclical process of *diagnosing*, *action planning*, *action taking*, *evaluating*, and *specifying*. His diagram of this cycle is reproduced in Fig. 5.10. Note that this model can easily be overlaid onto each of Duerk's programming cycles as a way of "filling them in" with more content. Certainly, Susman's cycle is descriptive of what designers go through in the design process. In reference again to Dickey's project, the series of sketches in Figure 5.11 illustrate cyclical iterations, each cycle culminating in a drawing. Figure 5.11A shows an

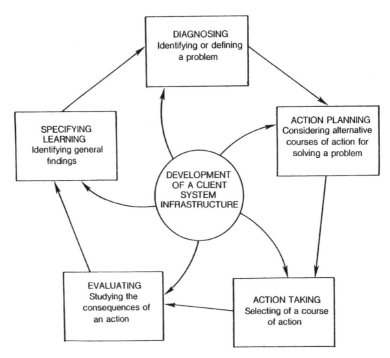

Figure 5.10 Gerald Susman's action-research diagram of the stages of knowledge-finding in a practical concrete context. We suggest this process is very like the process of generating a series of figural schemes, each scheme reflecting renewed attempts at diagnoses, evaluation, decisions to act (draw) in a certain direction, etc. Courtesy, Gerald Susman, Penn State University, and Roger Evered, Naval Postgraduate School.

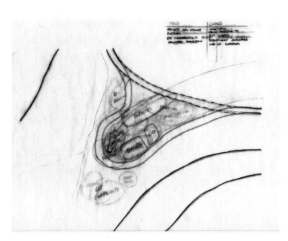
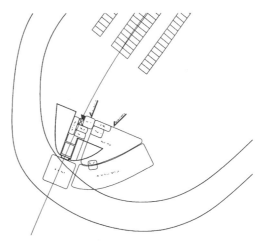
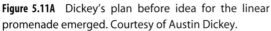

Figure 5.11A Dickey's plan before idea for the linear promenade emerged. Courtesy of Austin Dickey.

Figure 5.11B Dickey's plan during the time when the promenade connection to the parking lot first began to appear. Courtesy of Austin Dickey.

early Dickey plan of the wedding chapel; Figure 5.11B is after the conversation with his instructor, who suggested that the natural swale act as the basis of a promenade. This transformation occurred because *some* process of diagnosing, action planning, action taking, evaluation, and specifying took place in Dickey's mind. Action research can uncover these embedded stages in the iterative design process.

A more focused version of action research is "design-decision research," proposed by Jay Farbstein and Min Kantrowitz.[36] In action research, the researcher can still be outside of the concrete situation as he or she examines the iterative cycles of actions taken. Design-decision research embeds the researcher into the actual process; indeed, the authors underline the point that the "researchers" in their model can themselves be players in the process. In this sense, "researchers" and "designers" are "one community" and not two: facility programmers, architects, market analysts, communications consultants, in short, any player can be a kind of "new practitioner" who not only makes decisions, but also assesses those decisions from the perspective of research.[37] Farbstein and Kantrowitz give the example of a bank that wished to build a wing outfitted appropriately for its "high-value" customers. But in-depth interviews and focus group discussions revealed that the better approach would be to provide spaces for individualized personal contact, thus avoiding alienating other customers while providing the personal attention the management wanted for their elite clients. It is easy to see how these interventions can aid in the overall design process in an episodic fashion. It is also easy to see how, when design incorporates these approaches, research strategies addressed elsewhere in this book (for instance, in Chapter 7 on qualitative research) can be harnessed for design decisions. Farbstein and Kantrowitz themselves list many "phases" of a building's life cycle to which this approach can be applied: "planning, programming, feasibility studies, design, construction, operation, fine tuning, renovation, maintenance, repair and so forth."[38]

5.3.3 *Design as a Learned Skill: The Generator/Conjecture/Analysis Model*

Another way to conceptualize the coexistence of design with research—and one that can potentially include some of the elements of the previous approaches—is to regard design as a learned skill. In other words, rather than speculate in the abstract about the "black box" of design, let us learn how to do it better by practice, by a more explicit awareness of the attributes that characterize design in general, and by reflective assessments of the process. That is to say, let us incorporate in our design process, for instance, elements of action research and design-decision research. This is largely Bryan Lawson's approach in *How Designers Think: The Design Process Demystified*.

Lawson's work promotes a step-by-step construction of a "complete model of design constraints." This model puts in a systemic framework what Lawson means by design as a learned skill. The model has three categories: Generator (which includes factors that motivate design—client, user, legislator, designer), Function (symbolic, formal, practical, radical), and Domain (internal, external).[39] Simply put, a designer learns by developing a reflective awareness of how these design constraints work and interrelate, and by managing that awareness in design decision-making. Lawson's framework is similar to another "complete" model developed by J. Guilford termed the "complete structure of intellect"; this model is cited by both Jon Lang[40] and Gary Moore/Lynne Gay[41] (as well as by Lawson) in their discussions on design creativity. Guilford's three-category model is framed as Operations (evaluation, convergent thinking, divergent thinking, cognition, memory), Products (units, classes, relations, systems, transformations, implications), and Contents (figural, symbolic, semantic, behavioral). These kinds of frameworks constitute hypotheses about what a "complete" network of the factors in design process would contain. They try to combine into one system both empirical factors (e.g., client, legislator, etc.) and rational concepts (e.g., formal, symbolic, etc.). At minimum they serve as heuristic devices that can inform reflective thinking about design action. Beyond this, they are adequate theoretical frameworks from which new research investigations can be conducted.

Lawson cites Jane Darke, who describes the design process as one of "generator—conjecture—analysis."[42] Darke noticed that architects, when given design problems with very complex programmatic and social-cultural considerations, nevertheless tend to start by proposing very simple figural schemas. Over the design process, a schema is analyzed, refined, tested, analyzed again, and so on, until a more responsive schema emerges. Lawson, via Darke, conceives design as the process of integrating a "cluster of requirements" into an integrated solution. One can begin by accruing knowledge about any particular aspect of the design process. Lawson uses the window (our illustrative device as well in Chapter 2) as an illustration:

> The window is another unavoidably multidimensional component. As well as letting in daylight and sunlight the window is also usually required to provide a view while retaining privacy, and to offer natural ventilation. As an interruption in the external wall the window also poses problems of structural stability, heat loss and noise transmission, and is thus arguably one of the most complex of building elements.[43]

Lawson, as we also note in Chapter 2, underlines how one topic (the window) can be approached in multidimensional ways; the designer needs to learn these ways as part of his or her design process. "We are told that this strategy is intended to increase the amount of time spent on analysis and synthesis and reduce the time spent on the synthesis of bad solutions."[44] In this way, the initial general schema is refined toward a final solution reflective of systematic analysis.

Another Lawson approach is to divide "design" into strategic versus tactical considerations.[45] At the strategic level, Lawson holds that designers commonly rely not so much on precise theories as they do "on experience and rules-of-thumb." These come from normative, typological, symbolic, or simply observational sources. At this point, the design activity seems to correspond to Darke's initial schema. Lawson then addresses the next level, which he calls "design tactics and traps." Here he is quite specific about pitfalls that designers can fall into. For instance, there is the category trap: overlaying solutions that worked elsewhere on a new problem. And there is the puzzle trap, in which it is assumed that good design emerges when a graphic *pattern* that meets all of the listed criteria can be determined. There is the number trap, in which code regulations are blindly followed without thought to the effect on usable space. And there are the icon and image traps, the tendency of trained designers to be influenced by established typologies that may have little to do with the actual needs of the client. This consideration of strategy and tactics buttresses Lawson's overall claim that design is a process that can be learned—even though having that learning does not always guarantee good design.

5.3.4 *Design in Collaboration*

The preceding three models for the coexistence of design with research all implicitly emphasize the single designer. Much has been written recently on an alternative to this paradigm, namely, collaborative design. Architecture often emerges as a result of team effort, as opposed to the efforts of a single "star" architect. In today's post-industrial economy, in which projects are increasingly large and complex, the design process often calls for expertise in a wide variety of disciplines. How does this work? And in what ways? A consensus on this topic has yet to emerge. Here we summarize some investigations and position papers on the theme.

Darlene Septelka's study of an interdisciplinary design charrette at Washington State University (Box 5.2) brings up issues of the role of the architect in the larger context of the design process. Linda Groat has pointed out that the traditional images of the architect are those of the architect-as-technician and the architect-as-artist.

BOX 5.2

An Interdisciplinary Design Charrette

In a recent paper on an annual charrette in interdisciplinary design held at the Interdisciplinary Design Institute at Washington State University, Darlene Septelka found that students representing different design disciplines all recognized collaboration as an essential part of their professional education.* (The charrette is a three-day design exercise involving student teams, each comprised of a student architect, a student interior designer, a student landscape architect and a student in construction management.) Septelka also found that team members unreflectively tended to look to the architectural student as the "lead"; interior designers, landscape architects and construction managers tended not to act until the architect had designed something. Although 79% of all student respondents in a post-charrette survey felt the exercise was a positive experience, it is noteworthy that the architectural students expressed more frustration with the charrette, while comments from the interior designers and the construction management students were more favorable after the process than before. Also interesting in Septelka's study is the fact that

Figure 5.12 Interdisciplinary Design Charrette team at Washington State University. Photograph from authors' collections.

students overall reported an increase in trust and respect for team members while at the same time experiencing a decrease in regard for communication, collaboration, and teamwork. This could only mean that venues for cultivating collaboration other than in a frenetic three-day charrette should be identified and explored.

*Darlene Septelka, "The Charrette Process as a Model for Teaching Multidiscipline Collaboration," in *Proceedings of CIB W89: International Conference on Building Education and Research,* Georgia Institute of Technology College of Architecture and Clemson University, Atlanta, May 2000.

Both of these models not only set the architect apart from others (hence perhaps encouraging the "star" mentality), they also bring about disjunctures between what architects design and what everyday clients may want. Groat's alternative proposal is that of the architect-as-cultivator. Cultivator of what? Says Groat:

> Once we . . . foster environmental values that focus on the common good and reinforce the connectedness of people within an organization, a community, or society as a whole, we are then confronting the essence of cultural life. It is [at this point] that the model of the "designer-as-cultivator" comes into its own."[46]

Groat means to shift away from the model of the architect as sole technician or sole artist toward one that is sensitive to a larger communal mission of well-being. She structures her argument by borrowing seven ascending categories from Richard Barrett's book on organization theory *Liberating the Corporate Soul: Building a Visionary Organization.*[47] Barrett suggests that, in good organizations, individuals are encouraged to rise above self-interest to take on communal and ultimately global interests of well-being. Groat adapts this model for her new paradigm of the architect-as-cultivator (Figure 5.13). In short, the architect-as-cultivator encourages three things. He or she emphasizes process, by which Groat means the architect's spirit is collaborative and participatory. Second, the architect-as-cultivator encourages interdisciplinary design, where different disciplines contribute in concert to a solution; community is inherent in this process. Third, borrowing from the title of Barrett's book, Groat's architect-as-cultivator has "a sensitivity for the cultural as the soul of design." By this is meant a vision for the mission of the common good, with the architect motivating

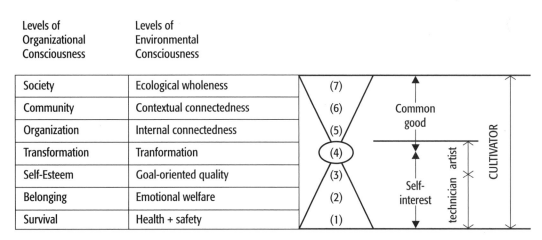

Figure 5.13 Groat's adaptation of Barrett's ascending levels of "consciousness" (from self-interest to global concern) for the architect-as-cultivator's design agenda. Use of original Barrett diagram courtesy of John Wiley & Sons.

his or her team to recognize that a successful environment "can only be realized by fully engaging the social and cultural milieu in which it is embedded."

5.3.5 Summary of the Episodic Ways of Relating Research to Design

Again, it is our view that none of the considerations we have summarized in the preceding subsections represent an overall strategy by which "design" can be subsumed under the umbrella of "research." Earlier in this chapter we outlined our view that these two domains are by nature rooted in different regions of human reason, and complicatedly so. Generative figural production is a different mode of inquiry from analytical research. The preceding considerations address ways that these two domains can coexist.

The reader is encouraged to look for connections between these different models. For instance, it is striking how Duerk's cyclical model for programming can be readily informed by Susman's diagram of action research. Farbstein and Kantrowitz's idea of the "new practitioner" who brings a research orientation to the design process may have similarities to the architect-as-cultivator Groat proposes. Certainly their observation that the current state of design practice has "muddied" (in the sense of blurred) so many roles so that "design is in the swamp" can be seen as an opportunity for Groat's architect-as-cultivator to emerge. Finally, Lawson's prescriptions for conjecture/analysis, and the itemized suggestions he makes for analytical inquiry and the avoidance of "traps," can be used as a framework for collaborative design processes as well.

5.4   SEVEN EXAMPLES

We conclude this chapter with a review of ways in which different kinds of research strategy, as addressed in Part II of this book, can be used to inform the design process.

5.4.1 Design and History Research

The strategy of history research is one of narrating an account of a past event or situation; it depends upon gathering as much empirical and deductive facts as can be identified. These are used as fixed points around which to weave, or "emplot," the narrative. Chapter 6 addresses emplotment, along with other forms of historical narrative, in detail. This kind of research is greatly beneficial to work in historic restoration. One firm with this specialty is John Milner Architects of Chadds Ford, Pennsylvania. For more than 30 years, Milner's firm has brought a variety of eighteenth-, nineteenth-, and early-twentieth-century structures back to life using meticulous research to determine their original appearance and the impact of alterations and additions over time. Milner employs architects, historians, archeologists, paint

Figure 5.14 The Muhlenberg House (originally built circa 1755), restored by John Milner Architects, Inc. The restoration was sponsored by the Historical Society of Trappe (Montgomery County, Pennsylvania) to commemorate the life of Henry Melchior Muhlenberg, patriarch of the Lutheran Church in America. It is open by appointment as a museum, and is the focal point of a cultural and leadership development center. Photograph by Don Pearse; courtesy of John Milner Architects, Inc.

color specialists and architectural conservators to document the physical evolution of buildings, and to plan and execute their restoration.

5.4.2 Design and Qualitative Research

In Chapter 7, we emphasize the *bricolage* aspect of qualitative research. This strategy seeks to piece together an in-depth account of a social context by means of a variety of tactics.

Charles Moore provides a fascinating account of qualitative research used in his St. Matthew's Church project in a suburb of Los Angeles; this is recounted in Andy Pressman's *The Fountainache: The Politics of Architect-Client Relations*.[48] The original church was destroyed by fire, and Moore's firm was hired by the parish with the requirement that any design proposal must be approved by two-thirds of the

Figure 5.15   The pergola at St. Matthew's Church, Los Angeles. Designed by Charles Moore. Photograph from authors' collections.

congregation—one that sometimes had trouble agreeing "what day it was." Moore's solution was to allow the design to emerge by collaborating with the congregation in four "open design charrettes" over a period of four months. During this participatory process, many different tactics were used to arrive at a design consensus. These included "awareness walks" of the site, where the congregation jotted down feelings and observations, then used found objects (Fruit Loops, cellophane, scissors, paper, even parsley) and made various configurations. In the second charrette, Moore's team showed slides of other church buildings; even though a dark wood building was a pre-charrette favorite, images of a white church by Aalto received many positive votes. During the third charrette, the congregation was given building shapes to work with to express their wishes. The team then took all of this input and developed some drawings and a model, all of which they left with the people for a month. In the end, 87% of the congregation approved the design.

Moore's approach reflects many of the characteristics of qualitative research, such as having no preset theory going into a research venue, and "living" with the people a design is meant for to develop "thick" accounts of how they perceive things. Said Moore, "Being a part of making that church was an opportunity to work toward an architecture filled with the energies not only of architects but of inhabitants as well, and helping people to find something to which they can belong."[49]

5.4.3 Design and Experimental Research

Examples of the laboratory testing of materials and construction assemblies abound. These affect the writing of codes and regulations for the construction industry, which in turn affect the design of built forms. Much of this research is experimental. In *Specifications for Commercial Interiors*, S. C. Reznikoff describes the testing that a variety of interior finish materials must undergo before they appear on the market. For instance, in the Steiner Tunnel Test and the Radiant Panel Test, Reznikoff summarizes experimental procedures whereby the flammability of carpet samples can be tested under laboratory conditions. The data from these experiments in turn become formalized into ASTM (American Society for the Testing of Materials) and NFPA (National Fire Protection Association) requirements, or regulations of agencies like them.[50]

Also, the construction industry is constantly inventing new materials that redefine how built forms can exist in the natural environment. One recent innovation is the material known as synthetic stucco (Dryvit® is the company name), a lightweight cementitious material that looks like conventional stucco when installed, but resists cracking and does not require painting. It can even be made to look like masonry without any of the need for the structural strength that masonry requires (Figure 5.16).

Figure 5.16   Arch made of cementitious material; the material can be made to look like masonry units while avoiding the weight considerations as well as the more costly construction process. Courtesy of Dryvit Systems, Inc.

5.4.4 Design and Correlational Research

We refer once again to Oscar Newman's study of high-rise versus low-rise public housing in New York City as an exemplary study of the relationship between building form and crime rate.[51] This research has been addressed in several places in this book (see 4.4.3, and Figure 8.11). The only note we wish to add here is about its effect upon subsequent design. Newman's findings enabled him to claim that "the new physical form of the urban environment is possibly the most cogent ally the criminal has in his victimization of society," and that, further, "crime . . . could be prevented architecturally."[52] In 1995, Henry Cisneros, then secretary of housing and urban development, issued a document that echoed Newman's position. Cisneros stated, "Today, the pendulum seems to be swinging back to an increasing recognition that . . . physical design does have a role to play in crime reduction."[53] Readers may refer to Chapters 4 and 8 for a more detailed account of Newman's work.

5.4.5 Design and Simulation Research

Simulation research, which we address in Chapter 10, can have a significant impact on design policy. One example is Rohinton Emmanuel's computer simulation studies of urban heat islands.[54] Emmanuel's work evaluates rule-of-thumb design criteria for housing in hot and humid urban areas, specifically in Colomba, Sri Lanka. Emmanuel's argument is that population increases in Colomba have led to increases in the heat emitted by built forms, producing the phenomenon known as an urban heat island (UHI). The result is that some "best case" design assumptions about how to mitigate heat in residential structures may not really be effective given the higher heating loads. Via computer simulation, Emmanuel found, for example, that assumptions about the double-glazing of windows proved insignificant for cooling load. On the other hand, lighter walls and better roof insulation decreased the cooling load significantly. Emmanuel concludes: "In the face of rapid urbanization and growing urban prosperity, mandating light exterior colors for urban buildings appears a prudent design requirement. . . . Such action could spare the nation from having to build up expensive thermal power generating capacity."[55]

5.4.6 Design and Logical Argumentation

As we will discuss in Chapter 11, logical argumentation is embedded in all modes of systematic inquiry; the logical construction is what makes an inquiry systematic in the first place. More specifically, we examine in Chapter 11 different ways that logical argumentation can be harnessed for architectural research, ranging from systematic theory-making to more episodic justifications for design action. One example of systematic theory, as well as many actual designs predicated upon that theory, can be found in the writings and work of Robert Venturi. In Chapter 11, we call his *Complexity and Contradiction in Architecture* a cultural/discursive type of systematic theory.

Figure 5.17 Guild House, an early postmodernist work by Venturi Scott Brown and Associates, Philadelphia. Photograph courtesy of Jeffrey Fama.

It will no doubt survive as an enduring statement of the postmodernist aesthetic of the late twentieth century. That it appeared early in this period renders its influence upon subsequent design analogous to the influence of Alberti's *Ten Books*, which emerged early in the Renaissance. Venturi's by now well-known categories (ambiguity, both-and, double-function, etc.) became guidelines for much of the design generated in postmodernist architecture.

5.4.7 Case Study and Multimethod Approaches to Research

Designers often use mixed-method research approaches without explicitly calling these approaches "mixed-method," or considering what they are doing "research." One example is the work of Dr. Liu Jiaping, professor of architecture at the Xi'an University of Architecture and Technology in Xi'an, China. Since 1996, Dr. Liu and his graduate students at the Green Architecture Research Center have been involved in designing sustainable cave dwellings in the village of Zao Yuan, in north-central China. The cave dwelling is a vernacular housing tradition that dates back to the Qin Dynasty (220 B.C.). Today, millions of rural Chinese still live in cave dwellings scat-

Figure 5.18   New "cave dwelling" units designed by the Center for Green Architecture at the Xi'an University of Architecture and Technology in Xi'an, China. The design team used ethnographic, survey, participant design, and experimental tactics to arrive at this design. Photograph from authors' collection.

tered over six provinces. The older dwellings, being simply tunnels dug into the sides of hillsides, tend to be damp, have no ventilation, and have very primitive sanitation systems. Dr. Liu's goal is to design and build new cave dwelling units that are sustainable while being sensitive to the cultural tradition of this Chinese building type. (The inhabitants of Zao Yuan, for instance, are very selective about the new designs that are proposed; they rejected one design because its greenhouse front did not look like a traditional cave with the arched front, emblematic of their culture.) To date, some 85 new units designed by the Green Architecture team have been constructed.

To collect their data, Dr. Liu and his students use a multimethod research approach that includes, at the tactical level, ethnographic, survey, participant design, and experimental methods. For instance, during the design phase, Dr. Liu and his team live right in the cave dwellings of Zao Yuan village for periods of more than a week at a time; they make note of their everyday experiences and gather to discuss their impressions. They conduct surveys; in one survey of 40 families, they found that over 70% of the townspeople were bothered by the humidity and dust inside the dwellings, but were quite content with the diffuse daylight that the arched opening allowed into the interior. During participant design exercises, the townspeople have the right to alter design proposals, and even reject them, as in the case of the greenhouse front. Finally, the experimental tactics used by the team involve the predesign collection of a wide range of environmental data ranging from indoor/outdoor air temperature to noise level, humidity, and natural light levels in the interior. The team then projects what these measures would be for the new units, using mathematical models.

5.5   CONCLUSION

We return to Austin Dickey's design thesis. How can the contents of this chapter inform what he did, and projects like his? We note that certain things Austin did could have been further clarified by more explicit tactics. For instance, Donna Duerk's text on programming is very helpful in this regard. For example, Austin's magazine survey can be categorized as a periodical search.[56] Duerk also recommends "casual observation"; in Austin's case, he could have gone to a wedding or two and made notes on the event, noting how the physical environment affected the behavior of the people.[57] Duerk also provides a useful menu of inquiry tactics involving different participants. In "group processes," participants are asked to share their design ideas for the project, and in "role playing," participants step "into the shoes of another person for long enough to discover the sets of concerns, issues, constraints . . . that are operating in the lives of other people."[58] All of this could have been done in Austin's case with outside individuals who have an interest in weddings or wedding chapels (such as friends who are getting married, or the owner of the local wedding facility).

BOX 5.3

Creativity and Research

When thinking about "design creativity," particularly in the context of its compatibility with research, something like Frank Gehry's Experience Music Museum in Seattle may come to mind. The originality of this building might lead some to assume that it was the result of pure fancy, or something on that order. And indeed it would be very difficult to frame a rule-based procedure to explain how one decision led to the next to yield this kind of highly expressive form. On the other hand, much research went into this project. The technical competence required to convey the concepts involved advanced computer graphics. The ability to construct these forms required sophisticated equipment and procedures, not to mentioned advanced knowledge of materials and project management. At the qualitative end of the spectrum, what cultural factors and forces in the social world would motivate this kind of form—and its reputation as an exemplar of the architectural design of its day? Refer to Figure 3.4 and the accompanying description of Ellen Berkeley's survey showing people's preference for Boston City Hall. Certainly research of a similar kind can be conducted for projects such as this one.

Figure 5.19A, 5.19B   Gehry's Experience Music Museum in Seattle. Courtesy of Zhenyu Wang.

If the Dickey wedding facility project were an actual commission in an architectural office, the real-project context could provide more opportunities for episodic research. Actual users, clients, neighbors, and other interested persons related to the project could be included in activities fitting Farbstein and Kantrowitz's "design-decision" research model. Furthermore, the project constitutes a concrete case to which Groat's vision of the architect-as-cultivator can be applied to derive a framework for action. That framework might look something like what Moore's team did in the St. Matthew project; certainly their approach offers helpful information on cultivating collaboration in the design process.

Architects armed with an awareness of how episodic research can inform their design processes will no doubt agree with Lawson's view that design can be learned. As such, we can learn to do it better over time.

5.6   RECOMMENDED READINGS

John Chris Jones's *Design Methods*, 2nd edition (New York: Van Nostrand Reinhold, 1992) and Bryan Lawson's *How Designers Think: The Design Process Demystified* (Oxford, UK: Butterworth Architecture, 1988) are two books that address the design process in systematic ways. As such, they provide much material for further investigation into the interface between design and research. Jones's work discusses the "black box" approach to understanding design alluded to in this chapter. (In Jones's book, the "black box" is opposed to what is called the "glass box," which is the view that the design process can be described by rule-based propositions.) Lawson's work addresses in detail the thesis that design is a learned activity.

Donald Schon's *The Reflective Practitioner* (New York: Basic Books, 1983) is useful in general in that it addresses decision-making in the concrete situation, rather than developing a theory that remains abstract. In specific, large portions of this work are devoted explicitly to the process of architectural design, particularly the culture of the design studio. Closely related to Schon's work is the article we cited by Gerald Susman, "Action Research" in the book *Beyond Method: Strategies for Social Research*, ed. Careth Morgan (Newbury Park, Calif.: Sage Publications, 1983).

Margaret Boden's *Dimensions of Creativity* (Cambridge, Mass.: MIT Press, 1994) surveys the theme of creativity from a wide range of perspectives. We highlighted Howard Gardner's chapter from this book; his study of the life patterns of seven creative individuals is highly revealing and, as we suggested, casts light on the question of how to evaluate creative output. For example, all of the creative individuals were fostered in encouraging (although not doting) settings, they alternately drew strength from and kept a distance from their colleagues, and they had distinct "breakthrough" periods in life. Gardner also found recurring cognitive and psychological traits. For instance, each creative individual had intellectual strength in apparently disparate fields of knowledge (e.g., in Einstein, mathematical ability with an advanced "spatial intelligence"). They also tended to be marginal relative to social groups—and enjoyed being that way ("indeed, when acceptance appears at hand [there is a tendency] to raise the ante so that one's marginal status is again firmly established").

The May 1979 edition of *Journal of Architectural Education* is a very informative edition in its entirety. The articles offer a range of perspectives (from architects to educators) on the relationship between research and design. Although several decades old, this edition is not exactly "historical" reading. It has a very contemporary sound in that the wide variety of opinions expressed on this subject are readily recognizable as still in circulation today. In one sense it underscores the difficulty (perhaps the impossibility) of ever arriving upon a single conceptual perspective that bridges "design" and "research." In our view, this edition of *JAE* is a "classic."

NOTES

1. Joseph Giovanni, "Terrain Vague: Zaha Hadid Transforms Landscape into Architecture in Shaping a Garden Pavilion in Weil am Rhein, Germany," *Architecture* (July 1999): 70–77.

2. This divide can be seen in a survey of various architectural educators and practitioners featured in the May 1979 issue of the *Journal of Architectural Education*. This entire issue is dedicated to the question of research in architecture.

3. A. Newell and Simon Herbert, *Human Problem Solving* (Englewood Cliffs, N.J.: Prentice-Hall, Inc., 1972).

4. Omer Akin, *Psychology of Architectural Design* (London: Pion Limited, 1986), 28–53.

5. Margaret Boden, *The Creative Mind: Myths & Mechanisms* (New York: Basic Books, 1990), 1–14, 118.

6. Ibid., 134–150.

7. Bill Hillier, John Musgrove, and Pat O'Sullivan, *Developments in Design Methodology*, ed. Nigel Cross (New York: John Wiley, 1984), 253.

8. Alan Chimacoff, "Figure, System and Memory: The Process of Design" in *Representation and Architecture*, eds. Omer Akin and Eleanor Wienel (Silver Spring, Md.: Information Dynamics, 1982), 139–146.

9. Salim Kemal, "Kant and his Predecessors," in *Kant's Aesthetic Theory* (London: Macmillan, 1992), 14–22.

10. Edmund Burke, "Recapitulation of Beauty," in *A Philosophical Inquiry into the Origin of Our Ideas of the Sublime and the Beautiful* (Notre Dame, Ind.: University of Notre Dame Press, [1757] 1968), 114–115.

11. Although not well represented in the architectural literature, Kant's thought has been very influential in Western thinking in general. In other words, we do not "resort" to Kant as a convenient philosophical means to defend our position. Kant's thought has influenced many lines of inquiry since its emergence in the late eighteenth century; it is unfortunate that the architectural literature, to date, has not made use of his work to any large extent. His system has been the gateway to elevating all kinds of topics of inquiry that, previous to Kant, would either not

have been proposed or would have been set aside as "mere sensed experience." For instance, it is through the headwaters of Kant's system that we get such areas of discourse as structuralism (Levi-Strauss, Piaget, etc.) and Hegel's ideas of communal consciousness. Ernst Cassirer's philosophy of symbolic form, which influenced Susanne Langer's theories of musical form, can be traced back to Kant. Our point is this: Many other realms of inquiry have recognized that their topic may be by definition nonpropositional in the scientific sense, but this has not stopped them from rationally coming to grips with the scope of their domains.

12. Immanuel Kant, *Critique of Judgment*, trans. Warner S. Pluhar (Indianapolis: Hackett Publishing Co., [1790] 1987), Sec. 1, 203.

13. Ibid., Sec. 67, 380 & Sec. 49, 313. For Kant, the mental faculties include the understanding, the imagination, the sensibility, the moral faculty; together, they are called the faculty of reason.

14. Ibid., Sec. 49, 314. An aesthetic idea is a "presentation of the imagination which prompts much thought."

15. Ibid., Sec. 49, 314.

16. Rudolf A Makkreel, *Imagination and Interpretation in Kant* (Chicago: University of Chicago Press, 1990), 119 (italics added).

17. Two instructors Dickey benefited from are Professor Douglas Menzies, who was the instructor of record for the thesis studio (academic year 1999–2000), and Professor Greg Kessler.

18. Kant, *Critique of Judgment*, Sec. 26, 255.

19. Chris Arnold, "The Clerk and the Ignoramus," in *Journal of Architectural Education*, vol. XXXII, no. 4 (May 1979): 2.

20. Clare Cooper Marcus, *House as a Mirror of Self* (Berkeley, Calif.: Conari Press, 1995).

21. "In most cases, we prefer not to use the word research to describe what we do, but rather the term inquiry. We have found that when we use the word research, too much can be expected in terms of the precision of the methodology, and too little in terms of the usefulness of the result." See Herbert McLaughlin, "Note on Research in Practice," *Journal of Architectural Education*, 32, no. 4 (May 1979): 15.

22. This term comes from John Chris Jones, who posits the "black box" and "glass box" models for studying design activity. The "black box" model presumes that we can never see into mind as it generates figural designs. See Chris John Jones, *Design Methods*, 2nd edition (New York: Van Nostrand Reinhold, 1992) 46–51.

23. Ernest L. Boyer and Lee D. Mitgang, *Building Community: A New Picture for Architecture Education and Practice.* (Princeton, N.J.: The Carnegie Foundation for the Advancement of Teaching, 1996), 53–57.

24. Ibid., 60.

25. Howard Gardner, "The Creators' Patterns," in *Dimensions of Creativity*, ed. Margaret Boden (Cambridge, Mass.: MIT Press, 1994), 143–158.

26. Gerald Weisman, "Environmental Programming and Action Research," *Environment and Behavior* 15, no. 3 (May, 1983): 383.

27. Donna P. Duerk, *Architectural Programming: Information Management for Design* (New York: John Wiley, 1993).

28. Ibid., 80.

29. Craig Zimring and Polly Welch, "POE: Building 20-20 Hindsight," *Progressive Architecture* (1988): 60.

30. Ibid., 55–56.

31. W. F. E Preiser and H. Rabinowitz and E. T. White, *Post-Occupancy Evaluation* (New York: Van Nostrand Rheinhold, 1988) 53–65.

32. Kurt Lewin, *Field Theory in Social Science*, ed. Dorwin Cartwright (Chicago: University of Chicago Press, 1976).

33. Donald Schon, *The Reflective Practitioner* (New York: Basic Books, 1983), 30–69.

34. Ibid., 76–104.

35. Gerald Susman, "Action Research," in *Beyond Method: Strategies for Social Research*, ed. Careth Morgan (Newbury Park, Calif.: Sage Publications, 1983), 95.

36. Jay Farbstein and Min Kantrowitz, "Design Research in the Swamp" in *Advances in Environment Behavior and Design*, vol. 3 eds. E. Zube and G. Moore (New York: Plenum Press, 1991), 297–318.

37. Ibid., 306–7.

38. Ibid., 304.

39. Bryan Lawson, *How Designers Think: The Design Process Demystified* (Oxford, UK: Butterworth Architecture, 1988), p. 227.

40. Jon Lang, *Creating Architectural Theory* (New York: Van Nostrand Reinhold, 1987), 60.

41. Gary Moore and Lynne Gay, "Creative Problem Solving in Architecture" (Berkeley, Calif.: AIA Education Research Project and The Graduate Division of the University of California National Science Foundation GE7439, University of California, Berkeley, September, 1967), 16–18.

42. Bryan Lawson, *How Designers Think: The Design Process Demystified* (Oxford, UK: Butterworth Architecture, 1988), 33–36.

43. Ibid., 43.

44. Ibid., 45. Lawson here is referring to John Chris Jones's work *Design Methods*, 2nd edition (New York: Van Nostrand Reinhold, 1992).

45. Ibid., 133–177.

46. L. Groat, "A Conceptual Framework for Understanding the Designer's Role: Technician, Artist, or Cultivator?" in *Design Professionals and the Built Environment: An Introduction*, eds. Paul Knox and Peter Ozlins (New York: John Wiley & Sons, 2000).

47. Richard Barrett, *Liberating the Corporate Soul: Building a Visionary Organization* (Boston: Butterworth-Heinemann, 1998).

48. Andy Pressman, *The Fountainache: The Politics of Architect-Client Relations* (New York: John Wiley, 1995), 59–65.

49. Ibid., 65.

50. S.C. Reznikoff, *Specifications for Commercial Interiors* (New York: Whitney Library of Design) 39–43.

51. Oscar Newman, *Defensible Space: Crime Prevention Through Urban Design* (New York: Collier Books, 1973).

52. Ibid., 2, 11.

53. Henry G. Cisneros, *Defensible Space: Deterring Crime and Building Community* (Washington, D.C.: Department of Housing and Urban Development, 1995), 1.

54. Rohinton Emmanuel, "Urban Heat Island and Cooling Load," in *Architecture, Energy and Environment* (Lund, Sweden: Lund University, 1999), 16-1–16-9.

55. Ibid, 16–8.

56. Donna P. Duerk, *Architectural Programming: Information Management for Design* (New York: John Wiley, 1993), 92–93.

57. Ibid., 94–95.

58. Ibid., 106–114.

Part II

Seven Research Strategies

Chapter 6

Interpretive-Historical Research

6.1 INTRODUCTION

In his study "The Home," Adrian Forty cites a character in an 1888 fictional work entitled *Mark Rutherford's Deliverance*. Here is Mr. Rutherford:

> At the office . . . nobody knows anything about me, whether I was married or single, where I live, or what I thought upon a single subject of any importance. I cut off my office life in this way from my home life so completely that I was two selves, and my true self was not stained by contact with my other self. (At) . . . the moment the clock struck seven . . . my second self died, and . . . my first self suffered nothing by having anything to do with it. . . . I was a citizen walking London streets; I had my opinions . . . I was on equal terms with my friends; I was Ellen's husband; I was, in short, a man."[1]

Forty presents a case that, from 1850 to 1950, the concept of the home underwent tremendous changes. This brought about transformations in how the home as a material object came to be designed. Forty provides four headings, each descriptive of a period within this larger time span. In each, he offers an interpretation of how social-cultural factors brought about material expressions of "home." The first heading (and the only one we will mention here due to space limitations) is "A Place for Anything but Work." Forty recalls how the Industrial Revolution drew many people from the countryside to the city to work in factories. This had the impact of separating home from workplace as two distinct concepts in the communal mind for the first time. The craftsman who worked at home now became a laborer in the factory, where his freedom was curtailed and he was "subordinated . . . to the rules and directions of the managers." This, in addition to the oppressive conditions at many of the workplaces, underlined the sense of separation between workplace and home. As a result, the home began to take on connotations of retreat, of haven, of an idealized realm in which the worker is anything but a worker. Figure 6.1 is an image from Forty's study, showing a London home interior in 1893. It shows how the home had become "a palace of illusions, which encouraged total dissociation from the world immediately outside."[2]

In this chapter and the next, we deal with what can be generally termed *interpretive research*, and this term needs immediate clarification. In a strict sense, all research involves interpretation. However, we define interpretive research specifically as *investigations into social-physical phenomena within complex contexts, with a view toward explaining those phenomena in narrative form and in a holistic fashion*. In this chapter, we aim to address instances in which the phenomenon is a *past* condition, relative to the researcher. Hence the title *interpretive-historical* research. In the next chapter, we address research into complex social-physical phenomena that are *contemporary* relative to the researcher. That chapter (7) is devoted to what we call *qualitative* research, and more will be said about it in that context.

Figure 6.1 London home in 1893 (from Adrian Forty): "a palace of illusions . . ." Permission of Royal Commission to the Historical Monuments of England.

The idea of subsuming "history"—which has its own disciplinary status in the academy, indeed, one of the oldest—under "interpretative research" might be questioned by some. Indeed, R. G. Collingwood has argued that historical inquiry is its own mode of knowledge.[3] On the other hand, on the terms in which we have conceived this book (that is, a consideration of various "ways of knowing" from the point of view of strategy and tactics), historical inquiry is very similar to qualitative inquiries in general. In each case, the researcher attempts to collect as much evidence as possible concerning a complex social phenomenon and seeks to provide an account of that phenomenon. This requires searching for evidence, collecting and organizing that evidence, evaluating it, and constructing a narrative from the evidence that is holistic and believable. Throughout the process, interpretation is the key. This activity can be generally captured by the diagram in Figure 6.2.

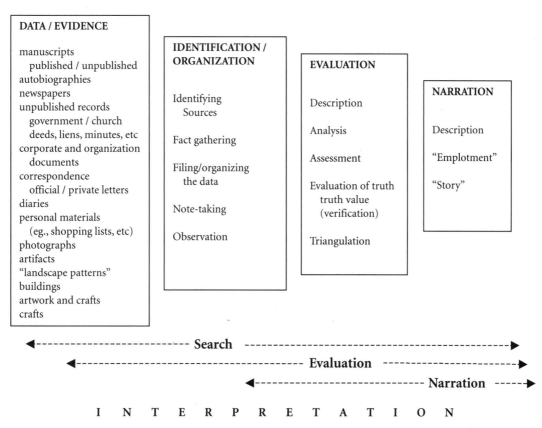

Figure 6.2   Chart of interpretive research.

Note that interpretation is active regardless of whether the task is evidence gathering, evaluation, or narration. Furthermore, the arrows beneath the columns suggest that the components of interpretive research are not contained in discrete "phases," but go on in parallel much of the time. For instance, Jacques Barzun and Henry Graff make the point that, even as the narrative is nearing completion, "you must keep an eye on events and publications for the latest relevant facts."[4]

In Forty's case, the interpretive-historical nature of the work is clear. A vast array of social-economic-political factors are brought into focus by the conceptual construct "the home." "The home" is also the means by which the holistic quality of Forty's account is achieved; that is, he does not just address social-economic-political forces randomly, but gives those forces roles in a coherent interpretive framework. Forty collects different kinds of data, such as written matter from the period (fiction, "how-to" books, advertisements, magazines), other scholarly commentaries, and photographs, as the basis for building his interpretation.

In this chapter, at the strategic level, we discuss the nature of historical narration (section 6.2), and provide a survey of four different "lenses" through which to view past phenomena (6.3). For heuristic purposes, 6.2 addresses considerations having to do with the nature of historical narrative as such, while 6.3 addresses some possible epistemological starting points that a researcher might bring to the construction of a historical narrative. We view both of these elements as falling under the umbrella of "strategy." Tactically, we deal with data collection (6.4) and general categories of evaluation (6.5). We conclude by considering one specific study (6.6), identifying the tactics used to frame the narrative.

6.2   STRATEGY: NARRATIVE AND ANALYSIS IN INTERPRETIVE-HISTORICAL RESEARCH

The interpretive researcher must eventually report what s/he finds in a narrative; and even while the research is in process, the findings are already being arranged in a narrational manner in the analyst's mind. How is history narrated? And in what ways could the narration be adjudged to be robust and believable? The *validity* of historical accounts starts with a demonstration that the events described occurred in the actual flow of time. A historical narrative cannot violate the sequence of that flow, or the coherent interconnectedness of its contents, in what Collingwood has termed "the one historical world."[5] A recent biography of Ronald Reagan, entitled *Dutch*, illustrates the problem that arises when a historical narrative's coherence is violated. The author of the work, Edmund Morris, chose to place a fictional character into his account of Reagan's tenure in the White House. While this may have some literary value, it is problematic as historical narrative. Morris's work is an instructive case of historical interpretation overstepping its bounds into fiction. Here we summarize three approaches to historical narration.

6.2.1 The Idea of History as Constructed of Narrative Sentences (Arthur Danto)

Danto proposes that historical accounts are by definition *narrative sentences*, a term that describes the nature of historical thinking and writing. A narrative sentence is one that necessarily involves two situations separated by time. And so the statement "The Thirty Years War began in 1618" is a sentence that must involve a beginning, which is 1618, and an end, which is the year 1648.[6] Someone making this statement before 1648 would make no sense, because no one could have known that the war would last 30 years. To illustrate his point further, Danto asks us to imagine an absolutely objective and exhaustive account of the flow of history documented by what he calls an Ideal Chronicle Machine, a gadget that rolls out *the* account of all possible events as time progresses. We could imagine the machine rolling out the Ideal Chronicle (the I.C.) of *all* the events of 1618. But even though all events are accounted for, the event we call the Thirty Years War cannot emerge via the I.C., either at the 1618 mark, or as the I.C. rolls by the year 1648. Only an observer removed from the objective flow of the I.C. could point to the flow, cull out the relevant facts as he or she sees them, and construct an account called the Thirty Years War. That construction is the narrative sentence.

Consider this statement made about Frank Lloyd Wright by William Cronon: "The faith of the Lloyd Joneses was more than just a religion for Wright; it also

Figure 6.3 Wright's mother's family. "The faith of the Lloyd-Joneses . . . would forever shape his speech and writing" (William Cronon on Frank Lloyd Wright). Courtesy Frank Lloyd Wright Preservation Trust.

schooled him in the moral rhetoric that would forever shape his speech and writing."[7] This is a narrative sentence. It involves two temporal conditions: a) the "faith of the Lloyd Joneses," his mother's family, which was no doubt a factor in his early life, and b) "the moral rhetoric that would forever shape his speech and writing." To be able to make the statement, Cronon must be standing at a point in time after Wright's life. Cronon's position is also a privileged one, for by making such an assessment of the Lloyd Joneses' influence upon Wright's "moral rhetoric," he discounts other possible influences upon that rhetoric. It is this removed position that the historian occupies that leads some to make comparisons between the historian's work and the work of, say, a storyteller. This connection to literature is considered as follows.

6.2.2 *Literary Metaphors for Historical Narratives (W. B. Gallie and H. White)*

As to the nature of the narrative itself, several theories argue that historical narratives are related in some way to literary forms. W. B. Gallie writes: "Every genuine work of history displays . . . features which strongly support the claim that history is a species of the genus Story."[8] Gallie goes on:

> The systematic sciences do not aim at giving us a followable account of what actually happened in any natural or social process: what they offer us is idealizations or simplified models. . . . But history, like all stories and all imaginative literature, is as much a journey as an arrival, as much an approach as a result. . . . Every genuine work of history is read in this way because its subject-matter is felt to be worth following—through contingencies, accidents, setbacks, and all the multifarious details of its development.[9]

Gallie is not saying that the historical narrative is identical to fiction; nowhere does he suggest that the rigorous tactics of evidence collection and analysis required for history research be set aside. Gallie instead is arguing for an essence of historical accounts. A story has a beginning, a development, a conclusion. It is an account of a set of events and details that carry the reader along in a coherent drama. Gallie holds that it is the same with historical accounts. That is why we enjoy reading them over and over again, even though the outcome is known.

Hayden White's position may be paired with Gallie's. White's literary argument for history has two main points. First, the historian is one who *emplots*: "Histories gain part of their explanatory effect by their success in making stories out of mere chronicles; and stories in turn are made out of chronicles by an operation which I have . . . called 'emplotment.'"[10] The historian must take the available evidence to weave together (emplot) a coherent account. But how does such an account achieve validity? White's answer is the second of his points: He appeals to literary types as measures of a historical story's coherence and robustness:

> The historian brings to his consideration of the historical record . . . a notion of the *types* of configurations of events that can be recognized as stories by the audience for which he is writing. . . . The important point is that most historical sequences can be emplotted in a number of different ways. . . . For example, what Michelet in his great history of the French Revolution construed as a drama of Romantic transcendence, his contemporary Tocqueville emplotted as an ironic Tragedy.[11]

White suggests that literary types "endow the events of our lives with culturally sanctioned meanings." In sum, both Gallie and White essentially make appeals to literature as a means to lend what might be called a validity-of-lived-experience to the historical narrative.

6.2.3 *The Role of Imagination and Comprehension in Historical Narratives (R. G. Collingwood)*

But how exactly is the narrative, story, or emplotment actually constructed? Collingwood's notion of the historical imagination is one answer to this question. Collingwood argues that the human imagination has an inherent ability to comprehend past phenomena in terms of coherent wholes, and he makes interesting connections between this ability and the ability to create art. Says Collingwood: "The historian . . . is always selecting, simplifying, schematizing, leaving out what he thinks unimportant and putting in what he regards as essential. It is the artist, and not nature, that is responsible for what goes into the picture."[12] The thrust of what Collingwood is saying is this: The product of this imaginative-narrative activity is not "weak knowledge." Rather, precisely *because* of the legitimacy of the human imagination when it functions in this way, the result is valid and robust knowledge. Now, of course, there are good and bad efforts at exercising the historical imagination; Collingwood certainly does not suggest that any attempt at historical narrative is legitimate just because of the role of the imagination. This brings up the next consideration.

6.2.4 *Analysis and Verification (Tosh and Barzun)*

History-as-story, the historical imagination and, indeed, "narration" itself does not guarantee accuracy and believability. A historical account is, after all, not a story in the fictive sense. Collingwood himself, his idealism notwithstanding, gives the decisive rule that any historical account must be part of the "one historical world."[13] By this he means that, while fictive stories have no obligation to be part of the continuum of empirical space and time, historical accounts are necessarily part of it. If any aspect of a historical account does not square with the logic of the connections within this continuum, that is grounds for doubting its believability. While Collingwood offers a philosophical argument for the need of accuracy, he does not provide the details for how to assure this in narration. Two works come to mind that may help. One is John Tosh's *The Pursuit of History*,[14] and the other is Jacques Barzun and Henry Graff's *The Modern Researcher*. (By the way, the lack of the word *history* in the Barzun/Graff work suggests these authors too conceive of historical writing as subsumed under a broader framework of inquiry; the term Barzun and Graff use is simply "research and report.")[15] Both Tosh and Barzun/Graff acknowledge that fitting an account dependably into the "one historical world" can be a big task. For Tosh, this is because historical sources "encompass every kind of evidence," and so each must be closely evaluated. For their part, Barzun and Graff cite the example of one researcher's 35 year trek in verifying the authorship of one 1879 document.[16]

Tosh points out the limitations of narration, which can suggest causal relations that are in fact not there, or "drastically simplify" a complex reality into something that renders the account untrue.[17] For Tosh, "analysis" is a kind of check to the other poles of "narration" and "description" in the overall project of historical research.[18] Tosh contends that analysis has come to play a larger role in historical writing in the last 100 years than it once did. In the 1991 edition of his book, Tosh identifies three components of analysis: textual authentication, validity of factual inferences, and weighing alternative interpretations.[19] We will return to Tosh's work in 6.4.

Barzun and Graff stress the need for "verification," a check against inaccurate narration. They point out that it is normal for anyone to sort through a variety of facts and claims in daily life to determine their veracity and usefulness. But historians must support their evaluations of each claim by "rationally convincing" argumentation.[20] This requires verification of the facts, and the authors cite a series of examples, under an array of headings, for how a researcher goes about the task of verification. We also suggest some in section 6.4 (see also Figure 6.7); suffice it here to say that many of these involve triangulating facts about an incident, via different sources, that converge to a point of agreement. If the triangulation cannot be achieved, the veracity of a claim is diminished.

6.3   STRATEGY: FOUR INTERPRETIVE LENSES

In this chapter and the next, it will become clear that under the umbrella of interpretive research are many variations on how subject matter can be interpreted. Here we consider four ways an interpretation of a historical subject can be framed.

6.3.1 Causal Explanations of History: The Idea of a "Covering Law"

The natural sciences have been accorded a great deal of respect in Western thinking. This is because science attempts to identify laws that regulate natural behavior, isolating causal connections and rendering those behaviors predictable. Gravity is such a law, as are the laws of thermodynamics and of motion. Armed with a general law, a researcher has a powerful means by which to examine any number of cases of natural behavior that fall under the dictates of that law.

History research has not escaped this idea. A leading proponent of a causal interpretation of history is C. G. Hempel (b. 1905). He is associated with the "covering law" of history, which posits no essential difference between the behavior of natural phenomena and the behavior of social phenomena.[21] General laws apply to both. The behavior of an object of nature, say, a planet, is covered by laws that are now well known. But covering laws for human society are much harder to isolate, because the "human sciences" are not yet sufficiently developed to formulate them. Thus, on Hempel's view, we do not yet have truly rigorous historical accounts. We only have (what he calls) *explanation sketches*, because any account is as yet unable to identify the covering law behind the phenomena it is describing. When a covering law *is* discovered, explaining an event covered by the law will be tantamount to predicting future events of that kind.[22]

In contrast, Karl Popper (b. 1902) rejects the possibility of large-scale predictions. His *The Poverty of Historicism* holds that the growth of human knowledge is not predictable, and so neither are actions based upon future knowledge.[23] Only small-scale predictions are conceivable in the realm of the social sciences. Popper calls this "piecemeal engineering," by which the social scientist, much like the natural scientist, takes small steps based upon *available* knowledge, observing the results, correcting mistakes, and eschewing any grand "utopian" claims to general predictions of the future, which Popper terms "prophecy."[24]

Popper's emphasis upon small-scale cause-effect relations is a useful modification of Hempel's covering law model for historical accounts; it does not index an account to grand laws as yet unknown. Critics of the covering law have noted that the human mind naturally looks for reasons for why a thing or an event is thus-and-so, without demanding that those reasons be laws having universal validity.[25] Danto gives the example of a dent in an automobile. The dent is there because some event caused it to be there, but Danto shows that the "cause" could be a variety of events, depending more upon the perspective taken in narration than upon any general law.[26]

6.3.1.1 Examples: Viollet-le-Duc, Choisey. The emphasis upon "scientific method" in the West predisposed many to think causally about the history of design. This tendency is particularly strong in theories that emerged during or after the Industrial Revolution. Eugene Emmanuel Viollet-le-Duc, for example, sought to revisit Gothic structures to explain their forms as the rational expression of necessary structural forces (see Box 6.1).

The work of Auguste Choisey (1841–1904) was influenced by Viollet-le-Duc's rationalism. In brief, Choisey's *Historie de l'architecture* (1899) posits that architectural form, as *effect*, is the result of the rational processes of construction, as *cause*: "Style

BOX 6.1

Causal Thinking in Architectural Design: Viollet-le-Duc

Eugene-Emmanuel Viollet-le-Duc (1814–1879) was one of the first thinkers of his day to assess architecture from a rationalist point of view. The images below are from his *Lectures on Architecture*. Consider Viollet-le-Duc's rationalist deductions on the style of the copper vessel. Its appearance: "exactly indicates its purpose. . . . It is fashioned in accordance with the material employed. . . . The form obtained is suitable . . . (for) the use for which it is intended."* There really is only one way in which the copper vessel is optimally designed, and human reason can discover this way by deductive processes. In the same vein, Viollet saw the architecture of the Gothic period as an expression of the reasoned analysis of structural forces. In short, form is the effect that is caused by structural principles. Analytical drawings such as the one shown here of Notre Dame Cathedral fill the pages of his works.

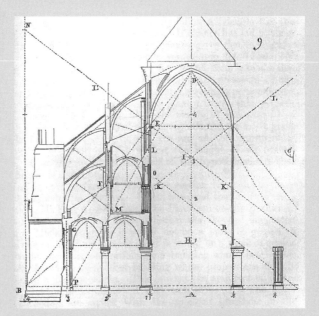

Figure 6.4A Illustration of copper vessel from Lecture VI of Viollet-le-Duc's *Lectures on Architecture*: "Thus . . . this vessel has style . . . first, because it exactly indicates its purpose; second, because it is fashioned in accordance with the material employed," etc. In short, here is an argument from *cause*.

Figure 6.4B Diagram from Viollet-le-Duc's *Dictionnaire Raisonnee* highlighting the rational factors behind Gothic framing.

*Eugene-Emmanuel Viollet-le-Duc, *Lectures on Architecture* (1872), trans. B. Bucknall, 2 vols. (New York: Dover, 1987), 1:180–181.

does not change according to the caprice of . . . fashion, its variations are nothing but those of processes . . . and the logic of methods implies the chronology of styles."[27] Following this rubric, Choisey sees the history of Western architecture as the result of causal factors. Thus he writes of the Doric pediment: "The pitch of the gable is that of the roof, which is governed by this double condition, that the rain should run off, and the tile should not."[28] And, on the layout of the Acropolis: "An oblique view is the *general rule*, while a view *en face* is a calculated exception."[29]

6.3.2 *History as the Movement of Absolute Spirit*

Another interpretive approach, derived from the thought of the philosopher G. W. F. Hegel, holds that history is the on-going evolution of a communal consciousness or mind (in German the word is *Geist*, translated as "mind" or "spirit"). Simply put, the communal consciousness is the sum of the individual consciousnesses of human beings, ultimately encompassing the consciousnesses of all individuals in a society at any one time. What is more, the whole is more than the sum of the parts. That is to say, the corporate consciousness, if not a mind of its own, at least has attributes of motivation and of will; these transcend the ability of any individual consciousness to fully grasp them. And so the single subject is always enmeshed in a much larger *zeitgeist* (spirit of the time) than he or she is able to comprehend. It is this larger-than-the-sum-of-the-parts quality to the communal consciousness that is represented by the word *spirit*. The influence of this approach upon architectural history at the turn of the twentieth century was enormous. Typical is this kind of wording from Le Corbusier:

> A great epoch has begun. There exists a new spirit. Industry, overwhelming us like a flood which rolls on towards its destined end, has furnished us with new tools adapted to this new epoch, animated by the new spirit.[30]

The modernists, in effect, assumed that their time was the fulfillment of Hegel's idea that the evolution of absolute spirit will culminate in a condition of complete knowledge. They conflated their exuberance over the possibilities of the machine with the idea that all of the past was merely preparation for a brave new world, which they implicitly held to be their world. Many works of history from this period, such as those by Pevsner and Giedion, are colored by this assumption of the modernist *zeitgeist*.[31] The title of Giedion's text, *Space, Time and Architecture*, is itself illustrative of the work's epistemological assumptions.

6.3.2.1 Example: Explanatory Power for Stylistic Transitions Through Time. The "movement of spirit" is one of the few interpretive approaches that could explain *transitions* from one style to another. Hegel's thought in general is concerned with the essential instability of any one "shape" of culture through time; the forces within a cultural system are always pushing toward newer horizons of understanding. Out of this emerge the changes in the visual attributes of the products of material culture. Heinrich Wolfflin's influential study *Renaissance and Baroque*, which posits explanations as to why the former style evolved into the latter, is an example of this kind of application of the Hegelian system.[32] Readers would do well to study this work, and see in it a forerunner of the twentieth-century histories referred to earlier.

6.3.2.2 Example: Explanatory Power for Stylistic Uniformity in a Given Period. The Hegelian system is also useful in explaining the *uniformity* of stylistic expression during a period of time. For all of the oversimplification that comes from categorizing art into periods, Hegel's philosophy explains why such categorizing basically *works*. The products of art in any given period do tend to look alike; Gothic art is Gothic art because of Gothic attributes, Renaissance art is Renaissance art because of Renaissance attributes, and so on. One just does not find a "Gothic artist" flourishing during Renaissance times. On Hegel's view, this is the communal spirit expressing itself in material forms. Moesei Ginzburg's *Style and Epoch*, in which he calls for the machine, the factory, and workers' housing to be the stylistic features of Russian architecture at the turn of the century, is an example of a work that affirms certain forms are right for a certain time.[33] (See Figure 11.14 and related text on Ginzburg.)

6.3.2.3 Example: Study of Individuals and Their Work. The Hegelian approach is also useful in its ability to render the backdrop behind specific individuals and their work more theoretically meaningful. The idea of someone being a "man for his time" has theoretical roots in this view. Even though the movement of communal spirit tends to devalue individual lives as such, Hegel invests heavily in special individuals as agents that bring about change. When dealing explicitly with history, Hegel calls such a person a *world historical individual.* The progress of communal spirit is very dependent on

> the activity of individuals, who are its agents and bring about its actualization. . . .
> The historical men, the world historical individuals, are those who grasp just such
> a higher universal, make it their own purpose, and realize this purpose in accor-
> dance with the higher law of the spirit.[34]

The artist stands in a similar position as one who is able to "grasp the higher universal," so as to "realize this purpose" in material forms. Of Alberti, for instance, Jacob Burckhardt says: "of his various gymnastic feats . . . we read with astonishment how, with his feet together, he could spring over a man's head; how in the cathedral he threw a coin in the air till it was heard to ring against the distant roof; how the wildest horses trembled under him."[35] Quite a fellow, that Alberti! Men such as Alberti were "historical men," who were able to take the various yearnings of the communal spirit of their time and convert them into material expression. It is fairly elementary to identify other names in the history of architecture that have played similar roles: Suger of St. Denis, or Frank Lloyd Wright, for instance.[36]

6.3.3 *Structuralism*

One question the Hegelian notion of communal spirit does not answer is why stylistic similarities in the products of material culture sometimes occur in widely dispersed cultures (that is, ones with little chance of contact). This is a question Claude Levi-Strauss addresses in his analysis of a number of widely dispersed cultural systems. One example is his study of the tendency for split representation of the human form in the decorative arts of the early Shang (Chinese), the Kwakiutl (Pacific Northwest) and the Maori (New Zealand) cultures.[37] Says Levi-Strauss:

> We reserve the right to compare American Indian art with that of China or New Zealand, even if it has been proved a thousand times over that the Maori could not have brought their weapons and ornaments to the Pacific Coast. . . . (If) historians maintain that contact is impossible, this does not prove that the similarities are illusory, but only that one must look elsewhere for the explanation. . . . If history . . . cannot yield an answer, then let us appeal to psychology, or the structural analysis of forms.[38]

When Levi-Strauss refers to history he means causal history, as the covering law model would have it. In this view of cultural development, similarity in style is necessarily the result of physical contact. Given the lack of historical evidence for such contact, Levi-Strauss appeals to structural analysis.

There are several texts that summarize structuralism, the one by Terence Hawkes probably being the most accessible.[39] Here we only summarize some important implications for history research that emerge from this strategy. First, systems of meaning have their own organic properties. Jean Piaget, for example, posits the characteristics of any structural system as self-contained, self-regulating, and self-transformative.[40]

Figure 6.5 Split face mask design after the kind referred to by Levi-Strauss. Courtesy of Angela Feser.

Language is such a system. The English language defines a clear, albeit widely diffused, conceptual area of "containment." It operates by a coherent set of rules that make reference to nothing outside of the system; it is self-regulating. It changes purely according to immanent conditions—consider the new meanings assigned to the words *mouse, surf,* and *memory* with the advent of computers—that is, the language is self-transformative.

Second, meaning rests not so much in entities themselves as in the relationships *between* entities. Ferdinand Saussure's thesis for language is that words, as well as the components of words (e.g., letters, in the case of alphabetized systems), only carry meaning when standing in relationship to other such signs. The entire network of these relationships constitutes a *langue*, the totality of the structural system, while any instance of the *langue* is a *parole*. The atomic components of the *langue/parole* system are *phonemes*, or the sound-images that make up the "material" of the language system. And, says Peter Caws, "the chief characteristic of the phoneme is simply that it is different from all the other phonemes—what it is in itself is a matter of comparative indifference."[41] Note that no reference to anything external to the system is necessary for meaning; meaning arising out of phonemic relationships is in this sense arbitrary, dependent only upon the agreement of the community that assigns such meaning.

6.3.3.1 Example: Deep Structures (Broadbent, Glassie). The idea of deep structure is derived from Noam Chomsky's theory of how the mind generates language. Chomsky holds that the mind has the innate ability to organize the world and to frame that organization into language. From these "deep structures" Chomsky generates a set of algorithms from which sentences are constructed. This theory has also been used to explain the generation of architecture. The reasoning is that architectural forms, as universal as human language, must also be generated from innate orientations within the mind. Broadbent et al. cite four such mental orientations of "structures": the building as container of human activities, the building as a modifier of climate, the building as a cultural symbol, the building as a consumer of resources.[42] These "structures" offer a basis by which built forms throughout history could be assessed in a way that transcends the bounds of any particular culture. This theory resonates in tone with Levi-Strauss's analysis of similarities of art and social systems in disparate cultures by means of "internal connections."

Another appeal to deep structure is the idea that the mind has embedded orientations that are expressed *geometrically* in the visible realm. Henry Glassie's taxonomy of the objects of Anglo-American folk architecture adapts Chomsky's theory of deep structures in this way:

> Down from the level of the observable there is a continuum of abstraction that becomes less detailed and more powerful as it modulates to lower planes. . . . at the lowest level of organization—a level comparable to that on which Chomsky's ker-

nel sentences may be found—there are base concepts that are specific structures of geometric entities to which designing rules are applied in order to derive the structures of specific components—the types of which actual artifacts are examples.[43]

Glassie proposes that an impressive range of Anglo-American folk architecture may be formally explained by a set of geometric "rules" that derive from a base concept of an "axially ordered pair of squares." For example, "a quantitative study revealed that 99.2 percent of the 2,193 barns surveyed could be understood in terms of this bilaterally symmetrical, tripartite concept"[44]

6.3.4 Poststructuralism

In poststructuralism, the idea of an orderly self-defining, self-regulating, and self-transforming system is questioned. Michel Foucault, for example, posits that historical periods merely come and go, each period understood as a web of discourses, only to be replaced by another period, understood as another web of discourses, and so on. Poststructuralism questions ontological value itself, suggesting that "reality" is a byproduct of "discourse," and hence subservient to it. This renders any notion of a universal or trans-historical understanding of "reality," in which certain ideational benchmarks remain constant (e.g., "language," "progress," "heaven," "nature," "man," and so on), a polite fiction. Any vestige of meaning as a substantive reality is denuded; discourse and not substance is the source of meaning. Paul Rabinow offers an example of this point of view in recalling a debate on "human nature" between Foucault and Chomsky. The structuralist Chomsky held that there is, in fact, a human nature. This is understandable in light of his theory of the universal capacities of the human mind for language formation and understanding. Foucault on the other hand rejected the idea of "a human nature" as a substantive reality, choosing rather to frame it as a notion that "designates certain types of discourse in relation to or in opposition to theology or biology or history."[45]

What is discourse? Poststructuralism understands discourse as something like the cultural manifestations of the trafficking of thought, distributed into various topical foci. These in turn are maintained by tacitly agreed-upon ways of seeing. The result is a web of meaning that defines an era. Instances of cultural manifestations may be a period's literature, arts, or professions. Topical foci are certain discursive headings that appear, subsumed under terms such as "nature," "pluralism," even "man." Ways of seeing are often reified into expressions of institutional power, such as political or economic structures, a moral code, the ecclesiastical class, and so on. In the debate on human nature, for example, Foucault simply suggests "practices" such as economics, technology, or politics as "conditions of formation" that make "human nature" possible. In other words, rather than an assumed and hence privileged view of human nature that transcends all cultures, Foucault sees "human nature" itself as a discursive product of a fairly recent Western way of seeing.

BOX 6.2

Los Angeles 1965–1992: A Poststructuralist Analysis

Edward Soja's study of Los Angeles in the period 1965–1992 is an illustration of a poststructuralist approach.* Soja takes two turbulent dates to bracket his study: the Watts riots of 1965 and the riots related to the Rodney King incident in 1992. Soja conceptualizes the Los Angeles of 1965–1992 as six intermeshed realities that involve everything from geographically distributed "exopolises" (each different, and larger, than the actual incorporated municipalities), to "flexcities" that are geographies related to shifts in patterns of economic production, to "cosmopolises" that, though local, depend upon the global economy. These then are intermeshed with social hierarchies that are "no longer easily definable by simple racial, ethnic, occupational, class, or immigrant status."** To this is added the police structure that inhabits this complex reality so as to enforce an unquiet peace. Finally, on all of this is overlaid the reality of Los Angeles as an endless agglomeration of "simcities" ("Korealand, Blackword, Little Tijuana . . . Funcky Venice . . .").† The reader leaves Soja's study with a sense of the density and complexity that is Los Angeles. It reinforces the poststructuralist idea that meanings and "knowledges" are much more indexed to a cultural time and place then previously assumed. For what it takes away by negating the idea of transhistorical knowledge, poststructuralism gives back in the possibility of grasping the immanent knowledge operating in any particular cultural-temporal space more deeply. Soja himself concludes his analyses on a typically open-ended poststructuralist note: "All that can be said in closing is that Los Angeles, as always, is worth watching."††

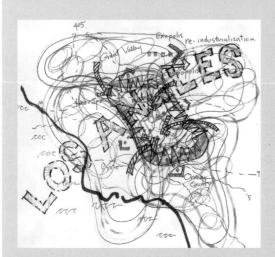

Figure 6.6   A student's graphic interpretation of Soja's analysis of Los Angeles. Courtesy of Angela Feser.

*Edward Soja, "Los Angeles, 1985–1992," in *The City: Los Angeles and Urban Theory at the End of the Twentieth Century*, ed., Allen J. Scott and Edward Soja (Berkeley, Calif.: University of California Press, 1996), 426–462.

**Ibid., 446.

†Ibid., 454.

††Ibid., 460.

A poststructuralist strategy of historical explanation, then, takes a period of time *as is*. This means two things. First, it does not explain a set of given conditions as obligated to previous conditions. The second follows from the first: While structuralism tends to take systems of human reality as universal ones (e.g., language, kinship relations, cuisine, manner of dress, and so on) poststructuralism does not look at transcultural systemic realities that somehow affirm "human-ness."

In poststructuralism, the material products of culture are parts of a larger immanent discourse, and so any historical assessment of architecture in this strategy is necessarily an assessment of the social/cultural discourse as well. As in the Hegelian paradigm, the individual artist may not be fully aware of the forces acting upon him or her. But in a departure from Hegel, here there is no obligation to a general sense of progress, or even necessarily to any sense of holistic communal identity. The historic era becomes simply the object-as-complex-reality, and an understanding of that reality consists of parsing the discourses that define it.

6.4   TACTICS: IDENTIFICATION OF DATA, ORGANIZATION, AND EVALUATION

Tosh lists six categories under which "historians and their writings are commonly classified." These are: politics, biography, ideas, economy, society, and mentality.[46] Architectural history research, because it so often focuses upon the material objects that constitute built environments, tends not to fall as easily under any one of Tosh's categories. The material object (it can range in scale from a copper vessel to the city of Los Angeles) is complicit with all of these categories. Thus the narrative must pull from what each category has to offer in order to weave its holistic account of the object in question. James Ackerman calls this the "direct experience of the artifact": "Though we do not read Newton's *Principia* to learn physics, or the Eighteenth Amendment to learn how to control the consumption of alcohol, we do visit the Acropolis at Athens and the Sistine Chapel to experience just what they have to convey."[47]

This said, one cannot *just* interact with built objects, many of which are either in decay, or in some way different from the condition in the period under consideration. The physical object cannot reveal much without the other tactics of the overall interpretive enterprise: evidence collection, evaluation, and narration (refer again to Figure 6.2). We give some guidelines and examples in this as well as in the next section.

The details of data collection and evaluation in interpretive-history research are many; an introductory text covering a wide spectrum of research methods for architecture cannot discuss them exhaustively. Here we provide a general table summarizing how Tosh and Barzun/Graff address these considerations (Figure 6.7). This table takes the one in Figure 6.2 and expands the content of the middle sections (identification, organization, evaluation).

	Identification	Organization	Evaluation / Analysis
DATA / EVIDENCE	Primary/secondary T28-29	Researcher's mind (B45) Accuracy B/G44 Love of order B/G44 Logic B/G45 Honesty B/G45 Self-awareness B/G46 Imagination B/G47	Authenticity External/internal criticism T51-54 Attribution B/G112 Social trend (falsification) B/G108
	Published/ unpublished T30		
	General/archival T34-35		
	Books/periodicals	Compilation B/G201 By topic By time By internal logical order	Clarification B119
	Public/personal T39-45		Audience B/G 29-30
	Official/colloquial T36-38		Difference between now and then T12 (for instance see "falsification on the increase" in B/G 108-112)
		Note-taking B/G25	
	Fact finding Catalogues B/G58 Encyclopedias B/G67 References B/G71 atlas, handbooks, etc Chronology B/G82 perpetual calendar B/G103	"Relatedness" of events T104	
		Composing B/G211	Fact versus idea B/G134
		Verification B/G96-133	Bias B/G185
		Scale/scope T99	Self-criticism B/G142
			Alternative interpretations T119 ('91 ed)
			Empathy T105 "post hoc propter hoc" T97
			Oversimplication T97

(beside the table to the right: **NARRATION**)

← **INTERPRETATION** →

Figure 6.7 Some considerations for data collection, organization, and evaluation taken from the Tosh and Barzun/Graff texts. Page numbers from their texts are provided here. In the Tosh case, pagination is from the 1984 edition except where noted.

Tosh's and Barzun/Graff's efforts may be summarized like this: the interpretive-historical narrative must be coherent and believable on the basis of how it fits into the logical connections demanded by Collingwood's "one historical world." Collingwood suggests "rules of method" for situating a historical narrative in this world.[48] For instance, the narrative must be localized in space and time, by which is meant that it cannot be situated in a make-believe space-time context. *Alice in Wonderland* and Dante's *Inferno* are not histories. A historical narrative must not only be consistent with the facts of its internal relationships in time and space, it also should be consistent with the single fabric of reality that is the one historical world. To be able to do this calls for what Collingwood terms *evidence*. "What is evidence . . . everything is evidence which the historian can use as evidence . . . this spoken utterance, *this building*, this finger-print . . . the whole perceptible world . . . is potentially and in principle evidence to the historian."[49] The historian uses the pieces of the perceptible world he or she has chosen as "pegs" to aid the imagination to "rediscover . . . (the) past," so as to re-enact that situation in his mind.[50]

Tosh is also helpful in surveying the various possible forms of written documentation.[51] He provides a balanced discussion of primary/secondary sources, published/unpublished matter, official/personal records, and so on. He underlines the fact that "identification," "organization," and "evaluation" do not occur sequentially, but are active in concert throughout the process. For instance, (official) records must be received as facts that someone deemed worthy of recording while personal (what Tosh calls "ephemeral") written matter—letters, lists, notes—can capture the context in a much more immediate way. Barzun/Graff adds an insightful section related to this issue. They argue that contemporary culture, where electronic and televised media are coupled with an emphasis on "free speech," tends to offer a great deal of material for the researcher, but at a lower level of real truth value. The press can print "fabrications" without risk because it can refuse to disclose the sources.[52]

Barzun and Graff suggest that good interpretation comes from good organization. This connection is most evident in their discussion of note-taking as the researcher interacts with the sources. They argue that note-taking, by which they mean writing down in one's own words a fact or a thought from the source, is a step taken "towards the first draft."[53] They include a discussion on the researcher's mind in this context. Barzun and Graff also suggest that certain traits and habits (love for order, honesty, dedication to accuracy, etc.) are helpful in organizing research. Furthermore, they suggest that a researcher's cultural background and values play a role in organization and interpretation as well. A moral bent will see events in terms of divine intervention over against the workings of natural law (e.g., Augustine); a nationalistic bent will send forward a particular people or nation as more important than others (e.g., Walter Scott); the theory of evolution brought about the idea that historical events were also the product of a long "genetic" chain.[54]

The veracity of claims made by the evidence must be assessed for their truth value. On this topic, Barzun and Graff give many examples of how different sources must be used to triangulate upon a claim. For instance, they mention that a letter purportedly written by John Stuart Mill, but only signed "J," appeared in the April 18, 1932 edition of *Le Globe*. How to verify that Mill indeed wrote the letter? Well, first, "research discloses two earlier allusions by the editors of the paper that 'one of the most powerful thinkers in London' intended to write a series of open letters" about this topic. Second, a note from one of the editors states that a letter from "M" is forthcoming. Third, the "J" letter was published three days after the promise stated in the "M" letter. Fourth, a letter clearly written by Mill a month later refers to "my letter which appeared in the *Globe*." And so on.[55] We now take a closer look at evaluation and analysis.

6.5   TACTICS: EVALUATIVE CATEGORIES IN INTERPRETIVE-HISTORICAL RESEARCH

In distinction to categories of *handling* the evidence (identification, organization, evaluation), this section suggests categories for *types* of evidence: determinative, contextual, inferential, and recollective.

6.5.1 *Determinative Evidence*

Of primary importance is evidence that can situate the object of study in the time and space of the one historic world. Dates are one obvious type of determinative evidence (Barzun and Graff, for example, list the perpetual calendar as one resource for date verification). And because architectural history research involves the material object, archaeological tactics that can pinpoint dates are useful as determinative evidence. Consider the transformations of the abbey church at St. Denis over the centuries (Figure 6.8). Here, archaeological methods were the tactics used to uncover different stages of the structure's evolution. Photographs may also serve as determinative evidence. Recently, the Associated Press issued this story:

> A negative of the 1906 photograph depicting the first person to scale Mount McKinley proves the climber actually was standing 15,000 feet below the summit. . . . Dr. Frederick Cook claimed he took the picture of his companion, Edward Barrill, after the pair scaled the Alaskan peak, which at 20,320 feet is the highest peak in North America. But researcher Robert Bryce told the Times that a print made from Cook's original negative shows geographical features in the background that were cropped when the explorer published the photograph. . . . Bryce found the photograph in some of Cook's papers recently donated to the archives at Ohio State University.[56]

Of course, computers provide us with new ways to analyze photographs—but they also provide new ways to alter them. This is a concern over photographic evidence that did not exist in years past.

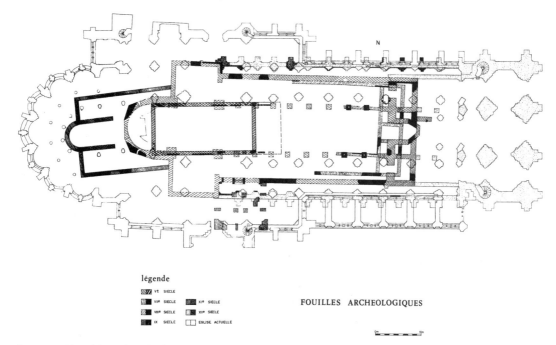

Figure 6.8   The abbey church of St. Denis in its various iterations: the evolving plan through time, based upon archaeological evidence. From Brankovic Branislav, *La Basilique de Saint-Denis: Les etapes de sa construction.* Courtesy Editions du Castelet, Boulogne, France.

6.5.2 Contextual Evidence

In architecture research, the elements of the built environment are often used to situate the object of inquiry *in context.* For example, in his study on the Abbott Suger, Otto von Simson makes the claim that the abbot's decisions about the portal design of the west façade of the church may well have been influenced by the Platonic ideas in the thought of Bernard of Clairvaux: "the increasingly cordial relations between the two men suggest that the art of St. Denis may reflect Bernard's ideas."[57] From the archives Simson first situates the building in time: "Suger's church, it will be recalled, postdates his reform of the monastery, undertaken at the insistence of St. Bernard."[58] Simson then uses other architectural objects, themselves situated in time, as contextual evidence. He compares the St. Denis portal design with the portal of the abbey church at Beaulieu in Languedoc, built shortly before the St. Denis portal, in the 1130s. The Languedoc design is one of "turmoil. . . . Innumerable figures seem to be crowded into a narrow space; the Apostles and angels . . . in wild agitation." In short,

Figure 6.9   Interior of St. Denis Cathedral. From authors' collections.

it is the style that St. Bernard found to be "most offensive." The St. Denis portal, on the other hand, is "serene and calm. . . . Clarity and simplification is noticeable throughout," reflective of the Platonic peace of an ideal world. Lastly, Simson's argument is built upon archival evidence: letters between St. Bernard and Suger.[59] "Bernard addresses Suger as his 'dearest and most intimate friend'; and unable to visit him, he requests the dying man's blessing."[60]

6.5.3 Inferential Evidence

Sometimes, by proximity of date, by reasoned interpretation, or by other logical deductions, one proposition is posited as very likely to be linked with another proposition, even though "hard" connections may not be available. Consider this: Wright's Robie House is one of this century's most photographed works of architecture, but for a study on how the house came to be, the photograph of Frederick Robie in his Robie Cycle Car may be more informative than photographs of the house itself. Daniel Hoffman's study of the house benefits greatly by inclusion of a photograph of the car (Hoffman's text is subtitled *The Illustrated Story of an Architectural Masterpiece*).[61] Robie's car speaks to the kind of man that would be attracted to the Robie House: an industrialist conversant with what technology can provide in the way of objects that connote progress—and one not afraid to embrace them.

Figure 6.10 Frederick Robie, with driver, in the Robie Cycle Car, designed and built several years before the construction of the Robie House. The photograph helps one understand the man who would have a house built with integrated ventilation systems, an attached garage, and structural steel cantilevers. Courtesy Frank Lloyd Wright Preservation Trust.

BOX 6.3

The Use of Inference in Researching the Work of Kirtland Cutter

Another example of inference may be found in Henry Matthews's work on the Pacific Northwest architect Kirtland Cutter. Matthews posits that Cutter's early design for his own house (1887) may have been influenced by the designs of A. J. Downing, on the basis of the popularity of Downing's work at that time (1850s): "... he must certainly have known Andrew Jackson Downing's popular and influential pattern book ..."* The claim is strengthened by visual similarities, although Matthews makes further inferences as to why the Cutter work is bolder. These are based upon Downing's own comments discouraging mere copying of the Swiss chalet's "defects," as well as upon Matthews's assumption that Cutter was influenced by the "real mountain architecture" that he saw on a trip to the Alps.**

Figure 6.11A Swiss chalet, from A. J. Downing's *Architecture of Country Houses* (1850), cited by Matthews in his text.

Figure 6.11B The Swiss chalet "type" that Cutter designed for his own home (1889). Use of both images courtesy of Northwest Museum of Arts and Culture, Eastern Washington State Historical Society.

---

*Henry Matthews, *Kirtland Cutter: Architect in the Land of Promise* (Seattle: University of Washington Press, 1998), 44.

**Ibid., 45.

6.5.4 Recollective Evidence

The interview in interpretive-history research targets memories rather than present-day reactions to things. To use the Robie example again, much of what we know about the events that led up to Frederick Robie's collaboration with Wright comes from an interview Robie's son conducted with his father some 53 years after the construction of the house. This interview can be found in Leonard Eaton's book *Two Chicago Architects*.[62] With recollection, all of the previous kinds of evidence may be involved. Recollection can lead to determinate information such as dates, and it can certainly yield contextual information. It is also inferential by nature, since the interviewee is drawing inferences about facts in times past. By the time the interviewer organizes the material that comes from the interview, it is necessarily an interpretation of an interpretation. The validity of recollective evidence, then, depends significantly upon who the interviewee is, what role he or she played relative to the object under study, what credibility he or she currently has, and how much of what he or she says can be corroborated by other evidence.

Figure 6.12 Frank Lloyd Wright: Robie House. This cantilever demonstrates the structural possibilities made possible by the technologies at the turn of the century in Chicago. Photograph from authors' collections.

The interview conducted by Robie's son is itself a historiographic issue. Robie characterized his selection of Wright this way: "I became rather interested in his views . . . and I thought, well, if he was a nut, and I was maybe, we'd get along swell."[63] Robie also said selecting Wright was "the best business deal I ever made."[64] The first comment reinforces the inference that Robie and Wright both had maverick temperaments, the one on matters of house design and the other in matters of industry. As to the second statement, the analyst must assess how much of this position is the result of the influence of Wright's stature upon Robie's "recollections" half a century later. This caution seems warranted by the following Robie recollection of the typical residence at the turn of the century:

> The idea of most of those houses was a kind of conglomeration of architecture, on the outside, and they were absolutely cut up inside. They were drafty. . . . I wanted no part of that. I wanted rooms without interruptions. I wanted the windows without curvature. . . . I wanted all the daylight I could get in the house, but shaded enough by overhanging eaves. . . . I certainly didn't want a lot of junk—a lot of fabrics, draperies, and what not. . . . I finally got it on paper . . . and displayed them to friends. . . . They thought I had gone nuts."[65]

This sounds like Mr. Wright himself! Wright led the way for "rooms without interruptions," he brought natural light into the interior (although other of his works, *and not necessarily the Robie*, are good examples of this), and he hated drapes. In other words, Robie's recollections may be more of a Wrightian manifesto than they are a report of the actual events. The interview in history research often has the effect of a hall of mirrors, piling interpretations upon interpretations. Even Robie's recollection of "the facts" may be more of an interpretation (informed intimately by subsequent developments) than an actual report.

We conclude this chapter by focusing on one further example of interpretive-historical research itemizing eight different tactics used. The reader is asked to consider how interpretation permeates the entire process, particularly in terms of the four evaluative categories we have just outlined.

6.6   TACTICS USED IN "INCA QUARRYING AND STONECUTTING" BY JEAN-PIERRE PROTZEN

Protzen's study focuses on the technique of Incan construction, from the quarrying of the stone to its installation. The study illustrates a variety of tactics that can be used to access a condition in the historic past. The reader is asked to become familiar with Protzen's article, which appears in the May 1985 issue of the *Journal of the Society of Architectural Historians* (references to this article below will only be by page number).

6.6.1 Tactic 1: On-Site Familiarity

Protzen acquired intimate knowledge of his topic by first-hand encounters with the site. From these came sketch maps, measurements and drawings, recordings of "innumerable blocks," field notes, and slides (footnote, p. 161). On-site familiarity was also essential for arriving upon conjectures that, in the completed narrative, have the weight of informed opinion. For instance, from the capital Cuzco, the physical distance of the two quarries Protzen researched led him to surmise that "the choice of rock type must have been of utmost importance to the Incas, or they would not have quarried sites so difficult of access and so far away." (p. 162). Or again, "the high degree of organization . . . is further indication . . . that quarrying was a very important operation . . . and not simply a routine matter" (p. 162). As we will see, most of the other tactics Protzen used also depended upon his presence at the site.

6.6.2 Tactic 2: The Use of Extant Documents

Protzen refers to many other studies, and he uses them either to corroborate his own findings or as a foil to what he observed. He cites a work by George Squire, who wrote of the Kachiqhata quarry in 1863. The fact that the earlier report "matches my own

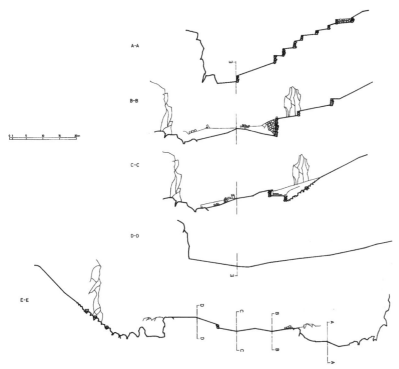

Figure 6.13 Protzen's sectional drawings, based upon site observations, of one of the Inca quarries. Courtesy Jean-Pierre Protzen.

observations very closely" lends credence to Protzen's point of view because it describes the site conditions more than 100 years closer to the actual period under study. This same tactic is used again later in the article, when Protzen uses José de Acosta's 1589 observations of fitted joints in a masonry wall ("without much mortar . . . it was necessary to try the fit many times") to defend his theory that the Inca masons did not use many sophisticated tools (p. 179; see also the reference to Outwater on the lack of tools, pp. 165–66).

6.6.3 Tactic 3: Visual Inspection

Visual observation uncovers site information that cannot be found any other way. For example, Protzen was able to determine that the two quarries he studied (Kachiqhata and Rumiqolqa) yielded different qualities of stone. The coarse-grained rocks from Kachiqhata were used in the buildings of the "religious sector," while the flow-banded andesite from Rumiqolqa, which is easier to be extracted in slabs, was used for sidewalks (p. 165). Also, the quarrying sequence becomes understandable under visual inspection: extraction of a block was often started before the ramp leading to it was finished; there are cases of partially dressed blocks not yet connected to the ramp. Finally, at Rumiqolqa, Protzen saw traces of how the rocks were quarried by means of a channel cut into the top of a cantilevered portion, and then holes worked into the channel of considerable depth. This also corroborates a report of the same technique surmised by Squires a century before (p. 169).

6.6.4 Tactic 4: Material Evidence

Protzen uses material evidence in a very focused way to support his larger hypothesis that the chief method of Inca stone dressing was by pounding. He noted that the whitish coloration of the pitmarks on the stones was consistent with the heat produced in pounding. Furthermore, he noted that the pitmarks were finer as they got closer to the joint edge. He theorized that they were made by "smaller hammers to work the edges." He found evidence to support this in the smaller slivers that lay in the surrounding area ("limiting myself to chips that I could pick up with my fingers, I found 43 slivers" p. 175). Finally, Protzen was also able to develop a hypothesis, consistent with his larger theory of pounding, of how the eye-holes so common in Inca masonry were made. "They exhibit a conical shape on either side of the perforated stone. This suggests that the pounding had been started from both sides until there remained only a thin membrane to be punched out." Based upon this, Protzen had grounds to dispute a theory of Hiram Bingham's, who suggested that the holes were bored with bamboo "rapidly revolved between the palms of the hands" (p. 176).

Figure 6.14 This image from Protzen's article shows the pitmarks that he observed diminishing in size as they get nearer the joint. Courtesy Jean-Pierre Protzen.

6.6.5 Tactic 5: Comparison with Conditions Elsewhere

Protzen looks to similar conditions in cultures elsewhere to speculate on technique. This approach is based upon the assumption that there are a limited number of ways a preindustrial culture can dress large masses of stone by hand. Of the evidence at Kachiqhata, Protzen had this to say: "The cutting marks on these and other blocks are intriguing. They are very similar to those found on the unfinished obelisk at Aswan, and the technique involved must not have been very different from the one used by the Egyptians, who used balls of dolerite to pound away at the workpiece until it had the desired shape" (p. 165).

6.6.6 *Tactic 6: Use of Local Informants and Lore*

Local informants as well as local lore proved useful. For instance, Protzen depended upon local lore to identify the west quarry of Kachiqhata as "the real quarry of Ollantaytambo" (p. 166). On the other hand, Protzen often cites local information just to question it or disagree with it. For instance, regarding certain needle-like blocks found at a quarry termed the Llama Pit, the author rejected the local opinion that they were for bridge construction (p. 167). He based his own view upon, again, educated conjectures from visual observation.

6.6.7 *Tactic 7: Reenactment/Testimonial*

Probably the strongest of Protzen's tactics, in terms of persuasive value, are his reenactments of the work the Inca stonemasons performed. Based upon his visual observations and deductions, Protzen reenacted both the dressing of the stones and the erection of a large masonry wall. In the first instance, he tested his theory that systematic pounding was the method of dressing by using a hammer of metamorphosed sandstone on a raw block of andesite. He learned the efficacy of different angles of pounding, as well as the utility of gravity as an aid in maneuvering the four-kg hammer. In the second instance, Protzen tested his idea of how large stones were fitted together in a wall of irregular jointure. He found that the dust produced from the

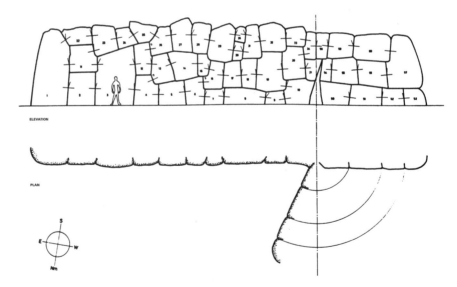

Figure 6.15 Drawing from Protzen's article, showing wall construction. Protzen enacted construction procedures to demonstrate his hypothesis that each new course can be cut to fit the profile of the course below it. Courtesy Jean-Pierre Protzen.

pounding of a bedding joint got compressed when an upper stone was placed upon the bed, indicating where further pounding was required. "Through repeated fitting and pounding, one can achieve as close a fit as one wishes" (p. 179).

The outcome of these reenactments is reported with the strength of a testimonial. With respect to the dressing of the andesite block, Protzen writes, "the work from rough block to the stage with one faced dressed took me only 20 minutes" (p. 173). This is impressive, and persuades the reader that pounding alone by a crew of trained persons can accomplish, without sophisticated tools, large amounts of dressed stone in a reasonable amount of time. With respect to wall construction, "it took me 90 minutes to complete the fit" (p. 179). This again makes believable the proposition that a large masonry wall can be erected by pounding.

6.6.8 Tactic 8: Identification of Remaining Questions

Finally, one element of a robust historical narrative is to clearly state what one does not know in the face of present evidence. For instance, after summarizing the local lore on an area designated as "quarrymen's quarters," as well as critiquing the view of another analyst (Emilio Harth-terre) on this subject, Protzen simply says that "the significance . . . of these structures remains to be established" (p. 164). And over against his theory that the Inca did not use many tools in their stonemasonry, Protzen acknowledges examples "throughout the territory that I explored" where there appeared to be clear cases of saw cutting and/or stone polishing. "What tools they used for this I do not yet know" (p. 178). Far from negating the validity of his ideas, Protzen's admission of ignorance on these matters instead underscores his credibility. Given the strength of his other tactics, his argument for pounding is still well supported. Future theories explaining the presence of sawed stone at certain locations may fit in as a corollary to his larger theory of pounding, as opposed to anything that would negate his ideas.

6.7   CONCLUSION: STRENGTHS AND WEAKNESSES

In this chapter we have argued that architectural history research is part of the larger domain of interpretive research; as such, this chapter and the next are similar strategically. The emphasis for interpretive-historical research is accessing evidence from the past, and we have provided an introductory overview of what this entails. At the strategic level, it entails epistemological points of view, acting as "lenses" through which past conditions are interpreted. Tactically, it entails fact-finding, fact-evaluation, fact-organization, and fact-analysis. It entails an interpretive imagination, that nevertheless does not spill over into fiction, but is rather guided by a mind that Barzun and Graff describe as having a love for order. It entails being aware of different kinds of judgments that can be made once enough evidence has been

BOX 6.4

History Research and Philadelphia's Bellevue-Stratford Hotel

Philadelphia's historic Bellevue-Stratford Hotel underwent extensive renovations in the late 1970s. Shown here is the rejuvenated lobby. It is the result of research and design by Hyman Myers, director of historic preservation for the Philadelphia firm VITETTA. For his research, Myers turned to the Philadelphia Historic Commission, the Library Company of Philadelphia, and the Historical Society of Pennsylvania. He consulted local newspapers (*Philadelphia Inquirer, Philadelphia Record*) from 1904 that provided stories on opening events and descriptions of the hotel at that time. Myers also conducted archival research on documents related to the hotel at the Athenaeum of Philadelphia and the University of Pennsylvania Fine Arts Library. Myers found some 20 original drawings (blueprints) of the building. He also consulted periodicals; he found material in a 1913 issue of the *Architectural Review* devoted to hotels in the USA. He also found a 1905 issue of *Architectural Record* that contained a series of product advertisements showing in detail who the craftsmen and artisans were who manufactured specific building elements for the original building.

Figure 6.16 The lobby of the Bellevue-Stratford Hotel (ca. 1979), Philadelphia. Hyman Myers, Director of Historical Preservation, VITETTA, Philadelphia. (Photograph by Nathaniel Lieberman). Courtesy: VITETTA Restoration Architects.

garnered. It entails the imaginative identification and use of specific tactics to access the object under study, as illustrated by Protzen's efforts. Finally, again at the strategic level, all of the above it entails the framing of a narrative that is at once holistic, in the sense that a story is holistic, and believable, in the sense that a well-investigated and well-documented report can be proven to describe an event that is part of the "one historic world." Figure 6.17 provides a summary of the strengths and weaknesses of interpretive-historical research.

Strengths	Weaknesses
• Interpretive-historical research is the only strategy that outlines how a narrative explaining past events can be framed. Other strategies, particularly in the qualitative range, because they also deploy written prose, can benefit from the narrative construction that this strategy provides. • Tactically, interpretive-historical research provides a means of "getting in" to a context or event in time past. This includes making use of archival, interview, archaeological, and other sources summarized in this chapter. The reader is encouraged to appreciate the harmony between these tactics and those summarized in the chapter on qualitative research (as well as correlational research), since the influence of past realities upon present circumstances are quite often hard to clearly isolate.	• The greatest limitation of interpretive-historical research is, of course, the fact that the object of inquiry is not empirically available for observation—and will never be. This is not like objects of other research inquiries that may also not be empirically observable (say, an atom or a distant galaxy) in that those objects are still extant in some ongoing ontological sense. Improvements in technology may lead to access to those objects in a different sense than the uncovering of new archival information (say) can promise for access to a past event. • The dependence upon emplotment and literary construction (that is, the similarities between historical narrative and "story") ought to alert the researcher—as well as the reader of research—to beware to avail himself or herself of multiple narrational perspectives on a historical event or object. • The means to measure the "accuracy" of a historical narrative is perhaps more flexible than guidelines for accuracy in some other research strategies. The productions of Collingwood's "historical imagination" need always to be checked by his other technical construct, the demand that the historical narrative always fit comfortably within the "one historical world." This is often not so easy to do.

Figure 6.17.   Strengths and weaknesses of interpretive-historical research.

6.8   RECOMMENDED READINGS

For a more detailed discussion of historical narration, we recommend the titles cited in this chapter. Arthur Danto's *Narration and Knowledge* (New York: Columbia University Press, 1985), insofar as it focuses on narration for this genre, can be regarded as foundational. It of course goes into much more depth than we were able to here on the narrative sentence; the passages dealing with the Ideal Chronicle Machine are also instructive. On the relationship between history and literary frameworks, we referred to W. B. Gallie, *Philosophy and the Historical Understanding* (New York: Schocken Books, 1964) and Hayden White, *Topics of Discourse: Essays in Cultural Criticism* (Baltimore, Md.: Johns Hopkins University Press, 1978).

With respect to historical imagination, R. G. Collingwood's *The Idea of History* (London: Oxford University Press, 1956) is seminal. One other work we did not mention in the text is Louis O. Mink's *Historical Understanding* (eds. Brian Fay, et al., Ithaca, N.Y.: Cornell University Press, 1987).

Often one comes across testimonials by historians on their work as narrative-emplotters. These offer first-hand insight into the historian's craft. Two brief but very informative testimonials are Stephen Ambrose's "Old Soldiers Never Die" and Jacques Barzun's "Wise Counsel." Ambrose's article is subtitled "History actually happens, but you can't trust the ones who make it." Barzun's is subtitled "A historian's historian talks about something that never was." Both can be found in the October 2, 2000 edition of *Forbes ASAP* magazine.

Hempel's essay on the covering law is a classic: C. G. Hempel, "The Function of General Laws in History," in *Journal of Philosophy* 39 (1942): 35–48. We also referred to Karl Popper's *Poverty of Historicism* (London: Routledge & Kegan Paul, ARK Edition, 1986) as a development of this idea.

The Hegelian view of history is most accessible in G. W. F. Hegel, *Introductory Lectures on Aesthetics*, trans. B. Bosanquet (London: Penguin, 1993). For a secondary commentary, see Jack Kaminsky, *Hegel on Art* (Albany, N.Y.: SUNY Press, 1970)

For more on structuralism, see Terence Hawkes, *Structuralism and Semiotics* (Berkeley, Calif.: University of California Press, 1977). On poststructuralism, see M. Foucault, *The Order of Things* (New York: Vintage Books, 1973), and *The Archaeology of Knowledge* (New York: Pantheon Books, 1972). And for a secondary commentary, see David Shumway, *Michel Foucault* (Charlottesville, Va.: University Press of Virginia, 1992).

Further examples (out of a countless number) of interpretive-historical research include: "The Factory as Republican Community: Lowell, Massachusetts," in John Kasson's *Civilizing the Machine* (New York: Penguin, 1976), pp. 55–106. Leo Marx, "The American Ideology of Space," in *Denatured Visions: Landscape and Culture in the Twentieth Century*, edited by Stuart Wrede and W. H. Adams (New York: Museum of Modern Art, 1988), pp. 62–78. C. M. Howett, "The Georgian Renascence in

Georgia: The Residential Architecture of Neel Reid," in *The Colonial Revival in America*, edited by A. Axelrod (New York: W. W. Norton, 1985), pp. 112–138.

NOTES

1. Adrian Forty, "The Home," in *Objects of Desire* (London: Thames and Hudson, 1986), 100.

2. Ibid., 101.

3. See R. G. Collingwood, *The Idea of History* (London and New York: Oxford University Press, [1940] 1956), 233.

4. Jacques Barzun and Henry Graff, *The Modern Researcher*, 5th ed. (Boston: Houghton Mifflin Co., 1992), 21.

5. Collingwood, *Idea of History*, 246.

6. Arthur Danto, *Narration and Knowledge* (New York: Columbia University Press, 1985), 152.

7. William Cronon, "Inconstant Unity: The Passion of Frank Lloyd Wright," in *Frank Lloyd Wright, Architect*, ed. H. Bee (New York: The Museum of Modern Art, 1994), 12.

8. Gallie, W. B. *Philosophy and the Historical Understanding* (New York: Schocken Books, 1964), 66.

9. Ibid., 67.

10. Hayden White, "The Historical Text as Literary Artifact," in *Topics of Discourse: Essays in Cultural Criticism* (Baltimore, Md.: Johns Hopkins University Press, 1978), 83.

11. Ibid., 85.

12. Collingwood, *Idea of History*, 236. Collingwood's derivation for the historical imagination largely comes from Kantian sources. In his *Critique of Pure Reason*, Kant holds that the imagination is one of the mind's *a priori* faculties and that the imagination has reproductive and productive modes (see Kant, *Critique of Pure Reason*, op.cit. A100–A102, A118). In the *Critique of Judgment*, Kant adds to the imagination's powers by positing it as *the* faculty involved in the creation of objects of art. (See Kant, *Critique of Judgment*, Sec. 1, 203). Collingwood's "historical imagination" is derived from these sources; it has the ability to picture things that are not empirically seen at the moment, and the end result of its work may be likened to art.

13. Collingwood, *Idea of History*, 246.

14. John Tosh, *The Pursuit of History* (London and New York: Longman Group, 1984).

15. See Jacques Barzun and Henry Graff, *The Modern Researcher* (New York: Harcourt Brace Jovanovitch, 1992), 3–13.

16. Ibid., 22–133.

17. Tosh, *Pursuit of History*, op.cit. 97.

18. Ibid., 94–95. It is noteworthy that Tosh connects "analysis" with the interpretive enterprise, while narration and description he considers "re-creation."

19. Ibid., 119.

20. Barzun and Graff, *Modern Researcher*, p. 99.

21. C. G. Hempel, "The Function of General Laws in History," in *Journal of Philosophy* 39 (1942): 35–48. "There is no difference . . . between history and the natural sciences: both can give an account of their subject matter only in terms of general concepts," 37.

22. Ibid., 39. "The preceding considerations [on prediction in scientific theories] apply to *explanation in history* as well as in any other branch of empirical science. . . . the expectation referred to is not prophecy or divination, but rational scientific anticipation which rests on the assumption of general laws" (Hempel's italics).

23. Karl Popper, *Poverty of Historicism* (London: Routledge & Kegan Paul, ARK Edition, 1986).

24. Ibid., 42–49.

25. "Thinking in terms of general concepts is so natural as to be very nearly unconscious. It is accordingly very easy to see why, in view of the psychological fact that the laws in question are never consciously entertained (or seldom so), philosophers would be tempted to say there is no general law, or that no general law is required to understand the explanation." See Arthur Danto, "The Problem of General Laws," in *Narration and Knowledge* (New York: Columbia University Press, 1985), 224.

26. Ibid., 233–234.

27. See Reyner Banham, *Theory and Design in the First Machine Age*, 2nd ed. (New York: Praeger, 1967), 24.

28. Ibid., 25.

29. Sergei Eisenstein, "Montage and Architecture," in *Assemblage* #10 (1989), 119. (Italics added in the case of "general rule.")

30. Le Corbusier, *Towards a New Architecture*, trans. F. E. Etchells (New York: Dover Publications, [1931] 1986), 227.

31. Nicholas Pevsner. *An Outline of European Architecture* (Baltimore: Penguin Books, [1943] 1974). Sigfried Giedion, *Space, Time and Architecture* (Cambridge, Mass.: Harvard University Press, [1949] 1967).

32. Heinrich Wolfflin, "The Causes of Change in Style," in *Renaissance and Baroque*, trans. K. Simon. (Ithaca, N.Y.: Cornell University Press, 1966), 73–88.

33. Moisei Ginzburg, *Style and Epoch*, trans. A. Senkevitch (Cambridge, Mass.: MIT Press, 1982), 77–102.

34. G. W. F. Hegel, *Reason in History*, trans. R. S. Hartman (New York: The Liberal Arts Press, 1953), 38–39.

35. Jacob Burckhardt, *The Civilization of the Renaissance in Italy*, trans. S. G. C. Middlemore (New York and London: Harper and Brothers, 1860).

36. Otto von Simson's study of Suger is noteworthy in this respect. While not Hegelian, von Simson in effect recognizes Suger as a kind of Hegelian world historical individual: "It is a drama played on two levels, the political and the theological, the human and the divine, and Suger is continually trying to render visible the ties that connect the two spheres. . . . He himself had forged and utilized the crises he chronicles, and it is this role, as well as his gifts as a historian, that irresistibly direct his narrative, and our eyes with it, toward the place where the historical and the providential intersect. This place is St. Denis." *The Gothic Cathedral* (Princeton, N.J.: Princeton University Press, 1974), 73.

37. Claude Levi-Strauss, *Structural Anthropology*, trans. C. Jacobson and B. Schoepf (New York: Basic Books, 1963), 245–268.

38. Ibid., 248.

39. Terence Hawkes, *Structuralism and Semiotics* (Berkeley, Calif.: University of California Press, 1977).

40. Ibid., 15–17.

41. Peter Caws, *Structuralism: The Art of the Intelligible* (New Jersey and London: Humanities Press International, 1988), 72.

42. Geoffrey Broadbent, R. Bunt, and C. Jencks, *Signs, Symbols and Architecture* (New York: John Wiley and Sons, 1980), 137.

43. Henry Glassie, "Structure and Function: Folklore and Artifact," in *Semiotica* 7 (1973): 328.

44. Ibid., 329.

45. Paul Rabinow, "Introduction," in *The Foucault Reader* (New York: Pantheon Books, 1984), 3–5.

46. Tosh, *Pursuit of History*, 27–47.

47. James Ackerman and Rhys Carpenter, *Art and Archaeology* (Englewood Cliffs, N.J: Prentice-Hall, 1963), 130.

48. Collingwood, *Idea of History*, 246.

49. Ibid., 243, 246–247. Italics added

50. Ibid., 296.

51. Tosh, *Pursuit of History*, 27–47

52. Barzun and Graff, *Modern Researcher*, 108–112.

53. Ibid., 27.

54. Ibid., 41–43.

55. Barzun and Graff, *Modern Researcher*, 112–114.

56. "Ascent of McKinley in 1906 Doubted," *Spokane Spokesman-Review*, 27 November 1998. Associated Press wire service.

57. von Simson, *The Gothic Cathedral*, 56–58, 111.

58. Ibid., 111.

59. Ibid., 110.

60. Ibid., 112.

61. Donald Hoffman, *Frank Lloyd Wright's Robie House* (New York: Dover, 1984), 3. (Italics added)

62. Leonard K. Eaton, *Two Chicago Architects and Their Clients: Frank Lloyd Wright and Howard Van Doren Shaw* (Cambridge, Mass.: MIT Press, 1969), 126–133.

63. Ibid., 9.

64. Ibid., 131.

65. Ibid., 127.

Chapter 7

Qualitative Research

7.1 INTRODUCTION

In her well-known book *Architecture: The Story of Practice*, Dana Cuff provides in-depth descriptions and analyses of architectural practice.[1] Throughout the book, she recounts in great detail the many interactions and processes that architects experience on a daily basis. With these observations as a foundation, she brings to light many of the underlying contradictions of the profession. These include, for example, the profession's tendency to celebrate the creative talent of the individual architect, even while most architects work in collaborative settings to bring to life complex building projects.

In introducing her study, Cuff describes in considerable detail how she went about her research. First and foremost, she persuaded three Bay Area firms to let her observe and participate in the life of each firm over a six-month period. In each setting, she observed meetings, interviewed firm members, participated in casual conversations, and took part in many informal social activities. Throughout these interactions, Cuff maintained two important principles: 1) that she should try to understand the dynamics of the profession from the point of view of the participants; and 2) that, at the same time, such insiders' perspectives had to be balanced by her "outsider's observations."[2] While Cuff insists on grounding her work in empirical reality, she also highlights the role of interpretation and meaning. As she puts it:

> Philosophically, what I value . . . is [a] rejection of positivist notions of the social world, embracing interpretation, meaning in context, interaction, and the quality of the commonplace.[3]

Figure 7.1   Meetings between architects, clients, and consultants are an esential aspect of the design process.

In another recent study, Linda Groat and Sherry Ahrentzen conducted a series of in-depth interviews with faculty women in architecture, the results of which were published in the *Journal of Architectural Education*.[4] The open-ended interview questions were developed to elicit the women's accounts of their professional careers, including: their initial motivations for entering the field; their experience of either discrimination or encouragement as faculty members; and their visions for the future of architectural education. Rather than selecting the women to be interviewed through random sampling, the authors' goal was to "maximize the variety and range of perspectives represented. . . . As consequence, our sample is heavily weighted to tenured women. . . . Yet because these are precisely the women who are most likely to exert influence within the academy, their perspectives merit serious consideration."[5]

Another key feature of their study was its inductive approach. The analysis of the in-depth interviews required a long, interactive process of identifying key themes, developing an elaborate coding scheme, and eventually synthesizing the results into the textual narrative for the article. The published article not only reports on the key themes culled from the "visions" section of the interview but also grounds these

Figure 7.2 An increasing number of faculty in architecture are women, and their perspectives on architecture are often different from those of their male colleagues. Photograph courtesy of Washington State University Spokane.

themes through illustrative quotations from individual respondents. Only after the major themes were identified did the authors consider the remarkable parallel to the recommendations of the 1996 Carnegie Foundation study of architectural education.[6] To be specific, five of the seven themes Groat and Ahrentzen identified correspond to those from the Carnegie study: ideals of a liberal education, interdisciplinary connections, different modes of thought, communicative design studios, and caring for students. Groat and Ahrentzen conclude that "these recommendations constitute a consistent and powerful argument for the visions for architectural education that any number of individual faculty women have been valiantly advocating for many years."[7]

7.2   THE STRATEGY OF QUALITATIVE RESEARCH: GENERAL CHARACTERISTICS

What the Cuff and the Groat/Ahrentzen studies have in common is that they can be categorized as qualitative research. Although this strategy can take many different forms, they typically have a number of important characteristics in common. Norman Denzin and Yvonne Lincoln, authors of a comprehensive three-volume handbook on qualitative research, offer the following "generic" definition:

> Qualitative research is multimethod in focus, involving an interpretive, naturalistic approach to its subject matter. This means that qualitative researchers study things in their natural settings, attempting to make sense of, or interpret, phenomena in terms of the meanings people bring to them. Qualitative research involves the studied use and collection of a variety of empirical materials.[8]

Within this definition four key components of qualitative research are identified. We will consider each of them in turn, using examples from architectural research to illustrate them.

7.2.1 An Emphasis on Natural Settings

By natural settings is meant that the objects of inquiry are not removed from the venues that surround them in everyday life. Cuff's primary material came from her in-depth observations and interactions at three architectural firms over a six-month period. In the Groat/Ahrentzen study, the value of the research is precisely due to its ability to highlight trends embedded in the context of the academic departments the subjects were a part of. In both these cases, the researchers used a variety of research tactics that placed themselves or their data collection tactics into the context being studied; the context did not have to be altered for the study to be conducted.

7.2.2 A Focus on Interpretation and Meaning

In both the Cuff and the Groat and Ahrentzen studies, the authors not only ground their work in the empirical realities of their observations and interviews, but they also make clear that they, as researchers, play an important role in interpreting and making sense of that data. To reiterate one of Cuff's points (quoted earlier), she intentionally employs methodological practices that embrace interpretation and meaning in context. Similarly, throughout the long process of interviewing the participants in their study, Groat and Ahrentzen routinely wrote and exchanged memos on their preliminary interpretations of the interviews, both to initiate the process of analysis and to guide the development of the remaining interviews. (See Section 7.3.1 and Figure 7.7 for details.)

7.2.3 A Focus on How the Respondents Make Sense of Their Own Circumstances

In the Cuff and Groat/Ahrentzen studies, it is clear that the researchers aim to present a holistic portrayal of the setting or phenomenon under study as the respondents themselves understand it. Cuff, for example, offers extensive and detailed descriptions of interactions among the multiple players in client meetings. For their part, Groat and Ahrentzen sought to understand how faculty women perceived three aspects of their experiences in architecture: their attraction to architecture as a career; their career experiences both in professional practice and in teaching; and their visions for architectural education.

Another good example of research that emphasizes how respondents make sense of their own experiences is Benyamin Schwarz's study of the design process in nursing home projects (discussed in Chapter 2).[9] In a series of case studies, Schwarz chronicles the dynamics of the design process from the distinct perspectives of individual stakeholders, each of whose point of view is well represented through extensive interview quotations. For example, in case No. 2, Schwarz describes the process as "a power struggle between the facility's development team and their architects, on one side, and the state regulators on the other."[10] One of the architects describes his severe frustration: "It's outrageous how much it costs to build a nursing home per square foot. . . . But you end up building in things that people don't even use. . . . An awful lot of regulations really do get in the way. [The reason for the regulation is] to limit the State's exposure in terms of how much money they're going to spend in the reimbursement system."[11]

For his part, the state regulator felt he represented the needs of the elderly residents: "The only reason that we set maximums was primarily to protect the people in the facility. Because we said that if there's limitation on reimbursement the applicants need to know that."[12] From the facility director's position, it seemed that state regulations forced a modification of the design that brought it closer to the more traditional nursing home, as indeed the design schemes in Figure 7.3 and 7.4 indicate. In the architect's opinion, the client had attempted to change state regulation through the design process, which "was not the right way to do it, but that's the way the client chose to do it."[13] Letting the various stakeholders speak for themselves and make sense of the process they experienced enabled Schwarz to clarify in a powerful way the "ideological contradiction" at the heart of the design process for long-term care settings.

7.2.4 The Use of Multiple Tactics

Denzin and Lincoln refer to this characteristic of qualitative research as bricolage. A bricolage is "a pieced-together, close-knit set of practices that provide solutions to a problem in a concrete situation."[14] Although not all qualitative studies employ multiple tactics (e.g., the Groat and Ahrentzen study), a good example of a multitactic qualitative study may be seen in Sherry Ahrentzen's "A Place of Peace, Prospect and

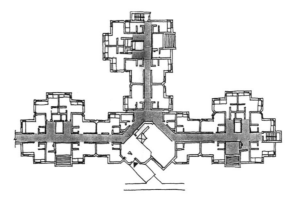

Figure 7.3 The floor plan for the initial cluster unit scheme, Schwarz, 1997. Drawing courtesy of Benyamin Schwarz.

... A.P.C.: The Home as Office."[15] Ahrentzen researched 104 individuals who work out of offices in their homes to gain an understanding of the "socio-spatial consequences" of such an arrangement. Specifically, she sought to uncover how these individuals perceived their neighborhoods in light of their homes being also their places of work. She also studied their attitudes to housing layout, as well as to how they "phenomenologically" viewed their home office. Her tactics are an excellent illustration of the bricolage approach: "This report is ... a cross-sectional survey design with self-administered questionnaire, face-to-face interview, a modified time diary, and photographs, sketches and a physical inventory of the home and workspace." To be sure, not every one of these tactics is exclusively qualitative, but the overarching research questions and the dominant mode of the research design are qualitative.

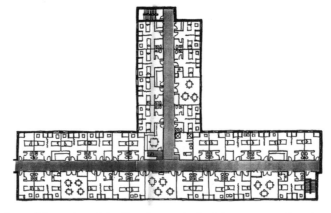

Figure 7.4 General floor plan of the first floor as built, Schwarz, 1997. Drawing courtesy of Benyamin Schwarz.

7.2.5 Other Aspects of Qualitative Research Strategy

To review, then, the strategy of qualitative research is one of first-hand encounters with a specific context. It involves gaining an understanding of how people in real-world situations "make sense" of their environment and themselves, and it achieves this by means of a variety of tactics. It acknowledges, rather than disavows, the role of interpretation in the collection and presentation of data.

Although the origins of qualitative research lie primarily in the social sciences, readers may already have remarked that this research design bears many similarities to the interpretive-historical method (see Chapter 6). Indeed, both strategies seek to describe or explain socio/physical phenomena within complex contexts, and both

---

Holistic. "The goal of qualitative research is to "gain a 'holistic' (systematic, encompassing, integrated) overview of the context under study." (Miles and Huberman, 1994, p. 6).

Prolonged Contact. "Qualitative research is conducted through an intense and/or prolonged contact with a 'field' or life situation." Hence, the emphasis in many studies on "fieldwork." (Miles and Huberman, 1994, p. 6).

Open Ended. Qualitative research tends to be more open-ended in both theoretical conception and research design than other research strategies (e.g. experimental or correlational) because it typically eschews the notion of a knowable, objective reality (Creswell, 1994, p. 44).

Researcher as Measurement Device. Since there is relatively little use of standardized measures—such as survey questionnaires, the researcher is "essentially the main 'measurement device' in the study." (Miles & Huberman, 1994, p. 7).

Analysis Through Words. Since an emphasis on descriptive numerical measures and inferential statistics is typically eschewed, the principal mode of analysis is through words, whether represented in visual displays or through narrative devices. (Miles and Huberman, 1994, p. 7).

Personal Informal Writing Stance. In contrast to the typical journal format of experimental or correlational studies, the writing style of qualitative work is typically offered in a "personal informal writing stance that lessens the distance between the writer and the reader." (Creswell, 1994, p. 43).

Figure 7.5 A summary of additional attributes of the qualitative research design. From J. Creswell, *Research Design: Qualitative & Quantitative Approaches* (Sage Publications, 1994); and Miles & Huberman, *Qualitative Data Analysis* (Sage Publications, 1994). Reprinted by permission of Sage Publications. © 1994 by Matthew B. Miles and A. Michael Huberman.

seek to consider the relevant phenomena in a holistic manner. Denzin and Lincoln's major collection of essays on qualitative research strategies includes a chapter by Gaye Tuchman titled "Historical Social Science,"[16] which argues that traditional distinctions between history and sociology have been largely abandoned. Tuchman concludes: "What remains in both fields is recognition that research is an interpretive enterprise."[17]

There are, however, major differences between the qualitative research design and the interpretive-historical strategy as defined here. The most obvious is temporal: whereas qualitative studies tend to focus on contemporary phenomena, interpretive-historical research has an historical focus. Data sources and collection techniques are likely to differ accordingly. Whereas qualitative researchers are more likely to be concerned with data collection involving people; historians typically rely on documents and other material artifacts.

Despite these differences, qualitative and interpretive-historical research remain closely related, demonstrating how permeable the boundaries of research strategies are. These two strategies are often combined, in fact, so that aspects of one can augment the characteristics of the other. For example, historical research may advantageously incorporate a focus on the social impact of particular buildings, styles, or city forms. Likewise, studies of contemporary environments may profit from analyses of historical archives and physical artifacts. This potential of combined strategies will be taken up in greater detail later in this book (see Chapter 12).

7.3   STRATEGY: THREE QUALITATIVE APPROACHES

In this section, we address three approaches to qualitative research: grounded theory, ethnography, and interpretivism. The last of these three should not be confused with the interpretive-historical strategy described in Chapter 6. Interpretivism is an approach that is strongly framed by the phenomenological perspective, whereas interpretive-historical research can accommodate many epistemological perspectives.

In each of the following sections we summarize the basic characteristics of each approach, including its strengths and weaknesses. We then present examples to show how the approach can be used in architectural inquiry.

7.3.1 Grounded Theory

In grounded theory, the researcher seeks to enter a setting without preset opinions or notions, lets the goings-on of the setting determine the data, and then lets a theory emerge from that data. Once the theory is proposed, other similar settings can be studied to see if the emergent theory has explanatory power.

The term *grounded theory* is associated especially with the work of sociologists Barney Glaser and Anselm Strauss and their research colleagues.[18] Strauss has described this approach to qualitative data analysis as "the development of theory, without any particular commitment to specific kinds of data, lines of research, or theoretical interests."[19] More recently, Strauss and Corbin offered this definition:

> In this method, data collection, analysis, and eventual theory stand in close relationship to one another. A researcher does not begin a project with a preconceived theory in mind (unless his or her purpose is to elaborate and extend existing theory). Rather, the researcher begins with an area of study and allows the theory to emerge from the data. . . . Grounded theories, because they are drawn from data, are likely to offer insight, enhance understanding, and provide a meaningful guide to action.[20]

An important, distinguishing feature of grounded theory is its use of an intensive, open-ended, and iterative process that simultaneously involves data collection, coding (data analysis), and "memoing" (theory building). Strauss's diagram, shown in Figure 7.6, suggests all combinations of movement across these three tasks.[21] Strauss draws a distinction between grounded theory research and other qualitative research: "This reexamination of all data throughout the life of the research project is a procedure probably engaged in by most qualitative researchers. But they do not usually double back-and-forth between collecting data, coding them, memoing."[22] In other words, in grounded theory research, it is assumed that the object of study

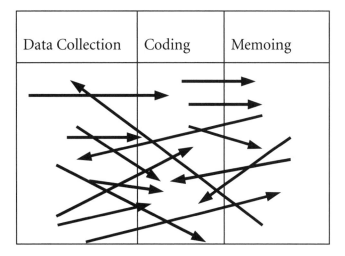

Figure 7.6   Phases of research coding. A. Strauss, *Qualitative Analysis for Social Scientists*, (Cambridge University Press, 1987). Reprinted with the permission of Cambridge University Press.

cannot be fully explained "on the first take." Instead, observation, data collection, and data structuring must take place in an iterative process before a theory can emerge.

The practice of "memoing" is a second distinguishing element of grounded theory. As Strauss describes it,

> Theoretical ideas are kept track of, and continuously linked and built up by means of *theoretical memos* [author's emphasis]. From time to time they are taken out of the file and examined and sorted, which results in new ideas, thus new memos. . . . *Sorting* [author's emphasis] of memos (and codes) may occur at any phase of the research. Both examination and sorting produces memos of greater scope and conceptual density.[23]

Although a number of authors have characterized grounded research as an exclusively inductive process, Strauss says this is a misconception. All scientific theories, says Strauss, "require first of all that they be conceived, then elaborated, then checked out."[24] Grounded theory research, he argues, requires both deduction (elaboration) and verification (checking out), equally as much induction (theory conception).

Groat and Ahrentzen's study of women faculty followed the grounded theory model, albeit somewhat informally. Groat and Ahrentzen began their inquiry without a particular theory in mind; they used the memoing technique throughout the sequence of 40 interviews; and they only developed the comparative analysis with the Carnegie study recommendations after they had completed the interview coding and memoing process. (See Figure 7.7.)

7.3.2 Ethnography

Although it also emphasizes in-depth engagement with its subject, ethnographic research differs from grounded theory in that the researcher's aim is not to create an explanatory theory that can be applied to many settings. Rather, ethnographic research culminates in a rich and full delineation of a particular setting that persuades a wide audience of its human validity.

Although ethnographic fieldwork was initially associated with anthropology, it has been adopted by a number of other disciplines, including sociology, human geography, organization studies, educational research, and cultural studies.[25] True to its anthropological roots, ethnography lays particular emphasis on the immersion of the researcher in a particular cultural context and on the attempt to ascertain how those living in that context interpret their situation. Although early ethnographic research reflected Western interest in non-Western societies, much ethnographic work in the twentieth century sought to investigate various sub-cultures within the West.

The overall characteristics of ethnographic work are fully consistent with the definition of qualitative research presented in this chapter. They include the holistic exploration of a setting using context-rich detail; a reliance on unstructured (i.e. not

PERCEPTION THAT ARCHITECTURAL EDUCATION REFLECTS A NAR-ROWING OF THE MIND. A number of women discuss the narrow focus, perspective, or intellectual inquiry in architectural education. Could these complaints stem from women whose educational background (or part of) was outside standard architectural education, hence they were exposed to other fields (e.g. Urban Studies, Music) that were more multidisciplinary and inclusive? I also wonder if this complaint may be a particular issue for those women whose own education/training was more "transformational," as discussed in the Aisenberg/ Harrington book and also discussed in Belenky et al's *Women's Ways of Knowing.*

SA to LG 10/14/92

ATTRACTIONS, REALITIES, AND MYTHS OF ARCHITECTURE. The meaning for architecture for women. This is a version of the hypothesis I outlined earlier: whether women architecture students tend to be motivated by more idealistic, socially-oriented goals than their male counterparts. If this is the case, the actual realities of architectural education and practice might lead to higher frustration and disappointment, and ultimately to more attrition. Within the context of this study, this hypothesis cannot actually be tested, but it is possible at least to determine the extent to which our sample actually holds idealistically, socially-oriented goals for architecture; the extreme frustration and attrition phenomena can not be measured without an extensive sample of deflected women.

In Sherry's discussion of the "narrowing of the field" concern expressed by many women, she speculated that this complaint might be more common among "women whose own education was more transformational." I think this is a good line to follow up. I suspect it may be true and also related to the tendency for women to come to architecture when they are older, i.e. after a broader range of life experiences.

LG to SA 11/2/92

Figure 7.7   A memoing sequence. Groat and Ahrentzen, 1997. Courtesy of Linda Groat and Sherry Ahrentzen.

precoded) data; a focus on a single case or small number of cases; and data analysis that emphasizes "the meanings and functions of human action."[26]

Perhaps the most distinctive aspect of ethnographic fieldwork is its reliance on "participant observation" as the primary mode of data collection. Although this term is frequently used to refer to a situation in which the researcher plays a naturally occurring, established role in the situation under study, the researcher may abide by this model to varying degrees. For instance, the researcher's identity outside the setting might be known by few or many; or revealed in more or less detail. The researcher may play his/her apparent role to a greater or lesser degree; or s/he may take the stance of either an insider or an outsider. Thus, participant observation allows for enormous variation in how the researcher observes and participates in the phenomena being studied.

Cuff's study of architectural practice serves as a good example of the ethnographic approach. Not only does Cuff use participant observation, she describes her research as following these ethnographic principles:

> [M]ost current ethnographic studies look at patterns of interpretation that members of a cultural group invoke as they go about their daily lives. Into the general knot of making sense of the world, an ethnography ties ideas about the group's knowledge, its beliefs, its social organization, how it reproduces itself, and the material world in which it exists.[27]

A recent doctoral dissertation in architecture offers another example of ethnographic research. In response to the intense modernization of her native Bangkok, Piyalada Devakula sought to identify the experiential qualities and meanings of the traditional Thai house, in both its original context and the present-day.[28]

With this goal in mind, Devakula chose four case study houses representing four distinct housing types: 1) a fully featured traditional house in its original form; 2) a lived-in and modernized traditional house; 3) a Western-style urban villa; and 4) a contemporary house designed to "capture" the traditional spirit. (See Figures 7.8. and 7.9.) Each case was studied using ethnographic field techniques such as participant observation and unstructured interviews. Devakula's identity as a researcher was known by the residents of the houses she observed. Although for the most part she simply observed the house's physical features and the activities of the family members within it, she also at times became involved in family and community activities. As an architect-researcher, Devakula was more concerned with the qualities of the physical environment and the way people living there experienced it than with other anthropological issues, such as family relations. Her description of her field work is informative:

> At each of the houses, I moved through the various little places in and around the houses, sat down once in a while, climbed up and down, looked at all the "things" that filled these houses. I also wrote field notes, did some sketches and took photographs. Many times, I "talked" to the people in the house, asked them about the house, or simply chatted away. Sometimes, I went to community events, and sometimes I simply played with the kids. Each time at the houses, something new and unexpected always came up. As the non-structured "interviews" and conver-

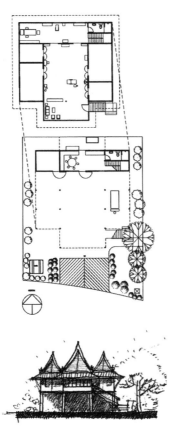

Figure 7.8 Ban Song Kanong, the modernized traditional house studied by Devakula, 1999. Drawing courtesy of Piyalada Devakula.

sations revealed much more than I could have expected, the open modes of data gathering allowed me to fully explore these fascinating worlds filled with colorful casts of characters and welcome the unexpected as a fruitful part of the experiences.[29]

Devakula derives a set of five experiential patterns in traditional Thai houses. These are discussed in considerable detail in relation to each of the four cases. It is only in her concluding chapter that Devakula introduces several relevant theoretical models that illuminate her empirically derived patterns. In this regard, Devakula's research reflects a primarily inductive stance that is characteristic of much, perhaps the vast majority, of qualitative research.

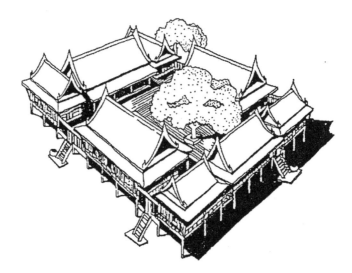

Figure 7.9 Tub Kwan, the traditional royal house studied by Devakula, 1999. Drawing courtesy of Piyalada Devakula.

7.3.3 Interpretivism

Interpretivism derives from the phenomenological tradition of the philosophers Edmund Husserl and Martin Heidegger and the work of scholars who have tried to adapt this tradition to the social sciences. A defining quality of this work, as described by Thomas Schwandt, is the shared "goal of understanding the complex world of lived experience from the point of view of those who live it."[30] True to the principles of the phenomenological tradition, proponents of this model of research "celebrate the permanence and priority of the real world of first-person, subjective experience."[31] Nevertheless, their approach is perpetually seeking to resolve the proverbial Cartesian split between subject and object, mind and matter. Or as Schwandt puts it: The interpretivist researcher must struggle with "[t]he paradox of how to develop an objective interpretive science of subjective human experience."

One well-known proponent of this strain of qualitative research is the anthropologist Clifford Geertz, author of the now-famous mandate that the researcher provide a "thick description" of the context under study.[32] Consider the wink of an eye. A "thick" (i.e. rich and full) description is one that describes not only the wink, but also what that wink can mean within the semantic systems of the culture in which it happens (the wink can mean something romantic, some kind of signal for action, or simply a muscle tic). More important, at a broader epistemological level, Geertz operates from the assumption that social facts are not "out there" as an objective reality. Rather, as Schwandt puts it, "the inquirer constructs a reading of the meaning making process of the people he or she studies.[33]

Figure 7.10   Attic window. Drawing by David Wang.

In blurring the distinction between science and literature, Geertz's stance is not unlike that of the historian Hayden White, who speaks of historical narrative as the process of "emplotment." (See Chapter 6 for a more complete discuss of White's perspective.) There is thus a powerful similarity between the interpretivist approach to qualitative research and the "literary" view of interpretive-historical research.

Cuff's study of architectural practice exhibits qualities of the interpretivist approach to research. For example, she insists on the value of interpretation both on the part of the respondents and on the part of the researcher. Moreover, Cuff also refers to Geertz's work, ethnomethodology (distinct from ethnography), and phenomenology—all orientations that are associated with interpretivism.

BOX 7.1

Qualitative Research: An Interpretivist Approach to Research Design

Clare Cooper Marcus's study of people's attachments to their homes, *House as Mirror of Self*, is a good example of what one might call applied phenomenology.* This book builds on work that she began many years ago with the publication of a now classic article entitled "The House as a Symbol of the Self."** Her approach to this material is particularly attractive in that she finds ways to access the phenomenological unity between a subject and her home—and can write about it—without using much of the jargon typically found in phenomenological writings. The following citation from the introduction to her book is useful in unveiling the phenomenological moorings of her methodology:

> So far as I was able, I attempted to approach this material via what philosopher Martin Heidegger called "prelogical thought." This is not "illogical" or "irrational," but rather a mode of approaching being-in-the-world that permeated early Greek thinkers at a time before the categorization of our world into mind and matter, cause and effect, in-here and out-there had gripped . . . the Western mind. I firmly believe that a deeper level of person/environment interaction can be approached only by means of a thought process that attempts to eliminate observer and object.†

Marcus was dissatisfied early in her research because her work had dealt primarily with house, but not home. It was not until a friend of hers "talked to the desert" that she discovered a way by which the precognitive realities of the "house-self dynamic" could be unearthed. She then developed tactics that involved asking a subject to talk to her house, and then to have the house "talk" back to her, supplemented by her respondents' attempts to capture the feelings in graphic form.

When Cooper Marcus turned to graphic exercises, as well as "talking to," rather than "talking about," environments of attachment, a phenomenological world opened up. For example, one individual, Bill, chafed at her suggestion that his love for remodeling was a "hobby." Bill's response: "The word hobby is an annoying word to me . . . this is not a hobby . . . this is a fundamental part of our existence."†† His insistence that the work of his hands is a "fundamental part of our existence" is profound in its conveyance of a sense of ontological unity between himself and his environment. In studies of a phenomenological nature, such use of words may also be data.

Figure 7.11 The sketch from someone who did not feel at home in his house. Excerpt from *House as a Mirror of Self* by Clare Cooper Marcus, copyright © 1995 by Clare Cooper Marcus, by permission of Conari Press.

Figure 7.12 A sketch of the house shared with a partner. Excerpt from *House as a Mirror of Self* by Clare Cooper Marcus, copyright © 1995 by Clare Cooper Marcus, by permission of Conari Press.

Figure 7.13 A sketch of a disliked suburban apartment and the route to visit friends in the city. Excerpt from *House as a Mirror of Self* by Clare Cooper Marcus, copyright © 1995 by Clare Cooper Marcus, by permission of Conari Press.

---

*Clare Cooper Marcus, *House as a Mirror of Self* (Berkeley, Calif.: Conari Press, 1995).

**Clare Cooper Marcus, "House as a Symbol of Self," in *Designing for Human Behavior: Architecture and the Behavioral Sciences*, ed. J. Land (Stroudsburg, Penn.: Dowden, Hutchinson & Ross, 1974).

†Clare Cooper Marcus, *House as a Mirror of Self*, 13.

††Ibid., 61.

BOX 7.2

Qualitative Research: An Interpretivist Approach to Studio

Accmmccording to architect Botund Bognar, a phenomenological approach in the studio can reverse the tendency of "rational" design, an attitude that reduces architecture "to measurable effects and results . . . which seriously limits architecture's primary grounding in human experience."* Bognar guided his students through several projects that entailed the following:

1. Recalling a place from memory and writing on how "sense of place" was achieved in that instance.
2. After being provided with a map of an actual locale, "picturing" the place's character, and then designing an appropriate intervention for it.
3. Getting to know a designated urban locale by walking in it, eating in it, riding a bus through it; and then mapping the boundaries, centers, zones, etc., of the location in a way that interprets its "character."
4. Identifying physical venues that felt "out of tune" and designing interventions to increase their sense of place.

These exercises emphasize direct experience between student and context and attempt to sidestep the reductivist tendency to design according to predetermined abstract concepts. They seek to recover the primordial unity between the experiencing subject and the context experienced, and make that unity a the source of design activity.

Figure 7.14 Students in a design studio. Here students are putting on paper design ideas for an urban park, having returned from a site visit. Photograph courtesy of Washington State University Spokane.

---

*Botund Bognar, "A Phenomenological Approach to Architecture and Its Teaching in the Design Studio," in David Seamon and Robert Mugurauer, eds. *Dwelling, Place, and Environment: Towards a Phenomenology of Person and World* (Malabar, Florida: Krieger Publishing Company, 2000), 185.

In the realm of architectural phenomenology, Gaston Bachelard's book *The Poetics of Space* is a classic work.[34] Bachelard uses vignettes from literature and poetry to weave an interpretive analysis of the significance of dwellings. In analyzing Bachelard's foundational work, Perla Kerosec-Serfaty observes that Bachelard "wants to show that the house is one of the strongest powers of integration for the thoughts, the memories and the dreams of men [sic],"[35] She then takes Gaston Bachelard's claim that the dwelling experience is a "total one" as a starting point for her own research study and conducts semidirected interviews of 96 homeowners on their feelings about their cellars and attics. From the results of these interviews she is able to identify eight qualitative categories that, in effect, parse Bachelard's original hypothesis of the total nature of the dwelling into an accessible conceptual framework. These categories are: appropriation, affluence and security, secrecy, keeping/throwing away, value, order and cleanliness, and continuity of generations.[36]

7.4 TACTICS: AN OVERVIEW OF DATA COLLECTION, ANALYSIS, AND INTERPRETATION

The exemplar studies described in the above discussions of grounded theory, ethnographic research, and interpretivism represent the diverse range of processes and tactics typical of qualitative research.

7.4.1 The Process

In their classic book *Qualitative Data Analysis*, Miles and Huberman describe the interactive relationship between data collection, data reduction, data display, and conclusion drawing/verifying this way:

> In this view the three types of analysis activity and the activity of data collection itself form an interactive, cyclical process. The researcher moves among these four "nodes" during data collection and then shuttles among reduction, display, and conclusion drawing/verifying for the remainder of the study.[37]

Strauss has described the interactive process entailed in the grounded theory approach. Figure 7.6 represents the back-and-forth cycles between data collection, coding and memoing.

7.4.2 Data Collection

Three of the exemplar studies discussed so far represent a diverse range of data collection processes. The Groat and Ahrentzen study of faculty women in architecture made use of in-depth interviews lasting up to three hours.[38] The Devakula study of

Thai houses involved several months of participant observation at four case study houses.[39] And Cooper Marcus's study of people's phenomenological experiences of their houses involved in-depth interviews in which people role-played a conversation with their home, as well as graphic sketches whereby the respondents sought to express their deeply held feelings. These data collection tactics and others are outlined in Figure 7.15.

Tactics	Interactive	Noninteractive
Interviews	In-depth interviews Key informants interviews Career histories	
Focus groups	Discussions guided to test in small groups Participants help construct the right questions	
Surveys	Multiple sorting Projective surveys (games)	
Observation	Participant observation	Nonparticipant observation stream of behavior Chronicles Field notes
Artifacts and buildings		Artifactual interpretation
Archival documents		Archival interpretation

Figure 7.15   The variety of data sources for qualitative research.

7.4.3 Data Reduction/Coding

Because qualitative research typically results in a vast amount of data (e.g., long interview transcripts, many pages of observation notes, graphic sketches or photographs), a major task in data analysis is to reduce the volume of data into manageable "chunks." Although there is no one way to begin, a common device is to code the "chunks" into various themes, often by making notes in the margins of transcripts or documents. In order to retain mindfulness in coding, it is often necessary to make use of a coding scheme that is clearly documented in some way, both for your ongoing use and for your records. Figure 7.16 reproduces a segment of interview transcript coding in Groat and Ahrentzen's study. As Miles and Huberman put it: "[I]f you are being alert about what you are doing, ideas and reactions to the meaning of what you are seeing will well up steadily."[40]

Figure 7.16 Coding of interview transcripts. Groat and Ahrentzen, 1997. Courtesy of Linda Groat and Sherry Ahrentzen.

7.4.4 Data Display

Most qualitative research studies make use of data displays, whether in the form of charts, graphs, or tables. Depending on the eventual publication format and readership, there is considerable variation in how extensively the study's analytical processes are represented by such data displays. Journal articles are likely to provide fewer, while books, dissertations, and professional reports and reports are likely to provide more, although many displays are likely to appear in appendixes. Figure 7.17 represents what Miles and Huberman label a "checklist matrix" which Devakula produced as she moved from raw fieldnotes to drawing her conclusions. Here Devakula is beginning to compare features of interest across all four of the houses in her study.

7.4.5 Drawing Conclusions and Verifying

Once the data has been coded, reduced, and displayed, the researcher gradually moves toward identifying patterns, providing explanations, and evaluating the findings. This is no small task, and a full discussion of the tactics involved is beyond the scope of this

	Tub Kwan	Songkanong	Chaipranin	101/1
• THE DWELLING The dwelling experience: what is it like to "live" in this house? See the roofs? Living off the ground or on the ground?	-n/a.	-the family spends most of the time home 'outside' the house.. either in the TaiToon, or out and around in the neighborhood.. walking around talking to friends and relatives. -no strong feeling of "living in a traditional Thai house".. "it's just another ordinary house," the daughter said. -the house was so transformed and the roofs joined together.. they don't see their eaves that much.	-the "living-on-the-second-floor" excitement (K.Nin).. light and airy, with nice panoramic view.. they just love it. -see each other a lot.. as every room looks down/out into the central Chaan.. also a sense of control and security. -see the roofs everyday.. -so in touch w/ the wind and the rain.. they hear the rain.. and they could sit down and watch it falling down the eaves... so close within their reach.	-very much living 'inside' the house.. which is very solid and ground bound. -little contact w/ the outside.. and it's hot to be upstairs in the afternoon; the floors however, especially that of the lower level, are nice and cool though. -there's hardly a chance to see the roof unless you really try looking up for it...too far out of reach. -it's hard to find a cozy spot to sit down and read a book, or relax, or even watch TV.. no back bone!
View: Food for the eyes - relationship w/ living spaces	-living spaces look out into the Chaan.. with the old Chand tree -looking from a protected shaded space into a bright open area. -not much scenery of the surroundings.. just the Chaan, tree tops, and the sky.	-the upstairs living space doesn't really have a view; yet the TaiToon and the Sala have strong visual connection with the alley.. and hence the people walking by. -from the TaiToon sitting area.. one also looks out to the various trees and flowers in the little front lawn.	-the living space here has an enormous void that connects it w/ the Chaan; the furniture in it was arranged to enhance that view. -the very urban surroundings (lots of high rise condos, etc.) were screened out by all the big trees and greenery in and by the Chaan.. the house is its own little world.	-the living space here is rather dark.. and cut off from the outside (all the windows and curtains closed!!). -the windows were rather high off the floor, where the family spends their time. -the formal guest receiving area is in a higher level.. and hence, with slightly better views.. yet never in use. -the best look-out spot = day bed.
Light: How? Any hierarchy?	-very hierarchical—the very bright Chaan, the shaded Rabiang, and the dark inner room. -special, wonderful dance of light filtered through the layers of green leaves of the old Chand tree.	-not very hierarchical.. the added roof over the central hall made the whole interior space rather dim.. despite a few spots of skylights. -uniform fluorescent lamps all over.	-there's an effect of being in a shade looking out to the bright Chaan.. but no true hierarchy. -the TaiToon is rather dark.. although the lighting effect at the tree well.. a mysterious and austere kind of effect .. is rather captivating. -the use of warm spot lights (and candles in the Chaan) helps generating a cozy feeling.	-dark interior and bright exterior.. but no strong connection—one is well-contained both when in the dim space (w/ perhaps the help of a uniform fluorescent light), and when out in the glaring sun. -the flat, uniform fluorescents at night don't help making the flat.. overflowing space any better.

Figure 7.17 Data display: checklist matrix. Devakula, 1999. Courtesy of Piyalada Devakula.

chapter. Figures 7.18 and 7.19 summarize the major considerations presented by Miles and Huberman in their chapter on the topic.[41] They remind us that "we keep the world consistent and predictable by organizing it and interpreting it. The critical question is whether the meanings you find in qualitative data are valid, repeatable, and right."[42]

7.4.6 Tactics in Exemplar Studies

Earlier in this chapter we described Ahrentzen's study of home offices as an excellent example of the multitactic approach typical of qualitative research.[43] Here we will explore the study in greater depth. The data sources that Ahrentzen employed included a self-administered questionnaire, face-to-face interviews, a modified time diary, photographs, sketches, and a physical inventory of the home and workplace. Among these, the self-administered questionnaire, in which respondents used rating scales, is more often associated with correlational design (see Chapter 8). The combination of photographs, sketches, and physical inventory provided a holistic picture of each homeworker's physical setting; the time diary yielded a robust picture of the worker's daily routines and activities; and the face-to-face interview of more than an hour's

Descriptive	Noting patterns, themes
	Seeing plausibility
	Clustering
	Making metaphors
	Counting
Analytical	Making contrasts/comparisons
	Partitioning variables
	Subsuming particulars into the general
	Factoring
	Noting relations between variables
	Finding interviewing variables
Explanatory	Building a logical chain of evidence
	Making conceptual/theoretical coherence

Figure 7.18   Tactics for generating meaning. From Miles & Huberman, *Qualitative Data Analysis* (Sage Publications, 1994), pp. 245–246. Reprinted by permission of Sage Publications. © 1994 by Matthew B. Miles and A. Michael Huberman.

Data quality	Checking for representativeness
	Checking for researcher effects
	Triangulation
	Weighting the evidence
Looking at unpatterns	Checking the meanings of outliers
	Using extreme cases
	Following up surprises
	Looking for negative evidence
Testing explanations	Making if-then tests
	Ruling out spurious relations
	Replicating a finding
	Checking out rival explanations
Testing with feedback	Getting feedback from informants

Figure 7.19 Tactics for testing or confirming findings. From Miles & Huberman, *Qualitative Data Analysis* (Sage Publications, 1994), p. 263. Reprinted by permission of Sage Publications. © 1994 by Matthew B. Miles and A. Michael Huberman.

length enabled Ahrentzen both to understand how each worker made sense of his/her experience and to verify or go into greater depth on issues that emerged from the other data sources.

One particularly useful line of inquiry involved a question posed to the respondents during the interview. If they could design an ideal home workspace from scratch, what would it be like? What would the layout be like? What rooms would be close by and what rooms distant? Another set of questions explored whether the meaning of home had changed for them as a result of telecommuting. Ahrentzen summarizes the responses this way: "Although for some home remained a positive refuge, for others that refuge quality was transformed into potential isolation and entrapment."[44]

The array of tactics found in this study certainly make it fit with what Denzin and Lincoln call a multimethod approach; the study also conforms to the other three components of Denzin and Lincoln's definition of qualitative research.[45] Ahrentzen's study has: 1) taken a naturalistic approach to the subject of the home office; 2) studied the experience of telecommuting in situ; and 3) attempted to understand the dynamics of an experience in terms of the meanings people bring to it.

BOX 7.3

Qualitative Research: Tactics for Practice

Among the best-known architects who have used qualitative research tactics to actively engage their clients are Charles Moore and Christopher Alexander. Moore's design process for St. Matthews Church is discussed in Chapter 5. Alexander's approach to design involves a robust combination of client participation, indigenous construction methods and materials, and primordial "patterns" that, he claims, usher positive emotion into built form. Although Alexander may not practice participant observation or conduct client interviews the way a scholar would, his design process engages people in informal versions of these qualitative methods.

Consider the Julian Street Inn in San Jose, California, a center that offers shelter for the homeless. As is typical of his approach, Alexander used collaborative tactics in the design and construction of this center. According to a documentary film on Alexander's work, his projects often do not employ a conventional "design-bid-build" process; rather, sketches derived from owner, builder and designer inputs are integrated into the process as construction moves along. Shown here is the dining room of the Julian Street Inn; the trusses were sketched after construction began. The current director states that this space energizes the life of the center.

Figure 7.20   Dining room in the Julian Street Inn, by Christopher Alexander. Drawing by Dave Wang.

Places for the Soul: The Architecture of Christopher Alexander (Videotape, 29 minutes). Berkeley, Calif.: University of California Extension Center for Media and Independent Learning, #37991 (609-642-0460).

Collaborative community design is another area of practice that involves people making sense of their own surroundings. It often displays resonant connections to the principles of qualitative research discussed in this chapter. Of course there are many varieties of collaborative design; we have in mind here the kind that involves the local citizenry in the making of architecture. Typically, designers enter into these projects with more of an open attitude; the very desire to have community input necessitates letting go of preset biases about what the final design form ought to be. One such example is the New Kensington Garden Center, realized through the efforts of a volunteer Philadelphia design organization called the Community Design Collaborative. The center's program director, Susan Frankel, wrote this about the project:

> The Center is located in the New Kensington neighborhood of eastern North Philadelphia along the Delaware River. . . . Landscape architect and Collaborative volunteer Michael LoFurno worked . . . with the New Kensington CDC, neighborhood residents, and Philadelphia Green. Michael took the group's ideas and turned them into a conceptual design for the garden center, which a cadre of

Figure 7.21   Presentation panel from the New Kensington Garden Center project. Courtesy of Community Design Collaborative of AIA Philadelphia.

Americorp volunteers would later build over an intense six-week period. . . . In a very short time the large, debris-strewn lot, no different from thousands dotting Philadelphia's landscape, was transformed into a local source for soil, compost, wood chips, and other basic gardening materials in large part thanks to volunteer efforts.[46]

7.5   CONCLUSION: STRENGTHS AND WEAKNESSES

The major strengths of qualitative research follow from its capacity to take in the rich qualities of real-life circumstances and settings. It is also flexible in its design and procedures, allowing for adjustments to be made as the research proceeds. As such it is especially appropriate for understanding the meanings and processes of people's activities and artifacts.

On the other hand, these very significant advantages come with some costs. Researchers wishing to employ a qualitative research design will find relatively few "road maps" or step-by-step guidelines in the literature; the researcher is thus obliged to exercise extra care and thoughtfulness throughout the research study. Another major challenge concerns the vast amount of unstructured data that must be coded and analyzed, a task that is enormously time consuming. It is no exaggeration to say that many researchers spend years working through the many facets of their qualitative data. Also, for researchers working in fields where a more rationalistic paradigm holds sway, the "trustworthiness" of qualitative data may remain suspect, despite the efforts of qualitative methodologists to show that such research can be systematic.

In the end, however, in fields such as architecture, the peer review processes of scholarly journals and conference groups tend to give credence to qualitative research, suggesting that it will remain an important model for some time to come.

Strengths	Weaknesses
Capacity to take in rich and holistic qualities of real life circumstances	Challenge of dealing with vast quantities of data
Flexibility in design and procedures allowing adjustments in process	Few guidelines or step-by-step procedures established
Sensitivity to meanings and processes of artifacts and people's activities	The credibility of qualitative data can be seen as suspect with the postpositivist paradigm

Figure 7.22   Strengths and weaknesses of qualitative research.

7.6   RECOMMENDED READING

Readers seeking introductory and readable texts on qualitative research may want to read one or both of the following: The chapter "Qualitative Methods" in Donna Mertens, *Research Methods in Education and Psychology* (Thousand Oaks, Calif.: Sage Publications, 1998), 158–190; The chapter "A Qualitative Procedure" in John Creswell, *Research Design: Qualitative and Quantitative Approaches* (Thousand Oaks, Calif.; Sage Publications, 1994): 145–170.

Readers seeking a more advanced and comprehensive review of qualitative research should consult Norman Denzin and Yvonna Lincoln's three-volume handbook, which includes: *The Landscape of Qualitative Research: Theories and Issues; Strategies of Qualitative Inquiry;* and *Collecting and Interpreting Qualitative Materials* (Thousand Oaks, Calif.: Sage Publications, 1998).

For more information on the grounded theory approach, there are several seminal texts: Barney Glaser and Anselm Strauss, *The Discovery of Grounded Theory: Strategies for Qualitative Research* (Chicago: Aldine, 1967); Anselm Strauss, *Qualitative Analysis for Social Scientists* (New York: Cambridge University Press, 1987); and Anselm Strauss and Juliette Corbin, "Grounded Theory Methodology: An Overview," in *Strategies of Qualitative Inquiry*, eds. Norman Denzin and Yvonne Lincoln (Thousand Oaks, Calif.; Sage Publications, 1998): 158–183.

For more information on ethnography, readers may want to consult the following: Paul Atkinson and Martyn Hammersley, "Ethnography and Participant Observation," in *Strategies of Qualitative Inquiry*, ed. Norman Denzin and Yvonna Lincoln (Thousand Oaks, Calif.; Sage Publications, 1998), 110–136; James Clifford and George E. Marcus, *Writing Culture: The Poetics and Politics of Ethnography* (Berkeley, Calif.: University of California Press, 1986).

For more information on the interpretivist approach to qualitative research, readers may consult the following: James Holstein and Jaber F. Gubrium, "Phenomenology, Ethnomethodology, and Interpretive Practice," in *Strategies of Qualitative Inquiry*, ed. Norman Denzin and Yvonna Lincoln (Thousand Oaks, Calif.; Sage Publications, 1998): 137–157; Clifford Geertz, *Local Knowledge: Further Essays in Interpretive Anthropology* (New York: Basic Book, 1983); Alfred Schutz, *The Phenomenology of the Social World* (Evanston, Ill.: Northwestern University Press, 1967).

Readers interested in specific exemplar works may want to consult: Dana Cuff, *Architecture: The Story of Practice* (Cambridge, Mass.: MIT Press, 1991); Clare Cooper Marcus, *House as Mirror of Self* (Berkeley, Calif.; Conari Press, 1995).

NOTES

1. Dana Cuff, *Architecture: The Story of Practice* (Cambridge, Mass.: MIT Press, 1991).
2. Ibid., 7.

3. Ibid., 6.

4. Linda N. Groat and Sherry Ahrentzen, "Voices for Change in Architectural Education: Seven Facets of Transformation from the Perspectives of Faculty Women," *Journal of Architectural Education* 50, no. 4 (1997): 271–285.

5. Ibid., 273.

6. Ernest Boyer and Lee Mitgang, *Building Community: A New Future for Architecture Education and Practice* (Princeton, N.J.: Carnegie Foundation for the Advancement of Teaching, 1996).

7. Groat and Ahrentzen, "Voices for Change," 273.

8. Norman Denzin and Yvonna Lincoln, *Strategies for Qualitative Inquiry* (Thousand Oaks, Calif.: Sage Publications, 1998), 3.

9. Benyamin Schwarz, "Nursing Home Design: A Misguided Architectural Model," *Journal of Architectural and Planing Research* 14, no. 4 (1997): 343–359.

10. Ibid., 349.

11. Ibid., 350.

12. Ibid., 349.

13. Ibid., 351.

14. Denzin and Lincoln, *Strategies for Qualitative Inquiry*, 3.

15. Sherry Ahrentzen, "A Place of Peace, Prospect, and a P.C.: The Home as Office," *Journal of Architectural and Planning Research* 7, no. 4 (1989): 271–288.

16. Gaye Tuchman, "Historical Social Sciences: Methodologies, Methods, and Meanings," in *Strategies of Qualitative Inquiry*, ed. N. Denzin and Y. Lincoln (Thousand Oaks, Calif.: Sage Publications, 1998), 225–260.

17. Ibid., 249.

18. Barney Glaser and Anselm Strauss, *The Discovery of Grounded Theory: Strategies for Qualitative Research* (Chicago: Aldine, 1967); Barney Glaser and Anselm Strauss, *Time for Dying* (Chicago: Aldine, 1968).

19. Anselm Strauss, *Qualitative Analysis for Social Scientists* (New York: Cambridge University Press, 1987).

20. Anselm Strauss and Juliette Corbin, *Strategies of Qualitative Inquiry* (1998): 12.

21. Anselm Strauss, *Qualitative Analysis for Social Scientists*, 19.

22. Ibid., 19.

23. Ibid., 18.

24. Ibid., 11.

25. Paul Atkinson and Martyn Hammersley, "Ethnography and Participant Observation," in *Strategies of Qualitative Inquiry*, ed. N. Denzin and Y. Lincoln (Thousand Oaks, Calif.: Sage Publications, 1998), 110–136.

26. Ibid., 111.

27. Cuff, 5.

28. Piyalada Devakula, "Experiential Characteristics and Meanings of the Traditional Thai House" (Ph.D. diss., University of Michigan, 1999).

29. Ibid., 43.

30. Thomas Schwandt, *Qualitative Inquiry: A Dictionary of Terms* (Thousand Oaks, Calif.: Sage Publications, 1998), 221.

31. Ibid., 223.

32. Clifford Geertz, *The Interpretation of Cultures: Selected Essays* (New York: Basic Books, 1973).

33. Thomas Schwandt, *Qualitative inquiry*, 231.

34. Gaston Bachelard, *The Poetics of Space* (New York: Orion Press, 1964).

35. Perla Korosec-Serfaty, "The Home from Attic to Cellar," *Journal of Environmental Psychology*, 4, no. 4 (1984): 305.

36. Ibid., 309–311

37. Matthew B. Miles and A. Michael Huberman, *Qualitative Data Analysis*, 2nd edition (Thousand Oaks, Calif.: Sage Publications, 1994), 12.

38. Groat and Ahrentzen, "Voices for Change."

39. Devakula, The Traditional Thai House.

40. Miles and Huberman, *Qualitative Data Analysis*, 67.

41. Ibid.

42. Ibid., 245.

43. Ahrentzen, "A Place of Peace."

44. Ibid, 284.

45. Denzin and Lincoln, *Strategies for Qualitative Inquiry*, 3.

46. Frankel, http://www.cdesignc.org/articles.html.

Chapter 8

Correlational Research

8.1 INTRODUCTION

During the 1970s William Whyte's study of urban plazas in New York City became a driving force in the revision of zoning codes for commercial high-rises.[1] When Whyte and his Street Life Project team began their research, New York City's zoning ordinance allowed developers to construct buildings with more floor space if they also provided public plazas. Some of the plazas that resulted were remarkably underutilized, while others seemed to be crowded with workers taking their lunch breaks.

Whyte wanted to understand why and to suggest guidelines for the design of successful plazas. So he and his team conducted a six-month study involving intensive observations of 18 representative plazas, counting the people using the space at specified time intervals with the aid of a video camera. By charting plaza use as a function of certain physical variables, they were able to identify several key design elements. Chief among them was the availability of sitting space. To support his analysis, Whyte presented charts that compared plaza use (number of people at the lunch hour) with the amount of open space available in each of the 18 plazas; there is no obvious relationship. However, a similar chart comparing plaza use with the amount of sittable space demonstrated that these two variables were more closely related.

Although Whyte and his team had completed most of their data collection and analysis within six months, their efforts to change New York City zoning ordinances took another two years. Happily, their proposed guidelines were eventually incorporated into a revised zoning code. New plazas were built to these guidelines, and just as important, many existing plazas were modified to meet the new zoning code.

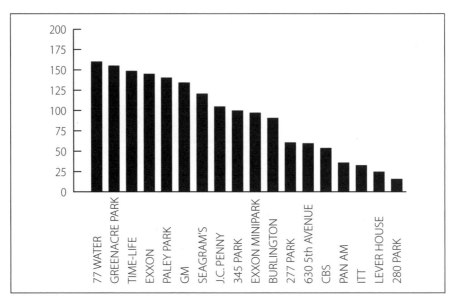

Figure 8.1   Plaza use: average number of people sitting at lunchtime in good weather. Courtesy of Project for Public Spaces, New York, New York.

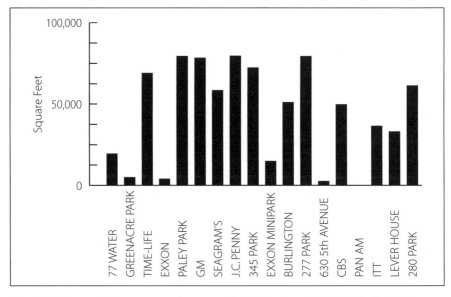

Figure 8.2   Amount of open space by square feet. Courtesy of Project for Public Spaces, New York, New York.

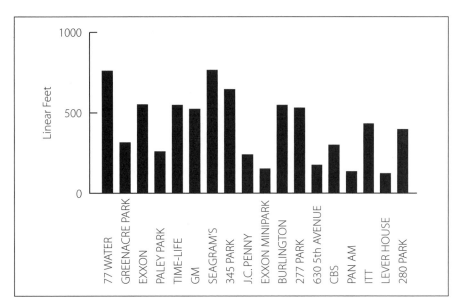

Figure 8.3 Amount of sittable space by linear feet. Courtesy of Project for Public Spaces, New York, New York.

Figure 8.4 Sittable space at 345 Park Avenue. Photo courtesy of Project for Public Spaces, New York, New York.

Much more recently, Joongsub Kim conducted a study of the "new urbanist" model of housing and neighborhood design. This trend, which represents a significant departure from conventional suburban development, has been generating debate within both professional journals and the lay press since the mid-1980s.[2] According to Todd Bressi, an underlying premise of new urbanism is that "community planning and design must assert the importance of public over private values."[3] In other words, it must enhance the sense of community. Among the goals that new urbanists seek to reach through design are social interaction and a greater sense of neighborhood attachment and identity, achieved in part through a more pedestrian-friendly layout.

To assess the extent to which these civic qualities are experienced in a new urbanist community, Kim studied the attitude of residents in Kentlands (a recently developed new urban community in Gaithersburg, Maryland) and in a conventional suburban neighborhood with similar demographic characteristics and located in the same town.[4] (See Figures 8.5 to 8.8.)

The principal tactic he employed was an extensive survey questionnaire that was distributed to every household in the two neighborhoods. In addition to some demographic and overview questions, Kim asked each resident to assess the extent to which specific physical features of the design facilitated their experience of the four key components of community identified in the literature: community attachment, pedestrianism, social interaction, and community identity. Residents were asked to respond on a five-point scale from "not at all" to "very much."

The Kentlands residents consistently rated their neighborhood higher by all four measures of sense of community. Single-family house and townhome residents gave the neighborhood an especially high rating. But even apartment dwellers in Kentlands expressed a slightly greater sense of community than single-family house residents in the conventional suburban group did. Kim thus concludes that new urbanist theory and practice deserves continued development and refinement.

8.2   THE STRATEGY OF CORRELATIONAL RESEARCH: GENERAL CHARACTERISTICS

The strategy used by both Whyte and Kim is that of correlational research. Broadly speaking, each study sought to clarify patterns of relationships between two or more variables, i.e. factors involved in the circumstances under study. Although details of two sub-types of the correlational strategy will be discussed in detail in section 8.3, it is useful first to clarify the overall characteristics of this research design. In the following subsections, we will review the general characteristics of this strategy: a focus on naturally occurring patterns; the measurement of specific variables; and the use of statistics to clarify patterns of relationships.

Figure 8.5   A Kentlands street and park. Photo courtesy of Joongsub Kim.

Figure 8.6   A Kentlands street with no visible edges. Photo courtesy of Joongsub Kim.

Figure 8.7   Orchard Village housing. Photo courtesy of Joongsub Kim.

Figure 8.8   Orchard Village with typical street-access garages. Photo courtesy of Joongsub Kim.

8.2.1 A Focus on Naturally Occurring Patterns

Both Whyte and Kim sought to understand naturally occurring patterns of socio-physical relationships. Whyte sought to understand the behavioral dynamics of plaza use, and in particular to find out what physical features would encourage their use. Similarly, Kim sought to understand the patterns of relationship between the physical attributes of two residential neighborhoods and residents' behavior (pedestrianism, social interaction) and perceived meanings (attachment, identity).

In both cases, the researchers wanted to clarify the relationship among a complex set of real-world variables. By variables we mean the range of characteristics (of physical features, of people, of activities, or of meanings) that vary with the circumstance or setting being studied and are also likely to affect the dynamics of socio-physical interaction. In its focus on real-world circumstances, correlational design is distinct from experimental design, the research strategy that will be discussed in Chapter 9. Whereas correlational design assumes that the researcher simply measures the variables of interest and analyzes the relations among them, experimental design depends on the researcher's active intervention.

8.2.2 The Measurement of Specific Variables

Both the Whyte and Kim studies focus on specific variables of interest that can be measured and quantified in some way. This is a feature that distinguishes correlational design from qualitative design. Although both strategies focus on naturally occurring patterns, qualitative research is more attentive to the holistic qualities of phenomena. (See Chapter 7.) As is typical for a correlational design, the researchers in Whyte's study employed observational tactics whereby the sheer number of people or their specific behaviors could be counted. Whyte's data documented exactly how many people were using a given plaza at particular times throughout the lunch hour. And once he identified "sittable space" as a key physical feature, he and his team could measure such attributes as the total lineal feet of sitting space and its various dimensions.

Other instances of correlational research, however, may focus less on observable behaviors than on people's attitudes, the meanings they ascribe to things, or even their perceptions of others' behavior. Such is the case with Kim's use of the survey questionnaire in the new urbanist and conventional suburban neighborhoods.[5] Kim sought to measure the extent to which the patterns of residents' sense of community might differ between the two neighborhoods.

Although the notion of measurement may seem straightforward, it can involve complex decisions. Researchers using the correlational research design must understand the implications of using different levels of measurement precision. Although we will define the main levels briefly here, readers who seek a more detailed discussion should refer to the list of references at the end of this chapter.

Categorical Measurement. In categorical measurement, the variable of interest is sorted into discrete categories, based on verbal or nominal terms. In Kim's study many of the demographic questions are designed for categorical measurement. For example, one survey question asked residents what mode of transportation they used to get to work; the categories provided for the answers were: walk; car; metrobus; metrotrain; other; and not applicable (for those who worked in the home). Similarly, in Whyte's study, if he had wanted to specify the kind of activities people were engaged in, the researchers' observations might have included the categories: sitting; standing; and walking.

Ordinal Scales. Ordinal measurement provides a greater degree of precision than categorical classification in that the variable in question, can, as the term implies, be *ordered* on some basis. In Kim's survey, for instance, some demographic questions provide a set of ordered categories. This is the case with a question about children's ages; six separate school-age categories from (1) preschool to (6) college are provided. Similarly, in a study of architects and nonarchitects' responses to a variety of building styles, Groat asked respondents to rank 24 building photographs according to their personal preference.[6] In this case, although the results reveal an order of preference, no assumptions about the interval of difference between one building and another can be made. Indeed, it is possible that the top two or three buildings are highly preferred, while the next building in order is much less favored.

Interval and Ratio Scales. A more precise measure still is one that specifies the exact distance (or interval) between one measurement and another. Any system that relies on an established and consistent unit of measurement—whether it is dollars, feet, or degrees of temperature—satisfies the criterion of an interval scale.

On the other hand, the validity of measuring attitudes and feelings on an interval scale is a topic of much discussion and some disagreement.[7] In the case of Kim's questionnaire, we might ask if it is legitimate to assume that respondents using the five-point scale—from very important (5) to not at all (1)—are employing a consistent increment of difference between responses of 4 and 5, for example. If we assume they are not employing a consistent interval of difference, then the attitudinal scale is in fact functioning as an ordinal measurement.

A further level of measurement precision is achieved with a ratio scale, whereby a zero point on the scale can be established. This means that something that measures 20 on a ratio scale is legitimately understood as constituting twice the quantity of 10.

In practical terms, there are few interval scales that are not also ratio scales, but one exception is that of temperature. We can not claim that 72 degrees is twice as hot as 36 degrees. On the other hand, we can assume consistent measuring intervals; the difference between 5 and 10 degrees is the same as the difference between 20 and 25 degrees.[8]

These distinctions among types of measurement frequently come into play in correlational research, because so many different variables—from demographic characteristics, to attitudes and behaviors, to physical properties—must be measured. And because different variables lend themselves to varying levels of measurement precision, great attention must be paid to establishing legitimate data collection instruments and appropriate modes of quantitative analysis.

8.2.3 The Use of Statistics to Clarify Patterns of Relationships

Another characteristic common to both the Whyte and Kim studies is their use of statistical measures to describe the relationships among variables. In his book *The Social Life of Small Urban Spaces*, Whyte relies primarily on graphic charts to represent the use patterns of the plazas he studied. For example, Figure 8.1 shows the average number of people using each of the 18 plazas in good weather; we can see that the most used plaza averages around 8 times more people than the least used. This use of statistics is called *descriptive* statistics because it simply presents, or describes, important relationships among variables.

Kim's study of residential developments employs, in addition to basic descriptive statistics, what are called correlational statistics. These statistical measures are used to "describe the strength and direction of a relationship between two or more variables."[9] For example, Kim presents the calculated correlations among all four of the measures of community, both for Kentlands and for Orchard Village (a pseudonym for the conventional suburban development). (See Figure 8.9) As it turns out, all four measures of community are highly and positively correlated with each other, for each neighborhood development. So, for example, in Kentlands, residents' ratings of the effect of various physical features on their sense of attachment have a similar pattern to their ratings for social interaction, and so on. In other words, in the perception of the residents, the role of the various physical features in achieving a sense of attachment, pedestrianism, social interaction, and sense of identity are quite similar. If the pattern of ratings on any two measures had been quite different, this would have been described as a negative correlation. All calculated correlation coefficients fall within a range of -1.00 (a negative correlation) to $+1.00$ (a positive correlation). A correlation coefficient close to 0 indicates no consistent linear relationship between variables, meaning the relationship cannot be graphed as a straight line.

Relationship among Q1, Q2, Q4 & Q7
(Orchard Village in parentheses)

Four Major Elements (K: based on 17 items only)
Q1: Community attachments
Q2: Pedestrianism
Q4: Social interaction
Q7: Community identity

	Q1 mean	Q2 mean	Q4 mean	Q7 mean
Q1 mean	1.000	.605 (.579)	.481 (.517)	.594 (.654)
Q2 mean	.605 (.579)	1.000	.639 (.662)	.514 (.530)
Q4 mean	.481 (.517)	.639 (.662)	1.000	.419 (.575)
Q7 mean	.594 (.654)	.514 (.530)	.491 (.575)	1.000

Findings:
Kentlands: Correlation is significant at the 0.01 level
Orchard Village: Correlation is significant at the 0.01 level

Figure 8.9 Relationship among questionnaire components. Courtesy of Joongsub Kim.

8.3   STRATEGY: TWO TYPES OF CORRELATIONAL RESEARCH

Within the general framework of correlational research, two major subtypes can be identified: 1) relationship and 2) causal-comparative.[10] Some correlational studies incorporate both of these subtypes. In the paragraphs below, we describe and analyze examples of both relationship and causal-comparative research.

8.3.1 Relationship Studies

Although all correlational studies seek to describe relationships among key variables, relationship studies focus more specifically on the nature and predictive power of such relationships.

One influential research project that sought to clarify relationships and predict outcomes is Oscar Newman's study of public housing in New York City.[11] To arrive at specific design guidelines for such housing, Newman's research team conducted an exhaustive investigation of the complex relationships between user demographics (including income and other socio-economic factors), the physical variables of the housing/site design, and the incidence of crime. Newman's team examined the extensive records of the 169 public housing projects managed by the New York City Housing Authority. As Newman explains, this vast amount of data, combined with the immense variety of building types and site plans, made it possible to "determine exactly where the most dangerous areas of buildings are, as well as to compare crime rates in different building types and project layouts."[12]

As a consequence of this extensive analysis, Newman and his team were able to identify consistent relationships and ultimately to propose a theory of "defensible space." Newman has defined the concept of defensible space as:

> a model for residential environments which inhibits crime by creating the physical expression of a social fabric that defends itself. . . . [It] is a surrogate term for the range of mechanisms—real and symbolic barriers, strongly defined areas of influence, and improved opportunities for surveillance—that combine to bring an environment under the control of its residents.[13]

Not only does this theory of defensible space define a relationship between environmental variables and behavioral consequences (a decrease in crime), but it also offers a predictive capacity that can be articulated as design guidelines, specifically: low-income housing that incorporates "real and symbolic barriers, defined areas of influence, and opportunities for surveillance" is likely to have lower crime rates. (See Figure 8.10.)

Similarly, in the case of Whyte's study, he concludes that higher levels of plaza utilization are associated with the combined presence of several variables, including: sittable space, proximity to street life, sun, water/fountains, trees, and availability of food from street vendors or cafes. Notice that Whyte (like other researchers employing correlational research) stops short of saying that sittable space causes plaza utilization. Indeed, there may well be hidden factors (such the experience of sociability) that explain the correlations Whyte found. Many high correlations—for example, between the number of ice cream cones and deaths by drowning—can be explained by hidden third factors, in this case hot weather.[14]

On the other hand, Whyte's research does enable him to *predict* the association of certain key variables (i.e. sittable space, proximity to street life, etc.) with higher levels of plaza use. The predictive accuracy of Whyte's work was the foundation for the design guidelines that were eventually embedded in new zoning codes and used by many architects and landscape architects.

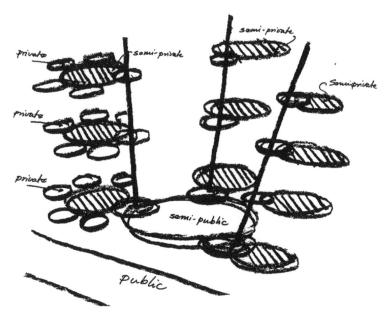

Figure 8.10   Newman's defensible space hierarchy in multilevel dwelling. Courtesy of Oscar Newman.

Likewise, Kim sought to understand and predict the relationship among various measures of community. As the correlations described in section 8.2.3 indicate, the patterns of ratings for each of the four measures of community are predictive of each other. With a similar goal in mind, Kim also asked residents of each neighborhood development two general questions about their sense of community. He first asked respondents to give their rating for: "Living in Kentlands (or Orchard Village) gives me a sense of community." He then sought their rating for: "The physical characteristics of Kentlands (or OV) give me a sense of community." Kim found the answers to these two global questions were highly correlated with the ratings for each of the four component measures of community. In other words, the respondents' overall assessment of sense of community is predictive of their assessment of physical features for each separate component of community, and vice versa.

Finally, Kim assessed the strength of the correlations he found using a test of statistical significance. Such tests—based on what is known as *inferential* statistics—enable a researcher to determine how likely it is that results are a consequence of a chance occurrence. In Kim's case, the correlations were found to be significant at the .01 level, meaning that there is only a 1 in 100 chance that the overall assessment of community is unrelated to the component measures.

8.3.2 Causal-Comparative Studies

Causal-comparative studies stake out an "intermediate" position between the predictive orientation of relationship studies and the focus on causality that characterizes experimental research. In causal-comparative studies, the researcher selects comparable groups of people or comparable physical environments and then collects data on a variety of relevant variables. The purpose of selecting comparable examples is to isolate the factor(s) that could reveal a "cause" for significant differences in the levels of measured variables.

Kim's study of Kentlands and Orchard Village serves as a good example of a causal-comparative study. Although he was certainly interested in studying the relationships among variables (such as the predictive relationship between overall and component measures of sense of community), his primary purpose was to determine the extent to which the differences between the physical characteristics of Kentlands and Orchard Village might contribute to differences in the residents' sense of community. In effect, Kim conceptualized the multiple physical features of each neighborhood as "independent" variables and the residents' perceived sense of community as a "dependent" variable. His research design has much in common with the experimental research strategy in that it seeks to ascribe causal power to a variable (or set of variables) for the measured outcome.

However—and this is crucial—the causal-comparative design can only ascribe cause in a provisional or hypothetical way. This is because causal-comparative research relies on naturally occurring variables (see section 8.2.1), as do all correlational studies. This is where it differs from experimental research (see Chapter 9), which characteristically involves a "treatment"—an independent variable that is manipulated by the researcher. To make the causal-comparative design persuasive, the researcher must establish the essential comparability of the examples studied. Unfortunately, there are often many obstacles to establishing the equivalence of the examples/groups in naturally occurring circumstances.

In the case of Kim's study, it would be hard to prove that the Kentlands and Orchard Village residents moved into their neighborhoods with equivalent attitudes toward sense of community. Indeed, a case could be made the Kentlands residents were enticed to move there precisely because they already had a greater affinity for community-oriented living; and if that is the case, the higher levels of sense of community measured in Kentlands, as compared to Orchard Village, are simply a consequence of those initial attitudes. To offset this argument at least in part, Kim can point to data gained from qualitative in-depth interviews and activity logs that suggest at least some residents' behaviors changed after moving to Kentlands including, their transportation patterns (more walking) and/or the quantity of social interaction. Even so, such a causal comparative study can only point to possible causation. It can not establish cause with the same degree of rigor associated with experimental designs.

Similarly, Oscar Newman sought to bolster his study of New York City public housing by including a causal-comparative component in his research design.

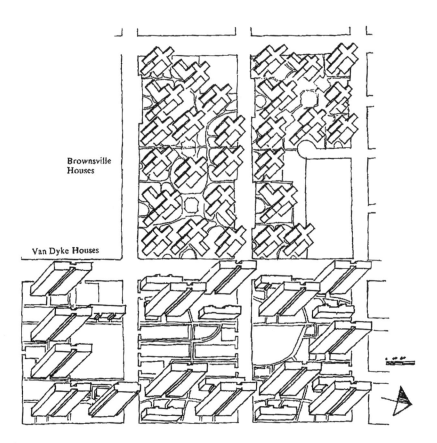

Figure 8.11 Plans of Brownsville and Van Dyke houses. Courtesy of Oscar Newman.

Newman's team conducted in-depth analyses of housing project pairs, comparable in virtually every respect except the physical design variables. Newman's rationale for this is quite clear:

> A fair test of hypotheses concerning the impact of the physical environment on crime therefore requires comparison of communities in which the social characteristics of the population are as constant as possible: where the only variation is the physical form of the buildings.[15]

Although Newman argues that the physical design unmistakably contributes to measured differences in crime rate between the two projects, he also acknowledges that his data can not provide "final and definitive proof" of the effects of physical design.[16] In fact, Newman suggests that the negative image of criminal behavior in Van Dyke

Figure 8.12 Van Dyke houses. Courtesy of Oscar Newman.

Figure 8.13 Brownsville houses. Courtesy of Oscar Newman.

Houses (the design *without* defensible space) contributed to the police department's pessimism about the value of their presence, a factor that in and of itself could contribute to the recorded higher crime levels there. Thus, like Kim, Newman can point to cause in the form of physical variables (a strength of the research design), but cannot establish it beyond doubt (a weakness of the design).

8.4   TACTICS: COLLECTING DATA

A wide range of data collection and analyses techniques are used in correlational research. Before we discuss them, four important issues must be acknowledged at the outset. First, we can only cite a few of the most common examples in the context of this chapter. Second, a number of data collection tactics are frequently employed in other research designs as well; for example, observational techniques are common in qualitative research as well as in correlational research. And third, virtually all of the tactics discussed here are described at length in other sources. To provide readers with an "entry point" to these more focused sources, we will provide key excerpts and the relevant citations, so that interested readers can pursue whichever of these topics seems particularly relevant to their work.

The fourth issue concerns a consideration that must be addressed prior to any data collection for correlational research, and that is sampling. On what basis does the researcher decide how many and which residents to interview about their satisfaction with a new building project in their city? Or, how many and which museum visitors should be observed for their choice of route through a new exhibit area? Although sampling is also a significant issue in other research strategies, it is especially vital in correlational research, because the goal of many correlational studies is to predict as accurately as possible the response or behavior of a large group of people, based on the patterns established by a smaller subset (i.e. sample) of that group.

We see this principle of prediction from a sample of respondents at work during election campaign, and in the development of commercial products. Poll results that predict election outcomes are based on surveys of a sample of likely voters, numbering perhaps a few hundred or several thousand. Similarly, manufacturers test their products—whether vacuum cleaners or toothpaste—on a small sample of consumers in the hope that they can predict the ultimate success of their product. In architecture, a designer might be interested in sampling users of a new workstation configuration before recommending that it be introduced on the other floors about to be renovated.

Within the vast literature on sampling, the most important concern to the researcher is the distinction between a *probabilistic* and *nonprobabilistic* sample. The goal of probabilistic sampling is to achieve a sample that is truly representative of the larger population. In practical terms, this usually means some form of *random* sampling (that can be achieved through a variety of procedural mechanisms), whereby each item or member of the population has an equal chance of being observed or interviewed. It is then possible to use inferential statistics to determine how likely it is that the results are a function of chance. Typically, researchers consider the .05 level of significance (i.e. a 5% likelihood of a chance occurrence) to be the minimum standard for generalization to a larger population. (See section 8.3.1 for an additional discussion of inferential statistics.) Readers who wish to make use of a probabilistic sampling procedure and to use inferential statistics to gauge their results should refer to some of the vast number of texts on this topic; several are listed among the references at the end of this chapter.

In a nonprobabilistic, or *purposive*, sample, the researcher is less concerned about generalizing to the larger population and more concerned about discovering useful patterns of information about particular groups or subsets of the population. For example, the architect of the office building renovation (described above) might find it more valuable to interview only those workers who had previously registered complaints about the new workstation. In this case, the architect is making a choice to discover the particular sources of dissatisfaction in the workstation design rather than to simply seek an overall level of satisfaction that fulfills the owner's general requirements for employee satisfaction. (Again, there are a variety of procedural mechanisms for deriving such samples; interested readers should review texts focused on the subject.)

We now turn to the variety of ways that a researcher might collect data for a correlational study. The range of data collection tactics discussed below is intended to introduce the beginning researcher to a broad range of techniques. Architectural practitioners will also find this discussion of value when soliciting critical information from clients, users, and other individuals involved in and affected by the design process.

8.4.1 Surveys

Among the variety of data collection tactics used in correlational research, the survey questionnaire is perhaps the most frequently employed. Indeed, its ubiquity is so well established that the terms *survey research* and *correlational research* are sometimes considered interchangeable. Our position, however, is that the survey questionnaire is just one of many possible data collection devices available for the correlational research design.

The great advantage of survey questionnaires is that they enable the researcher to cover an extensive amount of information—from demographic characteristics, to behavioral habits, to opinions or attitudes on a variety of topics—across a large number of people in a limited amount of time. However, achieving this breadth of information usually comes at the cost of in-depth understanding of the issues surveyed. Depth of understanding is more likely to be achieved through a qualitative research strategy for instance. (See Chapter 7 for more on qualitative research.) Nevertheless, the longstanding popularity of the survey tactic stands as a testimony to its usefulness in many circumstances.

Orchard Village Study

1. How important are these features to your feeling of attachment to Orchard Village

FEATURES of Orchard Village	very important	moderately important	some-what	minimally important	not at all
Residential density	(5)	(4)	(3)	(2)	(1)
Wetlands, public greens, tot lots, footpaths	(5)	(4)	(3)	(2)	(1)
Distance between sidewalks and houses	(5)	(4)	(3)	(2)	(1)
Architectural style	(5)	(4)	(3)	(2)	(1)
Block size	(5)	(4)	(3)	(2)	(1)
Club House-Recreation Complex	(5)	(4)	(3)	(2)	(1)
Overall layout of Washingtonian Woods	(5)	(4)	(3)	(2)	(1)
Street trees and other street landscaping	(5)	(4)	(3)	(2)	(1)
Overall size of Washingtonian Woods	(5)	(4)	(3)	(2)	(1)
Arrangement of houses on the block	(5)	(4)	(3)	(2)	(1)
Street width	(5)	(4)	(3)	(2)	(1)
Garage location	(5)	(4)	(3)	(2)	(1)
Onstreet parking	(5)	(4)	(3)	(2)	(1)
Lot size	(5)	(4)	(3)	(2)	(1)
Mixture of housing types	(5)	(4)	(3)	(2)	(1)
Overall design quality of housing	(5)	(4)	(3)	(2)	(1)
Street layout	(5)	(4)	(3)	(2)	(1)

Figure 8.14 Questionnaire segment of sense of community. Courtesy of Joongsub Kim.

Joongsub Kim's study of new urbanism (to which we referred earlier in the chapter) represents a good example of the use of the survey as a tool to gather broad—rather than in-depth—information.[17] Kim selected the survey as a tactic precisely because he wanted to compare residents' *overall* assessment of the "sense of community" achieved in a new urbanist development and a conventional suburban development. Kim also wanted to find out the extent to which a variety of specific design features contributed to this sense of community. After an extensive literature review (see Chapter 3 for more on literature reviews), Kim concluded that sense of community could be understood as having four relatively distinct components: sense of attachment, social interaction, pedestrianism, and sense of identity. Thus the bulk of his questionnaire asked the residents to rate the extent to which a set of seventeen design features affected each component. (See Fig. 8.14)

Kim also posed a number of demographic questions to each of the neighborhood's residents. These questions achieved at least two purposes. First, they helped Kim establish the extent to which the populations of the neighborhoods were essentially equivalent; and in fact, the two communities are quite similar by almost all demographic measures. And second, they helped him assess the extent to which key subgroups (i.e. residents of different housing types) responded differently to the four measures of community. As it turns out, single-family home and townhome residents indicate a higher level of sense of community than either apartment or condominium residents. (See Figure 8.15 for a list of key issues a researcher must address in developing a survey questionnaire.)

General Considerations	Examples of New Urbanist Research

1. <u>Goals</u>
Determine main topics to be covered
 	
Clarify the purpose of each question
	Kim's topics were:
	   overall sense of community
	   4 components of community
	   demographic characteristics

2. <u>Response Formats</u>
Evaluate advantages of closed vs.
   open-ended format
	Sense of community questions used
	   5-pt. closed scale
	Demographic questions used combination
	   of closed and open formats

3. <u>Clarity in Phrasing the Questions</u>
Use short sentences
Avoid making 2 queries in a single question
Avoid framing questions in the negative (not, never)
Avoid using ambiguous wording
Employ non-threatening language
	Reviewed question design with others
	   knowledgeable in research and the
	   respondent sample
	
	Piloted questionnaire with respondents

4. <u>Question Order</u> Use logical sequence of topics Start with interesting, nonchallenging issues Don't place important items at end of long survey	Survey starts with sense of community questions Full page demographic questions last
5. <u>Format</u> Use appealing, but simple graphics Avoid prominent or flashy design	Simple, understated graphics Though long, did not appear dense
6. <u>Instructions</u> Explain reason, context for survey Provide description(s) of what respondents expected to do Explain where respondents turn in survey	Introductory explanation provided Surveys were hand-delivered Provision for return mailing

7. <u>Ethics</u>
State provisions for keeping individual
   responses confidential
	Statement of confidentiality provided
	Survey submitted to university human
	   subjects review board

Figure 8.15 Considerations in the design of a survey questionnaire. First column adapted from D. Mertens, *Research Methods in Education and Psychology*, Sage Publications, 1998, pp. 115–117. Reprinted by permission of Sage Publications.

BOX 8.1

Tactics for Correlational Research: Using Surveys in Practice

In architectural practice, survey questionnaires can provide important information for ongoing projects. In his facility planning and predesign consulting service, architect Lawrence Stern frequently develops questionnaires to assess how physical design can support both individual and work group practices. For a recent planning project for an expanding Internet solutions organization, Stern developed a questionnaire to help the client organization wrestle with competing notions of appropriate work spaces; some employees envisioned a lively, free-flowing space evocative of the open-ended and fast-paced economic environment of dot-coms; while others envisioned more conventional individual workspaces that would provide privacy and respite from distracting activity. (See Figure 8.16 for Stern's individual preference questionnaire.)

Individual Name: _____

1. For each of the following attributes, indicate your preferences on the accompanying scale:

   - Physical Order (the need to feel your physical surroundings are predictable and ordered)
     Ordered - Free-flowing
   - Ambient noise (the preferred noise level of your work environment)
     Quiet (calm) - Loud (very active)
   - Distractibility (how your concentration is affected by nearby people and activities)
     Easily distracted - Not easily distracted
   - Sociability (how much you like to chat with co-workers while at your individual workplace)
     Introverted - Extroverted
   - Connectedness (what type of physical environment do you need to do your work)
     Exposed - Secluded

2. Overhearing co-worker telephone conversations or discussions may be beneficial. Indicate how frequently you would like to be able to hear the following:

	Always	Sometimes	Rarely	Never
• Your projects' requirements	_____	_____	_____	_____
• Other projects' requirements	_____	_____	_____	_____
• Informal information about your client	_____	_____	_____	_____
• Informal information about other clients	_____	_____	_____	_____
• Work group practices and methodology	_____	_____	_____	_____
• Company procedures	_____	_____	_____	_____
• Social event planning with co-workers	_____	_____	_____	_____

Figure 8.16   Sample survey in project planning phase. Courtesy of Lawrence Stern.

As it turned out, Stern was able to identify the clearly different sentiments of two groups of employees: the more creative software designers and the more technically oriented staff. The design-oriented staff considered themselves to be "not easily distracted" and were inclined to want more exposed, free-flowing spaces; whereas the technical staff considered themselves more "easily distracted," requiring more ordered and secluded space. As is often the case with small-scale projects with a limited number of users, Stern did not apply statistical measures of significance to his results, which demonstrated divergent tendencies between the two employee groups on several scales of the questionnaire.

Although surveys are most frequently used by researchers investigating social-cultural interactions or perceived meanings of environments, they can also be very effective tactics for a variety of other architectural research topics. A good example of correlational research in the environmental technology area is Raja et al's study of thermal comfort.[18] The goal of this research team was to investigate the use of various control mechanisms by workers in naturally ventilated office buildings. More specifically, the researchers sought to explore the effect of outdoor temperatures on indoor temperatures, especially the effect of office workers' use of environmental controls during peak summer months. To investigate this phenomenon, the researchers used the survey tactic for obtaining information from over 900 office workers in 15 buildings in two cities in Great Britain. Subjects were asked to report on thermal sensation and preference, clothing, activity, and use of controls (such as windows, fans, etc.); researchers also recorded the thermal environment close to each subject, as well as the outdoor temperature. The results of the study are based chiefly on an array of correlational analyses of the numerous variables. In general, the authors find that the availability of controls is key both to better building performance (i.e., the modification of indoor thermal conditions) and user satisfaction. They also make specific recommendations for the calculation of simulation models for naturally ventilated buildings.

8.4.2 Observation

Various forms of observation represent another frequently used set of tactics for data collection. In Whyte's study of urban plazas, the primary observation tactic was time-lapse film. At each plaza a camera was placed in a location that enabled filming of the pedestrian areas, usually a second- or third-story window or terrace perch. In an extensive appendix to his book, Whyte describes in useful detail the equipment and procedures used in the plaza study. Perhaps the most insightful section deals with figuring out what to look for. Indeed, establishing appropriate coding categories for

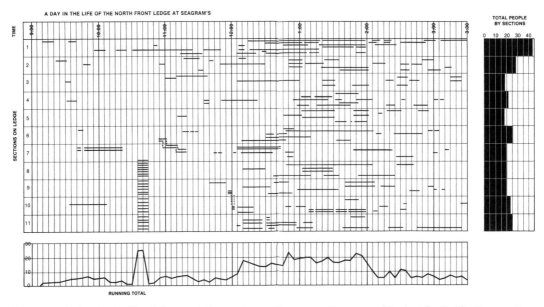

Figure 8.17 A day in the life of the north front edge at Seagrams. Courtesy of Project for Public Spaces, New York, New York.

activities recorded on film can be a painstaking task. On the other hand, the great advantage of observation tactics is that even a "simple" numbers count, such as represented in a day in the life of the ledge at Seagram (see Figure 8.17), can provide a detailed and powerful view of the human ecology of a particular setting.

In the realm of architectural education, Mark Frederickson's study of design juries is also notable for its extensive use of observations.[19] His goal was to monitor jury and student interactions, with a special focus on the possibility of gender and/or minority bias. Frederickson videotaped a total of 112 juries at three architecture schools. Like Whyte, he needed to decide explicitly what activities and interactions of the jury process needed to be specified, coded, and measured. The variables identified by Frederickson included both time/frequency measures (such as length of each student's presentation, length of jury comments, etc.) and content/process categories (such as collaborative idea building, use of rhetorical questions, and interruptions).

BOX 8.2

Tactics for Correlational Research: Using Observations in Practice

In the realm of architectural practice, Harrigan and Neel in their book *The Executive Architect* clearly make the case for incorporating systematic observation techniques:

> Many design decisions . . . will be influenced by observation results, which makes it essential to devise a thorough observation program. The observer cannot simply follow his or her eye, for any observer may be overwhelmed by the complexity of the situation to such a degree that the approach becomes random and loses it representativeness. . . . A program of systematic observation is undertaken because it is possible to establish justified design objectives for a new facility by observing existing facilities and the activities of users. The time spent is . . . justified when one is confronted with a situation that is new, or one that is complex or highly variable.*

The authors go on to describe the range of variables that might be observed (including demographic characteristics, specific activities, and user reactions) and how they might be structured. They also address some of the issues of sampling and coding already discussed in this chapter. Figure 8.18 summarizes Harrigan and Neel's assessment steps for the preparation of systematic observation in architectural practice.

While preparing for a program of systematic observation, the critical questions to be asked are:

- Have we chosen a study site that will help achieve our informational objectives?
- Will the site be available to us?
- Under what restrictions will we be operating?
- Will we have to be on the site continually, or can we set up a sampling scheme?
- If so, should we observe activities every day, hourly, or at another time interval?
- Will the selected time periods be representative of the activities that occur at other times?
- To what degree will our presence affect the situation?
- Will there be uncertainty about what to observe?
- Will the observers be consistent in what they pay attention to and what they document?
- If it is anticipated that there will be a problem with consistency of observations, how much training should we give observers?
- Do our observational goals match up with the situation, or should more effort go into their development?

Figure 8.18   Assessment steps for systematic observation.

---

*John Harrigan and Paul Neel, *The Executive Architect: Transforming Designers into Leaders* (New York: John Wiley & Sons, 1996) pp. 311–312.

One of Frederickson's key findings is that women students are more likely than male students to be put at a disadvantage during their juries. As Figure 8.19 indicates, women students are more likely to be interrupted during their initial presentations to juries; and they are also more likely to receive shorter jury sessions overall. These differences are statistically significant at the .05 level, meaning that there are only 5 chances out of 100 (or 1 out of 20) that these results are due to chance. In other words, interruptions and shorter jury time are strongly correlated, overall, with female gender.

Figure 8.19 Gender and ethnic dynamics in juries were the subject of Frederickson's research. Courtesy of Taubman College of Architecture and Urban Planning, University of Michigan.

Verbal Participation and Interruptions of Female and Male Students

	Interruptions to Student Introduction (Isp)	Total Duration of Each Jury (Tottime)
All Students	0.61	19.60
(N=112)	(p<.05)	
Female	0.76	17.50
(N=34)	(p<.05)	(p<.05)
Male	0.54	20.61
(N=78)	(p<.05)	(p<.05)

Figure 8.20 Verbal participation and interruptions of female and male students. © 1993 ACSA Press, Washington, D.C.

Content Variables

	Mean	School 1	School 2	School 3
Collaborative Idea Building per Min. (Ib)	.14	.08	.10	.25
Nonrhetorical Questions per Min. (Real)	19	.10	.14	.32
Rhetorical Questions per Min. (Rhet)	.05	.08	.02	.03

Figure 8.21 Content variables analyzed by school. © 1993 ACSA Press, Washington, D.C.

Another way that Frederickson analyzed the data can provide useful feedback to the schools he studied. Figure 8.20 shows his analysis of the content of jury comments at each of the three schools. The contrast between schools #1 and #3 is particularly strong. At school #3, there is a much stronger student-centered focus, evidenced by the greater emphasis on collaborative idea building and associated questions; whereas at school #1 there is a much higher incidence of rhetorical questions, suggesting that the jurors are more inclined to ask questions to make a point rather than to initiate dialogue.

8.4.3 Mapping

Probably the best-known example of the use of a "mapping" technique is Kevin Lynch's study *The Image of the City*.[20] In an effort to assess the way the physical characteristics of cities were experienced and understood by ordinary people, Lynch conducted interviews with residents of three U.S. cities—Boston, Jersey City, and Los Angeles—and asked them to sketch maps of their city. Figure 8.22 represents the

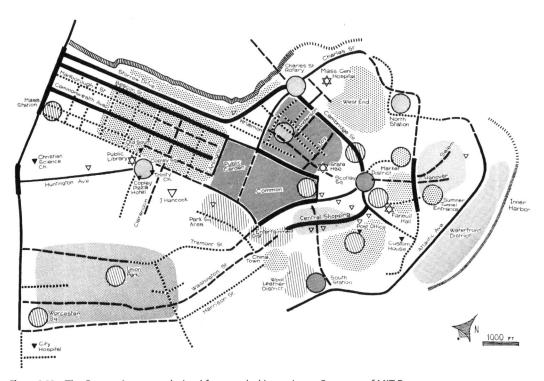

Figure 8.22   The Boston image as derived from verbal interviews. Courtesy of MIT Press.

composite maps derived from the interviews with Boston residents, while Figure 8.23 represents the composite map derived from the residents' sketch maps. Lynch concludes that overall there is a very high correlation between the two sets of maps for all three cities.

From these sets of mappings, Lynch was able to derive his now famous five general categories of urban features: path, edge, node, landmark, and district. All five types of features were delineated in each of the three cities. On the other hand, the density of these imageable features varied from city to city. Figure 8.24 shows the relative impoverishment of the composite Jersey City sketch map, compared to that of Boston.

Anne Lusk's more recent study of greenway bicycle paths is an excellent example of how mapping can been used as a basis for formulating design guidelines.[21] A long-time volunteer and activist in the greenway movement, Lusk wanted to discover the frequency of and distance between "destination" places along the greenway path. Recognizing that there might be important differences between different types of bikeways, she selected for study a total of six greenways nationally recognized for

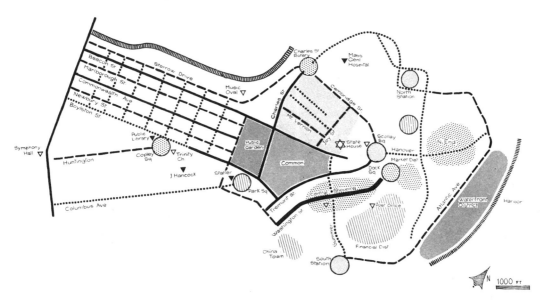

Figure 8.23 The Boston image as derived from sketch maps. Courtesy of MIT Press.

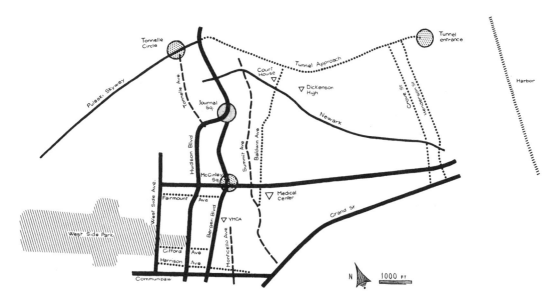

Figure 8.24 The Jersey City image as derived from sketch maps. Courtesy of MIT Press.

their aesthetic qualities: two scenic, rural trails; two urban trails; and two rails-to-trails greenways. At each site, Lusk asked greenway users to apply stickers representing different qualities of physical features to greenway maps she provided. Figure 8.25 provides the mapping instructions; and Figure 8.26 represents a composite map

---

Bicycle Path/Greenway Survey

This voluntary survey is being conducted through the University of Michigan for a Ph.D. dissertation on the determination of attractive destinations and their features on a multi-use path. We would like you to help us identify the locations of these destinations and to also list the elements that make that destination preferred. Please use the attached stickers on the survey. Out of a trial of 6 survey techniques, use of the stickers emerged as the most effective technique.

First, use the following code for the stickers, placing them as appropriate, on the map. You do not have to use all of the categories of stickers and you can use as many or as few stickers as you like.

Second, beside the spangley star sticker for the destination or destinations, please describe the area or features so that the destinations can be located. Also, please assign a number in order of preference to the destinations with #1 being the most preferred destination. You can have as many or as few destinations as you like.

Third, on the additional sheet of paper, please list the destinations located by you on the map according to the rank order with #1 being listed first. Below each destination, please list the preferred features at this destination and identify with a check, the top three or four features at each destination.

   1. Put a plain star by one or more areas that serve as the place or places you start on the path.

   2. Put a spangley star by one or more areas that serve as destinations or places, which even though you may pass by, you feel you have "arrived."

   3. Put a smiley face circle by the places which you particularly enjoy and/or look forward to.

   4. Put squares by places that serve primarily as way-finders (visible cues about your location) that might be attractive or unattractive.

   5. Put a line of small dots by stretches that you find appealing.

   6. Put a long bar or many bars at the places or stretches where you are bored.

   7. Put bugs/ants by individual places or things that you find unappealing.

   8. Put an arrow/pointer indicating the direction where you enjoy a view.

Figure 8.25   Mapping instructions for Lusk's greenway study. Courtesy of Anne Lusk.

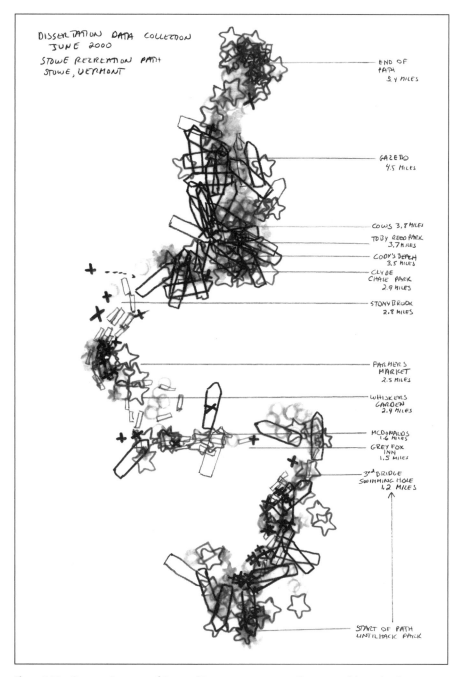

Figure 8.26 Composite map of Stowe, Vermont greenway. Courtesy of Anne Lusk.

for one of the greenways. Lusk was then able to measure distances between collectively established destination points using an odometer. Distances for each greenway were established and then general patterns for each greenway type were identified. Figure 8.27 represents a typical destination along the Stowe, Vermont greenway; it is a place where multiple features of interest converge, including cows to watch; a shady glen as a place to rest; a picturesque view of the mountains; and a lay-by large enough for people to interact with each other. Lusk was also able to determine that major destination points along the greenway occur about every two miles. These findings are comparable, i.e. correlated, to those of destination points on the other greenways studied.

8.4.4 Sorting

Another tactic that can be highly effective in both research and practice situations is the sorting task. This typically involves asking a respondent to sort a set of cards (usually between 20 and 30) with either words or pictures represented on them.[22] In a *directed sort*, the researcher specifies a set of categories into which the cards must be sorted, such as a 5- or 7-point rating scale from highly preferred to least preferred. In a *free* sort, the respondent can establish whatever categories make sense to him/her. For example, s/he might choose to sort a set of buildings into functional types, including houses, commercial buildings, churches, etc. Or the respondent might choose to sort a set of houses by categories of traditional vs. modern styles. In a *multiple* free sort, the respondent is typically asked to sort the items as many times as possible.

Figure 8.27   Typical greenway destination. Courtesy of Anne Lusk, photo by Jeff Turnaw.

Figure 8.28   A respondent beginning the sorting task. Photo by Linda Groat.

Other versions of the sorting task procedure (including examples such as the Q-sort and F-sort) can be found in some of the more specialized research methods books focusing on correlational research.

In a class for beginning architectural students, Groat has used the sorting task to clarify the design dialogue between the architect-student and a friend who serves as the client. The student is asked first to do several sortings of the 20 Xerox photos of houses both to familiarize her/himself with the sorting process and to elicit his/her own categorizations of the houses. Next, the student conducts an interview with the "client," who does his/her sortings of the houses. There is also a column at one edge of the sortings record sheet (See Figures 8.29 and 8.30) for each student and "client" to indicate a rank for each house in order of preference. Finally, the student is urged to discuss the similarities and differences in the sorting categories and the ranked preferences with his/her client. So, for example, if both architect and client sort according to building materials, but the client prefers wood shingles while the architect prefers expansive glass with steel, there is a clear difference of approach to work out. If both architect and client sort the houses according to the degree of exposure to landscape and sunlight, it may be that this agreement can serve as a device for resolving the conflict over materials.

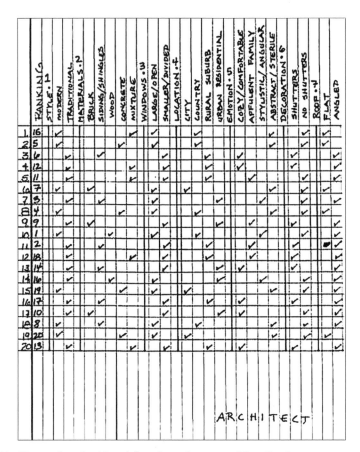

Figure 8.29   The student "architect's" sortings. Courtesy of Sara Stucky.

In a research context, both the preference rankings (an example of ordinal measurement as described in section 8.2.2) and the nominal sorting category designations can be subjected to statistical measures such that correlations between rankings and sortings can be investigated. However, the modest use of the sorting task in a practice setting—between client and architect, or among a small number of client/users—often serves more as a creative foundation for dialogue than as the basis for specific measures of correlation.

The essays that students have written about this experience suggest that a visual exercise such as the sorting task can be a very effective alternative to simply asking clients to state their preferences in a conversation or interview. Indeed, by sorting out alternative design elements and articulating the categories that come to mind, many

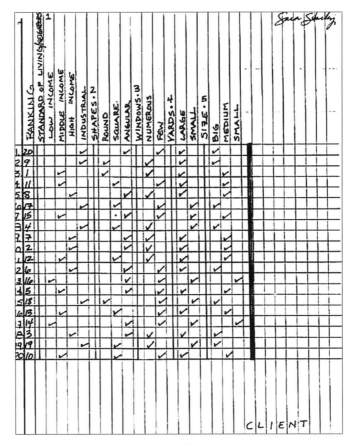

Figure 8.30 The "client's" sortings. Courtesy of Sara Stucky.

nonarchitects begin to experience architecture in ways that they might not otherwise be aware of or know how to express.

Reflecting on the use of the sorting task, Frances Downing found that her respondents—even the very busy professionals—quickly became captivated by the sorting process. (See Box 8.3.) Downing recounts:

> The memories that participants related were generally characterized by profound personal involvement. Soon it was evident that the information collected was central to the life of a designer: the reason why so many had made their career choices seemed bound up in the small white [sorting] cards with names of a history of places written on them.[23]

BOX 8.3

Tactics for Correlational Research: The Sorting Task

Frances Downing has used the sorting task to great effect in uncovering architectural designers' use of image banks in their design process.* Downing was interested in finding out the extent to which beginning architectural students, graduating architectural students, and practicing architects differed in the way they thought about and used design imagery in their work. Her procedure involved asking her respondents a series of evocative questions (e.g., As a child, what places did you live in that remain particularly memorable?) to elicit meaningful place images. As respondents named these images, the name of each image was recorded on a small card for use in the sorting task. Once all the images evoked by the questions had been recorded, the respondents carried out as many *free* sorts as possible.

Downing conducted her study at two different architecture schools, and included practicing professionals from the schools' respective regions. She found some intriguing differences of emphasis between the two groups of students and the professionals. Using a combination of inferential statistics for nominal data (see sections 8. 3.1 and 8.4) and multivariate statistics (see section 8.5), Downing was able to dis-

Figure 8.31   A memorable image that might be experienced in youth.
Photo by Linda Groat.

---

*Frances Downing, "Image Banks: Dialogs Between the Past and the Future," *Environment and Behavior* 24, no. 4 (July 1992): 441–470.

cover that, in general, the more experienced architects (especially the practicing professionals) were more inclined to integrate or combine vernacular images from prearchitectural experiences with the more high-style images from their professional education and experience. Entering students, by contrast, were less able to integrate the two types of images. Downing concludes architecture programs may be failing to help students make sense of their own experience of place while facing the challenge of creating place in their professional roles.

Figure 8.32 A memorable image that might be experienced during professional education. Photo by Linda Groat.

8.4.5 Archives

Yet another, though certainly less frequently used, tool for data collection is provided by archives. Newman's study of defensible space put an existing data base to extremely effective use. Newman is quite explicit about how the precision and wealth of data kept by the New York Housing Authority contributed to the success of his study. Newman explains that the wealth of demographic variables measured by the housing authority included age, income, years of residence, previous backgrounds, and history of family pathology. Similarly, the housing authority's police force maintained extensive records that included not only the nature of the crime or complaint, but also the precise location of the incident in the housing project.

These data on demographic characteristics and the presence/location of criminal behavior were then correlated with data on the physical properties of the various housing projects. The physical quality of the housing projects was measured in terms of a great range of variables, including numbers of residents, size of housing site, population density, number of housing stories, and plan type. Newman explains: "With this data it has been possible to determine exactly where the most dangerous areas of buildings are, as well as to compare crime rates in different building types and project layouts."[24]

One particularly influential and notable correlation discovered by Newman is that of the relationship between crime rate and building height. Newman concludes: "Crime rate has been found to increase almost proportionately with building height" for the projects administered by the New York Housing Authority.[25]

8.5   TACTICS: READING ABOUT AND UNDERSTANDING MULTIVARIATE ANALYSES

Up to this point in the chapter, our discussions have touched on some of the most typical descriptive and inferential statistical analyses entailed in doing correlational research. In this section, we will briefly describe a few examples of some of the more complex data analyses that can be deployed. We do not assume that either students or professionals at the beginning stages of learning about or doing research will employ these complex statistics; but we do anticipate that both students and practitioners who choose to read about research findings during a literature review may well find it useful to understand the intent of such complex analyses. To this end, we will describe in the chapter segments that follow three types of multivariate statistical procedures: multiple regression; factor analysis; and multidimensional scaling. More experienced researchers who wish to actually employ such statistical tactics may want to refer to some of the detailed texts listed at the conclusion of the chapter.

8.5.1 Multiple Regression

In correlational research that seeks primarily to understand and predict relationships among several variables, multiple regression is frequently employed as an analytical tool. It is one of several devices that can be used to describe the strength and direction of relationships among two or more variables. More specifically, it is appropriate for interval or ratio data where the researcher has hypothesized several independent variables that can predict the value, or measured outcome, of another variable. In such cases multiple regression can provide a mathematical equation that indicates the amount of variance that is contributed by each of the independent (or predictor) variables.

An example of how multiple regression might work in environmental research is provided by Olusegun Obasanjo, who studied the effect of the urban environment on adolescents.[26] Obasanjo used a survey questionnaire that measured adolescents' subjective experience of various social behaviors; cognitive functioning; and environmental quality (i.e. housing quality, neighborhood quality, and access to restorative resources). Restorative resources, as defined by Obasanjo and based on well-known research by Stephen Kaplan, are defined as places and experiences that are likely to enable people to experience the quality of being away, thereby overcoming mental fatigue.[27] Thus, Obasanjo included such questions as whether the respondents had quiet places to go in their neighborhood, whether they ever had the opportunity for nature experiences such as camping, etc.

Obasanjo used a series of multiple regression analyses to sort out the relationships among the many variables being measured, particularly the predictive association of the three sets of physical environment measures with either positive or negative social behaviors, such as delinquency or mental illness. For instance, Obasanjo found that housing quality and access to restorative resources accounted for the variation in perceived support from family at a statistically significant level. (See Figure 8.33.) Additionally, perceived neighborhood quality, along with housing quality and restorative resources, accounted for the variation in perceived support from friends. (See Figure 8.34.)

Space does not permit a complete description of the relationships among the many demographic, social, and physical variables that Obasanjo measured. Of particular interest to environmental designers, Obasanjo was able to establish statistically significant relationships between the *lack* of housing quality, neighborhood quality, and restorative resources and tendencies toward psychological illness and mild delinquency.

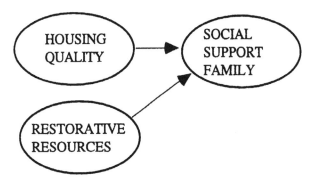

Figure 8.33   Effect of environmental experience on social support from family. Courtesy of Olusegun Obasanjo.

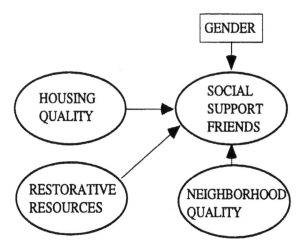

Figure 8.34   Effect of environmental experience on social support from friends. Olusegun Obasanjo.

8.5.2 Factor Analysis

Like multiple regression, factor analysis depends on interval or ratio data. But instead of using key variables to predict the outcomes of other variables, factor analysis aims to articulate an overall structure or pattern among variables. More particularly, factor analysis enables the researcher to identify thematic clusters of variables known as *factors*. Each factor is comprised of several variables that share similar patterns of responses or observations.

A good example of the use of factor analysis to uncover the underlying structure among environmental design variables is provided by Kim's research on new urbanist and conventional suburban developments.[28] As described in earlier segments of this chapter, Kim used a survey questionnaire to clarify the impact of a variety of physical features on residents' sense of community in the two neighborhood developments.

What Kim discovered is that even though the new urbanist residents rated their sense of community more highly than the residents of the conventional suburb, the underlying factors influencing their assessments of specific design features were remarkably similar. For example, in the evaluation of community identity, the same three factors were identified for both neighborhood developments: community plan;

Q7: Distinctive Character		Factor group themes					
		Kentlands			Orchard Village		
Q7	**Physical features**	**Com. Plan**	**Com App.**	**Ame.**	**Com. Plan**	**Com. App.**	**Ame.**
11	Street width	.77			.70		
14	Lot size	.76			.62		
5	Block size	.75			.62		
3	Distance between sidewalks and houses	.73			.65		
10	Arrangement of houses on the block	.71				.72	
12	Garage location	.69				.82	
1	Residential density	.66				.51	
17	Street layout	.59				.67	
16	Overall design quality of housing		.78			.86	
4	Architectural style		.71			.72	
15	Mixture of housing types		.70			.63	
7	Overall layout of Kentlands (or W.W)		.46			.67	
6	Club house-recreation complex			.75			.74
8	Street trees and other street landscaping			.63		.59	
9	Overall size of Kentlands (or W.W)					.59	
13	On street parking				.81		
2	Lakes (or Wetlands), public greens, tot lots, footpaths						.85
	Mean	4.20	**4.70**	4.27	3.45	4.02	**4.21**
	Alpha	.89	.77	.43	.89	.92	.62

Figure 8.35   Factor analysis of community identity. Courtesy of Joongsub Kim.

community appearance, and amenities. In Figure 8.35, the relevant physical variables associated with each factor are indicated. However, the relative salience of the three factors and the specific variables associated with them are somewhat different. Whereas the community appearance factor was most salient for the Kentlands residents (see mean score in bold), the amenities factor was more salient to the Orchard Village residents' sense of community.

8.5.3 Multidimensional Scaling

Multidimensional scaling analysis offers more flexibility than either factor analysis or multiple regression. Depending on the particular computer program used, it can make use of nominal data as well as interval or ratio data. In addition, because the outcome of the analysis is represented graphically, it may hold some inherent appeal for architectural researchers.

The overall goal of multidimensional scaling is similar to that of factor analysis in that it reveals an underlying pattern or structure among the variables analyzed.

However, some multidimensional scaling programs (such as the Guttman-Lingoes series or LIFa from University of Liverpool) allow for a greater degree of interpretive flexibility than is possible with factor analysis. Whereas factor analysis typically results in numerical designations for the degree of salience of each variable within a factor, multidimensional scaling results in a graphic plot that locates the relationship among all variables spatially. Two points (variables) plotted in close proximity mean that these variables represent a similar pattern of responses or observations; distant points (variables) on the graph represent a dissimilar pattern of responses or observations.

Linda Groat's research on architects' and laypeople's understanding of architectural style employs a form of multidimensional scaling that accepts the nominal data derived from a sorting task.[29] Groat was interested in investigating the extent to which architects and laypeople (in this case a group of accountants) responded differently to modern vs. postmodern styles. Some architectural theorists and proponents of postmodernism had speculated that laypeople would find postmodern buildings more appealing and meaningful than modern buildings. So Groat asked her respondents to carry out a set of free sorts of building photographs that represented a range of modern to transitional to postmodern styles.

Figure 8.36 represents the multidimensional scalogram analysis plot of a typical architect's set of sortings. Groat's interpretation of the plot reveals that basic *stylistic* categorizations underlie the architect's sortings, regardless of whether the architect

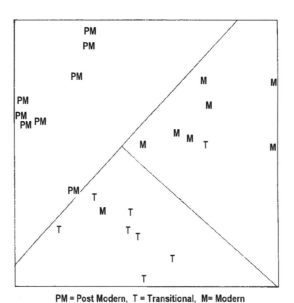

PM = Post Modern, T = Transitional, M= Modern

Figure 8.36 Underlying structure of architects' sortings.

had consciously sorted according to materials, geometric form, preference, or any other criteria. Lines have been drawn to indicate that the plot can be understood in terms of three stylistic regions that, with minor exceptions, correspond to the designations employed by architectural critics of the time.

On the other hand, Figure 8.37 represents a typical accountant's set of sortings. In this case, it is not possible to find any distinct stylistic regions. Groat interprets this result to mean that the accountant's sortings do *not* reveal an underlying stylistic conceptualization in the way the architect's plot does.

The sortings of all 20 architects and 20 accountants were subjected to the same multidimensional analysis procedures. Groat was able to determine that while *no* accountant's plot revealed a postmodern stylistic region, the plots of 10 architects *did* reveal a postmodern region. Further statistical analyses confirmed that this difference in response rate between the architects and accountants was significant at the .001 level, meaning that there is only one chance in a thousand that these results would be a chance occurrence.

As a result of this study, Groat concluded that the argument put forward by postmodern proponents at that time—that laypeople would respond more favorably to postmodern buildings than to modern buildings—was flawed. Indeed, even among the architects, only half revealed a consistent underlying stylistic differentiation between modern and postmodern styles.

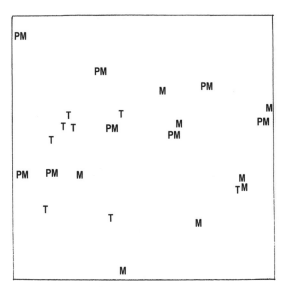

PM = Post Modern, T = Transitional, M= Modern

Figure 8.37 Underlying structure of accountants' sortings.

8.6   CONCLUSIONS: STRENGTHS AND WEAKNESSES

As the many research examples described in this chapter demonstrate, the correlational strategy is well suited for exploring the relationship among two or more variables of interest. Unlike experimental research, in which a variable is purposefully manipulated by the researcher, correlational research seeks to document the naturally occurring relationship among variables. This characteristic means that it is particularly appropriate in circumstances when variables either *cannot* be manipulated for practical reasons or *should not* be manipulated for ethical reasons. (See Figure 8.38.)

Because correlational research can accommodate the study of many variables measured in a variety of instances, the strategy is especially appropriate when the researcher seeks to understand a situation or circumstance *broadly*, rather than *in depth*. In other words, one of the strategy's great advantages is its potential for studying a wide range of variables. However, its consequent disadvantage is that a robust and deep understanding may not be achieved.

Finally, researchers who choose to employ a correlational strategy will have to bear in mind the distinction between causality and prediction. By revealing consistent patterns of relationships among variables, correlational research can predict whether certain physical features may be associated with certain social outcomes. But that is not the same thing as establishing the physical variables as the cause of those outcomes. Researchers who seek to establish direct causality between variables will need to turn to experimental and quasi-experimental strategies. They are the subject of the next chapter.

Strengths	Weaknesses
Can clarify the relationships among two or more naturally occuring variables	Researcher cannot control the levels or degrees of variables
Well suited to studying the breadth of a setting or a phenomenon	Less well suited to exploring the setting or phenomenon in depth
Can establish predictive relationships	Cannot establish causality

Figure 8.38   Strengths and weaknesses of correlational research.

8.7   RECOMMENDED READING

Readers interested in a more detailed overview of correlational and causal-comparative research, and their related tactics, can refer to Donna Mertens's textbook *Research Methods in Education and Psychology* (Thousand Oaks, Calif.: Sage Publications, 1998). In addition to her chapter on correlational research design, readers may also want to refer to her chapters on sampling (chapter 10), data collection (chapter 11), and data analysis (chapter 12).

For those particularly interested in survey research, two very useful sources are Robert Marans, "Survey Research," in Robert Bechtel, Robert Marans, and William Michelson, eds., *Behavioral Research and the Environment* (New York: Van Nostrand-Reinhold, 1987) pp. 41–81; and Donna Mertens, "Survey Research," in *Research Methods in Education and Psychology* (Thousand Oaks, Calif.: Sage Publications, 1998), pp. 105–143.

Students and professionals who are particularly interested in tactics for correlational research in practice and other applied settings may find two books of particular value. Several chapters in John Zeisel, *Inquiry by Design* (Monterey, Calif.: Brooks/Cole Publishing Co., 1981) describe tactics that are especially relevant to correlational research, including: "Observing Environmental Behavior" (chapter 8), "Standardized Questionnaires" (chapter 10), "Asking Questions" (chapter 11), and "Archives" (chapter 12). In addition, John Harrigan and Paul Neel, *The Executive Architect* (New York: John Wiley and Sons, 1996) includes a chapter on "Knowledge Development" (chapter 7) that describes the use of various research tactics in practice settings.

Other more specialized chapters or articles on some of the data collection tactics referenced in this chapter include David Canter, Jennifer Brown, and Linda Groat, "The Multiple Sorting Procedure," in Michael Brenner and David Canter, eds., *The Research Interview* (London: Academic Press, 1985) pp. 79–114.

For students and researchers who want to learn more about specific statistical applications, there are dozens of such books available. In addition to the chapters in Mertens that have already been cited, a classic and useful book is H. Blalock, *Social Statistics* (Tokyo: McGraw-Hill International Student Edition, 1979). A more advanced, comprehensive text is Thomas Black *Doing Quantitative Research* (Thousand Oaks, Calif.: Sage Publications, 1999).

Finally, readers who wish to study the details of the influential exemplars of correlational research may wish to refer to Oscar Newman, *Defensible Space* (New York: MacMillan Company, 1972); and William Whyte, *The Social Life of Small Urban Spaces* (Washington, D.C.: The Conservation Foundation, 1980).

NOTES

1. William Whyte, *The Social Life of Small Urban Spaces* (New York, NY: Project for Public Spaces, Inc., 1980).

2. Joongsub Kim, Sense of Community in Neo-Traditional and Conventional Suburban Developments (Ph.D. diss., University of Michigan 2001).

3. Todd Bressi, "Planning the American Dream," in *The New Urbanism: Toward an Architecture of Community*, ed. Peter Katz (New York: McGraw-Hill, 1994).

4. Kim, Sense of Community.

5. Although the survey questionnaire may be the most common tactic for gaining an understanding of people's opinions and perceived meanings, a great many other response formats—such as mapping, the sorting task, and the like—are also possible. See section 8.4 later in this chapter for a more complete discussion of these tactics.

6. Linda N. Groat, "Meaning in Post-Modern Architecture: An Examination Using the Multiple Sorting Task," *Journal of Environmental Psychology* 2 no. 1, (1982): 3–22.

7. H. Blalock, *Social Statistics* (New York: McGraw-Hill Book Co. 1960), pp. 12–18.

8. Ibid., 15.

9. Donna Mertens, *Research Methods in Education and Psychology* (Thousand Oaks, Calif.: Sage Publications, 1998), p. 332.

10. Mertens presents a more hierarchically structured typology. She uses the terms causal-comparative and correlational to designate two primary categories. Then, within correlational, she includes both relationship and prediction subtypes. We have chosen to simplify Mertens's hierarchy in part because pure "prediction" studies (which typically involve the study of a theorized outcome some months or years after the initial measurement of key variables) are relatively rare in architectural research. Mertens, *Research Methods*.

11. Oscar Newman, *Defensible Space: Crime Prevention Through Urban Design* (New York: Macmillan, 1972).

12. Ibid., xiv.

13. Ibid., 3.

14. Mertens, *Research Methods*, 94.

15. Newman, *Defensible Space*, xv.

16. Ibid., 48.

17. Kim, Sense of Community, xxx.

18. Iftikhar A. Raja, J. Fergus Nicol, Kathryn J. McCartney, and Michael A. Humphreys, "Thermal Comfort: Use of Controls in Naturally Ventilated Buildings," *Energy and Buildings*, 33 (2000): 235–244.

19. Mark Frederickson, "Gender and Racial Bias in Design Juries," *Journal of Architectural Education* 47, no. 1 (September 1993): 38–48.

20. Kevin Lynch, *The Image of the City* (Cambridge, Mass.: MIT Press, 1960).

21. Anne Lusk, Greenways' Places of the Heart: Aesthetic Guidelines for Bicycle Paths (Ph.D. diss., University of Michigan, 2002).

22. David Canter, J. Brown, and Linda Groat, "The Multiple Sorting Procedure," in *The Research Interview*, eds. Michael Brenner and David Canter (London: Academic Press, 1985) pp. 79–114.

23. Frances Downing, "Conversation in Imagery," *Design Studies* 13, no. 3 (July 1992): 297.

24. Newman, *Defensible Space*, xiv.

25. Ibid., 27.

26. Olusegun Obasanjo, The Impact of the Physical Environment on Adolescents in the Inner City (Ph.D. diss., University of Michigan, 1998).

27. Stephen Kaplan, "Beyond Rationality: Clarity-Based Decision Making," in *Environment, Cognition, and Action: An Integrated Approach*, eds. Tommy Garling and Gary Evans (New York: Oxford University Press, 1991); S. Kaplan, "The Restorative Benefits of Nature: Toward an Integrated Framework," *Journal of Environmental Psychology* 15 (1992): 169–182.

28. Kim, Sense of Community.

29. Linda N. Groat, "Meaning in Post-Modern Architecture."

Chapter 9

Experimental and Quasi-Experimental Research

9.1 INTRODUCTION

Research on the performance of various building components constitutes a significant and longstanding domain within architectural research as a whole. Although much of this research has focused on improving building technologies in the industrialized world, a study by Givoni, Gulich, and Gomez focuses instead on radiant cooling by metal roofs, a significant issue for housing in developing countries.[1] Givoni et al. noted that although corrugated metal roofs are effective for cooling in the evening, they tend to overheat houses in the daylight hours. The researchers hypothesized that the installation of operable hinged interior insulating plates under the roof would reduce daytime heating without interfering with the nighttime cooling function of the metal roofs.

To test this hypothesis the researchers built a small-scale mock-up of the typical house (termed a *test cell*) whereby the heating/cooling effect of various test conditions could be measured. (See Figure 9.1.) Givoni et al. tested three distinct conditions of insulation operation: 1) with the insulation panels closed both day and night; 2) with the insulation panels open at night and closed during the day; and 3) with the insulation positioned as in condition 2, but with the addition of a small ventilating fan from midnight to 5 am. In addition, two levels of thermal mass (as represented by water-filled bottles) were also tested.

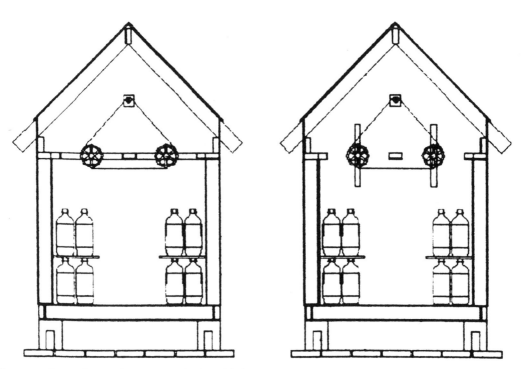

Figure 9.1 Test cell unit, showing panels closed (left) and open (right), Baruch Givoni et al., 1996. Courtesy of American Solar Energy Society, Inc.

Based on their tests of these conditions, the authors concluded that the combination of insulating panels and fan venting (condition 3) provides better daytime cooling than the insulation without the fan ventilation. On the other hand, no appreciable difference in cooling was noted as a consequence of the thermal mass condition. Finally, based on these data, the authors were able to develop predictive formulae for calculating the indoor maximum temperature as a function of the swing of the outdoor temperature.

Taking on a very different research topic, Ann Sloan Devlin sought to discover the extent to which gender might have an effect on how job applicants are evaluated in architectural practice.[2] She hypothesized that "women architects would be less favorably rated than male architects," especially at the more senior level.[3]

To test this hypothesis, Devlin created both a junior-level and senior-level resume, the junior level with four years of architectural experience and the senior level with 13 years of experience. Copies of each resume type (junior and senior) were created using a fictitious female name; an equal number of copies carried a fictitious male name. Each resume included a career objective, professional experience, affiliation, registration, education, skills, honors and awards.

Respondents in the study were more than 200 architects (156 men and 48 women) licensed in the state of Connecticut, but representing all regions of the country. Respondents were told that the study was about "the perception architects have of the characteristics possessed by those practicing architecture." These respondents then received one of the four fictitious resumes and were asked to evaluate the candidates on a seven-point scale in the following areas: technical aspects of the job, administrative aspects, interpersonal aspects, contribution to growth of firm's client base, creative contribution, advancement, and overall ability. Respondents were also asked whether they would accept or reject the candidate for hire.

The most salient result of Devlin's study was that the "male architect respondents were more likely to hire male applicants than female applicants as senior architects."[4] Devlin reached this conclusion by comparing the hiring decisions of the respondents in relation to the four resume conditions (male or female; intern or senior), using inferential statistical measures (see Chapter 8, section 8.3.1). She concludes that women in architecture may indeed "experience discrimination as they advance through the ranks."[5]

9.2   STRATEGY: GENERAL CHARACTERISTICS OF EXPERIMENTAL RESEARCH

These two studies may seem to be worlds apart. On a thematic level, the Givoni et al. study tackles an aspect of environmental technology, while the Devlin study seeks to clarify the dynamics of gender discrimination in architectural practice. The research contexts are also very different. The former is conducted in a laboratory setting, while the latter makes use of a real-life or "field" setting. The variables being investigated are quite different as well. The Givoni et al. study considers only physical variables; whereas the Devlin study focuses on behavioral and social conditions.

Despite these notable differences, the Givoni et al. and Devlin studies are alike in that they are both examples of the experimental research design. Many readers are likely to read into that factual statement either a commendation of high praise or an invitation to criticism. This is because experimental research is so frequently portrayed as the standard against which all other research strategies should be judged. In general, readers who adhere to the postpositivist system of inquiry are likely to see the experimental strategy as the essence of "scientific" research. On the other hand, many researchers who adhere to a naturalistic or emancipatory paradigm have argued persuasively that the experimental design is either inappropriate or insufficient for research about certain social and cultural phenomena. We will address some of these concerns later in this chapter. (See section 9.6.) We would argue that, as with the other research strategies, experimental research can yield either outstanding or flawed research, depending on how appropriately it is applied to a particular research question.

What then are the underlying commonalities that define the Givoni et al. and Devlin studies as experimental research? Briefly, the defining characteristics of an experimental research design include the following: the use of a treatment, or independent variable; the measurement of outcome, or dependent, variables; a clear unit of assignment (to the treatment); the use of a comparison (or control) group; and a focus on causality.[6] These five characteristics will be discussed in some detail in the following chapter segments.

9.2.1 The Use of a Treatment, or Independent Variable

In each of the two studies described above, the researchers are seeking to study the impact of one or more specific, identifiable variables on the phenomenon under study. In the case of the metal roof study, the researchers are seeking to test the thermal impact of several conditions, both in isolation and in combination, including: *insulation*, *venting fan*, and *thermal mass*. Similarly, in her research on gender issues in professional practice, Ann Sloan Devlin is seeking to clarify the impact of *gender designations* on how architects evaluate job applicants. Although quite different in nature, these variables are in each case *manipulated* or *controlled* by the researchers in some specified way, and so they are considered to be *treatments* in the experimental strategy.

9.2.2 The Measurement of One or More Outcome Variables

In each of these studies, the researchers were able to specify the impact of the experimental treatment by carefully measuring certain outcome measures, or dependent variables. For Givoni et al.'s study of metal roofs, the dependent variables were the *temperature readings for indoor areas* of the test cell environments including both the attic and the indoor living environment. The researchers were able to ascertain how much the indoor temperatures were cooled by the several experimental conditions (see Figures 9.2 and 9.3). In a similar way, Devlin was able to assess the impact of gender designations through two measures: a questionnaire instrument whereby prospective employers could register their *evaluation* on a 1-to-7 rating scale, and a *hiring decision* to accept or reject. Again, although quite different in nature, both the temperature and evaluation measures are the outcome measures (or dependent variables) of these experiments.

9.2.3 The Designation of a Unit of Assignment

In each of these studies, the researchers have applied the experimental treatment to a specified *unit of assignment*. In the case of Givoni et al.'s research, the treatment conditions (various combinations of insulation, venting fans, and mass) are all applied to a *test cell*. This test cell was a small-scale mock-up of a metal-roofed residential unit in a hot climate, a 1-meter cube with metal gabled roof. (See Figure 9.1.) On the other hand, in Devlin's study the unit of assignment was not an inanimate object, but rather the *individual architects* who were asked to evaluate the fictitious job applicants. Each of these "units"—whether test cells or individual architects—received a treatment manipulated by the researcher(s).

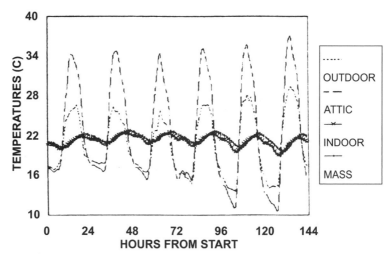

Figure 9.2 Control conditions: insulating panels closed day and night. Courtesy of American Solar Energy Society, Inc.

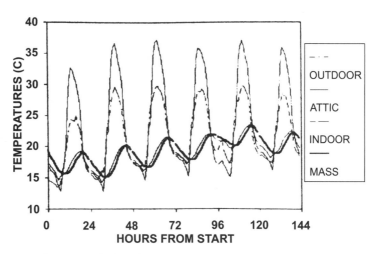

Figure 9.3 Insulating panels closed during the day and open at night. Courtesy of American Solar Energy Society, Inc.

9.2.4 The Use of a Comparison or Control Group

Most experimental studies measure the impact of treatments against a comparison or control group. The control condition in Givoni et al.'s study is achieved with the insulation panels closed both day and night so that no heating or cooling occurs. In all other conditions, i.e. the treatment conditions, the insulation panels are closed during the day and opened at night to allow for cooling. In other words, the control condition is defined as one to which the treatment is *not* applied. In Devlin's study, all architect respondents received some treatment, one of four combinations of male or female applicant, at a junior or senior level. In this case, the different treatments are compared against each other.

9.2.5 A Focus on Causality

The combined purpose of the defining features of the experimental research design (i.e. treatment, outcome measures, unit of assignment, and control or comparison groups) is to enable the researcher to credibly establish a cause-effect relationship. In general, the experimental researcher is seeking to ascertain and measure the extent to which a treatment causes a clearly measured outcome within a specified research setting, whether in a laboratory or in the field.

Although the underlying structure of the experimental research design is essentially consistent across diverse topic areas, researchers vary in the extent to which they take "causality" for granted.[7] Experimental research in environmental technology (such as the metal roof study) is more likely to take causality for granted than research in socio-cultural aspects of architecture (such as the gender designation study). This is because environmental technology, like much research in natural science, tends to incorporate the following characteristics: 1) the use of laboratory settings where relevant variables can be easily controlled; 2) dependent variables that are in many instances inert, and therefore not likely to change except as a consequence of the treatment; 3) explicit theories that enable researchers to specify the expected effects of a particular treatment; and 4) instruments that are calibrated to measure such effects. Given these conditions, causality can often be assumed without much discussion or argument.

In research that involves people's reactions or behaviors, or more complex arrays of variables in field settings (as in Devlin's research), researchers tend to be more explicit about how they have met the basic requirements of experimental design. Likewise, in drawing their conclusions, researchers who explore socio-physical dynamics in architecture tend to emphasize the conditions and limitations of a causal interpretation. Devlin, for example, qualifies her conclusion that male respondents tend to rate senior female applicants less positively than senior male applicants. Devlin mentions two limitations to a causal interpretation: 1) many respondents explained that they found it hard to rate the applicants because the resume information was so limited; and 2) the response rate was only 30% and therefore the extent of generalizability to the larger population of architect employers is limited. Such problems and limitations in experimental research will be discussed in greater detail in segment 9.5 of this chapter.

9.3   STRATEGY: DISTINGUISHING BETWEEN EXPERIMENTAL AND QUASI-EXPERIMENTAL RESEARCH

So far in our discussion, we have discussed only the general requirements of experimental research, without recognizing the very important distinction between experimental and quasi-experimental designs. This distinction rests on the manner in which the units of assignment (whether test cells, people, etc.) are selected. Although the goal for both experimental and quasi-experimental research is to achieve comparability among the units in each treatment group, such comparability is more precisely established in experimental research through random assignment. In contrast, the quasi-experimental research design is often employed in field settings where people or groups cannot be randomly assigned for either ethical or practical reasons. In such cases, the researcher seeks to ascertain or establish effective comparability across as many variables as possible. These considerations are discussed in greater detail below.

9.3.1 Random Assignment in Experimental Research

Random assignment plays an important role in experimental research when there is reason to believe that the units of assignment are not completely equivalent. It is considered the most effective way to ensure the essential comparability of treatment groups so that the observed differences in outcome measurements can be credibly attributed to the treatment.

In the gender discrimination study, Devlin was able to employ random assignment, even though the respondents were not conducting their evaluations in a laboratory setting. By choosing to manipulate the resume conditions rather than depend on the real-life applicant resumes received by these architects, Devlin could randomly assign the architects (registered in Connecticut, Devlin's home state) to the various resume conditions. This provides a greater level of assurance that the gender of the applicant actually had an effect on the male architects' evaluations.

On the other hand, experimental research based on inert materials (such as the Givoni et al. study) does not necessarily require such randomization measures. In most circumstances, the essential comparability of test cells or mock-ups can be assumed either because: 1) materials of the same physical specifications are used; or 2) the same physical unit can be reused in a different treatment condition. As a consequence, the authors of the metal roof study can claim that, given certain specified climatic conditions, the different measured cooling outcomes can be attributed to the differences in treatment conditions.

9.3.2 Nonrandom Assignment in Quasi-Experimental Research

As mentioned earlier, research studies conducted in the field frequently entail situations in which random assignments cannot be achieved for either ethical or practical reasons. For example, if a researcher wanted to test the effect of four lighting systems on employee productivity in four separate office areas, it is unlikely that managers would agree to assign their employees randomly to the four office areas in a way that would disrupt important work group functions.

In this situation, researchers would likely adopt a quasi-experimental design in which they would identify four *existing* work groups, each of which would receive a different lighting treatment. In doing so, the researchers would attempt to find work groups comparable in as many respects as possible, including their task or work objectives, mix of job types, gender mix, age range, level of education, etc. If, for instance, the work groups' tasks were quite dissimilar, it would then be more difficult to attribute measured differences in productivity to the lighting treatment rather than differences in the tasks.

Another example of quasi-experimental design is a small research project conceived and conducted by students in one of Groat's research methods classes.[8] The students had raised the issue of a small gallery area near the school offices that had been created to function as both an exhibit space and a lounge area for faculty and students. The students observed that the space was seldom used as a lounge. Discussion soon revolved around what sort of changes would have to made for the area to function more as a lounge and social space. The students hypothesized that the gallery would be used more if the arrangement of furniture were less formal and if small screening elements were used to block the view through the glass wall along the doorway side of the space.

The students' research design involved two sets of observations of the space. The first observations recorded people's use of the space in its existing condition; and the second recorded its use under the experimental treatment. The observations were made on the Monday (studio day) and Tuesday (nonstudio day) of two successive weeks, starting at 8:30 in the morning and continuing to 7:30 at night. Each observation period was of 15 minutes duration, starting on the half-hour and ending at 45 minutes after each hour.

The experimental treatment condition, used in the second two-day observation period, was designed to create a more "inviting" ambience; it entailed alteration of the furniture arrangement, lighting levels, and ambient sound. (See Figures 9.4 and 9.5.) More specifically, the following alterations were made: addition of screening elements to create more visual privacy from the hallway windows; relocation of some furniture elements for more privacy and to create groupings; lowering of fluorescent lighting

Figure 9.4 Existing condition of the gallery space, from Janice Barnes et al. Photo courtesy of Barnes et al.

Figure 9.5 Modified condition of the gallery place. Photo courtesy of Barnes et al.

levels; addition of incandescent table lamps; introduction of reading materials on the tables; use of soft background music; and introduction of plants.

The students also developed a one-page observation sheet that included the following information: a count of the number of people using the space during that observation period; a plan of the gallery including the furniture arrangement in which the people's movement and activities were mapped; and a coding system by which people's specific activities could be described (i.e. speaking, writing/reading, sleeping).

The general conclusion that the students were able to draw was that although the numbers of people using the space did not change substantially, the average amount of time each person spent in the gallery increased, and the nature of their activities changed as well. (See Figures 9.6–9.11.) Indeed, by the second day of the treatment condition, the proportion of staying activities was more than double that of the previous Tuesday in the control condition.

How much of this change can be attributed to the treatment effect? The circumstances of the field setting did not allow the students to assign gallery users randomly

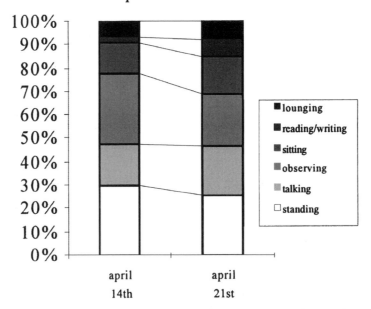

Figure 9.6 Comparison of observed activities for the existing and modified conditions, Mondays. Courtesy of Barnes et al.

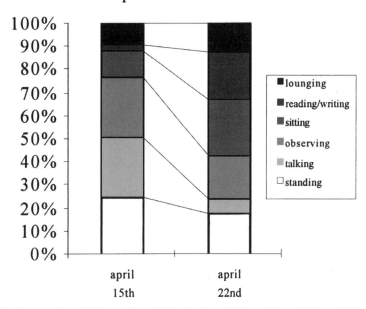

Figure 9.7   Comparison of observed activities for the existing and modified conditions, Tuesday. Courtesy of Barnes et al.

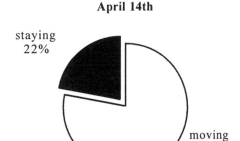

Figure 9.8   Moving/staying activities for the existing condition, Monday. Courtesy of Barnes et al.

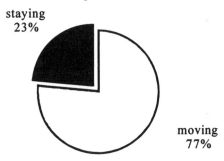

Figure 9.9   Moving/staying activities for the existing condition, Tuesday. Courtesy of Barnes et al.

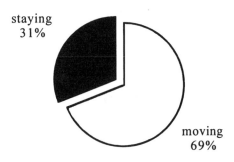

Figure 9.10   Moving/staying activities for the modified condition, Monday. Courtesy of Barnes et al.

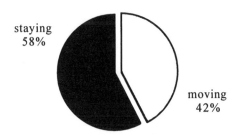

Figure 9.11   Moving/staying activities for the modified condition, Tuesday. Courtesy of Barnes et al.

to the two conditions, and so they adopted a quasi-experimental design. Since no specific measures of the gallery users were taken, it is not possible to gauge precisely how the users of the control condition compared with those in the treatment condition. Still, there were no obvious indicators that the groups were substantially nonequivalent. It is therefore likely, but not certain, that the "informal, inviting" condition did encourage a change in the use patterns of the gallery space.[9]

9.4   DIAGRAMMING EXPERIMENTAL RESEARCH DESIGNS

From the experience of the architectural design process, we know that it is often helpful, sometimes even essential, to diagram the singular qualities of a design concept or parti. In a similar vein, experimental researchers have devised a way of diagramming the particular details of experimental research designs, using the following coding system:

{R = Random assignment}

{X = Experimental treatment}

{O = Observation of dependent variables (e.g., pretest or posttest)}

Although there are a great many standard experimental research designs that use an established nomenclature,[10] we will limit our discussion to the three exemplar studies that have been discussed thus far in the chapter.

The Givoni et al. study of radiant cooling is represented below. Each row represents, from left to right, the sequence entailed in each treatment condition.

	O	{Observation only, with no prior treatment}
X1	O	{Treatment 1, and subsequent observation}
X2	O	{Treatment 2, and subsequent observation}
X3	O	{Treatment 3, and subsequent observation}

This notation system conveys the following essential points about the design of this study: 1) there is no explicit attention paid to random assignment, since all the relevant procedures deal with standardized inert materials; 2) there are three different treatment conditions in addition to the control condition; and 3) only posttest (i.e. no pretest) observations are made.

Devlin's study of gender issues in architectural practice presents a slightly different research design in the following respects: 1) random assignment is an explicit and important consideration for establishing comparability across treatment groups; and 2) there is no explicit control condition. However, as in Givoni et al.'s study, no pretest observations are made. Thus the notation system for this study can be represented this way:

R	X1	O	{Random assignment, followed by treatment 1, observation}
R	X2	O	{Random assignment, followed by treatment 2, observation}
R	X3	O	{Random assignment, followed by treatment 3, observation}
R	X4	O	{Random assignment, followed by treatment 4, observation}

The student study of behavioral patterns in a gallery space presents a slightly more ambiguous research design. This is because the researchers did not clarify the extent to which the people who experienced the original gallery arrangement were the same people who experienced the modified arrangement. (This could have been achieved by asking users if they had come into the gallery anytime during the previous Monday or Tuesday.) If the gallery users had been substantially the same group, then the notation of the research design would be as follows:

| O | O | X | O | O | {Two observations, treatment, followed by two observations}

This design is known as a single-group interrupted time-series design. Two pretest observations were made, after which the treatment (physical modification) was applied, followed by two posttest observations.

On the other hand, if the two sets of users were substantially or completely different, then it would be more accurate to diagram the research design in the following way:

| O | | O | {No treatment, two observations only}
| X | O | O | {Treatment, followed by two observations}

This second diagram presumes that the group that experienced the original gallery arrangement constitutes the control group, whereas the group that experienced the new arrangement was the experimental treatment group. Both control and treatment groups were observed twice, the treatment group only as a posttest.

Readers who choose to make use of experimental research procedures are advised to consult some of the books referenced at the end of this chapter for further examples of experimental designs. These diagrammatic notations can be exceedingly useful to the researcher for clarifying the precise nature and assumptions of the selected experimental design.

9.5   TACTICS: THE SETTINGS, TREATMENTS, AND MEASURES FOR EXPERIMENTAL RESEARCH

Experimental research can involve a wide variety of tactics. The experimental setting can range from a highly controlled laboratory to less well-controlled field site. Similarly, the treatment conditions can range from highly calibrated physical manipulations to categorical, nonphysical conditions, such as the gender designations in Devlin's study. And finally, measurement of the outcome variables can range from the precise calibration of a physical change (such as that of air temperature in the Givoni et al. study) to the more descriptive index of a behavioral response (such as in Devlin's study).

In the sections that follow, the broad range and combinations of tactics available to experimental and quasi-experimental research will be discussed in the context of several specific research studies.

9.5.1 Tactics Used in the Example Studies

Before considering additional examples of experimental research, we would like to characterize more explicitly the tactics used in the studies cited above. For instance, Givoni et al.'s study of radiant cooling employs the sort of tactics typically associated with experimental research in environmental technology. The construction and treatment of the test cells was carefully monitored within a university lab setting. The physical treatment conditions of the test cells could be precisely specified and controlled by the experimenters; and likewise the outcome measures of air temperature could be exactly measured by laboratory instruments. (See Figure 9.12 for a complete summary of the tactics used in the experimental studies cited earlier in this chapter. See Figure 9.16 for a summary of tactics used in studies cited in the remainder of the chapter.)

Study	Setting	Treatment	Outcome Measures
1. Radiant cooling (Givoni et al.)	Lab	Environmental modifications Modification insulation venting mass	Instrumented measures air temperature
2. Gender issues (Devlin)	Field	Resumes gender and seniority	Attitudinal response applicant evaluation hiring decision
3. Gallery behavior (Barnes et al.)	Field	Environmental modifications furniture lighting ambient sound	Behavioral change staying/moving screens

Figure 9.12 Summary of tactics in cited studies.

The Devlin study represents a set of experimental procedures starkly different from the Givoni et al. study. Indeed, one could argue that the combination of the setting, treatments, and measures in Devlin's study places it at the opposite end of the spectrum. First, the research setting is not only a field setting, but one that is dispersed across the country, in the many offices where the architects received the resume. Second, although the treatment conditions were conveyed physically in print through gendered names and stated levels of employment experience, the physical and interactive reality of a real-life applicant was absent. And finally, the outcome measures of evaluation and employment decision were rendered through scores on a questionnaire. In all of these ways, the focus of the study was on the social-cultural implications of non-physical treatment conditions, measured through attitudinal responses.

The student study of the architecture gallery, though quasi-experimental in design, represents an intermediate range of tactics. Although the study employs a field setting rather than a lab, this setting is relatively small and easily manipulated by the researchers. The treatment conditions are all physically based (e.g., arrangement of furniture, the type of lighting); they can be clearly specified and measured. And although the outcome is behavioral and requires some interpretation, the standards for counting people and classifying behavior are easily established.

9.5.2 Occupant Comfort from Air Movement: Using a Lab Setting, Physical Treatments, Instrumentation, and Subjective Measures

Although much environmental technology research relies on combining lab settings with exclusively instrumented measures of physical outcome variables, many other variations of lab setting research are possible. One example is a study by Edward Arens et al. concerning the use of personally controlled air fans to achieve cooling and perceived comfort.[11] The goal of this study was to evaluate the effectiveness of using fans, instead of compressor-based air conditioning, to achieve cooling comfort. The study was conducted in an environmental chamber (i.e. lab setting) where individual subjects could be exposed to a controlled range of warm temperatures. (See Figure 9-13.) The environmental chamber was designed to "appear as a realistic residential or office space."[12]

The 119 subjects (57 female, 62 male) were divided into two comparison groups. One group was asked to control the fan settings "in a naturally fluctuating outdoor mode"; and the second group used the fan's constant mode, "in which the inherent turbulence of the airstream was at higher frequencies than in the fluctuating mode."[13] During both experimental protocols, the subjects' time in the experimental chamber included two distinct activity segments generating two distinct metabolic rates: one that included both sitting and step-climbing (1.2 met), and another that was entirely sedentary (1.0 met). Throughout all sessions, the subjects experienced a range of temperatures from 25 to 30 degrees C. Thus the treatments represented a combination of both lab-based controls and behavioral regimens.

Figure 9.13 Environmental chamber. Photo by Marc Fountain, courtesy of Prof. Edward Arens.

The outcome measures included both instrumentation and subjective ratings of comfort. The former involved recording the subject's choice of fan speed; the latter used a seven-point scale from cold to hot indicating how the subject experienced the temperature of the environment. More than 80% of the subjects at the 1.2 met condition were able to maintain comfort up to 29 degrees C. As a result, the researchers were able to conclude that within certain temperature zones, the use of personal air fans can serve as an effective alternative to mechanical air-conditioning.

9.5.3 Experimental Validation of Simulation: Using a Lab Setting, Physical Treatments, and Instrumented Measures

Environmental technology research sometimes employs a combination of experimental and simulation strategies. Medved and Novak's study of double-pane windows, described briefly in Chapter 2, is an example of this combined strategy.[14] The researchers' objective was to evaluate the effectiveness of a double-pane window design with a screen and a siphon forming a semi-open cavity. (See Figure 2.1.) They used a mathematical and numerical modeling (simulation) strategy, which they then validated through experimentation.

BOX 9.1

Experiment: Energy Conservation in Housing

Malcolm Bell and Robert Lowe sought to test the impact of various energy-saving techniques in housing administered by the Housing Authority of York, United Kingdom.* (See Figure 9.14.)

In this field-setting experiment, the authors measured the impact of energy-saving improvements in modernized housing against a "control group of dwellings in the same modernization scheme but with no additional energy efficiency works."** The 21 houses in the experimental group were modernized with a combination of clearly specified physical treatments: insulation, draft-proofing of doors and windows, central heating with gas-condensing boiler, and a gas fire as a secondary heat source. The 11 houses in the control group, with no additional energy efficiency works, were well matched with the experimental houses in terms of their initial energy consumption. As a consequence, any consistent differences in energy consumption could be attributed to the experimental treatment.

Monitoring measures included internal temperatures and gross energy consumption for the entire period, both of which were based on instrumentation. Although the difference of 5536 kwh between the experimental and control groups is statistically significant at the .03 level, the measured savings are about half of what was predicted by energy modeling. Further investigation, including interviews with residents, indicated that some residents used the secondary heat source, the gas fire, so often that the energy efficiency of the gas boiler was compromised. The monitoring of energy-efficient modifications in this real-world housing setting thus provided important insights about the limits of conservation hardware when not accompanied by changes in human behavior.

Figure 9.14 Typical house type in Malcolm Bell and Robert Lowe's energy-efficient modernization study. Reprinted from *Energy and Buildings* 32 (2000), with permission from Elsevier Science.

---

*Malcolm Bell and Robert Lowe, "Energy Efficient Modernization of Housing: A UK Case Study," *Energy and Buildings* 32 (2000): 267–280.

**Ibid., 272.

The experimental design, in this case, involved the use of a laboratory setting, physical construction of the treatment condition, and instrumented measurement of the outcome variables. The lab setting was a temperature-controlled room into which a large "hot box" was placed; the hot box was a cube, on one side of which the double-pane window design was installed. In the first series of experimental treatments, the temperature inside the hot box was higher than in the controlled chamber; whereas in the second series of experiments, the air inside the hot box was cooled. Outcome measurements included the following: thermacouples measured air and surface temperatures; bulb thermometers measured radiation temperature; and flux sensors measured heat fluxes. (See Figure 9.15.)

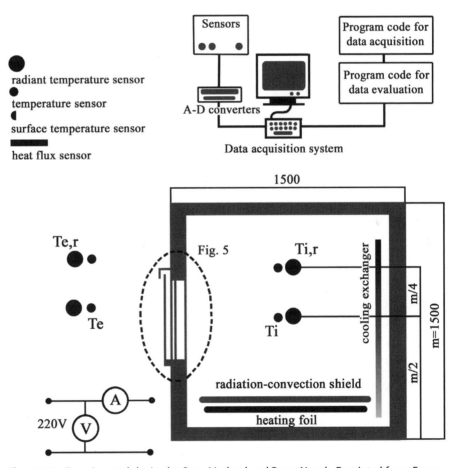

Figure 9.15 Experimental device by Saso Medved and Peter Novak. Reprinted from *Energy and Buildings* 28 (1998), with permission from Elsevier Science.

1. Personally controlled air fans (Arens et al.)	Lab	Physical treatments temperature activity level fan type	Instrumented measures and behavioral response fan speed choice perceived comfort
2. Energy use in housing (Bell and Lowe)	Field	Environmental modifications gas boiler insulation draft proofing secondary heat	Instrumented measures internal temperature gross energy consumption
3. Window pane design (Medved and Novak)	Lab	Environmental change hot box temperature radiation temp heat fluxes	Instrumented measures temperature measures
4. Perceptions of facades (Stamps)	Lab	Treatment of facade features	Perception of architectural mass

Figure 9.16 Summary of tactics in cited studies.

On the basis of the combined simulation and experimental strategy, Medved and Novak conclude that the double-pane design that includes a cavity with a "y" siphon provides good thermal insulation and shade protection. The researchers were able to validate a simulation model using limited experimentation; and that simulation model was used to achieve a much broader performance analysis of the windowpane design for specified climate conditions.

BOX 9.2

Experiment: A Study of Facade Treatments

Stamps's study of the effects of design features on people's perceptions of architectural mass uses an experimental research strategy, and in that regard it is unusual.* Many, probably most, studies of nonarchitects' or users' responses to building facades employ a correlational strategy involving assessments of actual buildings. Stamps's research strategy involved the use of computer-generated sketches of building facades that systematically varied the architectural treatment of each facade. Based on a previous pilot study, four key variables were identified as having a potential impact on respondent assessments; these variables were: visual area, partitioning of facade elements, fenestration, and articulation (e.g., bays or notches) of the facade plane. Using an experimental research protocol that enabled multiple treatments to be combined across a limited number of stimuli (i.e., the facades), Stamps generated the nine facade examples represented in Figure 9.17. A survey research firm was asked to recruit a random selection of respondents from the area. Each respondent was asked to view paired sets of the facades and indicate which facade appeared to be more massive.

The results of Stamps's study indicate that the most influential variable by far was visual area, which can be modified in situ by setback requirements. Fenestration treatments had a much more modest impact on perception of mass; and both articulation of the facade plane and the partitioning of facade elements had minimal impact.

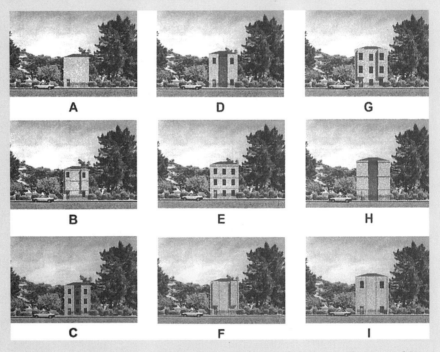

Figure 9.17   Computer-generated facade stimuli from Arthur Stamps. Courtesy of Pion Limited, London.

---

*Arthur Stamps, "Measures of Architectural Mass: From Vague Impressions to Definite Design Features," *Environment and Planning B: Planning and Design* (1998): 825–836.

9.6   CONCLUSIONS: STRENGTHS AND WEAKNESSES

Of all the research design strategies commonly employed by researchers, the experiment is, in all likelihood, the most controversial. On the one hand, experimental design is considered by postpositivist researchers to represent the highest standard of research.

> The best method—indeed the only fully compelling method—of establishing causation is to conduct a carefully designed experiment in which the effects of possible lurking variables are controlled. To experiment means to actively change {x} and observe the response {y}.[15]

This quotation crisply encapsulates the essence of what is seen as experimentalism's major strength: it is the most credible device for determination of causality.

On the other hand, the experimental design is widely criticized for a variety of reasons by researchers representing both the naturalistic and emancipatory paradigms. Most criticism centers on the following issues: 1) efficacy and accuracy; 2) misapplication of experimental procedure, or 3) ethical concerns. (See Figure 9.18.)

Efficacy and Accuracy. The essence of the argument concerning the efficacy of experimental method is that most real-life settings and socio-cultural phenomena are far too complex to be reduced to a small set of treatment and outcome variables. Moreover, the laboratory setting is seen less as a "neutral social environment" than as a "specific social environment that exerts its own effects."[16] Critics argue that instead, settings and phenomena must be studied in natural settings, in all their complexity. As Michelle Fine and Susan Gordon put it,

Strengths	Weaknesses
Potential for establishing causality	Reduction of complex causality reality to identify "casual" or independent variables
Potential for generalizing results to other settings and phenomenon	Misuse by overgeneralization to different ethnic, gender populations
Ability to control all aspects of experimental design enables attribution of causality	Overemphasis on control yields ethical problems, dehumanization

Figure 9.18   Strengths and weaknesses of experimental research.

If you really want to know either of us, don't put us in the laboratory, or hand us a survey, or even interview us separately alone in our homes. Watch me (MF) with women friends, my son, his father, my niece or my mother and you will see what feels most authentic to me. These very moments, which construct who I am when I am most me, remain remote from psychological studies of individuals or even groups.[17]

Misapplication. Critics who cite the misuse or misapplication of experimental protocol frequently focus on the way biases or oversights can inadvertently influence the results of such research. This critique is articulated quite clearly by the well-known feminist researcher Shulamit Reinharz. She argues:

[P]ublication practices and experimental design highlight differences and hide similarities between groups. Overgeneralization that masks differences in race, age, education, and other factors is clearly inappropriate and possibly dangerous. Too often studies done on white populations are generalized to all groups, just as studies done on men are generalized to all people, thereby producing distorted results.[18]

A number of feminists and others affiliated with the emancipatory paradigm have proposed a more nuanced and pragmatic perspective whereby the experimental research design is actually employed to reveal gendered and racist practices. Indeed, Devlin's study of gender discrimination in hiring is an example of this trend. Implicit in this use of the experimental method is the belief that, given the power and respect it commands in so many quarters, feminist and other emancipatory research will only be seen as credible if it is conveyed in the form of the dominant experimental paradigm.

Ethical Concerns. The core of the ethical concerns that have been raised about experimental design is that the manipulative control exercised by the researcher puts research subjects in an essentially powerless position. Treatments are often applied to subjects without their consultation. A potentially advantageous treatment (i.e. better lighting or gender-neutral pedagogy) might be withheld from the "control" group of subjects. Even using the term *subjects*—as opposed to people or individuals—tends to dehumanize those who participate in such studies.

In the end, it would seem that the experimental research design offers both profound strengths and potentially serious weaknesses. The former include the ability to attribute causality, as well as prestige and credibility in some circles. Indeed, in some areas of research—notably in the more technical areas—the premises of experimental work remain unchallenged, although such work is now frequently complemented by computer simulation models. The shortcomings of the experimental model include inappropriate simplification of complex research issues; the potential for misapplication; and the potential for serious ethical problems. However, even Reinharz argues that despite its apparent weaknesses, researchers may do well to exploit its strengths:

> Combining the strengths of the experimental method with the strengths of other methods is probably the best way to avoid its weaknesses while utilizing its power. Similarly, combining the strength of research with the power of other forms of persuasion is probably a useful approach for creating change.[19]

The notion of combining distinctly different research strategies is one that has become increasingly popular among researchers in diverse fields and disciplines. It is a topic to which we will return in Chapter 12.

9.7   RECOMMENDED READING

For readers who would like a general discussion of experimental and quasi-experimental research design, there are two classic books: Donald T. Campbell and J. C. Stanley, *Experimental and Quasi Experimental Designs for Research* (Chicago: Rand McNally, 1966); and Thomas D. Cook and Donald T. Campbell, *Quasi-Experimentation: Design & Analysis Issues for Field Settings* (Boston: Houghton-Mifflin, 1979).

For readers who would prefer a more compressed overview of experimental and quasi-experimental design, Donna Merten's chapter "Experimental and Quasi-Experimental Research," *Research Methods for Education and Psychology* (Thousand Oaks, Calif.: Sage Publications, 1998) is quite readable. A briefer, more prescriptive reference on how to conduct experimental research is provided by John Creswell in a chapter segment entitled "Components of an Experimental Method Plan," in *Research Design: Qualitative and Quantitative Approaches* (Thousand Oaks, Calif.: Sage Publications, 1994): 126–142.

NOTES

1. Baruch Givoni, Michael Gulich, Carlos Gomez, and Antulio Gomuz, "Radiant Cooling by Metal Roofs in Developing Countries," *Proceedings of the 21st National Passive Solar Conference* (Boulder, Colo.: American Solar Energy Society, April 1996): 83–87.

2. Ann S. Devlin, "Architects: Gender-Role and Hiring Decisions," *Psychological Report* 81 (1997): 667–676.

3. Ibid., 670.

4. Ibid., 667.

5. Ibid., 674.

6. Thomas D. Cook and Donald T. Campbell, *Quasi-Experimentation: Design and Analysis* (Boston: Houghton Mifflin, 1979).

7. Ibid.

8. Janice Barnes, Kaninika Bhatnagar, Fernando Lara, Satoshi Nakamura, Pirasri Povatong, Tien Chien Tsao, and Victoria Turkel, "Results of a Quasi-Experimental Treatment in the Architecture Gallery" (unpublished student paper, University of Michigan, 1997).

9. Despite these conclusions, a major obstacle to changing the furniture arrangement on a permanent basis was that the intended lack of visibility meant the security of the exhibits could not be monitored from the offices across the hall. As a result of this quasi-experiment, then, the student group made a policy recommendation to the administration that a separate student/faculty lounge area should be provided. At this writing, more than three years later, a new lounge is being built.

10. John Creswell, *Research Design: Qualitative and Quantitative Approaches* (Thousand Oaks, Calif.: Sage Publications, 1994); D. Mertens, *Research Methods in Education and Psychology* (Thousand Oaks, Calif.: Sage Publications, 1998).

11. Edward Arens, Tengfang Xu, Katsuhiro Miura, Zhang Hui, Marc Fountain, and Fred Bauman, "A Study of Occupant Cooling by Personally Controlled Air Movement," *Energy and Building* 27 (1998): 45–59.

12. Ibid., 46–47.

13. Ibid., 47.

14. Saso Medved and Peter Novak, "Heat Transfer through a Double-Pane Window with Insulation Screen Open at the Top," *Energy and Building* 28 (1998): 257–268.

15. D. Moore and D. McCabe, *Introduction to the Practice of Statistics* (New York: Freeman, 1993).

16. Shulamit Reinharz, *Feminist Methods in Social Research* (New York: Oxford University Press, 1992), 100.

17. Michelle Fine and Susan M. Gordon, "Feminist Transformations of/Despite Psychology," in *Gender and Thought: Psychological Perspectives*, ed. M. Crawford and M. Gentry (New York: Springer-Verlag, 1989), 106

18. Reinharz, 107.

19. Ibid., 108.

Chapter 10

Simulation and Modeling Research

10.1 INTRODUCTION

Rem Koolhaas is in Amsterdam and his client is in Chicago—but here they are chatting in the entry of the Campus Center at the Illinois Institute of Technology. The Campus Center is designed by Koolhaas, so architect and client have much to talk about as they experience the space. And yet this event is taking place before the building is even constructed. The encounter is by means of CAVE (Computer Assisted Virtual Environments), an innovative technology developed at the University of Illinois Chicago. CAVE enables participants to meet in a *virtual* space, while in reality they may be thousands of miles apart. Koolhaas and his client can interact in real time, their speech and even gestures captured by the technology. (See URL reference at note 25.)

Simulation research comes out of a general human fascination with the replication of real-world realities. Many art forms are essentially simulative. At the very beginning of Western ideas, Plato warned of the deceptive nature of copies of reality, while Aristotle valued the cathartic experience of viewing simulations of real life (specifically, theatrical performances). Both of these points of view relate directly to simulation research proper: the disadvantage of a loss of accuracy in replication, on the one hand, and the benefit of studying dangerous or otherwise harmful situations at a distance, on the other. While replications in art also yield knowledge of a kind (perhaps knowledge linked to aesthetic experience, or moral feeling), simulation research is characterized by the generation of data, in a propositional form, that can be returned to the real-world context for its benefit. In this chapter we first summarize some of the uses of simulation research, then present its major strategies and tactics.

10.1.1 The Uses of Simulation Research

Simulated contexts have many uses; the Koolhaas CAVE example, in which client and architect are able to experience a proposed design in "virtual reality" before moving ahead to build it, offers obvious benefits. A more standard use for simulation research is that it can yield information about *dangerous conditions* without placing people in harm's way. Simulations of building behavior in severe natural occurrences such as earthquakes or high winds have obvious utility.[1] Flight simulators enhance piloting skills in difficult circumstances without placing the pilots in jeopardy. A standard exercise in beginning courses in architectural structures involves loading a model bridge with weights until the point of structural collapse; clearly, these simulated incidents instruct without placing anyone in danger.

Related to danger is the question of *ethics*. Readers might recall the movie *The Truman Show*, in which the main character lives his entire life on a huge stage set complete with town, townspeople, beach, even storms at sea, all controlled externally by the producers, all unbeknownst to Truman. This is an example of what *cannot* be done with actual simulation research because of the obvious ethical problems; one just cannot "fool" people into simulated roles. Actual simulation research works in the opposite direction: it can circumvent ethical impossibilities because the replicated context is one that gets at issues of human interaction and behavior without placing the actors into compromising positions. One study that comes to mind involved simulations with clothed individuals that produced data on the use of toilet grab bars.[2] Clearly, observing people in the actual use of the toilet is not desirable or socially acceptable. The computer is also increasingly used to circumvent ethical obstacles to research. A paper by Feliz Ozel, for instance, outlines how a computer program can "predict" behavior in fire egress emergencies, obviously without placing actual persons in harm's way.[3] Of course, the fact that the actors were clothed in the case of the grab-bar study, and the fact that human behavior was "coded" into computer language, in the case of Ozel's study, both raise concerns about the accuracy of the data; the lack of real-world spontaneity is an embedded limitation of this research strategy.

Simulation research is useful when dealing with questions of *scale* and *complexity*. Current computer technology is well able to simulate natural as well as artificial phenomena at both the micro and macro ends of the scale. Clifford Pickover notes that computers can "simulate the tiny forces binding molecules . . . the support structures of huge skyscrapers . . . the behavior of the economy," and so on.[4] Users of computerized Geographic Information Systems (GIS) construct models predicting urban growth, transportation networks, and other large-scale built phenomena. These computer models manage extremely complex databases. For example, a recent program developed at the University of Washington to model urban growth (called UrbanSim) can be coupled with GIS technology. In one study, it identified 350,000 "objects" (households, developers, commercial units, etc.) in a projection of the growth of Eugene, Oregon.[5] These complex computations are only possible with computer technology.

The computer aside, simulation research is useful for studying the *subjective dimensions of human behavior* in relation to built environments. In the Netherlands, full-size mock-ups of entire residences are sometimes mandated before actual construction can proceed. The process allows architects to learn under research conditions why some people prefer certain environments and not others. It also allows the occupants of the future spaces to take part in the design process. Simulation in cases like this humanizes the design process: laypeople are empowered to shape their own living environments by experiencing and responding to the actual spaces before they are built.[6]

Simulation research is often used in *materials testing*. Many building components undergo tests replicating real-world stresses before being sold on the commercial market. Such tests are often mandated by government regulations. The Underwriters Laboratories (UL), for instance, specify the fire ratings of wall and ceiling assemblies by testing mock-ups under simulated fire conditions; UL numbers exist for many such assemblies, and code enforcement agencies usually require construction drawings to label all building assemblies with the appropriate UL designation. Manufacturers also impose performance standards upon the products they

Figure 10.1   Full size mock-up of residential spaces in Amsterdam: Resident participation in these simulated environments is mandated prior to actual construction of the design. Courtesy of Plenum Press.

make and sell: windows, doors, roofing, wall materials, and so on. Related to materials testing is the issue of *cost savings*. Large and complex architectural projects often require mock-ups of certain portions of the work to aid designers in product selection and/or design before materials are ordered in bulk. It is not uncommon for building specifications on larger projects to require the contractor to construct mock wall cladding systems (for instance) as part of the project bid, so that a value analysis can be performed before final design decisions are made.

In a general sense, simulation research is useful both in *developing theory* and in *testing theory*. This is a point made by William Crano and Marilynn Brewer.[7] They note that simulation research is often useful at an "intermediate" point of knowledge acquisition. That is, when a logical explanatory system has been framed (see Chapter 11), simulation research can help test, or at least enact, that conceptual system in an empirical venue. This is particularly true for theory-driven proposals for how physical environments can enhance (or otherwise alter or benefit) some aspect of life. For instance, full-size residential simulations provide data for affirming or disproving theoretical preconceptions; they can also provide material for new theory-making.

10.2   THE STRATEGY OF SIMULATION RESEARCH

Simulation research involves controlled replications of real-world contexts or events for the purposes of studying dynamic interactions within that setting. Colin Clipson calls these replicated contexts "virtual worlds" and the contents of these contexts "synthetic elements." The philosophical assumption in this approach, in Clipson's words, is that: "synthetic elements of the virtual world are accurate representations of the real world in all effects. . . . The experience of these elements is similar to what one would experience in the real world."[8] Increasingly powerful computer applications such as CAVE affirm this statement in new ways.

10.2.1 Representation versus Simulation

Simulations should not be confused with representations. We use the word *representation* to denote a fixed image that stands for a "real" object because the image has measurable qualities that describe and depict the real thing. By this definition, architectural drawings are representations. Photographs, the images that much of architectural education is dependent upon, are also representations (although studies of the efficacy of photographs as "simulations" have been done).[9] To-scale architectural models are representations as well. All of these remain "merely" representational unless they are included in a larger research program in such a way that the manipulation of specific factors results in useful data that can be applied back into the real-world context under study.

Figure 10.2 A to-scale model of a proposed church interior constructed by students in an interdisciplinary design studio at Washington State University at Spokane. Courtesy of Matthew Melcher.

For our purposes, *simulation occurs when a replication of a real-world context (or a hypothesized real-world context) contains within it dynamic interactions that are the result of manipulated factors. These interactions are reflective of interactions actually occurring in the real world, and a simulation research design is one that is able to collect data on these interactions for application into the real-world context.* Simulation studies can certainly make use of fixed representations such as drawings, to-scale models, and photographs. The key, however, is that a controlled replication must be defined and that specific data comes out of the replication. A good example is a study utilizing photographs (slides) and to-scale models of nursing homes. Rather than bringing elderly people to the actual buildings, researchers showed them models and a series of slides of the spaces. It was shown in this case that those experiencing the simulated environments had a better "working knowledge" of the buildings than those who actually visited them. The latter group experienced difficulty finding places out of sequence from their initial site exposure, but the group who participated in the simulation did not experience similar difficulty (they in fact found places not included in the simulated visit).[10] In another study, Rachel Kaplan summarized findings in which rough to-scale models of apartment complexes were found to be equivalent to high-detail models of the same complexes in terms of citizen groups' ability to assess a building's layout.[11] In both these instances, still representations were used such that subject interaction with them in prescribed ways produced data useful for application in the real world.

Figure 10.3   One frame of a continuous sequence showing sunlight and shading relationships through the course of a day. Readers can view this "winter solstice animation" on *http://www2.arch.ttu.edu/per100s/design/students/delao/proj3/final/animations.htm*. Courtesy of Robert Perl, Texas Tech University.

Now, even though the above distinction between representation and simulation is clear at a theoretical level, computer technology has blurred this distinction somewhat in practice. An architectural renderer could once demonstrate virtuosity by casting shadows in an "artist's rendition" of a design project that matched the actual shadows on the building when the project was built. It is now a matter of inconsequence for any of several commercially available computer programs to dynamically depict a building's shadows as the sun moves through the course of a day, at any location on earth, in any season (Figure 10.3). While the artist's rendition is at best an accurate representation, the computer images must be considered simulation. And the dynamism does not necessarily require time-lapse movement. For example, computer programs can now routinely depict not only correct natural lighting angles in renderings of architectural settings, they can also calculate the visual quality of the *reflected* light as natural light interacts with the kinds of surfaces scheduled in the design. This also is closer to simulation, because it provides real-world information in ways that yield measurable, and useful, data.

BOX 10.1

Computer Rendering and Simulation

Computer simulation is also useful for spatial models. The Lightscape rendering program not only renders the effects of light in a space by calculating diffuse as well as sharp lines of lighting, the program can also "walk" a viewer through a series of designed spaces. The program computes the correct foot-candle values for all surfaces scheduled in the design, calculating how each scheduled material will affect the reflected light. For artificial lighting, Lightscape accepts light fixture data from manufacturers and includes this in its calculations. These kinds of programs underline the blurring between mere representation and simulation.

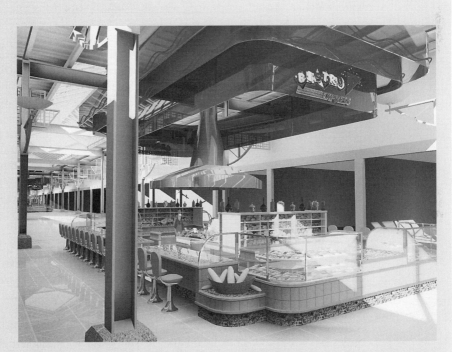

Figure 10.4 Computer rendering of an eatery at the Cherry Hill Mall, Cherry Hill, New Jersey. Software used: DataCAD 7 (3D model), Lightscape 3 (Radiosity Processing and Ray-traced Rendering), Micrografx Picture Publisher 7 (Image and Material Editing), Visual Reality 2 (Seamless Textures). Hardware used: 486 DX4/100 (model), PentiumPro 200 (rendering). Courtesy of Stephen Mallon, architect, Wyndmoor, Pennsylvania.

10.2.2 Types of Simulation Models

For our purposes, *model* and *simulation* are closely related terms. The term *model* is used to denote more than just static representations such as a particular scale model of a building. Rather, a model is a replication that aims to abstract natural laws and/or social-cultural factors that are involved in the interactions of the real world.[12]

A model can exist in a variety of forms, from the mathematical, consisting of abstract numerical expressions, to the physical, such as the simulated toilet area for testing grab bars. Clipson lists four types of simulation models: *iconic, analog, operational,* and *mathematical.*[13] The first two have more to do directly with physical contexts, iconic denoting the testing of materials or products and analog denoting a "dynamic simulation of an actual or proposed physical system." Flight simulators are of these varieties. *Operational* models deal with people's interaction within physical contexts, but the emphasis is more upon the data generated by role-play. *Mathematical* models are systems of numerical coding that capture real-world relationships in quantifiable abstract values.

While Clipson's typology offers a useful overview of the range of simulation models (and we make use of his terminology in this chapter), perhaps it is not as clear about the extent to which the computer is an increasingly present factor in each type. (Clipson's article appeared only in 1993, less than ten years before this book was written; this underlines how rapidly computers are affecting simulation research). In this chapter we treat the computer as a tactical tool in simulation research (see section 10.4), but its increasing power must be recognized as something that may eventually affect how simulation is understood at the strategic level. For instance, the Ozel study of human behavior in fire emergency situations (an analog or operational simulation under Clipson's typology) illustrates how human free agency can more and more be represented as a coded factor in computation-based (essentially mathematical) models. We therefore propose the general term *computer models*, with the understanding that it intersects all four of Clipson's typologies as a powerful *tactical* category that can fundamentally transform how each model type can be operationalized. By computer models we mean two-dimensional images on the computer screen that create the illusion of three-dimensional depth. The computer can create other kinds of depth as well. "Depth" can mean the ability to dynamically depict sequences of perspective views through time. Or it can mean the ability to represent dynamically changing conditions (such as stresses in a building structure). Or it can mean the ability to stack many layers of spatial information that yield new data when selectively intermixed together. Depth can even denote a computer's ability to project human actions. The key attribute is the computer model's power to convey *dynamic* spatial and/or temporal (and in Ozel's case behavioral) information via the two-dimensional computer screen. The power of the computer, which continues to increase, must thus be regarded as a significant factor in transforming all four of Clipson's typologies at least at the operational level.

10.2.3 Relationship of Simulation Research to Logical Argumentation

We have already noted Crano and Brewer's point that simulation research can be used to empirically test a theoretical position—which can then yield data for more theory-making. Insofar as the theoretical system is a product of logical argumentation, the *conceptual* framework of that theory, as a system, and the *simulational* framework of a model in simulation research makes for an informative comparison. First, the framework of a logical system is essentially conceptual; it is systematic reasoning expressed in language and/or signs. This is explained in detail in the next chapter (Chapter 11). A logical system can *explain* dynamic interactions but cannot actually *demonstrate* them. On the other hand, the simulational framework by its very nature is able to demonstrate dynamic interactions and to yield empirical outputs. This *demonstrative* capability is at the heart of why simulation research can add to (or negate) the claims of a purely logical (that is, a conceptually expressed) theory. This leads to the second point of comparison. While systems of logical argumentation strive for universal applicability, a simulational system is designed to *enact* a particular case, or at most a limited number of cases, of the general theory. A third connection is this: insofar as a computer model can be made of any of Clipson's four types of simulation study, the strategy of logical argumentation becomes more enmeshed with simulation research. This is because any computer program is necessarily a formal-mathematical system, that is, a domain of logical argumentation (see Chapter 11).

10.2.4 Relationship of Simulation Research to Experimental Research

Experimental research isolates a context and identifies variables that can be manipulated to see how they affect other variables (see Chapter 9). Simulation research also isolates contexts and manipulates variables; in these respects it is related to experimental research. Some cases of experimental research use simulation comfortably as the primary tactic; Clipson's iconic category (e.g., testing of materials or building products) is often experimental research operationalized by simulation. But simulation research recognizes that cause-effect relationships are usually not clear in real-world contexts, which often involve probabilistic factors, that is, variables and interactions that are hard to precisely isolate beforehand. Simulation research is simply able to bring out certain interactions in higher relief for study and data collection. Consider an example. John E. Flynn *et al.* arranged a space in a lighting laboratory to look like a conference room.[14] They then asked 12 groups (96 subjects total) to react to six different lighting combinations of overhead down-lighting and wall-lighting. The authors sought to measure four factors: evaluative impression, perceptual clarity, spatial complexity, and spaciousness. Among other results, they found that overhead down-lighting scenarios, regardless of the foot-candle intensity, were rated "hostile" and "monotonous" compared with options involving wall-lighting. The point for us is that the tactic in this experiment was a simulation—six lighting scenarios in a simulated conference room.

10.2.5 Relationship of Simulation Research to Correlational Research

As we saw in Chapter 8, correlational research examines interactions between two or more variables in their free co-variation in natural (or real-world) settings, and not in the sense of one factor *causing* another factor. To the extent that co-variation of multiple factors is evident in simulation research, it bears a resemblance to correlational research. But in general, the external manipulation of variables makes simulation research essentially different from correlational research; the independent variable does not play a role in correlational studies.

BOX 10.2

The Bridge at Alton, Illinois

On November 12, 1997, the PBS *Nova* television series featured "Super Bridge," a documentary on how a new bridge across the Mississippi River was conceived, designed, and built for the city of Alton, Illinois.* The Old Clark Bridge, "designed in the days of the Model A Ford," was no longer serviceable for the city; a new bridge was needed. The following is a portion of the documentary dialogue.

> Narrator: The Army Corps of Engineers has built an exact model of the Mississippi where it flows past Alton between the old bridge and the site of the new bridge. Even the tricky currents and eddies are perfectly reproduced. The point is to see how the river, the old bridge and the new bridge will interact. In their design for the new bridge, the engineers have put one tower, or pier, right at the edge of the shipping channel, and the other pier as close as possible for the shortest, and thus cheapest main span.... With the help of a little confetti, the first problem with the Illinois pier was quickly revealed.
>
> Tom Pokrefke: As the flow moves downstream, the confetti on the surface actually has to separate and go around the pier itself. And navigation would not want to be around all that turbulence right around that pier.
>
> Narrator: Too much turbulence might spell disaster for the barges traveling up and down the river . . .

The results led the designers of the bridge to relocate the pier.

**NOVA #2416, "Super Bridge," November 12, 1997 (PBS). Available through NOVA online transcripts: http://www.pbs.org/wgbh/nova/transcripts/2416bridge.html

Figure 10.5 The bridge over the Mississippi River at Alton, Illinois. During pre-design, the Army Corps of Engineers constructed a model of the river, simulating even the currents and eddies of the water, to determine the optimal location of the piers. Courtesy Greater Alton/Twin Rivers Convention and Visitors Bureau.

10.2.6 Relationship of Simulation Research to Qualitative Research

For simulation research to be meaningful, the researcher must often supplement it with activities that are not directly within the domain of simulation. This is particularly true for analog or operational types of simulation involving human behavior. For instance, data often have to be collected about the subjects previous to their participation in the simulation. This can involve interviews, checking records or documents, or other kinds of qualitative field work that have little to do with simulation strategy. We give some examples in section 10.3.2. Simulation can also be a tactic in interpretive-historical research—that is, qualitative inquiries into past events or conditions. We provide a clear example of this in Chapter 6, in which a researcher reenacted how Inca masons might have dressed the stones for their large masonry constructions.

10.3   TACTICAL CONCERNS

Replicating the real world is a difficult proposition, particularly if the goal is to obtain useful information from the replicated world to guide action in the real one. It involves four general areas of concern: completeness of data input, accuracy of the replication, "programmed spontaneity," and cost/workability. These concerns also reveal the limitations of simulation research. Ways to overcome them are a large part of the tactics of this research strategy.

10.3.1 Accuracy of Replication

A replication must accurately reflect the real-world context as much as possible. In simulations of physical objects or materials, this is addressed by using full-size mock-ups. Additionally, the simulation should take place with as many connections to the real-world setting as possible. In iconic simulation, a product or material needs to be tested in the very conditions (thermal, wind, geologic, etc.) the real object will be situated in. The color durability of window frames, for example, can be tested by placing the full-size window in intense sunlight conditions for a prolonged period of time; or simulation might need to involve mechanical devices that can replicate the effect of sunlight. The same goes for a window's resistance to wind and rain: performance can be evaluated by mechanically replicating wind and rain forces impinging upon the full-sized window. In analog or operational simulations, the actors involved should be individuals who are actually from the setting. Robert Marans documents a study of hospital rooms that went through several mock-up iterations before the study was completed, each one made more "real" after assessing the simulated actions of the players (doctors and nurses) acting as themselves.[15]

In analog or operational simulation involving human factors, even when the roles are played by the people who belong to the actual setting, the spontaneity of human free agency cannot be fully replicated (see below). And of course, for example, in the testing of the operation of hospital rooms, the individual receiving care in these instances, for obvious ethical reasons, cannot be a real case. At the tactical level, the goal of simulation entails cutting the divide between the replicated world and the real world to as fine a difference as possible without losing the advantages of using a simulated event in lieu of the real one.

10.3.2 Completeness of Input Data

Related to accuracy is completeness of input data. The simulated enactment, whatever form it takes, is often dependent upon a variety of preenactment data collection tactics that are separate from the simulation research strategy itself. In Ozel's computer modeling of human behavior in fire emergencies, she had to "calibrate" the performance of her BGRAF computer model with the events of an actual fire by having the computer simulate human behavior in a mathematical re-creation of the event. That is, she compared the computed outcome with the records of what the actual people did. This required collection of data from the real event (where the fire started, the location of the 94 persons on the floor at the time, and so on). She concludes her paper by noting that relevant field notes from actual fire emergencies are so scarce that it is difficult to test the accuracy of the patterns of behavior derived from computer simulations—and so it is incumbent on the researcher to go and collect her own field data.[16]

Of course, the reason the calibration is needed in the first place is that Ozel's approach required the *translation* of three real-world realities into terms the computer could understand: the physical environment, the projected conduct of human beings during a fire emergency, and the behavior of the fire. All three must then be programmed into the computer in a way that brings them together in dynamic interactions, and that yields outcomes predictive of human behavior in actual fires. This process of translating real-world realities into computer language is more a work of logical argumentation (Chapter 11) than of simulation research. In Chapter 11, we note that internal coherence in a logical system is no guarantee that the system is accurately explaining a situation. Insofar as computer simulations are logical systems, the risk is even greater in that a program that "works" is no guarantee that the real-world data has been completely and accurately coded into the program.

A different concern for completeness of data is illustrated by R. J. Lawrence's paper on the use of spatial simulations in participant residential design.[17] Lawrence wanted to create a simulation in which people interacted with full-scale mock-ups of house interiors. But first, data had to be available to interpret the *meanings* of the decisions made by participants as they arranged the spaces to their liking. Specifically,

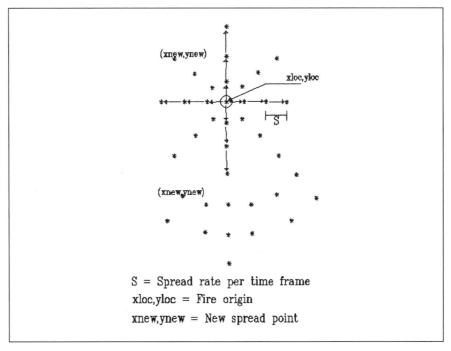

Figure 10.6   Spread of a fire in a building, coded into computer terms. From Ozel's study of human-space behavior in a fire emergency. Courtesy of Plenum Press.

Lawrence wanted to find out how participants' past and present housing experiences affected the choices in giving shape to their next home. To do this, he had to collect information via interviews, which coupled the simulation design with tactics from qualitative research. He also had to develop space syntax diagrams of the participants' past and present home plans, drawing from logical frameworks developed by Hillier, along with ones by March and Steadman. The study illustrates the complexity in discerning what kind of data must be included in the research design before a simulated study can have meaning.

If the example from Ozel illustrates the need for *field work* and accurate *logical translation* of real-world realities into computer language, and if Lawrence's work illustrates the need for a variety of preparatory *qualitative tactics* before the actual simulation, the emerging field of GIS modeling provides yet another kind of need for completeness of input data. This is the need to *harmonize* data from a variety of databases. Rapidly advancing computer power has made possible the "coupling" of large databases from different sources for the creation of highly complex computer models. Say a GIS operation seeks to project a city's future expansion so as to prescribe the location of new transportation corridors. This would entail incorporating a city's demographic data into a larger operation that also involves economic data, land-use data, transportation data, and utilities data, all rolled into a seamless computational framework. (See Figure 10.9 below.) It is clear that incomplete data in any one of these stores of information will negatively affect the outcome. Harmonizing the data, then, denotes two things. One is to make sure that the databases are all equally complete and up to date. The other is to make sure data in all stores are expressed in coordinate systems that are compatible with each other. The technical term *metadata* is used to describe this "data on the data," and there are now federal standards on the development, quality, storage, maintenance and use of metadata databanks, regulated by the Federal Geographic Data Committee (FGDC).[18]

10.3.3 "Programmed Spontaneity"—How Far from Reality?

Another concern of simulation research is the need to encourage spontaneity on the part of the players in an analog or operational simulation. Clipson suggests various tactics to address this need. First is programmed surprise, in which the participants in a simulation are not aware what the researchers have programmed to happen ("to achieve a high degree of realism, the simulation is designed to include elements of uncertainty and the consequent high level of tension"). Second, enactments should be conducted as close as possible to sites in which the event has actually occurred in the past (Clipson is here using terrorist attacks as the example). Third is use of the *empathic* model, in which a role is played for prolonged periods of time, in the real world, by the participant. The example is offered of a 26-year-old who with meticulous make-up and costuming transformed herself into an 80-year-old woman—and lived in this role for three years, three to four days per week. Another tactic is to have the key roles played by professional actors, while all other participants play themselves in their real-life occupations. Clipson suggests that participants who can internalize their roles will be more successful in generating realistic outcomes.[19]

10.3.4 Cost and Workability

The above considerations all raise the issue of expense. The mind can conceive of many simulation designs that are nevertheless difficult to enact largely because of *cost* and a related problem, *workability*. Iconic simulation requires the availability of the actual product or material, and then these must be exposed to complex replicated environmental conditions. Analog and operational simulations require not only mockups of physical objects or surroundings but also many individuals to play the parts. As we have seen, the key roles are sometimes played by professional actors. Mathematical models demand a great deal of time in translating real-world realities into computer logic; additionally, the increasing need to bring together preexisting databases into one modeling operation means further expense. Hence, many of the examples cited in this chapter come from funded research efforts, or from research and development departments in industry.

However, more episodic (and hence less costly) simulations can have heuristic value while lowering expectations for strict data outcomes. For example, students can simulate experiences of design and/or practice, with the understanding that, aside from any systemic data that might be produced, the experience itself constitutes a worthwhile "outcome." Full-size mock-ups of student designs are one example. At Ball State University, Professor Wes Janz describes this third-year undergraduate studio assignment, along with its heuristic value:

> The project was the design of a pedestrian canopy for a public plaza on the Ball State campus. About halfway into the project, each student constructed a full-scale mock-up of a section of the canopy and hauled it across the campus in order to locate the mock-up in the exact place it was designed for. . . . The students interviewed passers-by regarding their designs, watched persons interacting with the mock-ups, and sketched a three-frame sequence that studied the pedestrian interaction with the canopy from a variety of distances. For the final presentation ten days later, each student selected a key detail of the canopy which he/she then mocked up at full-scale as well. This was in addition to plans, sections, small models, and perspective of the final canopy design. . . . Among the benefits to the students are the realization that the small, important models they do become infinitely more complex (and interesting) as they approach ideas about material, connection, and a way of thinking for the project."[20]

At Washington State University, Professor Nancy Clark-Brown designed a studio project in which her students simulated the practice sequence of programming, design development, schematic design, working drawing, and construction phase submittals. Because the studio had an interdisciplinary mix of architecture, interior design, and landscape architecture students, each student played the role of his/her discipline. The project itself was fairly simple: an "intervention" into a transitional space such as a monumental stairway or a corridor. A key thrust of the effort was the operational simulation of actual practice. Clark-Brown programmed restrictions into the process that mirrored limitations faced by the practitioner in real life: time restraints, budget restraints, construction restraints, and so on:

> [The] design process model provided a structure representational of a model used by professional design teams to structure project deadlines. . . . After defining the project goals and designing the intervention students completed a working drawing set to construct the project from. The construction time allotted was two hours and they were given a budget of $100.00 maximum per team for the purchase of materials. Students were allowed to prefabricate pieces necessary to the construction process prior to the installation of the project.[20]

Figure 10.7 Intervention installation in a grand staircase (translucent panels at the monumental landing). The exercise gave an interdisciplinary team of design students (in architecture, interior design, landscape architecture) the opportunity to simulate a process of design, documentation, and construction with real-world time and financial constraints. Photograph courtesy of Professor Nancy Clark Brown, Washington State University.

Clark-Brown reports one heuristic outcome: "Students expressed a greater appreciation for the orientations of the distinct disciplines and made connections between them in the design process."

Another answer to the constraints of cost and workability is again the computer. While certainly not without cost, the computer's ability to substitute a computed simulation for one requiring physical mock-ups and/or human actors must be regarded as a potentially foundational shift in simulation research altogether. As we have noted, all four of Clipson's simulation model typologies can already be operationalized as computer models. There is no reason to think that computer models will not increase exponentially in their power to simulate all aspects of the natural as well as the social-cultural "real world." We now summarize some uses of computer modeling.

10.4   THE COMPUTER AS A TACTICAL TOOL

This section describes more explicitly the ways the computer can be used as a tactical tool in simulation research. First, research is being conducted on the ability of computers to replicate the generation of figurative design schemas by means of rule-based operations, once an exclusively human capability. This in itself is a kind of simulation research. In Chapter 5, we cite Margaret Boden's work with ACROBAT-Aaron, a computer that can generate "original" graphic schemas of human figures (see Figure 5.6). The computer is far from being able to "design a building from scratch," but we are unwilling to rule out this possibility. A more common subject of research is how computers and humans can generate design on an *interactive* basis. A joint project of researchers at Carnegie-Mellon University and the University of Adelaide is SEED (Software Environment to Support Early Phases in Building Design). This project pushes beyond traditional CAD paradigms, in which the computer is essentially used as a sophisticated pencil. SEED can propagate the implications of a human design decision throughout a design. Thus, changing the dimension of one room leads to alterations of other room sizes. Also, based upon a store of past instances of a given problem, the computer can show the designer a range of feasible solutions. The computer can also evaluate the merits of a particular design decision.[22]

Computer simulation also aids in the design and operation of "intelligent buildings." Jong-Jin Kim describes this scenario involving the use of an "intelligent card" (IC):

> When an employee enters a main entrance lobby using an IC card, the central building administration system sends an elevator to the lobby. As the person proceeds and enters his/her office, the IC card sends instructions to turn on the lights and the air distribution unit. In the evening, IC cards help to determine whether a space is occupied and, if it is unoccupied, the environmental systems are turned off automatically.[23]

Kim describes an automated system that anticipates future conditions and responds to the demands of those conditions. The conceptualization of these systems falls within the domain of simulation research, and depends upon the construction of mathematical models.

Mathematical models in turn draw upon mathematical-formal modes of logical argumentation (see Chapter 11). Energy simulation programs for buildings are often mathematical systems that represent, for instance, equipment performance under a given set of circumstantial parameters. We have already noted how the power of the computer increasingly makes possible different *kinds* of mathematical models, to the extent that human behavior can be computed.

Related to pure mathematical models are mathematical-spatial models, such as those made possible by GIS software programs. In these, a great deal of numerical data is represented spatially (that is, with graphics that denote spatial relationships, usually in plan), resulting in a graphic model of a projected condition. Figure 10.9 lists some of the databases brought together into a single GIS operation to determine the suitability for wildlife habitat of the Mirabeau Point area of Spokane County in the state of Washington (Figure 10.9).[24]

Figure 10.10 shows just a small portion of the spatial outcomes that these layers of information, when combined, can produce. GIS technology is currently being used by public agencies, corporations, real estate conglomerates, and research entities within academic settings, more than it is in the design professions. Its potential for architecture, however, is enormous, particularly as more and more geopolitical information is stored into databases around the world. Architectural companies can use GIS to project future spatial conditions in a variety of areas that can be of interest to clients. GIS can be used to produce transportation network projections, demonstrate population growth and demographic patterns, project business district and/or residential district evolution, optimize site selection criteria (or conduct comparative site studies), or quantify climate factors affecting building orientation and form. The ability of GIS to translate projections into two-dimensional images makes it useful not only for design but also for marketing.

Then there is "virtual reality." We define this term as computer environments that maximize participant interaction with the simulated context; the participant feels that he or she is able to freely interact with some or all of the elements of that context just as he or she can in a "real" setting. The CAVE capability referred to earlier is certainly at the cutting edge of this kind of simulation research, in that the technology is able to fully immerse the participant into a computer-replicated world. In addition, CAVE is able to "bring together" distant parties in one virtual setting, where both spoken and gestural communication can take place. There are currently 16 sites in U.S. academic institutions, with about the same number scattered in U.S. government and industry sites. Seventeen more CAVEs or CAVE clones are scattered worldwide.[25]

At present, CAVE technology is too expensive to be widely used. But virtual reality can also be nonimmersive, and much less costly. Leonard Temko's research at

BOX 10.3

Computer Simulation for History Research

The power of computers has opened a new line of research into historic structures. A recent study used computer modeling to show that the ornamental tracery on the hammerbeam trusses in London's Westminster Hall, built in 1395, plays a *structural* role. The authors contend that the load-bearing behavior of these trusses has escaped thorough analysis through the years because of their complex configurations. The computer changes this: It can process a large body of information in short periods of time, and it does this accurately without needing to "round off" numbers. After a truss has been coded into a computer model, a series of "what if" scenarios can be calculated."* In the study's truss diagrams reproduced below, the lower one shows the much larger bending moments (dark areas) in a scenario in which the computer has deleted the ornamental tracery from the calculations.

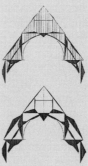

Figure 10.8B Computer models of the Westminster Hall truss using Finite Element Analysis. The lower diagram reveals larger bending moments when the ornamental tracery is deleted from the calculations. Courtesy of Stephen Tobriner.

Figure 10.8A Westminster Hall interior. By Sir Frank Baines, interior perspective, from Report on . . . Westminster Hall (1914).

---

*Toby E. Morris, Gary Black, and Stephen O. Tobriner, "Report on the Application of Finite Element Analysis to Historic Structures," in *Journal of the Society of Architectural Historians* 54 no. 3 (September 1995), 336–347.

Spokane County	University of Wash.	EPA	Census ESRI	Wash. Dept. of Ecology	NCRS	Wash. Dept. of Nat'l Res
Topography Parcels Bldg. footpr't Roads	Fish/wildlife Land use Wildlife corr. Veg. zones Wetlands Spotted frog	Watershed boundaries Digital elevations	Income data Population Schools	Hazardous sites Point source pollution sites	Soils	Rock substrate conditions

Figure 10.9 Chart of GIS sources. This figure gives an idea of the different kinds of data, from different sources, required for the project described. These are not necessarily root sources for each set of data. Rather, the headings indicate where this particular project turned to for information.

the University of Michigan involves external and interior spatial replication of canonical buildings (Schroder House, Villa Savoye, etc.) in the form of monitor-based "nonstereoscopic" simulations.[26] This means that the viewer is not immersed in the simulated context, but views the changing scenes on the computer screen in sequences that he or she can control. The viewer is able to navigate in and around each building and experience the spatial progressions, usually at eye level, although he or she can also "fly" through the spaces. The simulation is accomplished by readily available software: AutoCad Release 14, Kinetix 3D Studio Max, and Virtual Reality Modeling Language (VRML 107). Temko's research is also appealing in that he seeks to

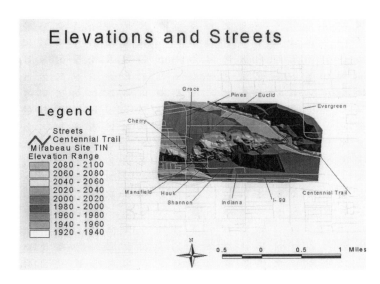

Figure 10.10 A small portion of a much larger board detailing suitability for wildlife habitat in a certain region of the state of Washington. Shown here is street information overlaying geological data. Courtesy of Tracy Morgan Grover, Washington State University.

broaden the applicability of virtual simulation to *general* architectural education. He likens the ability to depict canonical designs three-dimensionally in virtual reality to the revolution in perception brought on by perspective drawing. It is easy to see how this modeling technology can be used in instruction, from the design studio to history classes.

10.5   CONCLUSION: STRENGTHS AND WEAKNESSES

We considered simulation's relationship with neighboring strategies earlier in this chapter. We conclude by noting that simulation may be particularly suitable for use as a tactic in other research strategies. The data from simulation can be buttressed with data yielded by other means for more robust results. This certainly was the case, for instance, in Protzen's reenactment of Inca masonry fitting (see Figure 6.15 and related text): had he only used the reenactment, his claims would not have been as strong as they were when supplemented by other tactical findings. Including data from other tactics can help overcome the limitations we made note of in section 10.3.

Further consideration ought to be given to what *prediction* can mean in simulation research. In the simulation literature, the word is often used without specific elaboration as to what it means. This is the case, for example, in both Ozel's and Hunt's research.[27] Certainly the use of the word suggests the close relationship simulation has with experimental research. But there may also be a tendency to call any grasp of what will happen in the future "prediction." Closer consideration suggests that simulation research provides various kinds of information about future conditions that can be loosely described as predictions, but that vary in the degree of certainty they project about the behavior of particular variables. For instance, in many cases it is more accurate to say that simulation can reveal *patterns* of future behavior. Neither Ozel's and Hunt's research can predict specific future behavior for *this* person in a fire emergence or for *that* resident in a relocation; but both studies are valuable for understanding future patterns of behavior.

Simulation research can *project* conditions in the future. Suppose a large supermarket chain wants to build its next set of stores in growing population areas. GIS modeling, coupled with data from demographic databases and economic growth models, can project the development of an urban area for several years into the future. This data indicates the best locations for the new stores. Thus, such data is also *prescriptive* because it aids in decisions on what to do next. The utility of this research is clear for architectural firms marketing to corporate clients with long-term building agendas.

We have already noted that computer power is affecting how simulation research is designed and enacted, and this leads us to wonder what computer technology will bring next. With ever-increasing computational power, simulation research may become more and more synonymous with the framing of mathematical-formal models. On the other hand, it is difficult to imagine that computers will ever eliminate the need for data collection involving direct responses from human beings, especially when the goal is to understand issues of subjective feeling or preference.

Strengths	Weaknesses
One of the aims of simulation research is to capture the complexity of real-world behaviors (both natural and social-behavioral) in ways that do not require reduction to a limited number of discrete variables, as is the case in experimental research. It is able to reveal unexpected results that can inform either further research and/or action in the real world. Simulation research provides a variety of ways of understanding the future behavior of a context (in terms of patterns of behavior, or projections of behavior) without needing to be predictive in the strict sense of the world. On the other hand, because of the harmony between this strategy and experimental research, simulation can often serve as a primary tactic of experimental research. Because all research strategies involve "the real world" in some way, simulation tends to be useful at the tactical level to a variety of other strategies. For instance, it is conceivable that simulated environments can readily reveal correlational connections. The reader might also ponder the similarities and differences between J. P. Protzen's reenactment of Inca stone masonry techniques (see Section 6.6) and "simulation." Even though Protzen's actions may be challenged as to whether or not they constitute an "actual" simulation, his careful research into the conditions informing that particular reenactment raises fruitful issues for considering the quality of knowledge that comes out of role-playing.	The project of replicating a slice of the real world is necessarily limiting in that there is no definable way to assure the completeness (that is, the accuracy) of the replication. "Make-believe" contexts simply are not the same as real-world ones. What is more, the proposition itself that the world can be "replicated" raises both philosophical and practical questions. The philosophy aside, we have noted the various limitations associated with some common types of simulation research: lack of spontaneity in role-playing, for instance, or the challenges associated with coding aspects of human behavior into computer equivalents. Simulation research can become very expensive very fast. As such it may be out of the reach of individual and/or unfunded research. Inherent in the challenge of many simulation designs is how a level of accuracy of replication can be achieved with resources that are at hand.

Figure 10.11 Strengths and weaknesses of simulation research.

10.6   RECOMMENDED READING

Readers can refer to Stephen Sheppard's *Visual Simulation* (New York: Van Nostrand Reinhold, 1989) for a somewhat different view from ours; his use of the word *simulation* is closer to our word *representation*. But his text is good in summarizing a variety of ways that still images can be used to inform on future (or even postconstruction) realities. Written with little engagement with the computer, this text is still useful in outlining various ways of conceptualizing what simulation/representation can do for design investigation.

For a general collection of papers on simulation research, we recommend a text we have cited liberally in this chapter: *Environmental Simulation*, edited by Robert Marans and Daniel Stokols (New York: Plenum Press, 1993). Clipson's article offers a good overview of simulation and modeling. Other works in this book we did not cite here include studies involving color perception, synthetic landscapes, and landscape simulation, as well as implications of simulation research for regulations and policy.

Ozel's work is one example of computer simulation of people-space interactions. Michael O'Neill's "A Biologically Based Model of Spatial Cognition and Wayfinding" is another example (*Journal of Environmental Psychology* 11 (1991): 299–320). O'Neill outlines two opposing conceptions of how to model the subjective processing of environmental contexts for wayfinding: the computational process model and a biologically based model.

Another example of computer simulation comes from Rohinton Emmanuel, who explores the impact of urban heat islands on code policies for residential design in Sri Lanka. Rohinton Emmanuel, "Urban Heat Island and Cooling Load: The Case of an Equatorial City," in *Architecture, Energy and Environment*, (Lund, Sweden: Lund University, 1999, LTH): 16-1–16-10.

We have cited some of the following works on GIS modeling, but not all. The first two are introductions to the field. Michael N. Demers, *Fundamentals of Geographic Information Systems*, 2nd edition (New York: John Wiley & Sons, 2000); Karen C. Hanna and R. Brian Culpepper, *GIS in Site Design* (New York: John Wiley & Sons, 1998); Peter A. Burrough and Rachael A. McDonnell, *Principles of Geographic Information Systems* (New York: Oxford University Press, 1998). This next text is a compendium of essays for reference: *Environmental Modeling with GIS*, ed. Michael F. Goodchild, Bradley O. Parks and Louis T. Steyaert (New York: Oxford University Press, 1993).

VisionDome is another example of a virtual collaborative environment. Refer to the following URL for further information.

http://www.labs.bt.com/people/walkergr/IBTE_VisionDome/

NOTES

1. Colin Clipson, "Simulation for Planning and Design," in *Environmental Simulation*, eds. Robert W. Marans and Daniel Stokols (New York: Plenum Press, 1993), 42–45.

2. John A. Sanford and Mary Beth Megrew, "Using Environmental Simulation to Test Code Requirements," in *Enabling Environments*, eds. E. Steinfeld and G. Scott Danford (New York: Kluwer Academic / Plenum Publishers, 1999), 183–206.

3. See Filiz Ozel, "Computer Simulation of Behavior in Spaces," in *Environmental Simulation*, eds., Robert W. Marans and Daniel Stokols (New York: Plenum Press, 1993), 202–211.

4. Cifford Pickover, *Computers and the Imagination* (New York: St. Martin's Press, 1991), 15.

5. Michael Noth and Alan Borning, "An Extensible, Modular Architecture for Simulating Urban Development, Transportation, and Environmental Impacts," University of Washington. This paper is currently being reviewed for publication. Alan Borning may be contacted at borning@cs.washington.edu.

6. Roderick J. Lawrence, "Simulation and Citizen Participation," in *Environmental Simulation* eds., Robert W. Marans and Daniel Stokols (New York: Plenum Press, 1993), 143–145.

7. William Crano and Marilynn Brewer, *Principles of Research in Social Psychology* (New York: McGraw-Hill, 1973), 117–118.

8. Clipson, "Simulation for Planning and Design," 29.

9. Stamps does suggest photographs are a kind of simulation. A. E. Stamps, "Use of Photographs to Simulate Environments: A Meta-Analysis," *Perceptual and Motor Skills*, vol. 71 (1990), 907–913.

10. Michael E. Hunt, "Research for an Aging Society," in *Environmental Simulation*, ed. Robert W. Marans and Daniel Stokols (New York: Plenum Press, 1993), 98.

11. Rachel Kaplan, "Physical Models in Decision Making for Design" in *Environmental Simulation*, ed. Robert W. Marans and Daniel Stokols (New York: Plenum Press, 1993), 68–73.

12. Adapted from this statement from Louis T. Steyaert: "To study [these types of processes], either individually or as part of a system, physically based laws (e.g., Newton's laws of motion) or other types of assumptions are usually made on how the processes actually work. These laws or assumptions can be expressed as mathematical or logical relationships; collectively they represent a model." In "A Perspective in the State of Environmental Modeling," in Michael F. Goodchild, Bradley O. Parks and Louis T. Steyaert, *Environmental Modeling with GIS* (New York: Oxford University Press, 1993), 18.

13. Clipson "Simulation for Planning and Design," 30–34.

14. John E. Flynn, Terry J. Spencer, Osyp Martyniuk, Clyde Hendrick, "Interim Study of Procedures for Investigating the Effect of Light on Impression and Behavior," *Journal of the Illuminating Engineering Society* 3, no. 1 (October 1973): 87–94.

15. Robert Marans, "A Multimodal Approach to Full-Scale Simulation," in *Environmental Simulation*, eds. Robert W. Marans and Daniel Stokols (New York: Plenum Press, 1993), 113–131.

16. Ozel, "Computer Simulation," 204–206, 211.

17. R. Lawrence, "A Psychological-Spatial Approach for Architectural Design," *Journal of Environmental Psychology* 2, no. 1: 37–51.

18. The Federal Geographic Data Committee approved the Content Standard for Digital Geospatial Metadata (FGDC-STD-001-1998) in June 1998. Listed (here) is a chronological events calendar (most recent first) on the FGDC major activities to harmonize the FGDC Metadata Standard (FGDC-STD-001-1998) with the International Organization for Standardization (ISO) Technical Committee (TC)211 Metadata Standard 19115 (previously known as 15046-15).

19. Clipson, "Simulation for Planning and Design," 45–49.

20. Statement by Professor Janz in an e-mail correspondence with the authors, October 2000.

21. Statement by Professor Nancy Clark-Brown given to authors, October 2000.

22. Ulrich Flemming and Robert Woodbury, "Software Environment to Support Early Phases in Building Design (SEED): Overview" in *Journal of Architectural Engineering*, 1, no. 4, (1995), 147–152. A related effort, also with the goal of the computer responding to human design decisions, can be found in the paper by Scott A. Arvin and Donald H. House, "Modeling Architectural Design Objectives in Physically Based Space Planning," in *Acadia 99*, eds. Osman Ataman and Julio Bermudez (Philadelphia: IKON, 1999), 212–225.

23. Jong-Jin Kim, "Intelligent Building Technologies: A Case of Japanese Buildings," in *The Journal of Architecture Science* 1 (Summer 1996): 124.

24. Student Project in the WSU Department of Landscape Architecture, LA 467 Regional Landscape Planning and Analysis, Tracy Morgan-Grover, instructor. Students on this project: Melissa Sweeney, Lynn Gearhart, Matt Rapelije, Katie Johnson, Brian Donnelly (EPA = Environmental Protection Agency; ESRI = Environmental Systems Resources Institute, Inc; NCRS = National Resources Conservation Survey).

25. Jason Leigh, Thomas A. DeFanti, Andrew E. Johnson, Maxine D. Brown, Daniel J. Sandin. "Global Tele-Immersion: Better Than Being There" (Proceedings of ICAT '97 Tokyo, Japan, December, 3–5, 1997. For additional literature see http://www.evl.uic.edu/cavern/cavernpapers/index.html

26. Leonard Temko and Emmanuel-George Vakalo, "An Online Catalogue of Virtual Reality-Based Morphological Analyses," ACSA Technology Conference, MIT, Summer 2000.

27. Ozel, "Computer Simulation," 192: "BGRAF is potentially a predictive tool." Also Hunt, "Research Aging Society," 89: "The concepts of controllability and predictability are readily applied to relocation."

Chapter 11

Logical Argumentation

11.1 INTRODUCTION

In the *Theaetetus*, Plato's Socrates likens the possession of knowledge to having birds in one's private aviary. At this point in the dialogue, Socrates and his companions have just rejected an analogy likening knowledge to imprints made on a waxen tablet. According to this view, when we've learned that $5 + 7 = 12$, the "12" is imprinted onto the waxen tablets of our minds. But if knowledge is indeed like a waxen imprint (that is, if the answer is so easy to *see*), why do we sometimes still make the mistake that $5 + 7 = 11$, or another wrong number? The aviary analogy solves the problem. Rather than waxen imprints, the knowledge we have can be likened to birds flying around in the aviaries of our minds, each bird standing for "a piece of knowledge." And those little birds can be hard to catch! So, if asked what $5 + 7$ equals, we can easily nab the wrong bird, even though the right one is somewhere "in there." This explains why we give wrong answers even when we know the right ones.[1]

The efforts of Socrates and his friends illustrate an attempt at *logical argumentation*, which can be provisionally defined as making sense of some aspect of the cosmos in a systematically rational manner. The human mind often encounters a seemingly disparate group of factors or phenomena that it somehow senses can be interconnected into an explanatory system. Once this system is framed, it gives clarity to those disparate elements under a general heading. In Socrates's case, that heading was knowledge, and the goal of the exercise was to frame a logical system that can explain any instance of knowledge. The waxen tablet proposal was not flexible enough to accommodate all instances of knowledge; the aviary proposal seemed better.

The architectural literature and related literatures include works whose primary attribute is an ability to give logical order to a set of previously disparate factors. The works tend to be ends in themselves; their entire mission seems to be to frame logical

Figure 11.1   It's hard to nab the right bird. Photograph from author's collections.

conceptual systems that, once framed, interconnect previously unknown or unappreciated factors in relevant ways. We consider these works examples of *logical argumentation*, and this in more than just the general sense that all theoretical works have logical coherence. For heuristic convenience, we propose placing these works on a spectrum ranging from those that depend upon mathematical rules, at one end, to those that draw their logical coherence from the cultural world views they are embedded in, at the other. In between these two extremes are logical systems that seem to blend elements of the two. This spectrum is shown in Figure 11.2.

Formal-mathematical systems depend heavily upon rule-based propositions that are readily adaptable to the computer. One example is architectural morphology, sometimes called shape grammar (see Figures 11.4, 11.5). The advent of the computer has greatly aided the development of these systems, which in turn often result in computer software that analyzes extant designs for their basic syntactic rationale, or generates new figurative schemas based upon a formal-syntactic rationale. As Figure 11.2 indicates, formal-mathematical systems are typically expressed by *equations* or

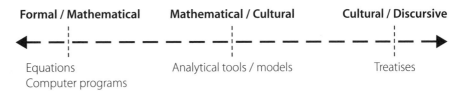

Figure 11.2   Spectrum of logical argumentation.

some other mathematical language. Computer software is another outcome of systems at this end of the spectrum.

At the other end are systems that have persuasive force because they capture a worldview and distill it into a logical argument with both theoretical clarity and rhetorical power. These systems use discursive language to anchor the validity of their claims to some larger transcendental venue (e.g., "nature," moral or ethical constructs, *a priori* reason, national identity, the machine) by systematic analysis and explanation. The result, if the explanatory system is successful, is its widespread acceptance, either as a normative basis for action in design, or as a way of understanding some aspect of human interaction with the built environment. This is because the work is able to somehow capture a culture's worldview in a discursive system that is perceived as a summary of its cultural "logic" relative to design action or style. As shown in Figure 11.2, we posit that these discursive works can be generally subsumed under the heading of *treatise*. There are many examples of the *treatise* in the literature; here we use Vitruvius's *Ten Books of Architecture* as an exemplar, but we will cite others as well. The term *treatise* is meant to emphasize the systematic nature of these works, in which detailed logical connections are provided in a variety of ways to frame an overarching argument.

In between these two poles are logical systems that share characteristics of both mathematical-formal systems and cultural-discursive ones. Like mathematical-formal systems, they may use numerical factors, equations, and rule-based propositions in their analyses of space and form, but with the view that the resulting data can shed light upon social-cultural values. An example is Bill Hillier and Julienne Hanson's *The Social Logic of Space*. This work frames a system in which an architectural plan is reduced to an abstract "map" (called a gamma map), along with a variety of numerical quantities, that unveil how patterns of social behavior relate to space adjacencies. The gamma map in effect becomes an *analytical tool*, and there are applications of this tool in the literature. In one of their own studies, the authors found that a great variety of English homes all have the same hierarchy of space adjacencies, a hierarchy linked to the values expressed in the social etiquette regulating contact between family and community.[2]

11.1.1 Primary Logical Systems and Secondary Research
in Logical Argumentation

We call logical systems that have broad explanatory power *primary logical systems*. These exist at a paradigmatic level; they not only frame a system with a very large explanatory scope, they also identify and define the internal technical terms and relationships that sustain the system. Once a primary system is in place, it has the ability to spawn many applicative (secondary) studies based upon the material it provides. These secondary studies usually do not expand the primary system with any new material. Rather, they tend to go deeper into the domain mapped by the primary system.

For example, shape grammar is a primary system; March and Stiny frame its general logical foundations:

> Architecture requires the delineation of one part of space from another. Such delineation, a configuration of lines, characterizes *shape*. The organization of a system of shapes gives space an *architecture*. Architecture in this sense may be applied to natural as well as to cultural phenomena, to works of nature and to works of man.[3]

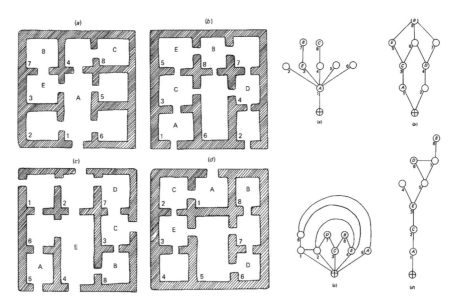

Figure 11.3 From Hillier and Hanson, *The Social Logic of Space*: The floor plans on the left are reduced to the gamma maps on the right. These maps are able to reveal patterns of spatial adjacencies. When the functional "label" each space carries with it is factored in, along with how many spaces removed each space is from the entry, patterns of adjacencies, reflecting social values, can be defined over a large sample of plans. By permission, Cambridge University Press.

The system posits that both natural and human-made forms are reducible to discrete rules regulating line-to-space relationships. Together these rules form a grammar that can describe the composition of extant works at an elementary level (perhaps uncovering traits unknown to the designer). It can also provide the basis for the design of new structures (see Figure 11.4). Now, if the system outlined by March and Stiny is the primary system, secondary studies use the parameters it sets forth. We provide an example of such a secondary study in Box 11.1.

Hillier and Hanson's *The Social Logic of Space* is also a primary system that sustains secondary studies. Here, all interior spaces and their adjacent relationships to other spaces, as well as to the outside, are reduced to the justified gamma maps. These are generated by designating each room as a circle with the lines radiating from it signifying the access points to and from the room (see Figure 11.3). The circles and lines are then rearranged to reveal how many rooms any particular room is removed from a starting point (usually the entry). This simple reduction creates a variety of patterns that manifest some of a culture's social presuppositions in a way the plans themselves do not immediately reveal.

In a secondary application of this system, Hanson uses gamma maps to assess house plans designed by Botta, Meier, Hejduk, and Loos to reveal how the space syntax of the plans reveal cultural attitudes (for instance, toward gender).[4] Another secondary application (although this inquiry does offer new concepts, and hence has primary characteristics) can be found in the work of John Peponis and others at the Georgia Institute of Technology, developers of the *Spatialist* computer software program. The program analyzes a floor plan for such factors as visual permeability to provide insight into the quality of the spatial experiences it can encourage or sustain.[5]

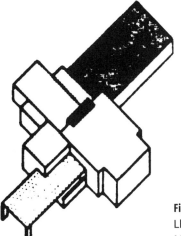

Figure 11.4 A "prairie house," after the style of Frank Lloyd Wright, by means of shape grammar rules. From March and Stiny. Courtesy Pion Limited, London.

BOX. 11.1

The Shape Grammar of Palladio's Villa Malcontenta

Apaper by Liou, Vakalo, and Lee entitled "Lines, Shapes, Spaces and Computers" takes a work mentioned by March and Stiny and develops a deeper analysis of its shape grammar characteristics.* The work is the Villa Malcontenta by Andrea Palladio. The authors propose that the Villa Malcontenta can be described by 47 (out of a total of 1,243) rules regulating line-to-space relationships. Their paper also describes a computer program (called ANADER) that can analyze building plans by the rules of the shape grammar. Indeed, one of the key traits of mathematical-formal systems is their compatibility with the computer.

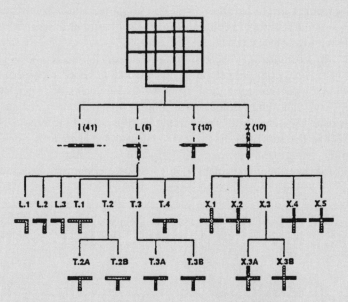

Figure 11.5   A sample of the "cells" that make up the rule-based shape grammar of Palladio's Villa Malcontenta. Courtesy Professor Shuenn-Ren Liou.

---

*S. R. Liou, E-G Vakalo, and Y. C. Lee, "Lines, Shapes, Spaces, and Computers," in *Pre-Symposium Proceedings of the 13th International Congress on Cybernetics* (Namur, Belgium: Institut D'Informatique, 1992) pp. 47–53. The paper is also available through Professor Shuenn-Ren Liou, Associate Professor, Department of Architecture, Tunghai University, Taichung, Taiwan.

The primary/secondary distinction also exists for cultural/discursive logical systems; Vitruvius's *Ten Books on Architecture* is an example of logical argumentation in the *treatise* form. We noted earlier that one characteristic of treatises is that they tend to root their claims in a larger transcendental realm (nature, history, the machine, etc.). That is, the "logic" of the argument is usually derived from its connections to the larger theme. In Vitruvius's case, the "logical" groundwork for architecture is seen within the larger system of nature:

> Therefore, since nature has designed the human body so that its members are duly proportioned to the frame as a whole, it appears that the ancients had good reason for their rule, that in perfect buildings the different members must be in exact symmetrical relations to the whole general scheme.[6]

John Summerson's *The Classical Language of Architecture* is an example of a secondary treatise built upon the primary logic of such treatises as Vitruvius's work. Summerson also affirms the connection of the classical forms to nature. He argues that human language is a phenomenon of nature, and that the classical orders also constitute a language system. A designer working within the rules of this system does not have the freedom to invent new rules willy-nilly, but can nevertheless experience great creative freedom, just as an author can use the preset rules of language to write an original story.[7]

Mathematical / Formal	**Mathematical / Cultural**	**Cultural / Discursive**
CAD / shape grammar:	Space syntax:	Design treatises:
Mathematical constructions and computer models	Formal models that are connected to social-cultural interpretations	Justifications for architectural action by appeal to larger transcendental contexts (nature, history, culture, the machine)
Exemplars:	Exemplars:	Exemplars:
March / Stiny (primary)	Hillier / Hanson (primary)	Vitruvius (primary)
Liou / Vakalo et al. (secondary)	Hanson (secondary)	Summerson (secondary)
	Peponis/Wineman et al. (secondary)	Many others ...

Figure 11.6   Spectrum of logical argumentation in more detail.

We now propose an expanded diagram of our spectrum. Although there are obviously other examples, we will treat the works listed in this diagram as exemplars, and refer to them repeatedly in this chapter.

11.2   STRATEGY: TRAITS OF LOGICAL ARGUMENTATION

Certainly any theory or research agenda must exhibit logical coherence, and we discussed this essential trait in our definition of "theory in general" in Chapter 4. It is not our intention here to draw rigid distinctions between logical argumentation and other kinds of theory. But we do want to shed light on a particular kind of research design that makes use of tactics ranging from mathematical to the discursive. What such inquiries have in common are the following traits.

11.2.1 Broad Systemic Applicability

Works in logical argumentation tend to have as a research outcome the framing of a conceptual system that has wide explanatory applicability. Indeed, these kinds of systems tend to lay claim, implicitly if not explicitly, to *universal* explanatory power on a variety of grounds, ranging from mathematical determinism, to various axiomatic certainties (e.g., *a priori* reason, numerical objectivity, invariant biological considerations, etc.), to rhetorical/polemical convictions that find acceptance from a large audience. And once an explanatory system is framed, it tends to become an internally self-contained conceptual system that resists further alterations or additions.

Shape grammar is one example of a system claiming broad applicability. Its validity is based upon the assumption that numerical relationships and equations logically express universal conditions that transcend localized cases. Refer again to the statement by March and Stiny cited above. Note the authors' goal of framing a system ("a system of shapes") that can explain a wide range of phenomena. Also note their use of the word *architecture*, now broadened to cover both natural and human-made objects. The shape grammar promises to be able to reduce such objects down to discrete rules that reveal syntactic connections, or can be programmed into a computer to design new forms.

Or consider the statement cited above from Vitruvius. The position taken is that the ubiquity of natural proportions—that is, the larger transcendental venue—ought to *logically* ensure the uniformity of proper proportions in buildings as well. Besides anchoring to "nature," Vitruvius's work also appeals to the larger principle of national identity.[8] Moreover, there is an implicit appeal to moral purity; this is most evident in how the masculine and feminine proportions of the orders imply moral attributes of solidity, strength, maternity, innocent maidenhood, and so on.[9] The "logic" of such a system lies partly in the way it "made sense" to a wide cultural audience, and for a long period of time. Vitruvius's treatise crystallized a culture's point of view of a particular style, and it was used as a justification for design action for centuries.

11.2.2   *Paradigmatic Innovation*

Exercises in logical argumentation tend to take a set of previously disparate factors, or previously unknown and/or unappreciated factors, and interconnect them into unified frameworks that have significant and sometimes novel explanatory power. In other words, primary logical systems tend to be innovative ones, so much so that they shape a discourse at a paradigmatic level. If the system is successful, it provides a new way of looking at old facts or existing phenomena. It is informative, for instance, to note the disparate factors that March and Stiny look to as *their* conceptual forerunners: Da Vinci's classification of central-plan churches, Dürer's typologies of the human face, Goethe's primordial *Urform* in nature, and Froebel's building blocks as a formal vocabulary.[10] Also, the idea of architecture as composed of discrete units syntactically linked is clearly traceable to developments in linguistics and structuralism emerging in the early nineteenth century. The point is that very few primary systems emerge *de novo*. Most draw instead from previous ideas. What is instructive is that these various ideas, themselves unrelated, can be the roots from which a new systemic paradigm grows.

Primary logical systems also have the ability to, as it were, uncover reality at a deeper level than what is seen on the empirical surface of things. And the reality that is uncovered reveals connections that unify the stuff at the surface. In March and Stiny's case, behind all natural and humanly made forms is a shape grammar composed of discrete rules. In the case of Vitruvius, behind all classical buildings is a vocabulary that is indexed to natural proportions. Hillier and Hanson's study of diverse English homes finds them to have the same hierarchy of space adjacencies linked to social values. In the more polemical instances at the discursive/cultural end of the spectrum, a building is beautiful if it has the attributes of the first primordial hut (Laugier).[11] Or: The essence of the new architecture is the principle of the machine, if we only had eyes to see! (Le Corbusier).[12] All of these instances appeal to underlying realities that unify a wide range of empirical appearances.

11.2.3   A Priori *Argumentation*

It is not surprising, then, that a common trait of systems of logical argumentation is reliance upon *a priori* principles. That is, any specific instance of a thing is only ratification of principles that the logical system in question has already identified as the enabling conditions for that thing. The power of the *a priori* is this: if it can be identified, then *necessary* consequences ensue from it. For example, March and Stiny cite a secondary work in which the prairie houses of Frank Lloyd Wright show the shape grammar "clarifying the underlying structure and appearance of known instances of style."[13] In other words, the shape grammar principles are an *a priori* explanatory reality relative to the instances of the prairie houses. We will present a deeper consideration of *a priori* and of *necessity* in section 11.3, when we address relational features of logical systems.

11.2.4 Testability

In Chapter 4, we presented Moore's list of the traits that constitute "theory." One of these is testability: A theory should be able to be tested, usually by empirical means. We noted, further, that one function of a "research method" is to conduct such a test. The method serves as an action agenda by which the claims of a theory can be verified or rejected. Systems of logical argumentation certainly also undergo testing. We suggest the following ways in which testability for these systems can be understood.

11.2.4.1 Testability for Mathematical-Formal Logical Systems: Quantitative Tools. The outcome of a mathematical-formal logical system is often a set of quantitative tools that can be used to diagnose empirical conditions. The work in shape grammar illustrates this clearly; its adaptability to the computer has resulted in many software programs that perform rule-based formal analyses. CAD programs in general fit into this category. Now, with CAD programs (that is, with computer software in general), the mathematical-formal systems that frame them are in a real sense tested with each use. We may not consciously regard each use as a test, but certainly the periodic upgrades manufacturers issue to a given program are based upon what is learned from extended use (read: testing) of the previous "releases."

11.2.4.2 Testability for Cultural/Discursive Logical Systems: Normative Standards. At the cultural/discursive end of the spectrum, successful logical systems are highly influential in shaping design opinion, and hence affecting normative standards for design action. Good treatises find acceptance because they "make sense" to a wide cultural audience, and the system is looked upon as the representative summary of that culture's worldview relative to style. In short, the system is accepted as "logical" within that cultural milieu. It is therefore not uncommon to find in each culture, or in each period of a culture's history, systematic works that seek to make sense of the times, to give focus to those times in a theoretical framework. Consider A. W. Pugin's treatise in favor of a pointed architecture, which appealed to the larger principles of national identity and Christian virtue.[14] Or consider John Ruskin's claim that ornamentation equals architecture; this was a response to the larger venue of the industrial revolution and its negative effects.[15] On the other hand, consider Adolf Loos's proposition that ornament equals crime; this was also in response to the larger venue of the industrial revolution, perhaps in its *positive* effects.[16] All of these arguments arose out of a certain interpretation of the "logic" of the times.

Now, these systems all have as a goal, implicit or explicit, the establishment of normative design standards. Their testability, then, must be understood in conjunction with their influence upon normative design action. Widespread influence affirms that the proposed system has struck a chord in expressing a culture's worldview; Pugin's, Ruskin's and Loos's positions can all be evaluated as "logical" according to this criterion. On the other hand, because these kinds of treatises are indexed to cultural venues, the tendency is for their influence to wane as the culture progresses to newer ways of understanding its place in the cosmos. "Testability" for the logic of a cultural/discursive treatise is therefore not dependent upon "falsification" of its claims; it is more indexed to the cultural underpinnings of its claims evolving to other principles.

Figure 11.7   Houses of Parliament, London, after the style of Pugin's "pointed" architecture. Pugin rooted his "logic" in the larger conceptual principles of national identity (that this style should be the national style) and morality (that this style is emblematic of Christian virtues and longing). Photograph from author's collections.

11.3   TACTICS: CHARACTERISTICS OF SYSTEMIC CONSTRUCTIONS:
DEFINITION, RELATION, RHETORIC

We turn now to some key components that make up systems of logical argumentation. Independent of their location on the spectrum, all logical systems tend to be
constructed of these components. Good logical systems tend to offer strong examples
of these components. Existing logical systems can thus be critiqued by an assessment
of their robustness and/or clarity in each of these areas.

11.3.1 Definition

The very construction of a system is fundamentally an attempt at *definition*; in this
sense, definition is the beginning, middle, and end of logical argumentation. Definition, for our purposes, is *the conceptual delimitation, in the form of words or signs, of
the scope of a system as well as its contents.*[17]
    Almost always, because of their novelty or paradigmatic status, primary systems
will identify a menu of *technical terms* that, together, make up the conceptual chassis
upon which the system is framed. If the system is influential, these terms are used
and/or elaborated upon by subsequent secondary works. The technical terms may be
new words (for instance, Alberti's term *lineaments*, cited below); more often they are
old words redefined. (Note again, for instance, how March and Stiny define the word
architecture in a way that is particular to the system they construct). It is impossible
to grasp the intent of a logical system without a thorough grasp of its technical terms.
Indeed, one difficulty with logical systems is the demand they place upon the human
mind to, as it were, learn a new language. The researcher constructing a logical system
ought therefore to be sensitive to the number of technical terms being introduced.
The more of them, the more likely it is that the system will be hard to comprehend.
On the other hand, economy of technical terms cannot compromise on a logical system's mission to explain thoroughly the issue under consideration.
    One way to appreciate how crucial the right technical terms can be for a system
is to play a mind game in which one proposes a limit of (say) three words that best describe a well-known systemic entity—for example, the personal computer sitting atop
one's desk. Of the following, which would be the best set of technical terms to describe the system: a) keyboard, screen, mouse, or b) CPU (the microprocessor), RAM
(random access memory), BIOS (basic input-output system)? Clearly it would be
(b). The first set of words are far too general (is it a piano keyboard, a movie screen?).
And even if it is clear we are talking about a computer, the words still describe empirical objects without identifying anything that is actually doing the *work*. On the
other hand, one can say that the three words in (b), although a good start, do not
completely describe a computer either. We would still need an *operating system*, perhaps a *hard drive*, certainly *software*, and so on (those knowledgeable in computers
will recognize these latter terms are dependent upon the first three).

What follows are some sample citations from various works of logical argumentation; they illustrate different kinds of definition. Sentences with this definitive tone are very common in these kinds of works:

1. "The basic marketing functions that must be performed by one or several individuals are the following: closer, counter, lead finder, coordinator, marketing manager/director." (Weld Coxe)[18]
2. "The whole matter of building is composed of lineaments and structure. . . . lineaments have [nothing] to do with material. . . . lineaments [are] the precise and correct outline, conceived in the mind, made up of lines and angles, and perfected in the learned intellect and imagination." (Alberti)[19]
3. "We define the shape of a building plan as a set of wall surfaces and a set of discontinuities. We define discontinuities to include the edges of freestanding walls and the corners formed at the intersection of two wall surfaces." (Peponis, Wineman, et al.)[20]
4. "we require of any building . . . that it act well; that it speak well; that it look well." (Ruskin)[21]
5. "It is useful to distinguish between *positive* and *normative* theory and between *substantive* and *procedural* theory." (Lang)[22]

These disparate sentences all have one thing in common: they state technical terms that amount to the chassis upon which the logical system is built. They are the building blocks used for *constructing* a system. How does one arrive at technical terms that amount to the structural foundations of logical systems? Are there any general characteristics of technical definitions that can be identified? The following subsections give some guidelines.

11.3.1.1 Definition: First Principles of Quantity.[23]   The identification (definition) of a first principle of quantity is one of the most common signatures of logical argumentation; it is one basic way to arrive at a technical term. In the *Metaphysics*, Aristotle says this about the sciences: "those with fewer principles are more exact than those which involve additional principles."[24] He thus suggests that the simpler system is always closer to the essence of something than a more complex one. Early philosophy often conceived of the cosmos as composed of a finite number of essential elements. For the Greeks, these were earth, air, fire, and water. In the East, the elemental number was five: water, fire, metal, wood, and earth.[25] It is no accident that Vitruvius's treatise begins with five "fundamental principles of architecture" (arrangement, eurythmy, symmetry, propriety, economy).[26] It is in this vein that Coxe lists five "basic marketing functions": closer, counter, lead finder, coordinator, marketing manager/director."

A first principle of *quantity*, then, is one kind of definition: the goal is to construct a conceptual system that can explain the widest scope of the phenomenon in question with the least (essential) number of fundamental principles that characterize that system. The names of those basic principles are invariably important technical terms. Consider again this statement by March and Stiny, noting the primary goal of identifying the fundamental quantities of the case:

> The way designs are distinguished depends on two main factors: 1) the rules used to compose the shapes that combine to represent them, and 2) the rules used to describe them in other terms pertaining to, for example, purpose, function . . . meaning, type, or form. Roughly speaking, rules of the first kind fix the syntax of designs, and rules of the second kind fix their semantics."[27]

Whether or not one agrees with their position, this is quite a bold statement in that it proposes an extremely wide scope of theoretical coverage: *all* designs can be reduced to these two "factors." But these kinds of bold lists, in which the fundamental essentials of a system are identified, are everyday occurrences in works of logical argumentation. They are perhaps even more common in cultural/polemical systems. Consider Gottfried Semper's "four elements" of architecture, in which he proposes that all architecture can be reduced to hearth, roof, enclosure, and "mound."[28] Or Laugier's "general principles of architecture": column, entablature, pediment, stories of a building, windows and doors.[29] Or Le Corbusier's *Five Points of a New Architecture*: supports, roof-gardens, free plan, the long window, the free façade.[30]

Consider a more recent example: Stuart Brand's *How Buildings Learn*.[31] Brand introduces the notion that a building can be conceived of in six layers (site, structure, skin, services, space plan, and stuff). The rate of alteration over time increases from the immobile site to the *stuff* on the interior that is moved about daily: chairs, phones, pictures, hairbrushes, etc. Brand here is constructing a logical system by identifying essential quantities.

11.3.1.2 Definition: First Principles of Quality. Intimately related to principles of quantity are principles of quality. In the West, philosophically speaking, an embedded assumption has been that a determination of essential quantity is necessarily a determination of essential quality. This attitude is implicit in the original Greek quest for "the good" (*eudaimonia*), which is not only *the* primary virtue (that is, a question of quantity), but also the *highest* aim of life (that is, a question of quality). Hence Aristotle, in arguing that a good science is one that defines essential quantities, notes also that the highest science is the study of the Good.[32]

This simultaneity of quantity and quality can be seen in today's systems of logical argumentation, in two senses, both of which flow from Aristotle's point of view. In some systems, there is an implicit argument for quality that comes with essential elements of quantity. In other words, once the quantity has been determined, the quality is necessarily determined as well. For example, in Laugier's mind, the components of the hut (column, entablature, pediment, etc.), which are elements of quantity, also guarantee quality: "The parts that are essential are the cause of beauty."[33]

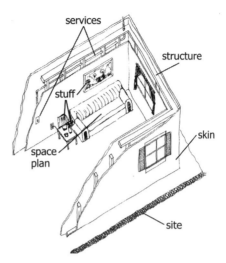

Figure 11.8 Student drawing illustrating the fundamental categories identified in Stewart Brand's theory for the rate at which building components change. The site hardly ever changes; as we go up (or into) the hierarchy, changes occur more rapidly. A building's "stuff" changes everyday. Drawing courtesy of Angela Feser.

(See again Figure 4.5). And here is Dana Cuff's theoretical statement about what constitutes excellent buildings: "I maintain that there are three principal evaluators of any building's quality and these are the consumers or the public at large, the participants in the design process, and the architectural profession."[34] This is immediately a statement of essential quantity as well as of essential quality.

In other systems, the argument for quality is explicit. There seems to be a human need to explain why something is *fundamentally* good and to accept that thing based on that explanation. Recall Viollet-le-Duc's well-known argument from function for the copper vessel (see Box 6.1): there is a *single* way of forming it because that was the *best* way.[35] Or consider John Ruskin's dictum that happy carvers produce happy buildings that, in turn, contribute to a happy society.[36] In these cases, there may or may not be elements of quantity. If there are such elements, in contrast to the first case, they are servants to the overall argument from quality (that is, they enumerate how the issue of quality can be broken down to essential principles).

11.3.1.3 Definition: First Principles of Origin. The question of origins is another kind of first principle. There are also two senses in which an argument from origin can work: the *genetic* sense and the *enabling* sense. Certainly the "hut theories" (Vitruvius,[37] Laugier, and R. D. Dripps,[38] to name three) are theories of genetic origin. Such theories assume that, because something originated in such and such a fashion, the present condition can be explained in that light. Consider Heidegger's treatment of "dwelling" in

Building Dwelling Thinking. In this work, Heidegger explores a host of old German words related to *bauen* (to build),[39] implying that uncovering the original meanings of the words is equal to uncovering the meaning of dwelling itself. This ascribes to early peoples a powerful capacity to express inmost essences—even though these peoples are typically viewed as "primitive" in many other ways. It all attests to the implicit respect for the explanatory power of origins. The *enabling* sense of an argument from origin can be illustrated, again, by Cuff's theory of excellent buildings. The complete title of her chapter is "Excellent Practice: The *Origins* of Good Building" (our italics).[40] Aside from positing that if the three ingredients (quantity) are in place, the building will be excellent (quality), Cuff also embeds in her title the implicit claim that these three quantities are the *enabling conditions* from which quality springs. Insofar as a definition of quantity also defines what enables the reality under consideration, that definition may also be an argument from origin.

11.3.2 Relationship

After the technical definitions have been clarified (and not all attempts at logical argumentation get past this hurdle), a systemic framework must demonstrate certain *relational* propositions that go a long way toward making the system logically coherent. Here we address some of these relational considerations.

11.3.2.1 Relation Between Terms: Necessity. By the laws of logic, necessity is that which is explicitly embedded in a proposition. For instance, given Mr. Jones, it is necessary that he is a man. Given that Mr. Jones is a bachelor, it is necessary that he is unmarried. Necessary relationships between the various terms of a logical system ensure the explanatory dependability of that system. Contrarily, if the relationships between terms are *contingent* rather than necessary; that is, if one proposition can lead to a variety of results, then the explanatory certainty of a system is greatly reduced.

Necessity in formal systems, such as in rule-based computer programs in shape grammar or space syntax, is based upon the logic of mathematics and numerical relations. For instance, Figure 11.5 shows the necessary geometric cell structures that emerge from the Villa Malcontenta. The cells are discrete and invariable, and this kind of reduction is useful in that the overall system promises to be able to explain the plans for a wide range of buildings *necessarily* predicated upon the underlying rules.

Necessity in cultural/discursive systems is of another kind. The *Oxford Dictionary of Philosophy* calls this *nomic* necessity, by which is largely meant the dependable patterns of nature's behavior. We mentioned earlier that cultural/discursive systems often ground their arguments in a larger frame of reference such as nature, culture, or the machine. Embedded in this is an argument from nomic necessity: Because the larger domain is thus and so, therefore architectural action must be thus and so. When Vitruvius argued that buildings must be "symmetrical" because nature had made the human body "duly proportioned,"[41] he was essentially arguing from nomic necessity. When Le Corbusier bemoaned "eyes which do not see" in his *Vers une architecture*, he was essentially chiding his fellow architects for not seeing a necessary connection, that being the logic of the machine in informing how the new architecture should be realized.[42] (Figure 11.9)

11.3.2.2 Relation Between Terms: Deduction / Induction. Related to necessity are deduction and induction. Deduction draws conclusions explicitly contained in a set of facts; again, given Mr. Jones, we deduce he is a man. That is, deduction involves *necessary* connections. In contrast, induction draws generalizations from given facts beyond what is embedded in just those facts. If Mr. Jones shows up at his office every day at 8 am, we feel able to read into this pattern of events a possible *general* pattern, to wit, that he will always show up at this time. This projection of a general pattern is an inductive operation. Now, once we have that general pattern, we can *deduce* from that generalization that Mr. Jones will indeed show up at 8 am the following day. But he may not. And if he does not, the weakness of our induced generalization is revealed. From this we may observe two simultaneous factors. First, induction involves contingency, and contingent propositions are never as strong as necessary ones. But second, induction can *do* more, in the sense that it promises (at least an illusion of) explanatory power for a larger reality than the observed instances. It is boring to just know that Mr. Jones is a man. It is more exciting to posit that he might actually show up tomorrow at 8 am. A system framed only on deduction has a tendency to restate the obvious, and so may not be of much use. But a system framed only by contingent (induced) connections is not a strong one, because the more contingency, the less the expectation that it can actually explain or predict. (Actually, there is a fair amount of philosophical literature that addresses just how complex deduction/induction is, to wit, that we cannot have the one without the other.)[43]

Figure 11.9 Le Corbusier's superimposition of various buildings over the ship *Aquitania*. Images such as this fill his *Vers une architecture*, with the aim of supporting the author's view that the machine age is the larger realm from which principles for architectural design must be derived. By permission, Dover Publications.

Any logical system, then, is a fine balance between deduced necessities and induced projections (which are essentially contingent). From a finite set of observed phenomena, certain deductions, argued to be necessary, are arrived upon. From these observed patterns, a general logical system is framed that promises explanatory power beyond the observed instances. This is the inductive aspect of logical argumentation. Now, the technical terms of a logical system can be thought of as forming the nexus of the deductive/inductive nature of a logical system. Insofar as they denote the necessary fundamentals of that system, they represent deductive processes of reasoning. Insofar as they, together, frame an explanatory system beyond specific instances, they represent inductive assumptions. Box 11.2 addresses Hillier and Hanson's system as an example of deduction/induction.

11.3.2.3 Relation Between Terms: Syllogistic Frameworks. A syllogism is constructed of a primary and a secondary premise leading to a necessary conclusion. The typical construction is as follows: A = B; C = A; therefore C = B. The typical example: all men (A) are mortal (B); Socrates (C) is a man (A); therefore Socrates (C) is mortal (B). In mathematical-formal systems, syllogistic relationships are taken up in the transitive nature of the logic (A=B; B=C; A=C). At the cultural/discursive end of the spectrum, it is not uncommon to have syllogistic *frameworks* embedded in logical systems. Because they are cultural/discursive, and because they encompass so many contingent assumptions, these frameworks cannot be considered pure syllogisms in any formal sense of the word. But they are framed in such a way that two related premises are given, out of which a deductive operation drives the theorist's point of view as an assumed *necessary* conclusion. In the Summerson work already cited, the syllogistic framework goes something like this: nature (A) relates to architecture (B); language (C) is natural (A); therefore language (C) relates to architecture (B). Or take a more

BOX 11.2

Induction and Deduction in a Logical System: Social Patterns in the Architecture of the Ambo Tribal Compound (from Hillier and Hanson)

We have already mentioned Hillier and Hanson's "gamma map" system in the study of English homes. They have also used the gamma maps to diagnose social-cultural values in non-Western venues. In one instance, the placement of wives' quarters so close to the exterior of a tribal compound (Ashanti) is connected with that culture's practice of wives remaining in their matrilineal groups; they do not cohabit with their husbands. Hence their relationships with the world outside are important.

This comes through in the gamma maps. In another tribe, one that practices patrilineal transmission of the family line (Ambo—see below), the wives live in the compound with the husband, and so their quarters are far removed from the entry area.* From these instances, the authors make the claim that the gamma map system is an analytical tool that can unveil large-scale social-cultural values embedded in floor plans—in Ashanti, Ambo, and implicitly, in all instances. This is the inductive step. If the system is workable, when we use it to analyze other instances of floor plans in the manner it prescribes, we ought to be able to *deduce* social-cultural patterns in those instances. For their part, Hillier and Hanson realize the inductive limits of their system, and they state this explicitly: "the larger buildings become, and more removed from intuitive experience, the more hazardous becomes the use of the abstract model to try to construct a sociological picture of a particular type of building.**

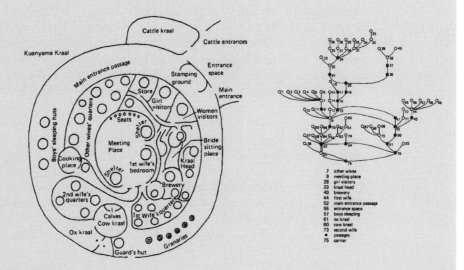

Figure 11.10   Hillier and Hanson's maps of the Ambo tribal compound. Figure on left is the architectural plan, while the figure on the right is the justified gamma map of the plan. Permission of Cambridge University Press.

---

*Hillier and Hanson, *Social Logic of Space*, 163–175.

**Ibid., 163.

complex instance, Semper's theory of the four elements of architecture. This argument may be syllogistically framed as in Figure 11.11 below.

Again, we want to make clear that these "syllogistic frameworks" are not syllogisms in any formal sense; the Semper and Summerson examples are clearly filled with contingent possibilities that would weaken the force of the frameworks as we have diagrammed them. But we highlight Semper's and Summerson's arguments in this way to illustrate how, embedded in cultural/discursive systems, is the same dependence upon necessity that is much more clearly exhibited in mathematical-formal systems.

11.3.2.4 Relation Between Terms: *A Priori / A Posteriori*. The notion of *a priori* (which means "previous to experience") also comes out of necessity. In contrast, *a posteriori* refers to facts or truths that are established as a result of experience. Logical systems are motivated by the need to identify *a priori* conditions so that those conditions can in turn be the basis for explaining particular instances of experience. In cultural/discursive logical systems, which look to larger domains (nature, culture, history, etc.), principles from those larger venues readily serve as *a priori* justifications for logical construction. Consider again Louis Sullivan's theoretical statement "form follows function"[44] (see Box 4.2). For Sullivan, the inner essence of nature in things is the necessary *a priori* for their subsequent expressions as matter. Nature is also the *a priori* for the Vitruvius argument already cited. (For Sullivan, it is almost a vitalistic force in nature that is *a priori* for material expression, while for Vitruvius it is the visible "symmetrical" qualities of natural forms that is the *a priori* for the orders.)

11.3.2.5 Relation Between Terms: Entailment/Implication. Entailment is sometimes related to the technical term *implication*, particularly in the context of a system. In other words, within a system, entailment can mean what any one component of that system necessarily implies for other components within the same system.[45] Entailment therefore

A	Architecture a) learns from nature, and b) is a means of embodying human ideas	B	When it does so, it increases in meaning and beauty
C	Original architectural constructions consisted universally of 4 elements of hearth, roof, enclosure, and mound	A	These 4 elements constitute an unreflective embodiment of human ideas in learning from nature and expressed in architecture
T H E R E F O R E			
C	The four elements (expressed truthfully) …	B	…result in an architecture of meaning and beauty

Figure 11.11   Semper's argument structured in a syllogistic framework.

applies to possibilities that the components of a system can offer, but it may not guarantee universal necessity. Entailment in short enriches a system by providing bases for formulating the implications of any proposition, and by giving the implications systemic backing (or by rejecting other proposed implications because they cannot be backed by the logic of the larger system). Peponis's *Spatialist* computer program, for instance, can identify the total possible "s-spaces" (defined as the stable geometric patterns in plan that result if all wall surfaces are geometrically extended beyond their end-points) and "e-spaces" (defined as the stable geometric patterns that result after all possible diagonals are drawn within a space) of a plan. The resulting patterns show what spatial textures a viewing subject experiences as he or she moves through a plan (see Figure 11.12). These total possible surfaces and spaces are an example of an en-

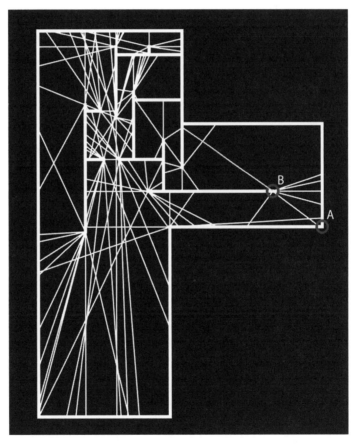

Figure 11.12 "e-lines" from the *Spatialist* computer program developed by Peponis et al. Courtesy of John Peponis.

tailment operation at the mathematical-formal end of the spectrum. In the Vitruvian treatise, entailment factors are abundant, in that the orders do not necessarily guarantee one single outcome in any application. Rather, Vitruvius teaches that the *implications* of a specific locale should be factored into the realization of symmetry, eurythmy, and so on ("I think it certain that diminutions or additions should be made to suit the nature or needs of the site, but in such fashion that the buildings lose nothing thereby").[46] It is entailment that gives us confidence that the resulting form will conform to the larger, more general, strictures of the orders.

11.3.3 Rhetorical Tactics in Cultural/Discursive Systems

We have noted that cultural/discursive systems depend upon rhetorical tactics to convey their arguments. Thus they also use the logic of persuasion. An audience will not come around to a particular point of view unless that point of view makes sense to it. For mathematical-formal systems, the "making sense" is less dependent upon cultural contingencies, since these systems are rooted in the logic of numbers. But even for cultural/discursive systems, which *are* complicit with social-cultural factors, the rhetorical devices used tend to be fairly consistent. Chaim Perelman and L. Olbrechts-Tyteca, in their important work *The New Rhetoric*, argue that in our everyday modes of thinking we must deliberate upon a multitude of factors that ultimately shape, not so much our grasp of abstract truth, but our *adherence* to one point of view over another.[47] The very need to deliberate implies the lack of absolute necessity in these matters; something "makes sense" because of other factors rooted in the logic of persuasion and rhetoric. We examine some of these elements here as they relate to logical argumentation in cultural/discursive systems.

11.3.3.1 Rhetorical Tactics: Naming. "One of the essential techniques of quasi-logical argumentation is the identifying of various elements which are the object of discourse: We consider this identification of entities, events, or concepts as neither arbitrary nor obvious, that is . . . it is justifiable by argument."[48] In this statement, Perelman and Olbrechts-Tyteca point out that definition (in the sense of the mere identification and explication of technical terms) can be a persuasive enterprise, or at least can have a persuasive component to it. The goal is to achieve a sense in the hearer that what is being defined has something to do with him or her not only at the level of cognitive reason, but also at the level of emotional or psychological identity. The tendency of cultural/discursive treatises to root their arguments in a larger transcendental realm (again, nature, morals, history, the machine, etc.) arises just because of their need to establish these levels of identification.

Now, one way to achieve identity with a larger realm is simply by *naming*. For instance, Ruskin's first principles of quality, that buildings must "act well . . . speak well . . . look well," makes a connection between architecture and moral considerations by a *nominative* leap that immediately grips reason at a provocative level. The claim is halfway to being legitimized just by the connection being made: how can we argue with morals? First principles of origin (in the enabling sense) also usually have this attribute: they are legitimate simply because of their nominative position in the argument. Consider again Semper's four elements. Hearth, roof, enclosure, and mound are concrete concepts that Semper simply culls out of the mythical past, as it were, by naming them. Of course not any name is acceptable; successful naming must give persuasive traction to the process of deliberation. In Semper's case, the four elements are, first, categorically distinct from one another; second, they seem to capture a complete representation of the major components of a dwelling without a suspicion of something being left out; and third, they seem to be descriptive of all instances of dwelling.

11.3.3.2 Rhetorical Tactics: Association or Disassociation. Another way to "make sense" to an audience is by *association*, a primary tactic by which cultural/discursive treatises connect to larger transcendental realms. It is quite important, for instance, that the Doric, Ionic, and Corinthian orders be associated with anthropomorphic ideas. The Doric is masculine; the Ionic matronly; the Corinthian maidenly. These are essential factors for their appeal and durability because they associate the physical forms with issues of character and human identity. (See Figure 11.13.)

Figure 11.13 The Erecthium in Athens. Here the association between the orders and the human form is explicit. Photograph courtesy of Eliot Price.

Consider any number of early modernist treatises in which association with the machine is the overarching means by which architectural design action is justified. Here is Moisei Ginzburg in *Style and Epoch*:

> It is precisely the machine, the main occupant and the master of the modern factory, which, having already exceeded its bounds and gradually filling all the corners of our way of life and transforming our psyche and our aesthetic, constitutes the most important factor influencing our conception of form.[49]

Related to association is *disassociation*. In the rhetorical tradition, dissent, or at least its possibility, is legitimate in its own right. To disagree with an established norm often demands a hearing, provided that the one who dissents is acceptable to the audience on other grounds. J. N. L. Durand, for instance, argued forcefully in a dissent against the Vitruvian position that classical proportions are derived from measurements of the human body. He measured a human foot, and claims he was not able to derive from it the building proportions that this venerated argument prescribes.[50]

Figure 11.14   Image of a crane from Ginzburg's *Style and Epoch*. Like Le Corbusier, Ginzburg looked to the machine as the larger paradigm from which to derive the design principles for modern architecture. Courtesy of MIT Press.

Durand's authority, apart from his own professional and academic standing, draws from the cultural ideas of his day, namely, the advent of the machine and the gradual departure from an anthropomorphic understanding of nature for a much more functional/utilitarian view. So, for the logical researcher at the cultural/discursive end of the spectrum, one question to be asked is this: Are there factors in contemporary culture that can be used as the bases by which to mount a dissenting point of view against precepts already accepted, but perhaps based upon outmoded cultural factors?

11.3.3.3 Rhetorical Tactics: Story. Along with association comes *story*, in which something that is named is amplified by an account that, on its face, is not provable. The origin of the Corinthian capital is a case in point: a "freeborn maiden" takes ill and passes away; her nurse places some of her belongings in a basket over her grave with a roof-tile on top to keep it in place. An acanthus plant eventually surrounds the basket with its leaves.[51] Vitruvius's account is very durable, still being recounted by Laugier in 1753. Summerson suggests that Vitruvius's "personalization" of the orders in this fashion opened the way for many such anthropomorphisms in the Renaissance; the Corinthian came to be associated with notions such as "virginal," "lascivious," and so on.[52] In the case of the story of the primordial hut as the origin of all architecture, the account has established such a legacy of treatises over the centuries that the story has become a kind of domain for logical argumentation unto itself. No one would literally accept the notion of a single historical hut with this much influence; and yet the account has become part of the canon.

Why do stories work? A story plays into our need for a workable account of beginnings; in this sense, it belongs under the rubric of the argument from origin. Because of this, the successful story is usually not of something that is temporally or physically nearby (that is, something that can easily be proven false on empirical grounds). Rather, a story makes a connection with the faraway in such a fashion that the mythical qualities, or at least the connotative or symbolic values, of the present object is enhanced or heightened. Finally, a workable story usually depends upon a tradition. We see how Dripps's work on the hut, for example, is readily able to continue that particular tradition; for Dripps to have started the hut myth from scratch, as it were, would have been much harder to do, and the arguments much less believable.

11.3.3.4 Rhetorical Tactics: Graphic Images. This is a device that is all too often neglected. Perelman and Olbrechts-Tyteca recount the story of the king who sees an ox on its way to sacrifice; he orders a sheep to take its place and later confesses that his decision was based upon having seen the ox and not having seen the sheep. They follow Piaget in positing: "The thing on which the eye dwells, that which is best or most often seen, is, by that very circumstance, overestimated."[53] Laugier's memorable image of the primordial hut (see Figure 4.5) in his *Essay on Architecture* has come to be *the* emblem of not only his argument, but of the entire hut tradition. Box 11.3 describes a more recent example, Robert Venturi's *Learning From Las Vegas*.

BOX 11.3

Graphic Persuasion in *Learning From Las Vegas*

The cliché "a picture is worth a thousand words" is perhaps more appreciated in popular culture (for example, in the advertising industry) than by those engaged in the task of framing a logical system. And yet the right picture in the right context really can be very powerful. This is because it acts to coalesce into one graphic image complex semantic realities that combine propositional facts with elements of feeling, psychological identity, and other factors not easy to describe in words. Robert Venturi's *Learning From Las Vegas,** one of the early treatises that influenced the post-modern movement in architectural design, is a work that illustrates how the graphic image can give focus to a way of life not possible to describe merely in words.

Figure 11.15   Tanya billboard in Las Vegas. Courtesy of Venturi Scott Brown and Associates, Inc.

*Robert Venturi, Denise Scott Brown, and Steven Izenour. *Learning From Las Vegas* (Cambridge, Mass: MIT Press, [1977] 1996).

11.3.3.5 Rhetorical Tactics: Implicit or Explicit Appeals to Group Identity. A cultural-discursive system emerges out of group experience, and it is to that group that it makes its primary appeal. For instance, Vitruvius opens his treatise by addressing the Roman emperor:

> When I saw that you were giving your attention not only to the welfare of society in general and to the establishment of public order, but also to the providing of

public buildings intended for utilitarian purposes, so that not only should the State have been enriched with provinces by your means, but that the greatness of its power might likewise be attended with distinguished authority in its public buildings, I thought that I ought to take the first opportunity to lay before you my writings on this theme.[54]

By this Vitruvius makes clear that his treatise aims to contribute to a coherent society, based on the implicit premise that the authority of the emperor should be expressed in the authority of its buildings. Centuries later, Pugin argued along the same lines of national identity, albeit somewhat more brusquely: "What does an Italian house do in England? Is there any similarity between our climate and that of Italy? Not the least. . . . We are not Italians, we are Englishmen."[55] At the level of design action (that is, not at the level of a treatise in this instance), here is Daniel Libeskind subtly invoking group identity to explain his choice of materials for his Jewish Museum:

I got the idea of using zinc from Schinkel. Before his very early death, he recommended that any young architect in Berlin should use as much zinc as possible. . . . In Berlin, untreated zinc turns to a beautiful blue-gray. Many of Schinkel's Berlin buildings . . . are built of zinc. . . . When you knock them, you can tell that they are just covers. That is very Berlin-like.[56]

Figure 11.16 Liebeskind's Jewish Museum, Berlin. Photograph courtesy of Henry Matthews.

The idea is to introduce concrete points in the argument that have resonance with some aspect of an audience's sense of *me*, or *us*. In the examples above, these were national identity, professional identity, and regional place and history. Given the right amount of elaboration, it is hoped that a level of subjective acceptance for the arguments, if not outright "bonding," takes place on these grounds.

11.3.3.6 Rhetorical Tactics: Dividing. Related to group identity, but more subtle, is what we term dividing. Identification can be encouraged by offering the audience two or more opposed or hierarchical groupings. "Making sense" is then dependent upon certain choices that the audience is asked to make, either for one group and against another, or about how the groups should be arranged in some sequence. Consider a case from Perez-Gomez. In his *Architecture and the Crises of Modern Science*, he distinguishes between *mathesis* and *mythos* (an argument from quantity), and argues that the mythical dimension is what has been lost in architecture (which immediately connects to issues of quality).[57] The very division between the two domains brings focus to his argument. Never mind that *mythos* (not to mention *mathesis*) can be defined in ways other than the way he chooses to handle the terms.

Alberti's use of division permeates his treatise: "The whole matter of building," for instance, is composed of *lineaments* and *structure*.[58] And a grasp of his point leads to the larger claim that, lineaments being a domain of the mind, an important division in the building arts must be between the architect who has the intellectual capacity to design buildings, and the "mere carpenter" who enacts the architect's wishes. So Alberti's is not only an abstract division, but also one that established group identities at a societal level.

It is a worthwhile exercise to see how the division between hand labor and the power of the machine has been handled in cultural/discursive systems. With Ruskin and William Morris, the division was clearly one of *segregation*: the machine and its byproducts (mass production, iron and steel, for instance) are inferior to handcraft. For Ruskin, the instant iron or steel is used to substitute wood or stone as a load-bearing material, the building "ceases . . . to be true architecture."[59] Ruskin's argument appeals to the larger venues of history (the long tradition of wood and stone construction by hand) and nature (cast iron does not exist purely in nature). On the other side of the Atlantic, Frank Lloyd Wright approached this question using *integration*. In a secondary work within this tradition, "The Art and Craft of the Machine" (actually a speech given to the Chicago Arts and Crafts Society in 1901), Wright argues for the integration of the machine as another tool in the production of art.[60] These two different positions on the same issue illustrate how "logical argumentation" of this kind does not guarantee one propositional result, but can lead in different directions depending upon how the argument is situated with respect to larger factors. For the European tradition the larger realms of historical truth (Ruskin), nationalism (Pugin), and handcraft (Morris) led to a rejection of the machine. For Wright, "nature" and "art" are the larger venues that include the machine as a tool; *because* of that subordinate position, on Wright's view, the machine is no threat. The logic can work both ways, depending upon the larger conceptual venue in which the logical argument is situated.

11.3.3.7 Rhetorical Tactics: Authority. The authority of any logical system is primarily dependent upon the coherence of its argumentation and, as a consequence, its explanatory power. But a system also gains authority 1) if it is spoken by an established voice, 2) if it is connected to a larger body of voices saying related things, or 3) if it can harness the energy of an emerging trend. We see instances of the first approach in many situations in everyday life. For example, manufacturers spend large sums linking their products to movie stars or famous athletes whose names have little to do with the product they are paid to endorse. In cultural/discursive systems, barring a direct endorsement by an established voice, a treatise gains authority if the positions of established voices are woven into its argument. When this is done, the new (usually secondary) system is more assured of connecting to already accepted theoretical positions. It did not hurt, for instance, that Venturi's *Complexity and Contradiction in Architecture*, written relatively early in the architect's career, appeared with an introduction by Vincent Scully, hailing it as "probably the most important writing on the making of architecture since Le Corbusier's *Vers une Architecture*."[61]

As for the second approach, it is not unusual for cultural/discursive arguments to emerge in topical "packs," as it were. Ulrich Conrads' *Programs and Manifestoes of 20th Century Architecture*[62] includes short works that by themselves would not attain the level of "treatise." But if taken as a "pack," the whole gives each more of a sense of logical coherence. And so arranged, the whole is also revealed to be the production of a particular trend in the worldview of a particular period. Indeed, the value of edited works in general is that they suggest a systemic character for a collection of separate voices.

In an instance of the third approach, the writing that accompanied the 1988 Johnson/Wrigley MOMA exhibit on "Deconstructivist Architecture" came at the emergence of a trend, and perhaps helped to legitimize "deconstruction" in architecture.[63] Here, aside from the authority of a Johnson, the authority of a MOMA, and the illusion of authority that comes with the textual sophistication, the success of the project comes from a synergy between all of these elements and the actual pieces displayed in the show. Additionally, it was fashionable at the time to associate with Jacques Derrida and the developments in poststructuralism and deconstruction. In short, from a *zeitgeist* point of view, it was just the right time and place for a "deconstructivist architecture."

11.4   TACTICS: SYSTEMIC TRACTION

How does one construct a logical system from scratch? Anyone one who has framed a logical system can attest to the creative dimension involved in the process. Here we list some clues that can be identified in extant systems indicating how a logical system can be framed.

11.4.1 By Mathematical Representation and/or Computer Modeling

A logical system may be framed by capturing the behavior of an empirical reality in mathematical terms. For example, in shape grammar, architectural plans (and in some instances, elevations) are captured by arithmetic "rules" that unveil underlying patterns. We have already mentioned several works in this vein; Palladio's Villa Malcontenta seems to be used as an exemplar in many such studies.[64] Figure 11.17 shows some geometric/arithmetic schemas developed by G. Stiny and W. Mitchell for analyzing Persian paradise gardens; the expressions regulate ways that fundamental geometries are "inflected."[65] As another example, here is Peponis et al.:

> From a computational point of view, the basis for computing the integration of a space is the formula $(k-2)(2d^{mean}-1)$, where k is the number of elements in a system, and d^{mean} (mean depth) is the average minimum number of transitions, from one space to another, that must be made to reach every other part of the system.[66]

What the authors mean to say is that spatial arrangements can be described by means of numerical expressions, and that once these expressions are found, their power to describe instances of those arrangements are great. Computer programs—such as Peponis' *Spatialist*—can then be developed in accordance with this premise. The key in this kind of system-making is to represent an empirical reality with a system of mathematical rules and relationships.

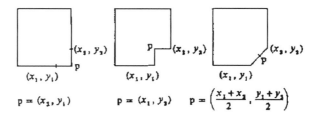

Figure 11.17 Geometric/arithmetic schemas developed by G. Stiny and W. Mitchell for analyzing Persian paradise gardens. Here are rules that dictate various truncations of a basic rectangular form. Courtesy of Professor George Stiny.

11.4.2 By Analogy

Logical argumentation can gain systemic order through analogy. A new system is then predicated upon a likeness between the attributes and/or behavior of its contents and the attributes and/or behavior of some other metasystem, usually existing in nature. One example is the parallel between biology and architecture. (Of course, the dependence of the classical orders upon anthropomorphic references is already a "biological" example, but here we have in mind an appeal to biology at a more foundational level.) D'Arcy Thompson's *On Growth and Form* is a seminal example of this approach.[67] Philip Steadman's *The Evolution of Designs* draws from Thompson's earlier work;[68] Steadman frames a systematic assessment of architecture with a series of analogies all having to do with the biological premise. These include·morphology and structure (the anatomical analogy), trial and error in design progress (the "Darwinian" analogy), tools as extensions of the physical body, and design process as a kind of biological growth.

11.4.3 By Categorization and Elaboration

Logical systems can be framed by categorizing the reality to be explained. The categories must have some claim to universality; this in essence is the purpose of identifying principles of quantity, quality, or origins, etc. Identifying persuasive categories often suffices to form the foundation of a workable logical system. For example, the chapter headings of Venturi's *Complexity and Contradiction in Architecture* amount to categories of postmodern design (e.g., "Ambiguity," "Both-And," "Double-Functioning"); these categories form the framework of his treatise. Categorization is also the tactic Christian Norberg-Schulz uses to tackle the notion of "dwelling." In *The Concept of Dwelling*, he holds that "when dwelling is accomplished, our wish for belonging and participation is fulfilled."[69] But this fulfillment is accomplished when architecture facilitates: 1) meetings for the exchange of ideas, products, and feelings, 2) the ability to come to agreement with a common set of values, and 3) a sense of "having a small chosen world of our own." These categories are further broken down into "modes" of dwelling: the collective, the public, and the private. Finally, the three modes are assigned architectural form-equivalents of urban space (the collective, or the settlement), institution (public buildings), and house (the private retreat). Then the author elaborates on how a category relates to dwelling:

> When we approach a settlement, the skyline is usually of decisive importance. What we perceive is a figure which rises from the ground towards the sky in a certain way. It is this standing and rising which determines our expectations and tells us where we are. . . . When we travel through a landscape, we are "tuned" in a certain way, and the settlement ought to offer an answer to our expectations.[70]

Essentially, this elaboration is grounded in the categorizations Norberg-Schulz previously established. The key in categorizing is for the taxonomy to be completely descriptive of the reality it aims to describe.

11.4.4 By Cross-Categorization and Elaboration

An additional means for framing logical systems is what we call cross-categorization. In Kevin Lynch's *The Image of the City*, five categories—paths, edges, districts, nodes, and landmarks—are posited as the fundamental components of a city's "imageability" (see Section 3.2.1). But Lynch gives his argument traction by citing examples of these abstract categories from Los Angeles, Boston, and Jersey City. These instances act as cross-categories in his overall framework. A more sophisticated deployment of this tactic can be found in the logical framework of Lisa Heschong's *Thermal Delight in Architecture.*[71] Heschong's system introduces the four technical terms (her first principles) *necessity*, *delight*, *affection*, and *sacredness*, and these act as categories that "intersect" with another pair of categories: *hearth* and *garden*. *Hearth* is used to describe the internal domicile, while *garden* is used to describe the incorporation of nature into human dwelling. These six terms form an orthogonal grid upon which she places a range of examples. (See Figure 11.18.)

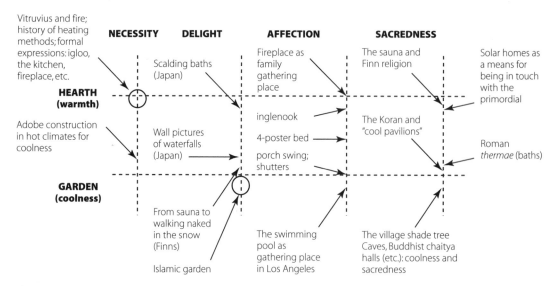

Figure 11.18 Diagrammatic of Heschong's structure for *Thermal Delight in Architecture*.

11.4.5 By Argument from Metaphilosophical Traditions

A logical system can be framed by drawing from the domain of a much larger philosophical tradition. Many treatises dealing with art and architecture use this approach. In the West, metaphilosophical traditions such as rationalism, empiricism, and idealism underlie most logical systems. There are also many more topical frameworks, such as linguistic philosophy and phenomenology. Ernest Gombrich's aesthetic system is rooted largely in psychoanalysis.[72] Many systems draw from political philosophy, such as Tafuri's *Architecture and Utopia*.[73] But the major metaphilosophical traditions alone provide rich material for building logical systems. Rationalism, which holds that the human mind has *a priori* powers that structure empirical experience, has generated a wealth of logical systems relevant to architecture. These include Ernst Cassirer's *Essay on Man* (in which he addresses art),[74] Susanne Langer's *Philosophy in a New Key*,[75] and, more recently, Roger Scruton's *Aesthetics of Architecture*.[76] From a base in empiricism, which holds that experience is the source of all knowledge, John Dewey's *Art as Experience* argues that art starts not with the relics in museums, but rather emerges when everyday experience finds fulfillment in full expression.[77] As for idealism, it has probably been the most influential metaphilosophical tradition for architectural treatises over the last one hundred years. Its emphasis upon the mind as the generator of reality, along with Hegel's idealist views on history (that of a corporate mind moving toward absolute knowledge) greatly influenced modernist manifestoes (see Section 6.3.3).

11.4.6 By Updating in Light of New Developments or Data

A logical system can be an update of an older system, now needing to be revamped in light of new developments. Alberti's *On the Art of Building in Ten Books* updates Vitruvius's treatise. Alberti's work evidences the clear influence of the revival of interest in all things Greek during the early Renaissance—so much so that it is more of a "Greek" text than Vitruvius's work. For instance, Alberti's notion that *lineaments* reside purely within the mind is a much clearer link to Platonic philosophy than anything found in Vitruvius. One can also detect the influence of Plato's *Republic* in Alberti's concern for the *polis*—and for the elevated position of the architect within it. Another example is Quatremère de Quincy's expansion of Laugier's hut theory (1753). Quatremère's work appeared some fifty years after Laugier's. Increased knowledge in archaeology, as well as great societal interest in this area, coupled with the emerging interest in language as such, all contributed to a need for a more flexible theory of architectural origins than that provided by the notion of a single primordial hut. And so Quatremère's system posits multiple primordial origins, symbolized by not only the hut, but also by the tent and the cave.[78]

11.5   CONCLUSION: STRENGTHS AND WEAKNESSES.

Logical argumentation constructs conceptual frameworks that have great explanatory power. These systems shape how we understand the world we live in. On the other hand, the utility of these systems can be limited in a number of ways, and we conclude this chapter by enumerating some of them. (See also the Strengths and Weaknesses Chart, Figure 11.19.) Logical systems tend to become outmoded with progress, or at

Strengths	Weaknesses
Of the strategies covered in this book, this strategy is perhaps the most ubiquitous in that any conceptual framework must exhibit logical coherence in some sense. Grasp of the principles outlined here can help frame any logical framework. Logical argumentation is very useful in providing theoretical foundations for a wide range of empirical manifestations. Some examples of this cited here are Hillier and Hanson's framework to reveal simple social-cultural patterns in a diverse array of floor plans, or the notion that disparate empirical forms can nevertheless be reduced to a "shape grammar." Logical argumentation, conceived of as a research strategy, is very powerful in being able to situate a large and diverse amount of extant theoretical literature into a single conceptual system. What is more, the tools of logic used to frame the system can make the explanation very economical. Insofar as the resulting theoretical explanation is based upon internal logical consistency, logical systems can be hard to refute. In this chapter we have tried to show that "logical" can transcend the boundaries of "mathematical" (numerically based knowledge) and "discursive" (rhetorically based knowledge) by demonstrating that foci as diverse as shape grammar theory, on the one hand, and Vitruvius's classical orders, on the other, can all occupy one spectrum of logical argumentation.	The first item under "strengths" may easily be a weakness as well: it may be hard to grasp why or how logical argumentation is a research strategy, since all frameworks need to have logical coherence. We have attempted to show that logical argumentation, as a research strategy proper, involves the framing of conceptual frameworks that explain a wide scope of a certain reality. Furthermore, they tend to culminate in the theoretical system itself as an outcome, rather than have the logical framework be a means to other outcomes. A weakness can be a lack of economy in technical terms. In other words, if a system proliferates in technical terms, it is an indication that essential foundations have not been clarified. Another weakness is that a system can lack the ability to explain a wide scope of reality. Systems of logical argumentation need to be constantly evaluated as to their accuracy. Internal logical consistency does not guarantee accurate explanatory power. For instance, proposed fundamental categories, while all relevant, may not be exhaustively descriptive—there may be other as-yet undefined categories. The theory of logical argumentation itself does not have a self-regulating mechanism, necessarily, that can alert the theorist to this lack; it must be tested by applying the proposed system to relevant venues, with the attendant critical evaluation. Also, as noted, some logical systems are time dependent, so that the passing of a social-cultural era may render a proposed system more of a historical item than one having current explanatory power.

Figure 11.19   Strengths and weaknesses of logical argumentation research.

least with changes in the empirical environment that spawned them. Therefore, most logical systems have a limited "shelf-life," after which they become more of a historical artifact than anything readily useful. Mathematical-formal systems change as new evidence emerges to alter established paradigms. This theme is addressed systematically by such thinkers as Thomas Kuhn[79] and Karl Popper.[80] Toward the cultural/discursive end of the spectrum, treatises that have "become history" are abundant. This is why many systems of this type (e.g., Vitruvius, Alberti, Laugier, Ginzburg) are as comfortable in history classes as they are in theory classes. It is also one reason why the moniker "history/theory" has currency.

Another limitation of logical systems is this: A system may not be an accurate representation of the reality it purports to explain *and yet still be internally consistent from a logical point of view*. Popper's theory of falsification has added much to the literature in this area insofar as mathematical-formal systems are concerned. For instance, Newton's law of gravity, in light of Einstein's theories, was proven to be lacking in its ability to describe a behavior of the cosmos, even though Newton's equations are logically correct. Parallels to this problem can also be found in cultural/discursive systems. Many (now historical) works on city form and planning written from a modernist perspective (for instance, Le Corbusier's *The City of Tomorrow and its Planning*) have been challenged by later works such as Jane Jacobs's *Death and Life of Great American Cities*. The issue of how a system logically connects to the reality it purports to explain is a fascinating one, and deserving of more research in its own right. The point for the logical researcher is that an internally coherent system does not guarantee an accurate depiction of an external reality.

Other potential problems of logical systems have to do with their economy and inherent utility. A good logical system, as we have pointed out, ought to provide a wide scope of explanatory coverage with an economical number of technical terms. Logical systems quickly become less useful when the opposite is true: a great number of technical terms attempting to explain something of uncertain or limited scope.

11.6   RECOMMENDED READINGS

A useful work we did not refer to in this chapter is William Mitchell, *The Logic of Architecture* (Cambridge, Mass: MIT Press, 1990). This work is strong on the mathematical-formal end of the spectrum; Mitchell addresses the logic of computation, and summarizes the theory of shape grammar. But Mitchell also provides support for a general theory of logical argumentation by describing several "worlds" that a logical system must situate itself in. These include "volumetric worlds," "point worlds," "surface worlds," and the worlds of language and of function.

For a general reference on the strategy and tactics of rhetorical persuasion *understood as a logical exercise*, we highly recommend Ch. Perelman and L. Olbrechts-Tyteca,

The New Rhetoric: A Treatise on Argumentation (Notre Dame, Ind.: University of Notre Dame Press, 1971).

A further development of the Hillier/Hanson work cited in this chapter is Bill Hillier's *Space Is the Machine: A Configurational Theory of Architecture* (New York: Cambridge University Press, 1996).

This chapter has cited many classic works in cultural-discursive logical argumentation: Vitruvius, Alberti, Laugier, Pugin, Loos, Wright, Venturi, and so on. Those readers interested in doing logical argumentation might find it very instructive to analyze these works in light of the tactics addressed here.

Many journal articles within the architectural literature as well as outside of it illustrate points made in this chapter. One of the best examples of the use of fundamental categories can be found in an article by Joseph Pine II and James Gilmore, "Welcome to the Experience Economy," *Harvard Business Review*, July–August 1998, pp. 97–105. This is a virtuoso handling of principles of quantity (with quality embedded). The authors argue persuasively that we are presently in an *experience economy*, having progressed through an *agrarian economy*, an *industrial economy*, and a *service economy*. (Note the technical terms by which they *name* four distinct categories.) They then use the illustration of the birthday cake. In an agrarian economy, families made the cake from scratch by mixing farm commodities realized from their own labor. In an industrial economy, the cake is made with ingredients premixed in boxes purchased from a store. In a service economy, parents order the cake ready-made and pick it up on the way home from work. In an experience economy, the entire family goes to Chuck E. Cheese or the Discovery Zone, and the birthday cake is often included as part of a much larger birthday *experience*. It takes little to imagine the built environments that accompany these evolving stages of economic growth; the agrarian homestead is quite different from the strip mall where the Chuck E. Cheese is located. Pine and Gilmore's logical system helps in connecting built form with economic factors.

Another journal article, this one within the architectural literature, is Alexander Tzonis and Diane Lefaivre's "The Mechanical Body Versus the Divine Body." While not a treatise or a logical system as such (it is perhaps a secondary example of logical argumentation), it addresses an instance of a shift in paradigms, and how that shift resulted in the need for updated logical systems. (Alexander Tzonis and Diane Lefaivre, "The Mechanical Body Versus the Divine Body: The Rise of Modern Design Theory," *Journal of Architectural Education*, September 1975, pp. 4–7.)

NOTES

1. Plato *Thaeatetus* 197(e)–199(b), in *Plato: Collected Dialogues*, trans. F. M. Cornford, eds. Edith Hamilton and Huntington Cairns, 14th printing (Princeton, N.J.: Princeton University Press 1989). Of course, Socrates moves on very quickly to show that the aviary solution is lim-

ited. For instance, why is it that in the *interchange* of right pieces of knowledge (that is, after we have the right birds in hand) we can still derive wrong judgments?

2. Bill and Julienne Hanson, *The Social Logic of Space* (Cambridge, UK: Cambridge University Press, 1984), 155–163.

3. L. March and G. Stiny, "Spatial Systems in Architecture and Design: Some History and Logic," in *Environment and Planning B: Planning and Design* 12 (1985): 31. Italics in text.

4. Hanson's paper, " 'Deconstructing' Architects' Houses," is a secondary work derived from the primary work she did with Hillier. The paper summarizes student investigations of four residences designed by "star" architects (Botta, Meier, Hejduk and Loos) along the lines of the gamma map theory. For instance, in the Botta house (Pregassona), Hanson and her students found it to be "treelike" in that the design restricted possibilities of movement from one space to another. They concluded that, for all of its formal attractiveness, the gamma map revealed limited possibilities in the plan for innovative cultural-functional lifestyles. They also suggest a possible segregationist view of gender relations in the house by dint of where the kitchen is located. See J. Hanson, " 'Deconstructing' Architects' Houses," in *Environment and Planning B: Planning and Design* 24 (1994): 675–704.

5. See *http://murmur.arch.gatech.edu/~spatial/*. Concept development by: John Peponis, Jean Wineman, Mahbub Rashid, Sonit Bafna, Sung-Hong Kim, Georgia Institute of Technology.

6. Vitruvius, *The Ten Books on Architecture*, trans. M. H. Morgan (New York: Dover, 1960), 3.1.4.

7. John Summerson, *The Classical Language of Architecture* (London: Thames and Hudson, 1980), 19–27.

8. Vitruvius, *The Ten Books*, 1 (preface). 2–3.

9. Ibid., 4.1.6–9.

10. March and Stiny, "Spatial Systems," 31–36.

11. Marc-Antoinne Laugier, *Essay on Architecture* (1752), trans. Wolfgang and Anni Hermann (Los Angeles: Hennessey and Ingalls, 1977).

12. Le Corbusier, *Towards a New Architecture* (New York: Dover Publications, 1986), 89–103.

13. March and Stiny, "Spatial Systems," 43. The secondary work cited is H. Koning and J. Eizenberg, "The Language of the Prairie: Frank Lloyd Wright's Prairie Houses," *Environment and Planning B* 8 (1981): 295–323.

14. A. W. Pugin. *True Principles of Pointed Christian Architecture*, 1841 (New York and London: St. Martin's Press, 1973).

15. "But if to the stone facing of that bastion be added an unnecessary feature, as a cable moulding, *that* is Architecture." John Ruskin, "The Lamp of Sacrifice," in *The Seven Lamps of Architecture*, 1880 (New York: Dover Publications, 1989), 9.

16. Adolf Loos, "Ornament and Crime" (1908) in *Ornament and Crime and Selected Essays*, trans. M. Mitchell (Riverside, Calif.: Ariadne Press, 1998), 167–176.

17. Philosophically speaking, "definition" is hard to define. Readers can consult any good dictionary of philosophy (such as the *Oxford Companion to Philosophy*) and texts dedicated specifically to addressing this term (such as John William Miller's *The Definition of a Thing*) if they wish to pursue it in an in-depth manner. See John William Miller, *The Definition of a Thing*, (New York: W. W. Norton, 1980).

18. Weld Coxe, *Managing Architectural and Engineering Practice* (New York: John Wiley & Sons, 1980), 58–64.

19. Leon Battista Alberti, *On the Art of Building in Ten Books* [1453], trans. Joseph Rykwert, Neil Leach, and Robert Tavernor (Cambridge, Mass.: MIT Press, 1994), 7.

20. John Peponis, J. Wineman, R. Rashid, S. Hong Kim, and S. Bafna, "On the Description of Shape and Spatial Configuration Inside Buildings: Convex Partitions and Their Local Properties," in *Environment and Planning B* (1997) 24: 762.

21. John Ruskin, *The Stones of Venice* (New York: E. P. Dutton & Co., n.d.), vol. 1, 33.

22. Jon Lang, *Creating Architectural Theory* (New York: Van Nostrand Reinhold Co., 1987), viii.

23. For this discussion on "quantity" and the following subsection on "quality" we are indebted to material from Chaim Perelman and L. Olbrechts-Tyteca, *The New Rhetoric, A Treatise on Argumentation* (Notre Dame, Ind.: University of Notre Dame Press, 1969). Perelman and Olbrechts-Tyteca treat these two terms under their general heading of "loci." Here, we have used these terms in another manner (under our heading of "definition"), but we recommend *The New Rhetoric* as an important work from which readers interested in logical argumentation can benefit.

24. Aristotle, *Metaphysics*, 982a.

25. A comparative review of these two lists may be found in Donald Munro, *The Concept of Man in Early China* (Stanford, Calif.: Stanford University Press, 1969), 29–32.

26. Vitruvius, *The Ten Books*, 1.2.13–16.

27. March and Stiny, "Spatial Systems," 40.

28. Gottfried Semper, *The Four Elements of Architecture and Other Writings*, trans. J. F. Mallegrave and W. Hermann (Cambridge, UK: Cambridge University Press, 1989), 101–102.

29. Laugier, *Essay on Architecture*, 11–38.

30. Le Corbusier, "Five Points of a New Architecture," in *Architecture and Design: 1890–1939*, ed. Tim and Charlotte Benton (New York: Whitney Library, 1975).

31. Stewart Brand, *How Buildings Learn* (New York: Viking, 1994), 2–23.

32. Aristotle, *Metaphysics*, 982b. "And that science is supreme, and superior to the subsidiary, which knows for what end each action is to be done; i.e., the Good in each particular case, and in general the highest Good in the whole of nature . . ."

33. Laugier, *Essay on Architecture*, 12.

34. Dana Cuff, *Architecture: The Story of Practice* (Cambridge, Mass: MIT Press, 1993), 196.

35. Viollet-le-Duc, "Lecture VI" in *Lectures on Architecture* [1872], trans. B. Bucknall (New York: 1987), vol. 1, 179–180.

36. John Ruskin, "The Lamp of Life," in *The Seven Lamps of Architecture* (New York: Dover, 1989), 173.

37. Vitruvius, *The Ten Books*, 2.1.1–2.

38. R. D. Dripps, *The First House* (Cambridge, Mass: MIT Press, 1997).

39. Martin Heidegger, "Building Dwelling Thinking," in *Basic Writings*, ed. David Krell (San Francisco: Harper Torchbooks, 1993), 347–363.

40. Cuff, *Architecture: The Story of Practice*, 195.

41. Vitruvius, *Ten Books*, 3.1.4.

42. Le Corbusier, *Towards a New Architecture*, 89–103.

43. Any deduction involves a tacit inductive step, which is the assumption that nature is uniform in its behavior. In other words, that Mr. Jones will continue to be a man (as opposed to turning into something else) assumes a lot about the coherence of the universe and its behavior. Such assumptions are essentially inductive patterns of reasoning. This is the position of David Hume: "For all inferences from experience suppose, as their foundation, that the future will resemble the past, and that similar powers will be conjoined with similar sensible qualities. If there be any suspicion, that the course of nature may change, and that the past may be no rule for the future, all experience becomes useless, and can give rise to no inference or conclusion." *An Enquiry Concerning Human Understanding*, 1748 (Indianapolis: Hackett Publishing Co., 1993), 24.

44. Louis Sullivan, "The Tall Office Building Artistically Considered," in *Kindergarten Chats and Other Writings* (New York: Wittenborn, Schultz, 1947), 207–208.

45. Antony Flew, ed., *A Dictionary of Philosophy*, 2nd Ed. (New York: St. Martin's Press, 1979), 164–165.

46. Vitruvius, *The Ten Books*, 6.2.4.

47. Perelman and Olbrechts-Tyteca, *New Rhetoric,* 13–17.

48. Ibid., 210.

49. Moisei Ginzburg, *Style and Epoch*, trans. A. Senkevitch (Cambridge, Mass.: MIT Press, 1982), 80–81.

50. J. N. L. Durand, *Summary of the Lectures on Architecture*, in *A Documentary History of Art*, vol. 3, ed. E. Holt (Garden City, Anchor, 1966), 206–207.

51. Vitruvius, *The Ten Books*, 4.1.9–10.

52. Summerson, *Classical Language of Architecture*, 14–15.

53. Perelman and Olbrechts-Tyteca, *New Rhetoric*, 116–117. It should be noted that the authors here mean verbal images: ". . . make present, by verbal magic alone . . ."

54. Vitruvius, *The Ten Books*, 1 (preface). 2–3.

55. Pugin, *Principles of Pointed or Christian Architecture*, 64–65.

56. Daniel Libeskind, *1995 Raoul Wallenberg Lecture* (University of Michigan, Ann Arbor. 1995), 40.

57. Alberto Perez-Gomez, *Architecture and the Crises of Modern Science* (Cambridge, Mass: MIT Press, 1994), 3–14.

58. Alberti, *Art of Building in Ten Books*, p. 7.

59. John Ruskin, "The Lamp of Truth," 41.

60. Frank Lloyd Wright, "The Art and Craft of the Machine," in *Frank Lloyd Wright: Writings and Buildings*, eds. Edgar Kaufman and Beb Raeburn (Cleveland, Ohio: The World Publishing Company 1960), 55–73.

61. Vincent Scully, introduction to Robert Venturi, *Complexity and Contradiction in Architecture* (New York: Museum of Modern Art, 1985), 9.

62. Ulrich Conrads, ed., *Programs and Manifestoes of 20th Century Architecture* (Cambridge, Mass.: MIT Press, 1970).

63. Philip Johnson and Mark Wigley, *Deconstructivist Architecture* (New York: Museum of Modern Art, 1988), 10–20.

64. The paper by Vakalo Liou, et al. has already been mentioned. Another article using the Villa Malcontenta prominently is G. Stiny and W. Mitchell, "The Palladian Grammar," in *Environment and Planning B* 5 (1978): 5–18.

65. G. Stiny and W. Mitchell, "The Grammar of Paradise," in *Environment and Planning B* 7 (1980): 209–226.

66. Peponis et al., "On the Description of Shape and Spatial Configuration," 771.

67. D'Arcy Thompson, *On Growth and Form* (London: Cambridge University Press, 1971).

68. Philip Steadman, *The Evolution of Designs* (London: Cambridge University Press, 1979).

69. Norberg-Schulz. *The Concept of Dwelling: On the Way to a Figurative Architecture* (New York: Rizzoli, 1985), 7.

70. Ibid., 33–34. There is significant lack of clarity in some of Norberg-Schulz's terms and phrases. For instance, what does it really mean that the settlement can "determine our expectations" or that it "tunes" us in a certain way? The problem in his logical system is an assumption that ephemeral subjective feeling can be indexed to formal typologies, almost as if given the latter, certain feelings would ensue. But this is essentially a fault in his reasoning; it is not a fault of the tactic of categorization as a means of framing logical systems.

71. Lisa Heschong, *Thermal Delight in Architecture* (Cambridge, Mass: MIT Press, 1997).

72. E. H. Gombrich, *The Story of Art* (London: Phaidon, 1971).

73. Manfredo Tafuri, *Architecture and Utopia* (Cambridge, Mass.: MIT Press, 1976).

74. Ernst Cassirer, *An Essay on Man*, 1944 (New Haven, Conn.: Yale University Press, 1972).

75. Susanne Langer, *Philosophy in a New Key: The Symbolism of Reason, Rite and Art*, 1942 (New York: Mentor Books, 1964).

76. Roger Scruton, *The Aesthetics of Architecture* (Princeton, N.J.: Princeton University Press, 1979).

77. John Dewey, *Art as Experience*, 1934 (New York: Perigee Books, 1980).

78. See Sylvia Lavin, *Quatremère de Quincy and the Invention of a Modern Language of Architecture* (Cambridge, Mass.: MIT Press, 1992).

79. Thomas Kuhn, *The Structure of Scientific Revolutions*, 1962 (Chicago: University of Chicago Press, 1970).

80. See various essays on "falsification" and scientific method by Popper in David Miller (ed.), *Popper Selections* (Princeton, N.J.: Princeton University Press, 1985).

Chapter 12

Case Studies and
Combined Strategies

12.1   INTRODUCTION

In 1961, Jane Jacobs wrote her classic book, *The Death and Life of Great American Cities*. Jacobs's book challenged the conventional wisdom of modernist-inspired urban renewal popular at that time. Her insights about how to maintain and foster the vitality of cities are derived almost entirely from vignettes of life in New York City.

However, the richness and depth of her many examples of the socio-physical dynamics of life in New York were powerfully persuasive; and, as a consequence, the book had an enormous impact on the planning and architecture professions nationwide. Moreover, the themes she identified were later observed and documented in other cities. In her introduction, she presents an articulate rationale for the strategy of her investigation:

> In setting forth different principles, I shall mainly be writing about common, ordinary things. . . . The way to get at what goes on in the seemingly mysterious and perverse behavior of cities is, I think to look closely, and with as little expectation as is possible, at the most ordinary scenes and events, and attempt to see what they mean and whether any threads of principle emerge among them. . . . I use a preponderance of examples from New York because that is where I live. But most of the basic ideas in this book come from things I first noticed or was told in other cities. . . . I hope any reader of this book will constantly and skeptically test what I say against his own knowledge of cities and their behavior.[1]

Figure 12.1   Cityscape in Brooklyn Heights, New York. Photo by Linda Groat.

In recent research on quite a different theme, Fernando Lara poses the questions: Why was modern architecture better received in Brazil than in Europe or the United States? How were the attributes of modernism promulgated in such a way that many working- and middle-class houses of the 1950s were built with visible attributes of modernism? And to what extent were these houses truly modernist?[2]

To explore these questions, Lara selected the Brazilian city Belo Horizonte as the focus of his study. Belo Horizonte was selected for at least two reasons: 1) the great number of 1950s popular modern houses in major sections of the city; and 2) the presence of one of the first and most significant ensembles of modernist public buildings, the Pampulha complex built in the early 1940s. Pampulha represents an officially sanctioned and close-at-hand example of modernism, known to the entire city's population.

In framing the contours of the study, Lara identified three tactics for collecting data: 1) archival research to ascertain the influence of various social, economic, cultural, and media transmissions; 2) formal analyses (of facade design and interior lay-

Figure 12.2　Part of the Pampulha complex, Belo Horizonte, Brazil. Photo courtesy of Fernando L. Lara.

outs) in a sample of 300 houses in two sections of the city; and 3) in-depth interviews with 20 to 30 residents of popular modern houses, many of whom are original owners. In this way, Lara has combined multiple data sources that address the broad cultural influences, the physical extent of modernist adoption and/or adaptation, and the residents' own understanding of their home in relation to the larger cultural context.

From the rich array of data obtained this way, Lara is able to explain in very detailed and nuanced ways how and why modernism came to infuse the building of

Figure 12.3　A typical popular modernist house, Belo Horizonte, Brazil. Photo courtesy of Fernando L. Lara.

middle-class residential areas of Belo Horizonte. Indeed, some of his analyses uncover unexpected patterns and relationships. For example, although popular magazines were full of both advertisements and stories about the artifacts of modernization, many of the families who built modernist-style homes were most influenced through personal connections and/or direct exposure to the homes of more well-to-do families.

Figure 12.4   A typical product advertisement, Brazil, 1950s.

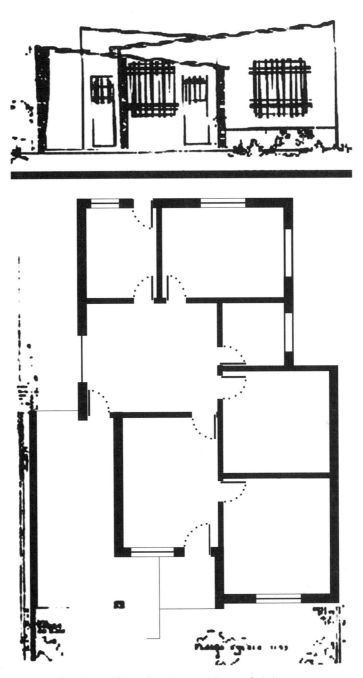

Figure 12.5   Typical facade and floor plan. Courtesy Fernando L. Lara.

Moreover, the application of modernist principles was often inconsistent or piecemeal. Often modernist features were applied to the facade of houses, while the interior layouts reflected the social traditions of premodernist houses.

These two studies illustrate two powerful, and sometimes overlapping, approaches to research design. Jacobs's study is a preeminent and well-respected example of the *case study* strategy; she uses the example of New York City—as a particular case—to explore the multiple socio-physical dynamics that contribute to the vitality of urban life. Although she may have gained insights from her experience in other cities, and others may have studied other cities in light of her conclusions, the heart and soul of her study is the particular case of New York City.

Lara's research is also a case study in that he focuses on the multifaceted dynamics that led to adoption and adaptation of modernism in one city: Belo Horizonte, Brazil. But his study also represents quite emphatically the power of *combined strategies*, in this instance the interpretive-historical and the qualitative strategies.

In the remainder of this chapter, we will examine in detail both the case study strategy and models for achieving effective combined strategies.

12.2   STRATEGY: GENERAL CHARACTERISTICS OF THE CASE STUDY

In the one of the most frequently cited books on case study research, Robert Yin provides the following definition: "A case study is an empirical inquiry that investigates a contemporary phenomenon within its real-life context, especially when the boundaries between phenomenon and context are not clearly evident."[3] To make the definition more clearly applicable to architectural research, we would amend Yin's definition to read: an empirical inquiry that investigates a phenomenon or setting. By deleting the word "contemporary" and adding the word "setting," we include historic phenomena and both historic and contemporary settings as potential foci of case studies.

What then are the primary characteristics of the case study? Briefly, there appear to be five particularly salient characteristics: 1) a focus on either single or multiple cases, studied in their real life contexts; 2) the capacity to explain causal links; 3) the importance of theory development in the research design phase; 4) a reliance on multiple sources of evidence, with data needing to converge in a triangulating fashion; and 5) the power to generalize to theory. These five characteristics will be discussed in detail in the following chapter segments.

12.2.1 A Focus on Cases in Their Contexts

The essence of the case study strategy is its focus on studying a setting or phenomenon embedded in its real-life context. As Yin describes it, the case study strategy implies much more than simply studying a phenomenon "in the field." Rather, it involves studying a case in relation to the complex dynamics with which it intersects. This definition of the case is clearly evident in both the Jacobs and the Lara studies. For instance, Jacobs's investigation of urban vitality in the case of New York City is clearly linked to a multitude of contextual factors and phenomena—from the rise of the automobile culture, to federal funding policies, to trends in planning theory. Similarly, Lara's study of modernist houses in the case of Belo Horizonte is linked to a wide range of issues, from the role of modernization in Brazil, to the economic prosperity of the 1950s, to the influence of local political leaders. As both of these examples demonstrate, the context of the case becomes virtually inseparable from the definition of the case itself.

BOX 12.1

Case Study: A 100 Percent Flexible Workspace

A combination of recent trends—including the globalization of markets, rapid growth of telecommuting and telecommunications, the shift toward collaborative work and project teams, and the increasingly flexible assignment of office space, such as hot desks—has led many organizations to reconsider how they plan for and use their office environments. In some organizations, the changes have been so profound that it is unclear how, or if, ongoing work practices are being supported by the design of the physical environment. Doctoral student Janice Barnes wanted to know: How can architectural design support the way project teams share knowledge in a 100% flexible workplace?

The focus of this case study was an office site within a consulting organization of over 130,000 employees, with operations in over 50 countries. The site was chosen because it had recently been designed by a local architectural firm to meet the workplace standards established by the organization in 2000. The design intention was to provide a 100 percent flexible workplace in which no person, even at the partner level, claimed a dedicated office. All office assignments were temporary; and extensive telecommuting was accommodated.* In addition to site visits for observations, Barnes conducted open-ended interviews with approximately 25 people, including members of various project teams; office support staff; facilities department staff members; human resources staff, a national facilities staff member; and several members of the architectural firm that had designed the site.

---

*Janice Barnes, Situated Cognition in Flexible Work Arrangements (Ph.D. diss., University of Michigan, 2001).

(continues)

BOX 12.1 (continued)

Barnes concludes that in this new environment, project teams most frequently share knowledge via an array of artifacts displayed in the team work room. These artifacts may include: reference documents from clients, workflow diagrams pinned to wall surfaces, diagrams from brainstorming sessions, etc. Few, if any, representations of knowledge are located or displayed in individual offices or cubicles. And since these offices are constantly reassigned, virtually no personalization of offices occurs. This new design standard for the workplace seems to serve the short-term interests of the project teams reasonably well, but interviews revealed that employees feel little, if any, attachment to the workplace and invest no energy in getting to know other employees within it.

Figure 12.6 Typical project team work room, with the artifacts representing the team's shared knowledge. Drawing by Fernando Lara.

12.2.2 The Capacity to Explain Causal Links

One of the most frequently discussed issues in research design is that of causality. As we discussed in Chapter 9, for instance, the experimental research design is fundamentally orchestrated so as to ascertain the causal capacity of the independent or treatment variable. By contrast, correlational design can identify patterns of relationships, but stops short of attributing cause. (See Chapter 8.) But we have also seen that both interpretive-historical and qualitative strategies can also address the issue of causality, albeit in a quite a different way than experimental research; both of these strategies offer the potential to uncover the multiple, complex, and sometimes overlapping factors that eventually lead to particular outcomes. It is in this latter sense that case studies can also identify causal links among an array of socio-physical factors and events.

In arguing that case studies can, like experiments, be *explanatory*, Yin suggests that they can also be either *descriptive* or *exploratory* in purpose.[4] Whether a particular case study is explanatory, descriptive, exploratory, or some combination of these is a function of the researcher's purpose—or more precisely the nature of the research question—rather than any limitation inherent in the case study strategy. To clarify his point, Yin develops a case study typology that distinguishes among both research goals and design structure. (See Figure 12.7.)

Using Yin's typology, we can classify Jacobs's work as a theory-building study that has both exploratory and explanatory purposes. The exploratory nature of her investigation is reflected in the following sentiment, quoted earlier at greater length: "The way to get at what goes on in the . . . behavior of cities is, I think, to look closely

	Purpose of Case Study		
Type of Structure	Explanatory	Descriptive	Exploratory
1. Linear-Analytic Typical article format: problem statement literature review methods results	X	X	X
2. Chronological (narrative sequence)	X	X	X
3. Theory-Building Sequence of chapters depends on logic of theory development	X		X
4. Unsequenced Sequence of chapters interchangeable		X	

Adapted from Robert Yin. Yin includes 2 other types not commonly employed in architectural research.

Figure 12.7 Typology of case study designs. Adapted from Robert K. Yin, *Case Study Research: Design and Methods* (Thousand Oaks, Calif.: Sage Publications, 1994) p. 138. Reprinted by permission of Sage Publications.

. . . and attempt to see what they mean and whether any threads of principle emerge among them."[5] But Jacobs also clearly intends to do more than just find out; she also wants "to *explain* [emphasis ours] the underlying order of cities."[6] And to this end, she identifies what she calls the most "ubiquitous principle" right off the bat in her introduction: "the need of cities for a most intricate and close-grained diversity of uses that give each other constant mutual support, both economically and socially."[7] This combination of exploratory and explanatory goals is clearly articulated in the four-part structure of her book. In Part One, the exploratory component is represented in her observations on the nature of cities. In Part Two, Jacobs lays out the heart of her explanatory argument by identifying four key conditions for city diversity. And finally, the next two sections discuss the implications of the diversity principle for the regeneration of cities, including specific tactics for achieving such regeneration.

Similarly, Lara's study of Brazilian modernism is driven primarily by an explanatory purpose. His basic research questions are these: Why and how was modernism so much more enthusiastically embraced by the Brazilian middle class than it was in the United States and most of Europe? Lara's research also reveals both exploratory and descriptive purposes. He seeks to explore the complex dynamics of modernism's infusion into Brazilian culture through multiple—and previously unexamined—materials, including: archives, documentation of the physical artifacts, and oral histories. At the same time, Lara's exhaustive mapping of modernist houses in two multiblock neighborhoods of Belo Horizonte is a descriptive feat of major proportions. In Yin's typology, Lara's study clearly represents the *linear-analytic* type of case study, which follows the traditional research article outline: problem identification, literature review, methods, results, discussion, and conclusions. (See Figure 12.7.) Not only does this organizing structure accommodate Lara's multiple purposes, but it is the most conventionally suitable for dissertation work.

BOX 12.2

Case Study: A Daylighted Building

Although researchers have been studying the potential of daylighting design as a contribution to energy conservation for a number of years, there is still relatively little information about its effectiveness in practice. Indeed, researchers from the Windows and Lighting Program at Lawrence Berkeley Laboratory reviewed more than 40 daylighted buildings published in architectural and engineering magazines, and discovered that there was no useful data on exactly how much energy could be saved from a "daylighted" building. The researchers chose to take up this challenge and conduct a case study of a San Francisco Bay area building that had recently been published for its daylighting features.* Their goal was to provide guidance to designers by validating their computer-based daylighting models and simultaneously to develop rigorous data that would be convincing to decision-makers.

Their yearlong case study entailed extensive monitoring of daylighting and electricity usage and numerous site visits to explore the more qualitative dimensions of the lighting conditions. Three aspects of the building design were assessed: the design configuration itself, including the central atrium space; the electric lighting system, including an indirect fluorescent system and separate task lighting; and the lighting control system intended to provide automatic dimming when daylighting was sufficient.

From this case study, the research team concluded that the architectural features were generally successful in providing sufficient ambient lighting, sometimes even displacing the use of task lighting. However, they also discovered that many of the photosensors were located inappropriately, thus compromising the overall lighting control system. In some building locations, there was significant potential for dimming that was not being realized; so the researchers recommended that the sensors be strategically relocated and the system recalibrated. Were the lighting control system reconfigured, the expected payback for the control system would be only 2.6 years, an outcome that is quite attractive in economic terms.

Figure 12.8 Although the central atrium is dramatic, it is relatively inefficient in providing light for adjacent spaces. The research team characterizes the atrium as "more a location of light than source of light." Photo by Timothy Hursley.

*C. Benton, M. Warren, S. Selkowitz, and J. Jewell, "Lighting System Performance in an Innovative Daylighted Structure: An Instrumented Study," *Proceedings of the 1986 Daylighting Conference*, Atlanta: American Society of Heating, Refrigerating and Air-Conditioning Engineers, 1989, pp. 286–291.

12.2.3 The Role of Theory Development

Despite the relatively open-ended and broad focus of the case study, Yin recommends that the case study research design be guided by theoretical development. As he puts it: "[T]heory development as part of the [research] design phase is essential, whether the case study's purpose is to develop or to test theory. . . . The complete research design [should embody] a 'theory' of what is being studied."[8] He then goes on to explain that by *theory*, he does not mean a "grand" theory; rather, the goal is to have "a sufficient blueprint for your study"[9] that will suggest what data must be collected and what criteria should be used for analyzing it. Perhaps it is fair to say that the role of theory development Yin proposes has some equivalent to the notion of "hypothesis" in much postpositivist research.

In both Jacobs's and Lara's studies, the role of theory development in the research designs is evident. As Jacobs reveals in her introduction:

> [M]ost of the basic ideas in this book come from things I first noticed or was told in other cities. For example, my first inkling about the powerful effects of certain kinds of functional mixtures in the city came from Pittsburgh, my first speculations about street safety from Philadelphia and Baltimore, my first notions about the meanderings of downtown from Boston, my first clues to the unmaking of slums from Chicago.[10]

These observations from other cities prompted the theoretical propositions underpinning her case study research in New York, as she put it, "at my own front door."[11]

On the other hand, it was Lara's observations of *dissimilarity* between 1950s middle-class housing in Brazil and the United States that prompted the theory development underlying his case study of Belo Horizonte. Thus Lara's research design was guided by his intention to *explain how* and *why* popular acceptance of modernism was so much more pervasive than in more developed industrialized countries in Europe or in the United States.

12.2.4 Using Multiple Sources of Evidence

Another key feature of the case study is its incorporation of multiple sources of evidence. Thus while Jacobs, as a resident and participant observer of her Greenwich Village neighborhood, focuses her attention and analytical insights on the case of New York City, she also draws heavily and freely on her observations of other cities, as well as from commentaries of officials and community leaders in New York and elsewhere.

Lara's case study is particularly notable for the range and variety of data sources, including: archives, oral history, artifactual inventories, as well as formal and spatial analyses. To be specific, the archival work included: 1) an examination of all issues of popular housing magazines from 1950 through 1959 that yielded hundreds of pages of articles about and advertisements of modernist housing and building products; and 2) a review of 25 house plans filed with the Buildings Office of Belo Horizonte. In addition, Lara conducted 21 interviews with family members, most often elderly widows, still living in their modernist-inspired houses of the 1950s. These interviews were particularly in important in uncovering the informal relationships and experiences that influenced the residents' choice of housing style. Lara and his research team also conducted a thorough artifactual survey of all houses within two multiblock neighborhoods to ascertain the proportion of modernist-inspired housing. Finally, Lara examined a sample of houses in order to: 1) classify them along a continuum of traditional to modernist, based on their use of specific facade design features; and 2) conduct both a visual and computer-based analysis of the spatial qualities of the floor plans.[12]

Figure 12.9   House plan diagrams. Courtesy of Fernando L. Lara.

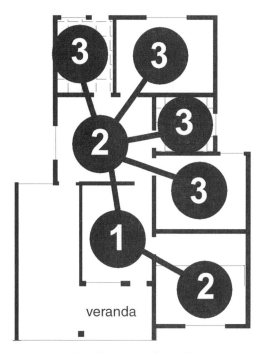

Figure 12.10   Depth analysis of a traditional house. Courtesy of Fernando L. Lara.

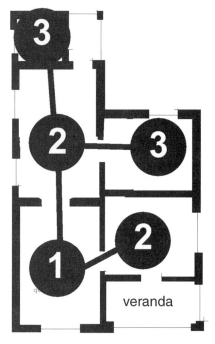

Figure 12.11   Depth analysis of a modernist house. Courtesy of Fernando L. Lara.

12.2.5 Generalizability to Theory

Although a conventional criticism of case study research is that there is no basis for generalizing from one case to other cases, Yin contests this argument vigorously. In effect, he argues that the premise of much correlational research, that one can only generalize from a representative sample to a larger population, is beside the point. Instead, he maintains, the case study's strength is its capacity to generalize to theory, much the way a single "experiment" can be generalized to theory, which can in turn be tested through other experiments. To substantiate his point about generalizability, Yin actually cites Jacobs's study. His insights are worth quoting in some detail:

> This approach is well illustrated by Jane Jacobs in her famous book [that] is based mostly on her experiences from New York City. However, the chapter topics, rather than reflecting the single experience of New York, cover broader theoretical issues in urban planning, such as the role of sidewalks, the role of neighborhoods parks, the need for primary mixed uses, the need for small blocks, and the

processes of slumming and unslumming. In the aggregate, these issues in fact represent the building of a theory of urban planning.

Jacobs' book created heated controversy in the planning profession. As a partial result, new empirical inquiries were made in other locales to examine one or another facet of her rich and provocative ideas. Her *theory*, in essence, became the vehicle for examining other cases, and the theory still stands as a significant contribution to the field of urban planning.[13]

In other words, the influence and power of Jacobs's case study lies in the robust theory she was able to achieve.

In a similar vein, the potential power of Lara's research is in the theoretical principles he is able to identify concerning the complex dynamics of modernization, political influence, indigenous architectural trends, etc. The implication of his case study is not that the acceptance or rejection of modernist architecture can be predicted and thereby generalized to other contexts; rather, its power will be to clarify how and why particular cultural factors can impact middle-class receptivity to architectural trends.

On the other hand, some advocates of the case study warn researchers that too great a focus on generalizing to theory can obscure the intrinsic value and uniqueness that each case offers on its own terms.[14] Robert Stake distinguishes between what he calls the instrumental case study and the intrinsic case study. For researchers using the former, the case is of secondary interest to the theory that can be established from it. In the intrinsic case study, the research is "undertaken because one wants better understanding of this particular case."[15]

12.2.6 Distinguishing the Case Study

The case study, as we have described it here, is a distinct research design. Although the research literature may sometimes employ the term "qualitative case study," this does not mean that the case study research design is equivalent to or necessarily associated with the qualitative research design. Indeed, there is no necessity for qualitative research to adopt a case study design (e.g., Groat and Ahrentzen, 1997). And by the same token, a case study can be based on exclusively quantitative data; or it may have a theory-driven focus rather than the more inductively oriented approach favored in much, though not all, qualitative research.

Similarly, the case study as a research design should not be confused with case study *teaching*. True, both practices are defined by their focus on the case. But in the pedagogical context, the case materials can be deliberately altered to serve particular instructional purposes.[16] Such a practice is obviously antithetical to the principles and purposes of research. On the other hand, case-study research and case-study teaching do both benefit from the robust and multifaceted character of the case focus.

12.3   STRATEGY: SINGLE OR MULTIPLE CASES?

Up to this point, we have focused on research examples of the single-case variety: urban vitality through the case of New York City, and popular modernism through the case of Belo Horizonte, Brazil. Indeed, the single-case study can be highly compelling and—as with Jacobs's study—very influential. On the other hand, there are times when a researcher may want to consider a multiple-case design. On what basis does one make such a choice? And if one does choose a multiple-case design, how many cases are needed?

There is no quick and easy formula for making the choice *between* single- and multiple-case design, or about the *number* of cases necessary for a multiple-case design. But two principles are paramount, and both of them build upon the special characteristics of the case-study strategy identified in the previous chapter section: 1) the nature of the theoretical questions, or research questions, involved; and 2) the role of replication in testing or confirming the study's outcomes.

As single-case studies, both Jacobs's and Lara's work sought to investigate sociophysical phenomena involving multiple and highly complex factors. Each study dealt with issues from the scale of very broad cultural trends to the more intimate moments of sidewalk interaction and supervision of children (in Jacobs's case) or familial relationships represented in house plans (in Lara's study). From a theoretical point of view, it made more sense for each of these researchers to uncover the very complex dynamics of one setting of interest than to look less deeply at more settings. And from a practical point of view, the level of complexity involved also suggested the virtue of a single-case design.

In other instances, a researcher may frame a theoretical question that is narrower in scope, and in which factors of importance may vary from one case to another. In these circumstances, the multiple-case design might be advantageous. This raises the question: How many cases are enough? Here the answer is essentially the same as with the single-case design: the power of generalizability comes from the concept of replication, rather than the concept of sampling. Yin explains this quite well:

> The decision to undertake multiple-case studies cannot be taken lightly. Every case should serve a specific purpose within the overall scope of inquiry. Here, *a major insight is to consider multiple cases as one would consider multiple experiments*—that is, to follow a "replication" logic. This is far different from a mistaken analogy in the past, which incorrectly considered multiple cases to be similar to the multiple respondents in a survey (or to multiple subjects *within* an experiment)—that is, to follow a "sampling" logic. [Emphases the author's.][17]

This quotation highlights not only Yin's insistence on the significance of the replication logic, but also another important principle, namely: "Every case should serve a specific purpose within the overall scope of inquiry."[18] To clarify what he means by this, Yin describes the distinction between *literal* and *theoretical* replication. A *literal* replication is a case study (or studies) that tests precisely the same outcomes, principles, or predictions established by the initial case study. In contrast, a *theoretical* replication is a case study that produces contrasting results but for predictable reasons.

For example, if in the future Lara seeks to replicate his findings on the popular acceptance of modernism in Belo Horizonte, he might seek to do so by conducting both literal and theoretical replications. In general, any other Brazilian case would be subject to the broad socio-cultural trends of modernization, political history and economy. However, a literal replication would also include other conditions similar to those found in Belo Horizonte, such as the existence of an iconic exemplar of modernism, built with the enthusiastic support of the city's political leadership. Without such conditions, another Brazilian case study would constitute a theoretical replication. Similarly, if Lara were to study the popular acceptance of modernism in another developing country, but without the overt support of modernism by the nation's president, this would also constitute a theoretical replication. With these considerations in mind, we will now consider two examples of multiple-case study designs.

12.3.1 A Multiple Case Study: Greenways. The goal of Anne Lusk's study of greenways was to develop design guidelines for people, agencies, and community organizations wishing to create new greenways or upgrade existing ones. In particular, she was interested in determining the desired frequency of qualitative features that would provide a sense of arrival or destination.[19] Although she considered many different research designs, including simulation (see Chapter 10) and correlation (see Chapter 8), she eventually came to the conclusion that the most useful guidelines would emerge from closely examining best practices, i.e., good exemplars of existing greenway design. To this end, she sent an inquiry to all members of a national greenway activist group, asking them to recommend the best greenways.

Although Lusk might have simply selected the top two or three to include in a multiple-case design, she also recognized that there were distinctly different "types" of greenways. Some, like the Stowe Recreation Path in Vermont, were in scenic rural areas and could take advantage of natural landscape features. Another group of greenways was in predominantly urban areas, often linking existing city parks but including more developed and densely populated areas. And yet a third set of greenways, such the West Orange Trail near Orlando, Florida, were a product of the "rails-to-trails" movement in which old railway right-of-ways have been converted to greenways.[20]

Given this typology of greenway conditions, Lusk decided to combine a *literal* and *theoretical* replication design. Thus for each greenway type—rural, urban, and rails-to-trails—she selected the two most highly regarded exemplars. In this way, she

Greenway Types		
Rural	**Urban**	**Rails-to-Trails**
1. Stowe recreation Path Stowe, Vermont	3. Lakeshore Drive Chicago, Illinois	5. Minuteman Trail Boston, Massachusetts
2. Vail Trail Vail, Colorado	4. Platt River Denver, Colorado	6. West Orange Orlando, Florida

Figure 12.12   Multiple case-study design by Anne Lusk. Courtesy of Anne Lusk.

achieved three *literal* replication pairs; and in addition, she was able to test the outcomes of each replication pair against two pairs of *theoretical* replications.

12.3.2 A Multiple Case Study: The Experience of Thai Tradition in Housing

The goal of Piyalada Devakula's study was to elucidate the experiential characteristics and meanings of the Thai tradition in housing. As in many other developing countries, many architects and laypeople in Thailand have expressed concern that the cultural identity of their architectural tradition has been lost in the development of modernized and Western-oriented housing.[21]

Because Devakula wanted to look deeply into the experiential qualities of Thai housing—as opposed, for instance, to looking more broadly at popular notions of stylistic features—she chose a case-study strategy. But this also presented some challenges. While she wanted to select a case (or cases) that would represent as full an embodiment of Thai tradition as possible, she also wanted to look at how contemporary Bangkok residents lived their lives in their houses. Having identified these two critical factors—the presence or not of traditional Thai design features and the accommodation of modern lifestyles—Devakula was then able to select four case-study houses representing different relationships between the two factors.

Devakula selected two case-study houses that represented the extreme versions of tradition and modernization. The first, the Tub Kwan Pavillion, had been a modest royal residence, but is now a museum and not used as a residence. At the other extreme, Sukhumvit 101/1 represents a contemporary Western-style villa house in Bangkok. The other two cases represent a confluence of traditional Thai housing features and modern styles. The Baan Song Kanong represents a traditional Thai house, nearly 100 years old, that has been modernized and continues to be a residence. In contrast, the Chaipranin House is an architect-designed house, built in 1994, but it embodies many traditional Thai features such as a raised courtyard design.[22]

	Tub Kwan Pavilion	Baan Song Kanong	Chaipranin House	101/1 House
Nature	Full-featured traditional Thai house	Living traditional Thai house	Contemporary Thai house w/ traditional characteristics	Modern villa-type house
Location	Nakhon-Pathom province (1 hour from Bangkok)	Phrapradaeng, Samut-Prakarn province (in the vicinity of Bangkok)	Sukhumvit 11 (near the heart of Bangkok)	Sukhumvit 101/1 (Bangkok suburban area)
Year of Construction	1911 (abandoned: 1920's; restored: 1970's)	Approx. 1900-1910's	1994	1978
Basic Spatial Organization				
Demographic characteristics of Inhabitants	N/A (currently unoccupied, but built as a summer palace)	Middle class Mon-based professionals	Upper middle class young professionals/ new family with young children	Middle class professionals
Interesting Features	Acclaimed as aesthetically the best example of existing full-featured Central Thai houses	Traditional built environment in transition, with pressing tension between modern living and traditional environment and values	A coexistence of the modern villa-type in-law's house and the courtyard-type new house, the presence of traditional extended family system in a new urban environment	A representation of both the typical middle-class villa-type living, a point of contrast to the traditional one, and a clarification of my background as an interpreter

Figure 12.13   The four case studies of Piyalada Devakula. Courtesy of Piyalada Devakula.

Within this set of four case studies, the Tub Kwan and the modern villa clearly constitute theoretical replications, since the outcomes one would predict for each are quite different. On the other hand, the modernized house and the new tradition-based design could conceivably represent a set of literal replications, depending on how extensive the modernization of the traditional house was and how robustly the traditional design was executed in the new house. As it turns out, the modernization of the traditional house was indeed extensive enough to alter its original experiential qualities. So in the end, the four case studies constituted *theoretical* replications, evidencing similarities and differences consistent with the fluctuation of the two defining issues of traditional design features and the accommodation of modern life.

12.4   CASE STUDIES: STRENGTHS AND WEAKNESSES

Many of the strengths of the case-study research design flow naturally from the defining characteristics already identified in section 12.2. The first four items listed in Figure 12.14 directly mirror those earlier section headings. However, those same characteristics also give rise to potential weaknesses. For instance, the embeddedness of the case study in its context can lead to such an expansion of scope that the study becomes unwieldy. And while the case study can uncover and explain causal links, the causality it describes is likely to be more variegated and multifaceted than that identified by an experimental design. Similarly, while the incorporation of multiple data sources can help confirm findings, it makes establishing the coherence of the study more challenging. Not least, although its potential for generalizing to theory represents an important strength of the case study, the theory remains tentative until confirmed by other case studies.

Taken together, these strengths and weaknesses lead to the more general assessment listed as item 5 in Figure 12.14. Indeed, the depth, complexity, and multifaceted quality of the case study contribute to its robustness as a research design. Examples such as Jacobs's study of city life reinforce the point that a case study, when done well, can be a particularly compelling form of research. On the other hand, there are fewer established rules and procedures for designing and conducting case study research. Almost by definition, the case study is conceived in terms of case-particular considerations; and great latitude is afforded the researcher in devising the overall research design and selecting particular combination of tactics. This contrasts quite sharply with the much more prescribed components of the experimental strategy, and with

Strengths	Weaknesses
1. Focus on the embeddedness of the case in its context	1. Potential for over-complication
2. Capacity to explain causal links	2. "Causality" likely to be multi-faceted and complex
3. Richness of multiple data sources	3. Challenge of integrating many data sources in coherent way
4. Ability to generalize to theory	4. Replication required in other cases
5. Compelling and convincing when done well	5. Difficult to do well; fewer established rules and procedures than other research designs

Figure 12.14   Strengths and weaknesses of the case study.

the measurement of clearly specified variables in correlation research. Although just "following procedures" in experimental or correlational designs by no means guarantees quality, it is even more true that the case study requires the researcher to carefully think through both the overall framework and the details of the research design.

12.5 COMBINED STRATEGIES: INTEGRATING MULTIPLE RESEARCH DESIGNS

Increasingly, researchers in many fields, including architecture, are advocating a more integrative approach to research whereby multiple methods from diverse traditions are incorporated in one study. Because each method of conducting research brings with it particular strengths and weaknesses (as we have noted in the previous chapters), many researchers believe that combining methods provides appropriate checks against the weak points in each, while simultaneously enabling the benefits to complement each other.

A term frequently used to describe the principle of combining strengths and neutralizing weaknesses is *triangulation*. (See also Chapter 2.) Originally a concept used in navigation and military strategy, it refers to the use of multiple reference points to locate the exact position of an object (Smith, 1975 as quoted in Jick, 1979).[23] In general, researchers advocate triangulation to address issues of research validity (or credibility in the naturalistic paradigm) and/or objectivity (or confirmability in the naturalistic paradigm).

A potentially confusing aspect of the discussion, however, is that different authors advocate the combining of methods at very different levels of the research process, including: topic areas; paradigms or ways of knowing; research design; and tactics in data collection. For example, in discussing the apparent paradigmatic dichotomy in architectural research, Julia Robinson offers a number of examples of integrative research described primarily in terms of specialty areas.[24] In particular, she describes Geoffrey Broadbent's work as combining the topics of design methods and human behavior;[25] Susan Ubbelohde's work as an integration of technology, history, and human behavior;[26] and Juan Paul Bonta's research as linking mathematics, art, and social science.[27]

Researchers in other fields have also tended to address the discussion of mixed methods at multiple levels of the research process. For instance, in the social sciences, where such discussions have been especially prevalent, many researchers (e.g., Jick, 1979; Creswell, 1994; and Miles and Huberman, 1994) have tended to use the terms *qualitative* and *quantitative* to refer both to the paradigmatic (system of inquiry) and tactical levels. Tellingly, Miles and Huberman emphasize the distinction between research levels to highlight the difference between a researcher's avowed epistemological stance and his/her actual practice:

In epistemological debates it is tempting to operate at the poles. But in the actual practice of empirical research, we believe that all of us . . . are closer to the center, with multiple overlaps.[28]

While we acknowledge the usefulness of discussing mixed methods at multiple levels of the research process, we will focus this discussion primarily at the level of strategy, or research design. For instance, how might a researcher go about combining the interpretive-historical strategy with simulation? Or the correlational strategy with the qualitative? Although there are no quick formulas for developing a research design in the first place, much less a combined strategy, Creswell does offer three general models that are suitable for our consideration: 1) the two-phase approach; 2) the dominant–less dominant design; and 3) the mixed methodology design.[29] In the following chapter sections we will discuss each model in turn, along with appropriate examples of actual research studies.

12.5.1 A Combined Strategy: A Two-Phase Design

As the term itself suggests, a two-phase research design involves combining two or more strategies in a sequence of distinct phases. The advantage of such an approach is that the particular procedures and standards associated with each strategy can be presented fully and distinctly. A disadvantage is that the project could lack coherence if the strategies are not conceptually well linked.[30]

An instructive example of a phased research design is represented by William W. Clark and Robert Mark's study of the buttress design of Notre Dame Cathedral.[31] The premise of their study is that while improved engineering analyses have raised the level of understanding of the technical innovation involved in Gothic architecture, architectural history has been slow to incorporate this knowledge. In particular, Notre Dame Cathedral in Paris is widely presumed to be the first example of an externally visible flying buttress; yet conflicting reconstruction drawings of the original buttress structure (subsequently renovated in the thirteenth and nineteenth centuries) leave unresolved the precise design of the original. Clark and Mark's research question, then, is simply: What was the original structural design of the Notre Dame buttresses?

The first phase of the research follows an interpretive-historical design, utilizing both archival and archaeological sources of evidence. Without going into great detail, the authors not only sort through virtually all the conflicting reconstruction documents but also carry out an exhaustive archaeological field examination of the Notre Dame structure. As a result of this investigation, they are able to conclude that the original nave scheme called for two ranks of buttresses that were relatively independent of each other. They conclude: "The evidence of both archaeology and drawing argues in favor of a much simpler form for the first flying buttress . . . than has been previously envisioned."[32]

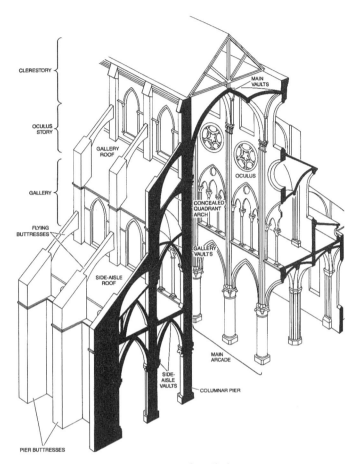

CLERESTORY

OCULUS STORY

GALLERY

FLYING BUTTRESSES

GALLERY ROOF

SIDE-AISLE ROOF

SIDE-AISLE VAULTS

PIER BUTTRESSES

MAIN VAULTS

OCULUS

CONCEALED QUADRANT ARCH

GALLERY VAULTS

MAIN ARCADE

COLUMNAR PIER

Figure 12.15 Schematic isometric restoration, after Clark.

Next, the authors conduct a comparative case study of the cathedral at St. Martin at Champeaux, whose buttresses "most closely resemble" the first ones built at Notre Dame.[33] Historical documents show that the church at Champeaux actually belonged to the Bishop of Paris from the twelfth century; and the authors cite other historical links as well. Again the combination of archival documents and archaeological fieldwork lead the authors to conclude that the nave buttresses at Champeaux provide "an independent means of confirming" much of the evidence recorded in nineteenth century drawings and still preserved at Paris.[34] Moreover, the example of Champeaux also appears to clarify some details no longer preserved at Notre Dame. In sum, the authors conclude that the comparative case study of Champeaux seems to confirm their proposed reconstruction of Notre Dame's original buttress.

Finally, in the third phase of the study, Clark and Mark turn to a simulation strategy. Specifically, they seek to analyze the structural behavior of the original buttress design that was confirmed in the first phases of their research. To conduct the analysis they construct a scale epoxy model of a typical structural bay which is then tested in a photoelastic laboratory "under simulated gravity and wind loadings."[35] Based on this simulation model, they conclude that the original structural system would have been feasible for supporting the cathedral, though some "cracking distress would have become evident" in two areas of the windward buttressing.[36] And this, they speculate, may represent a previously unknown factor underlying the decision to renovate the cathedral in the 1230s, approximately 45 years after the nave was built.

This study represents well the possibility of combining what may seem like highly contrasting research designs: the interpretive-historical and simulation. It also underlines the often intersecting territories of combined strategies and of the case study designs. In this instance, one might characterize Clark and Mack's study as a case study of the structural design of Notre Dame Cathedral, divided into three distinct phases, one of which is a comparative case study.

On the other hand, it is possible to employ a two-phase research design without adopting a case study design. For example, Ahrentzen and Groat conducted an extensive study of the status and viewpoints of women faculty in architecture that used a correlational design for the first phase and a qualitative design for the second phase.

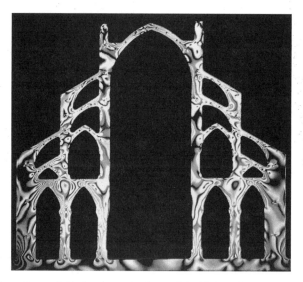

Figure 12.16   Notre Dame de Paris, photoelastic model with interference pattern of stress intensity. Courtesy of Robert Mark.

In the first phase of the research the authors employed a survey questionnaire that was sent to all faculty women in architecture, as well as a shorter survey that was sent to architecture program chairs.[37] Although the bulk of their report from this phase took the form of descriptive statistics, it also highlighted the relationships between how program chairs and faculty women perceived of women's status in their schools.

In the second phase of the research, Groat and Ahrentzen used the faculty women's perceptions, especially their responses to two open-ended questions, as a basis for developing the protocol for in-depth phone interviews with approximately 40 faculty women respondents.[38] In this phase, in contrast to the survey phase, there was no intention of achieving a random sample of respondents; rather, "the goal was to maximize the variety and range of perspectives."[39] The sample of respondents was more heavily weighted to tenured women, precisely the group of women who are most likely to exert some influence within the academy. The interviews themselves entailed three broad themes: attractions to architecture as a career, career experiences, and visions of architectural education. The outcome of this second phase was an analysis of the extent to which faculty women's perspectives mirrored the recommendations of the Carnegie Foundation study of architectural education (1996).

12.5.2 A Combined Strategy: A Dominant–Less Dominant Design

As its name suggests, the dominant–less dominant design entails the insertion of one type of research design within the framework of a distinctly different research design. The advantage of this design is that the overall coherence of the study is easy to maintain, as it is vested in the dominant research design. The less dominant design is then used to provide a particular aspect of the study with greater depth and/or validity. The consequent disadvantage is that the full and potentially complementary strengths of the less dominant design will not be fully realized.

A useful example of this dominant–less dominant design is Joongsub Kim's study of new urbanism in Kentlands and a comparable conventional suburban design, described in considerable detail in Chapter 8.[40] Earlier we characterized Kim's study as a causal-comparative design, under the more general category of the correlational strategy. This indeed is the dominant strategy of the study. The primary means of data collection was a detailed survey questionnaire designed to elicit from residents of the two neighborhoods their perceived sense of community. The questionnaire asked the respondents to evaluate the extent to which they believed that various physical features affected their responses to four different indicators of community: sense of attachment; pedestrianism; social interaction; and sense of place identity. As is typical of the correlational strategy, various statistical calculations were used to assess the relationships among multifaceted variables measured in the study.

However, included in Kim's study is a secondary element: in-depth interviews with approximately 130 residents, which generally conform to a qualitative research strategy. Kim had several reasons to incorporate such interviews as a less dominant component in his study. First, he wished to explore in a more open-ended fashion and in greater depth some of the themes from the survey questionnaire, for instance: narrative vignettes of the kind of social interactions they had with their neighbors; and how such interactions affected their sense of community. A second reason Kim chose to include the qualitative interviews is that he had no way to establish the comparability of the two different neighborhood groups, a weakness of his causal-comparative design. Do Kentlands residents evaluate their sense of community more highly because the people who chose to move there are more community-minded in the first place? Through the interviews, Kim was able to establish that many—though not all—residents had moved to Kentlands without any particular intention about social interaction, pedestrianism, or community sensibilities, but once in residence their habits and inclinations had changed.[41] Thus, as a consequence of these interviews, Kim was able to address directly a potential threat to the validity and interpretation of his study.

BOX 12.3

Combined Strategies: The Perception of Safety on Buses

For a project funded in part by the Great Lakes Center for Truck and Transit Research and the Ann Arbor Transportation Authority, Ann Lusk combined correlational and qualitative strategies.* Using a mixed-methodology design in which both strategies were used with equal emphasis, Lusk sought to identify the physical features of buses and bus stops that convey a sense of safety to prospective passengers. The goal was to increase ridership by improving bus image and safety, especially among people who would otherwise use their cars.

To elicit potential riders' perceptions of safety, Lusk assembled groups of people from diverse backgrounds in both Ann Arbor and Detroit. Her respondents included people of different ages (including the elderly, who often depend on public transportation), ethnic backgrounds, and income levels. She then showed sets of slides covering distinct aspects of bus design (e.g., bus fronts, bus sides, entry sequences, bus stops), asking respondents to rate each slide according to how safe the bus element made them feel. This portion of the study used numerical rating data that could

---

*Anne Lusk, Bus and Bus Stop Designs Related to Perceptions of Crime. Federal Transit Administration. Office of Research, Demonstration and Innovation. FTA MI-26-7004-2001.8. 2001.

be analyzed so as to uncover relationships among ratings of different respondent groups or among the specific physical features being evaluated.

Once the respondent group had completed their rating sheets, Lusk employed a focus group format to discuss the most positively and most negatively rated examples. Through this qualitative component of her study, Lusk was able to uncover the underlying reasons for people's ratings and explore the more subtle nuances of their reactions. Figures 12.17 through 12.20 indicate some typical focus group comments associated with particular bus features.

Figure 12.17 UnSafe: "I don't want to get on this bus because I don't know who is inside." Photo courtesy of Anne Lusk.

Figure 12.18 Safe: "This is the best bus because you can see all the way through." Photo courtesy of Anne Lusk.

Figure 12.19 UnSafe: "This looks like a prison bus." Photo courtesy of Anne Lusk.

Figure 12.20 Safe: "This bus is smiling." Photo courtesy of Anne Lusk.

12.5.3 A Combined Strategy: Mixed-Methodology Design

The mixed-methodology design represents the most complete level of integration among two or more research designs. In this model, the researcher conducts aspects of both strategies in roughly comparable sequences, and with approximately equal degrees of emphasis. The advantage of such an approach is that the strengths of each research design can complement each other, while the weaknesses of each design can be substantially offset. On the other hand, the mixed methodology may well require a level of familiarity with multiple research designs that is uncommon for people trained in a very specific research tradition. Moreover, some "purists" may find the combination of research designs too unconventional and therefore suspect.

A good example of a mixed methodology design is represented by Lara's study of popular modernism in Brazil, which we have already described in considerable detail as a case study. In fact, it is clearly both, as we have noted earlier in this chapter. Because the case study strategy typically makes use of multiple sources of evidence, it may frequently entail the combination of not just data collection tactics but also distinct research designs. Indeed, in Lara's study the combination of interpretive-historical and qualitative designs is virtually seamless. Within the historical-interpretive design, he has included: extensive archival research on the portrayal of modernism in popular media; archival documentation of modernist house plans in the city offices of Belo Horizonte; an artifactual inventory of all the houses in two multi-block areas of the city; and a detailed stylistic analysis of each house facade within the neighborhood inventories. Also note that Lara has, even within this interpretive-historical strategy, incorporated not only verbal and visual data (e.g., the media analyses) but also more quantitative data (e.g., the housing inventories).

Lara simultaneously weaves a qualitative research design into his study. Included within this component are open-ended interviews with 21 original residents of popular modernist homes in Belo Horizonte, and detailed spatial analyses of the house plans, linked with the residents' commentaries on the social dynamics of their family life. Just as Lara incorporates both quantitative and qualitative data and analyses in

Strategies	Tactics: Data Sources
Interpretive-Historical	Housing inventory of 2 neighborhoods Stylistic analysis of all houses Archival documentation of houses in city records Verbal / visual analyses of media representations
Qualitative	In-depth, open ended interviews with original residents Configurational analyses of representative house plans Computer-based spatial analyses of house plans

Figure 12.21   Diagram of combined strategies of Fernando Lara.

the interpretive-historical component, so too he incorporates both quantitative and qualitative elements in this segment of his study. For example, the floor plan analyses depend on quantitative measurements as well as social history provided by the residents. And verbal, qualitative analyses of the floor plans are complemented by computer-analyses of "spatial depth." In sum, Lara's deft and complementary use of two research strategies, as well as both quantitative and qualitative tactics, makes this study a very robust example of the mixed methodology design.

12.6   COMBINED STRATEGIES: STRENGTHS AND WEAKNESSES

Figure 12.22 briefly summarizes the relative strengths and weaknesses of the three models of combined strategies that were presented above in each of the separate chapter segments. The chart suggests that while there is much to be gained in integrating different research designs, the researcher may also find that combining strategies may require a higher level of sophistication in research methodology than would be expected if s/he were to use a more conventional approach. It is still the case that in many academic disciplines, and certainly in architecture, particular research designs are often taken for granted as the preferred method for research in particular topic

Model of Combination	Strengths	Weaknesses
1. Two-phase	Each strategy can be presented fully and distinctly	Potential lack of connection and coherence
2. Dominant – less dominant	Potential for maintaining coherence through emphasis on dominant design Less dominant design can provide depth and validity	Complementary strengths of less dominant design not fully realized
3. Mixed methodology	Potential to maximize strengths and minimize weaknesses of each design	Need for level of sophistication in multiple research design Mixed methodology too unconventional for some purists

Figure 12.22   Strengths and weaknesses of combined strategies. Adapted from J. Creswell, *Research Design: Qualitative & Quantitative Approaches* (Thousand Oaks, Calif.: Sage Publications, 1994) pp. 177–178. Reprinted by permission of Sage Publications.

areas. This means that many researchers have been exposed to and trained primarily in one, perhaps two research strategies; as a consequence, it may require considerable effort to break the pattern and augment the preferred strategy with a suitably complementary strategy.

Even if the researcher is knowledgeable about multiple research strategies, there still remains the challenge of how to combine strategies in an effective and coherent way. The two-phase design may put the overall coherence of the study at risk if the two research strategies are very different. On the other hand, the dominant–less dominant design tends to maintain the coherence of the study by placing one strategy in a secondary role, thus compromising the potential strengths of that strategy. Finally, the mixed methodology model tends to present the greatest challenge for the researcher in reconciling and integrating two (or more) disparate strategies. Yet, if done well, it may yield the greatest pay-off, since it may realize the complementary strengths of the combined strategies most fully.

Despite the assorted pitfalls and challenges, it is our contention that combined research strategies in architecture represent an enormous opportunity. By definition, architecture is a multidisciplinary professional field. Yet to date, much architectural research has remained within the confines of subdisciplinary topic areas, such as environmental technology or architectural history.

Certainly there will always be a valuable role for research efforts in traditionally defined areas; but likewise there are many other important topic areas that defy easy categorization. Should research on environmental comfort or on energy conservation habits of building users be considered environmental technology research or behavioral research? If it is both, then shouldn't some combination of the research designs typically used in each tradition be combined so as to investigate the phenomenon or setting in a more effective and multifaceted way?

Because there are, at this point, fewer established rules and procedures for designing combined research strategies, the researcher who uses them must exercise more care and build on a greater range of knowledge in research methodologies. But despite this greater challenge, we believe that architectural research that combines strategies represents an important and necessary frontier in our field.

12.7   RECOMMENDED READING

For readers interested in using the case study research design, Robert Yin's *Case Study Research: Design and Methods*, 2nd ed. (Thousand Oaks, Calif.: Sage Publications, 1994) is both valuable and extremely readable. For additional commentary on case studies, see Robert Stake's "Case Studies" chapter in Norman Denzin and Y. Lincoln, eds., *Strategies of Qualitative Inquiry* (Thousand Oaks, Calif.: Sage Publications, 1998), 86–109. Stake's discussion, however, is limited to consideration of case studies within the framework of qualitative research.

Discussion of the use of combined strategies is best represented by the chapter "Combined Qualitative and Quantitative Designs" in John Creswell's *Research Designs: Qualitative and Quantitative Approaches* (Thousand Oaks, Calif.: Sage Publications, 1994), 173–192. For a discussion much more particular to the architectural realm, readers can refer to Julia Robinson's article "Architectural Research: Incorporating Myth and Science," *Journal of Architectural Education* 44, no. 1 (November 1992): 20–32. However, Robinson's discussion tends to focus more on the paradigmatic and tactical levels than actual research design. Another useful article, but focused on methodological examples in the administrative and business realms, is Todd Jick's "Mixing Qualitative and Quantitative Methods: Triangulation in Action," *Administrative Science Quarterly* 24, no. 4 (December 1979): 602–611.

Finally, an excellent exemplar of case study research is the one cited extensively in this chapter: Jane Jacobs, *The Death and Life of Great American Cities* (New York: Random House, 1961). A reference for both case study and combined strategies design is Fernando Lara, Popular Modernism: An Analysis of the Acceptance of Modern Architecture in 1950s Brazil. (Ph.D. diss., University of Michigan, 2001).

NOTES

1. Jane Jacobs, *The Life and Death of Great American Cities.* (New York: Random House, 1961), 13, 23, 25–26.

2. Fernando Lara, Popular Modernism: An Analysis of the Acceptance of Modern Architecture in 1950s Brazil (Ph.D. diss., University of Michigan, 2001).

3. Robert K. Yin, *Case Study Research: Design and Methods*, 2nd ed. (Thousand Oaks, Calif.: Sage Publications, 1994), 13.

4. Yin, *Case Study Research.*

5. Jacobs, *Great American Cities*, 23.

6. Ibid., 25.

7. Ibid., 23–24.

8. Yin, *Case Study Research*, 27–28.

9. Ibid., 28.

10. Jacobs, *Great American Cities*, 25.

11. Ibid., 25.

12. Lara, Popular Modernism.

13. Yin, *Case Study Research*, 37.

14. Robert E. Stake, "Case Studies," in *Strategies of Qualitative Inquiry*, eds. Norman Denzin and Yvonna Lincoln (Thousand Oaks, Calif.: Sage Publications, 1998), 86–109.

15. Ibid., 88.

16. Yin, *Case Study Research*, 10.

17. Ibid., 45.

18. Ibid., 46.

19. Anne Lusk, Guidelines for Aesthetic Greenways: Determining the Preferred Frequency and Features of Attractive Destinations on a Multi-Use Path (Ph.D. diss., University of Michigan, 2001).

20. Ibid.

21. Piyalada Devakula, A Tradition Rediscovered: Toward an Understanding of Experiential Characteristics and Meanings of the Traditional Thai House (Ph.D. diss., University of Michigan, 1999).

22. Ibid.

23. Todd D. Jick, "Mixing Qualitative and Quantitative Methods: Triangulation in Action," *Administrative Science Quarterly* 24 (December 1979): 602–611.

24. Julia Robinson, "Architectural Research: Incorporating Myth and Science," *Journal of Architectural Education* 44, no. 1 (November 1990): 20–32.

25. Geoffrey Broadbent, *Design in Architecture* (Chichester, United Kingdom: Wiley, 1973).

26. Susan Ubbelohde, "Oak Alley: The Heavy Mass Plantation House," *Eleventh Annual Passive Solar Conference Proceedings*, American Solar Energy Society (1986).

27. Juan Paul Bonta, *Architecture and Its Interpretation: A Study of Expressive Systems in Architecture* (New York: Rizzoli, 1979).

28. Matthew B. Miles and A. Michael Huberman, *Qualitative Data Analysis* (Thousand Oaks, Calif.: Sage Publications, 1990), 4–5.

29. John W. Creswell, *Research Design: Qualitative & Quantitative Approaches* (Thousand Oaks, Calif.: Sage Publications, 1994).

30. Creswell describes the strengths and weaknesses of the three models in terms of combining paradigms, but his analysis is just as applicable to the challenge of using combinations of research designs.

31. William W. Clark and Robert Mark, "The First Flying Buttresses: A New Reconstruction of the Nave of Notre-Dame de Paris," *The Art Bulletin* 66, no. 1 (March 1984): 47, 65; Robert Mark and William W. Clark, "Gothic Structural Experimentation," *Scientific American* 251, no. 5 (November 1984): 176–185.

32. Clark and Mark, "The First Flying Buttresses," 57.

33. Ibid., 60.

34. Ibid., 62.

35. Ibid., 63.

36. Ibid., 63.

37. Sherry Ahrentzen and Linda Groat, *Status of Faculty Women in Architecture Schools*, (Washington, D.C.: Association of Collegiate Schools of Architecture, 1990); Sherry Ahrentzen and Linda Groat, "Rethinking Architectural Education: Patriarchal Conventions & Alternative Vision from the Perspectives of Women Faculty," *The Journal of Architecture and Planning Research*, 9, no. 2, (Summer 1992): 95–111.

38. Linda Groat and Sherry Ahrentzen, "Voices for Change in Architectural Education: Seven Facets of Transformation from the Perspectives of Faculty Women," *Journal of Architectural Education*, 50, no. 4, (May 1997): 271–285.

39. Ibid., 273.

40. Joongsub Kim, Sense of Community in Neo-Traditional and Conventional Suburban Developments (Ph.D. diss., University of Michigan, 2001).

41. Ibid.

Epilogue

LINDA GROAT

In the first segment of this epilogue, my intent is to summarize and draw connections among the strategies and purposes we have presented in the preceding chapters. In his segment, David Wang will highlight the larger implications of this book and the role that research can play in architecture.

At the end of each semester in my research methods course, I challenge the students to come up with a diagram that represents the terrain of research methods that they have just explored. Whatever two- or three-dimensional form is generated, the requirement is that any proposed research design could be logically located within that diagram. The diagrams are always inventive, and the discussions both provocative and lively. Invariably, I learn something new about the similarities and differences among the various strategies; or I am struck by an entirely new concept as an organizing dimension for the diagram.

The diagram illustrated here is the last best "take" to emerge from those discussions. Although it is certainly only one of many ways that the research methods domain might be diagrammed, it does reflect the underlying structure of this book. The basic diagrammatic form is a cylinder. The circle element is defined by pie-shaped wedges, one for each of the six main research strategies. At the center of the circle, there is a "core" that represents case studies and/or combined strategies. The periphery of the circle, on the other hand, represents the more distinct and focused exemplars of each particular strategy. Finally, the vertical dimension of the cylinder represents the purpose or outcome of research, defined by the dimension from theory to design (i.e. action or applied research).

An important feature of the diagram is the sequence of the research strategies within the circle. There may well be good arguments for one or another alternative sequence; but in the order represented here, each strategy is neighbored by others with common traits. Indeed, starting with the interpretive-historical strategy and moving

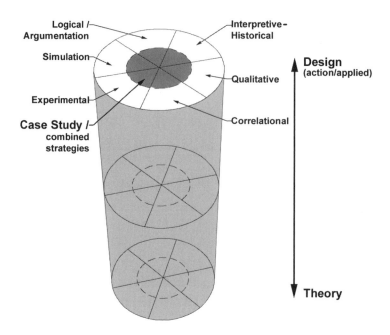

Figure E.1   A conceptual framework for research methods.

clockwise, the diagrammed sequence reflects the chapter order of this book. Qualitative research, like the interpretive strategy, emphasizes a holistic treatment of the research subject, but with contemporary rather than historical focus. Correlational research likewise focuses on naturally occurring circumstances, but makes use of more quantitative data. Experimental research shares with the correlational design the use of measurable variables, but with a requirement for a treatment controlled by the researcher. Simulation research likewise involves control and manipulation of the simulated elements, but it can eliminate the need for extensive real life testing. Logical argumentation shares with simulation an emphasis on abstraction, but it also entails a self-contained system of logical order. And finally, interpretive-historical research depends on a constructed logic of interpretation, but that interpretation is based on documents or artifactual evidence. And so we come full circle.

This diagram can help the researcher clarify the nature and structure of his/her proposed study. Just as a schematic diagram or parti in design can serve as a touchstone for the architect throughout the design process, so too can a heuristic device such as this help the researcher to *define* and *sustain* the essential quality of his/her research design. To illustrate, we can "locate" on the diagram a few of the research studies that figured prominently in the previous chapters. For instance, Benyamin

Schwarz's study of the design process in nursing homes (described in Chapters 2 and 7) would be firmly located within the qualitative segment of the circle; its location on the theory–design dimension might be best represented somewhere near the midpoint, but perhaps a bit more toward the theory end. This is because it offers no obvious or immediate application to a design setting. On the other hand, the analysis and conclusions are very much tied to the particular "ideological contradictions" inherent in the design process for long-term care facilities.

A second example is Rohinton Emmanuel's simulation research on design criteria for housing in hot, humid urban areas, specifically in Colomba, Sri Lanka (described in Chapter 5). Emmanuel's goal was to simulate the impact of different building designs on heating loads. Through this study, he was able to determine that whereas double-glazing of windows was ineffective, the combination of lighter walls and better roof insulation was very effective in mitigating heat gains. Because Emmanuel's research offers immediate and very practical applications, this study would be located at the design or application end of the theory–design dimension. His study would be very clearly located within the simulation domain of the diagram.

Finally, Lara's case study/combined strategies research on popular modernism in Brazil would clearly be located within the "core" of the strategy circle. As discussed in Chapter 12, Lara's study is not only a case study of Belo Horizonte during the 1950s, but it also combines both qualitative and interpretive research designs. In addition, its research purpose is positioned decidedly at the theoretical end of the spectrum; Lara's conclusions represent an important and insightful perspective on modernism's acceptance among the middle class, but it is not likely to have an immediate or practical application in a design setting.

With these examples in mind, we invite readers to make use of this diagram in whatever way might seem fruitful. For instance, readers might consider examples either of their own research or of studies described in recent publications. How might those research examples be located within this conceptual framework? Are there ways in which contrasts and comparisons might be revealed? The terrain is there to be explored; we hope many of you will do so.

DAVID WANG

Ernest Boyer, in *Scholarship Reconsidered*,[1] argues for a multifaceted understanding of what *scholarship* can mean. Addressing an academic audience, he suggests that this term should overcome the dichotomy represented by the more traditional categories of "teaching versus research." The same theme is addressed again, now explicitly targeted at architecture, in Boyer and Lee Mitgang's well-circulated study *Building Community: A New Future for Architecture Education and Practice*.[2] Four categories are proposed for an expanded understanding of scholarship:

1) a scholarship of discovery
2) a scholarship of integration
3) a scholarship of application
4) a scholarship of teaching

These headings are a constructive way to situate the present book into a larger conceptual venue. This larger venue has to do with the ongoing discourse on the role of research in architecture. I would like to take Boyer and Mitgang's four headings and consider briefly how the chapters of this book can fill out what each can mean.

With respect to a scholarship of discovery, I hope this book has conveyed the message, if not explicitly then at least implicitly, that architectural research is in many ways synonymous with discovery. Of course, the discovering that we architects do when designing figural schemas that end up as built forms—those acts of inspiration and enlightenment—may be different from the discovering that comes with research. We have addressed this tension, most directly in Chapter 5, but also at the beginning of Chapter 3. However, we have also argued that the latter is very valuable if we want to perform the former in a more informed way. Research and design are not incompatible. In fact they strike me as very compatible; to use the analogy of marriage, they make a very good couple. But like any marriage, rich rewards and deep insights about life await the pair (that is to say, they await to be *discovered*), only if the parties do not hold grudges, learn to set aside differences (in fact value them), and find ways that the strengths of one can gently but valuably make up for the weaknesses of the other. It is my hope that designers who use this book will find ways and means in the research methodologies presented to richly inform their approaches to design. It is also my hope that researchers who use this book will see that what they do is not divorced from design; that, in fact, contributing to a richer understanding of how design can enhance our stay on this earth ought to be a goal of any research in architecture. If designers and researchers could see this basis for unity, *that* would certainly be discovery, quite aside from the contents a design agenda integrated with research can yield in the way of discovery.

This flows naturally to considering what a scholarship of integration means. For me (and I think this is also the thrust of the Boyer and Mitgang text), integration in this case means an appreciation of the interdisciplinary nature of architectural inquiry. I addressed this in my portion of the preface, but it will not hurt to revisit the theme in the epilogue. And perhaps here I can use more of an exhortative tone. It is my conviction that robust architectural research is hard to do unless we as architects engage with the research methods of disciplines that neighbor our field. Not much elaboration on this is needed here, since the chapters of this book, if they are anything, are reflective of this stance. On the other hand, in my travels in various architectural circles, I have come across the following opinion, often firmly held: because architecture encompasses so many diverse elements of knowledge, the nature of architectural demands of the classroom. My students have taught me which ideas "work," and which do not, both in a theoretical sense, and in the pragmatic sense of the *communication* of ideas. I look forward to more such testing and refining in the fires of the classroom, and I offer this book as evidence that I am trying to live up to Boyer and Mitgang's fourth category. And so I conclude this book with the same statement I gave at the beginning: I dedicate my efforts herein to my students, who always keep me learning.

NOTES

1. Ernest L. Boyer, *Scholarship Reconsidered: Priorities of the Professoriate* (Princeton, N.J.: Carnegie Foundation for the Advancement of Teaching, 1990).

2. Ernest L. Boyer and Lee D. Mitgang, *Building Community: A New Future for Architecture Education and Practice* (Princeton, N.J.: Carnegie Foundation for the Advancement of Teaching, 1996).

3. Vitruvius, *The Ten Books on Architecture*, trans. M. H. Morgan (New York: Dover, 1960), 1.1.4–7.

4. Boyer and Mitgang, *Building Community*, 57.

knowledge just *is* interdisciplinary, and so we do not need to interface with ciplines. My own view is quite opposite of this position. Indeed, in my less moments, I think this position smacks of an uninformed elitism. The ti matter is this: Precisely *because* architecture encompasses diverse elements edge, we ignore the knowledge other disciplines can teach us to our own p

Once upon a time, "being interdisciplinary" was not a problem for arc architecture. To begin with, the idea of "interdisciplinary" had not beer Vitruvius's formula for the education of an architect included mastery in a of fields: medicine, music, mathematics, philosophy, and so on.[3] And he all of this without being aware that he was promoting any new-fangled n chitecture needing to be interdisciplinary. But I think the tremendous ei now give to specialization, dictated by the workings of our very comp economic world, as well as by the explosion of knowledge in all fields, against an ability for even the most energetic amongst us to keep up with a evant knowledge that is on offer. As already mentioned, one of Linda's ai for this book has been to take research typologies from different disciplina to place them into a single-source reference for architects. I kindly ask re this as an attempt on our part to integrate the knowledge provided by fields into the field of architectural inquiry.

There is then the scholarship of application. For Boyer and Mitgang the exploration of "how knowledge can be applied to consequential prob vice to the community and society."[4] In other words, they see the schola plication as coterminous with acts of social service. Of course I agree w this book gives not a few examples of action in the social arena. But I thii answers the call for applicative scholarship at a deeper level. I am referrir made in Chapter 4, namely, that a research method already occupies ar position. That is to say, given a theory, its viability is often demonstrated l method (or methods) that provides tools for testing its claims. This boo ing the strategies and tactics of a range of research methodologies, can viewed as providing material for how and what kinds of applicative sch be undertaken. In short, I see this book as not only responding to Boy gang's call for applicative scholarship, but providing grounds for *enactin* scholarship in a systematic manner.

Finally, what of the scholarship of teaching? At many universities, th spoken tension between the teaching that a faculty member does, on th and all of the other responsibilities he or she undertakes, on the other. often the teaching is less valued when weighed in the balance with a facul research, or service to the university. At least that is the subtext I seem to I admit I do not know how this book can contribute to solving this d widespread level; after all, we are dealing with research here. But I can say sonal level: The contents of the chapters I have written have largely con

Personal Names Index

Subject Index